Mary Shelley in Her Times

Mary Shelley in Her Times

Edited by Betty T. Bennett and Stuart Curran

The Johns Hopkins University Press
Baltimore and London

© 2000 The Johns Hopkins University Press
All rights reserved. Published 2000
Printed in the United States of America on acid-free paper
9 8 7 6 5 4 3 2 1

The Johns Hopkins University Press
2715 North Charles Street
Baltimore, Maryland 21218-4363
www.press.jhu.edu

Library of Congress Cataloging-in-Publication Data will be found
at the end of this book.
A catalog record for this book is available from the British
Library.

ISBN 0-8018-6334-1

To Bill and Stuart Buice

To honor them as they honor the Romantics

Contents

Preface and Acknowledgments

Mary Wollstonecraft Godwin (1797–1851), as her given names eloquently testify, was a child of the radical 1790s: her first major publication, *History of a Six Weeks Tour* (1817), evinces the impress of her mother's *Letters Written during a Short Residence in Sweden, Norway, and Denmark,* and her second, *Frankenstein* (1818), was influenced by and dedicated to her father. By the time she was thus marking these family continuities, however, she was already in association with a second radical circle of the English Regency, one that positioned itself against Europe's rapidly entrenching postwar conservatism. The famous Geneva summer of 1816, for most students of literary history, is now more often identified with Mary Shelley's first novel than with the writings of Lord Byron and P. B. Shelley contemporary with it. From these influences, and with the perspective of a highly gifted, intellectual woman educated both in the culture of her own era and in the contexts of the broader literature and history of western civilization, she shaped a literary voice singularly alert to the significant political, economic, and social changes that inaugurated the world as we know it today.

Her intellectual range is not the only element that set Mary Shelley's experiences apart from those usual for her day. Her lengthy stay in Scotland as an adolescent, the Geneva summer, and the five years she spent in Italy (1818–23) extended her sense of geography and history as well as literature onto a pan-European plane, giving her a perspective rare among writers of the day and rarer still among prominent female writers.

After P. B. Shelley drowned in 1822, she reentered the London literary world in 1823 alone and on a different footing from when she had left it. Though *Frankenstein* had made its indelible imprint, she was no longer "a part of the Elect" (*MWSL* 1:450). But despite her deep sense of loss and her concerns about raising her one surviving child, Percy Florence, she pursued the literary path she had cultivated for herself since childhood. Blending knowledge of a remarkable breadth of past and contemporary history, literature, languages, and philosophy, she enunciated in her works an enduring humanistic vision of the future. Mary Shelley spent more than three decades at the center of Great Britain's literary world, as it negotiated the profound transition between its Romantic and High Victorian cultures. By birth, education, associations, and experience, she was virtually unique in the place she held through the shifting modes of her times. Her six novels, a novella, five volumes of biographical lives, two travel books, and her many short stories, essays, and reviews, not to mention her monumental editions of P. B. Shelley's writings, reveal a writer of singular calling and a thinker of consequence.

To celebrate the notable artistic and intellectual range of Mary Wollstonecraft Shelley, in terms of her own era and ours, the Keats-Shelley Association of America, in May of 1997, her bicentennial year, hosted an international conference bringing together notable scholars from around the world to assess the totality of her achievement and legacy. This volume represents an integration of the principal concerns articulated at that conference.

Among the categories to which the authors continually revert are Mary Shelley's debts to Wollstonecraft and Godwin; other influences on her thought from the 1790s; her relations with P. B. Shelley, Byron, and the "Satanic School"; her position in Regency culture; her cosmopolitanism; her place in the transitional literary scene of the 1820s; her later career in Victorian England; her politics and her representations of history; her uses of science and other contemporary thought; the genres of her writing; and her trajectory as a female writer. Lest one unnecessarily constrict our sense of the "times" in which Mary Shelley lives, the final essay in this volume, by way of a historical postlude, focuses directly on a contemporary author whose confrontations with Mary Shelley have occurred throughout her career and have largely impelled their own trajectory.

The essays are meant to stand on their own. But in their affinities — and differences — they speak to establishing Mary Shelley's works at a level that truly recognizes her cosmopolitan historical concept of the human experience and its potentialities. Taken together, the essays in this volume offer fitting testimony to Mary Shelley's place as an important Romantic author; but more than that, they testify to a visionary perspective that endures to influence cultures yet to come.

With pleasure, we wish to acknowledge the many colleagues whose special contributions have made this volume a reality. For particular praise, we would like to single out Dr. Doucet D. Fischer for integrating our conference activities with the exhibition contemporary with it mounted by the New York Public Library and curated by Doucet Fischer and Stephen Wagner, curator of the Carl H. Pforzheimer Collection of Shelley and His Circle. The Graduate School and University Center of the City University of New York was notably generous in its support of our aims, and that they were realized to their fullest possibility is in great measure owing to the care of Professor Joseph Wittreich of the English Department, Provost William Kelly, and President Frances Degan Horowitz. Dr. Nora Nachumi watched over the welfare of all the conference participants with diligent kindness. The American University and the University of Pennsylvania have supported both the conference and the assembling of these essays, and we wish to acknowledge their unflagging commitment to the success of both undertakings. We are also indebted to members of the Department of Performing Arts of the American University for their performance of *Frankenstein* at the conference, especially Professor Gail Humphries, who directed the performance, Professor Valerie Morris, then chair of the department, and the remarkable cast of students and graduates who so well imbued with life both creature and scientist. Also at American University, we wish to thank Alexandra Meadows, Tisha Brady, and, particularly, Kathleen Kennedy-Corey, for their assistance with any number of the conference preparations.

We are grateful to the Directors of the Keats-Shelley Association of America for providing the support that made the conference a reality. And finally, we wish to acknowledge the very special support given us by William T. Buice, III, President of the Keats-Shelley Association of America, and his wife, Stuart Buice, and we dedicate this volume to these very special friends.

Abbreviations

References to the writings of Mary Shelley, unless otherwise indicated, cite the respective volumes of *The Novels and Selected Works of Mary Shelley* (London: Pickering and Chatto, 1996): *F* (*Frankenstein*); *Fa* (*Falkner*); *L* (*Lodore*); *LM* (*The Last Man*); *M* (*Matilda, The Fields of Fancy, and Miscellaneous Writings*); *PW* (*Perkin Warbeck*); *TW* (*Travel Writings*); *V* (*Valperga*). The shorter fiction of Mary Shelley is cited from *Mary Shelley: Collected Tales and Stories,* ed. Charles E. Robinson (Baltimore: Johns Hopkins Univ. Press, 1976), as *CT. The Letters of Mary Wollstonecraft Shelley,* 3 vols., ed. Betty T. Bennett (Baltimore: Johns Hopkins Univ. Press, 1980–88) are cited as *MWSL. The Journals of Mary Shelley 1814–1844,* ed. Paula R. Feldman and Diana Scott-Kilvert (Baltimore: Johns Hopkins Univ. Press, 1995) are cited as *MWSJ.*

William Godwin's *Enquiry Concerning Political Justice,* ed. Mark Philp, vol. 3 of *The Political and Philosophical Writings of William Godwin* (London: Pickering, 1993), is cited as *PJ; The Enquirer,* vol. 5 of the same edition, ed. Pamela Clemit, is cited as *E.* Quotations from P. B. Shelley's poetry are taken from *Shelley's Selected Poetry and Prose,* ed. Donald H. Reiman and Sharon Powers (New York: Norton, 1977); where this edition is cited for prose or for a particular page of the verse, it is abbreviated as *PBSPP.* Verse not contained in that volume is cited from the Oxford Standard Authors edition (*OSA*) of *The Complete Poetical Works of Shelley,* ed. Thomas Hutchinson (1905, rev. G. B. Matthews 1970). *The Letters of Percy Bysshe Shelley,* ed. Frederick L. Jones (Oxford: Clarendon Press, 1964) are cited as *PBSL.*

The editors, preferring some rhetorical awkwardness and personal distancing to an unintended blurring of identities or a reinforcement of the cultural prioritization of the male surname, have rigorously separated the wife and husband under the denomination of Mary Shelley and P. B. Shelley.

Mary Shelley in Her Times

1 : "Not this time, Victor"

Mary Shelley's Reversioning of Elizabeth,
from *Frankenstein* to *Falkner*

ℬETTY 𝒯. ℬENNETT

Mary Shelley created in her first and last novels two characters who, like philosophic bookends, reflect, extend, and comment on each other and the works in which they appear: Elizabeth Lavenza in *Frankenstein* (1818) and Elizabeth Raby in *Falkner* (1837). Beyond their given names, the two Elizabeths share other important attributes, including their being partial or total orphans, Catholic lineage, and surrogate families. The similarities of the women, however, seem dramatically eclipsed by their sharply different roles in the novels they inhabit: from a minor player in *Frankenstein*, *Falkner*'s Elizabeth, some two decades later, takes center stage. This marked transposition might lead to the assumption that the coincidence of their names is just that: a coincidence. But exploring the circumstances of the Elizabeths reveals a remarkable relationship between the two. Out of the matrix of their similarities, fused with their critical distinctions, Mary Shelley created in her final novel not a reversal or denial of her early Romantic ideology, as many commentators have argued, but rather a reversioning of *Frankenstein* that affirms the author's remarkably consistent reformist sociopolitical ethos.

Mary Shelley's reversioning in *Falkner* is consistent with both Shelleys' works, in which they commonly retold canonized stories.[1] But this instance is extraordinary in its reflexivity. If *Frankenstein*'s future may have been doubted in 1818,[2] by 1835, when Mary Shelley began to write *Falkner*, there was ample evidence that the scientist and the Creature held a permanent grip on society's imagination, permeating all levels of the culture, including newspapers, parliamentary debate, theatrical productions, inexpensive or pirated reprints, and translations. Rarely does an author create an instant myth; usually such meteoric candidates fade within their own era. Mary Shelley, then, had an unusual opportunity that went beyond bringing out a second, revised edition of her work, as she did in 1831. Unlike almost any other author, she could draw on an earlier, already semicanonized public myth that she herself had written to create negative and positive prints of the same Romantic etching. While her reformist ideology remained unchanged, however, her second "printing," *Falkner,* recontextualized her philosophy to reach an increasingly middle-class and materialist Victorian society, one that had largely turned away from Romantic radical politics to take its tea and literature in the more secure confines of Romantic aesthetics.

First, let us look at the 1818 Elizabeth, passively introduced into the novel, as is everyone else in Victor Frankenstein's circle, through his third-person controlling lens, a metaphor itself for his commanding power over their lives. Elizabeth Lavenza in the first edition is the child of Frankenstein's deceased aunt. Her father, about to remarry, proposes to send her from her native Italy to be raised as the senior Frankenstein's "own daughter, and educate her thus" (*F* 23). The father packages his request with both a carrot and a stick, commodifying the child much as one might in a business negotiation. The carrot, practical and mercantile, is a guarantee that the child will retain her mother's fortune. The threat—which surely must have nettled the second Mrs. Godwin—he couches in a question: "Reflect whether you would prefer educating your niece yourself to her being brought up by a stepmother" (*F* 23).[3] Frankenstein's father, a basically kind man, immediately fetches his sister's little girl to Switzerland and the safety of his own family.

But what exactly does this proffered safety mean in terms of the inhabitants of her sanctuary? From the perspective of Frankenstein's mother, Caroline Frankenstein, she now has possession of the "most beautiful child she had ever seen," who "shewed signs even then of a gentle and affectionate disposition." Frankenstein reveals his mother's immediate determination, "to bind as closely as possible the ties of domestic love" by considering "Elizabeth as [his] future wife; a design which she never found reason to repent" (*F* 23). Nor does Frankenstein, whose narrative nullifies each of Lavenza's potential strengths by counterbalancing them with an ingrained subservience. For example, Lavenza was "docile and good tempered, yet gay and playful as a summer insect . . . her feelings . . . strong and deep, and her disposition uncommonly affectionate. No one could better enjoy liberty." But this is quickly modified by, "yet no one could submit with more grace than she did to constraint and caprice." Frankenstein could allow his perfect female her "luxuriant" imagination given her ability to submit; her "light and airy" figure that was "capable of enduring great fatigue" because, at the same time, "she appeared the most fragile creature in the world." In sum, Frankenstein acknowledges, "I admired her understanding and fancy, I loved to tend on her, as I should on a favourite animal." Not surprisingly, despite their great differences, they "were strangers to any species of disunion and dispute" (F 23). Every one, including the servants, adored Elizabeth Lavenza.

The safety given Lavenza, in terms of the tacit privilege born of wealth that pervades the life of the Frankensteins, clearly exacts the heavy toll of a passivity that reflects her position in the family and in society. Her docility is as much a given as her aunt's ordaining that she would be her first cousin's wife, situating her in what some critics have regarded as a quasi-incestuous marriage. Mary Shelley's refiguration of Lavenza as an orphan of a Milanese nobleman in the *Frankenstein* of 1831, a more conservative time, has supported that suggestion. But marriage between first cousins was not regarded as incestuous in England in that period, though one might argue incest is implied because the two are raised in the same household. Peter L. Thorslev Jr., however, has cogently argued the significance of incest among the Romantics as "a symbol of the Romantic psyche's love affair with self and of its tragic isolation in an increasingly alien world."[4] This import would situate the near-relationship of Lavenza and Frankenstein as another example of Frankenstein's egocentricity.

Even without the suggestion of incest, in 1831 Lavenza's role in terms of that egocentricity is unchanged, symbolized by the fact that Caroline Frankenstein in that text gives the four-year-old Lavenza to the five-year old Victor Frankenstein "as a pretty present" (F 192). In the 1831 revision, Mary Shelley additionally intensifies Frankenstein's ownership of Lavenza as well as her functioning as a symbol "of the psyche's love affair with self," by the transfer of an 1818 epithet. In the first edition, Lavenza referred to Justine Moritz as "my more than sister" (F 62), a hyperbolic acknowledgment that breaks the barriers of class to assert devotion of one woman for another. In 1831, however, the phrase belongs to Victor Frankenstein, who twice describes Lavenza as his "more than sister" (F 192). In male-female relationships, this hyperbole doesn't break the societal gender barriers between the two but rather, I would suggest, increases Frankenstein's "psyche's love affair with self."

The revision also provides Mary Shelley one of a number of opportunities to underscore the generally implicit politics of *Frankenstein*. By removing the child's genealogy from that of the family Frankenstein in 1831, she introduces, however briefly, the existence of altruistic and humane values through the story of Lavenza's father, who sacrifices his freedom, and perhaps his life, in the name of liberty.

In both versions, from the family's point of view, Lavenza dutifully fulfills the traditional expectations of a girl in her circle and her era. But what of Lavenza's attitude towards her place in society and her role in life? For the most part, all we know of her interior life is one narrative remark to the effect that to her the world "was a vacancy, which she sought to people with imaginations of her own" (*F* 24) and what we may guess from her actions. For example, Lavenza learns to draw not because she enjoys it but to please her aunt. Even her study of Latin and English with Frankenstein, which suggests an enlightened educational agenda for girls, proves rather to be part of an indulgent agenda, more of a plaything for the children of a wealthy family than a serious system of education directed towards developing reflective moral and ethical values. Frankenstein underscores that carelessness of attitude in his retrospective comment: "I cannot help remarking here the many opportunities instructors possess of directing the attention of their pupils to useful knowledge, which they utterly neglect" (*F* 25). In *Frankenstein* 1831, Frankenstein's parents' "spirit of kindness and indulgence" continues, but Lavenza's education is limited to reading poetry and admiring nature on her own while Frankenstein attends a local school. This new comparison emphasizes the limitations on Lavenza's sphere of knowledge at the same time that it further condemns society's relegation of women to the status of puppets.

Parental neglect concerning education proves to be a critical turning point in Frankenstein's own life. When as a boy he questions his father about Agrippa, his question is tossed aside "as sad trash" (*F* 25). Had his father taken the time to explain, Frankenstein asserts, "my ideas would never have received the fatal impulse that led to my ruin" (*F* 25–26). In *Frankenstein* 1831, Mary Shelley spells out that the failure of Victor Frankenstein's education includes his lack of interest "in the structure of languages, . . . the code of governments, . . . the politics of various states" (*F* 194), all disciplines she regarded as essential to the development of an educated citizen of the world. Lavenza, the product of the same societal code as Frankenstein's, responds to her education as expected for a woman: she is, except for one major incident in the novel, silent.

Apart from that incident, which I will return to, the remainder of Lavenza's role in the novel is relatively sparse, consistent with her societal role. In Chapter 2, when she contracts scarlet fever, she serves as the unwitting catalyst to Caroline Frankenstein's death and a warning about female assertiveness, however benevolent. At first, Caroline Frankenstein yields to her family's appeals not to attend her niece. When the girl's life is threatened, however, she nurses Lavenza, who survives, while the aunt/mother is punished for her "imprudence" (F 29) — defiance of the family's judgment, which surely means the father's — by herself falling victim. Caroline Frankenstein's death plays out in two ways: First, tending a fatally ill relative is women's work — no sacrifice is too great. Second, the exchange of Caroline Frankenstein's life for Elizabeth Lavenza's melds the concepts of incest, egocentricity, and male domination. To reinforce this connection, in one of Caroline Frankenstein's last acts, she addresses Lavenza and Frankenstein as "my children," joins their hands together, and reminds them of her hopes for their union. She also informs Lavenza that she "must supply my place to your younger cousins." Her mothering complete, she then resigns herself "cheerfully to death" (F 29), as much a victim of the dominant power system as its proponent. Lavenza, now ersatz mother, wife, and fiancée, immediately begins her assigned duties of contributing "to the happiness of others, entirely forgetful of herself" (F 30).

Little wonder that in Chapter 4 Frankenstein's feverish attempt to forget his horror at the Creature he had constructed from dead limbs results in a construct made of other dead limbs. When he dreams he embraces Lavenza, blooming with health, he finds her lips "became livid with the hue of death; her features appeared to change, and I thought that I held the corpse of my dead mother in my arms; a shroud enveloped her form, and I saw the grave-worms crawling in the folds of the flannel" (F 40). This dream has been variously interpreted as an expression of Mary Shelley's suppressed guilt about her own mother's death, her own unconscious suppression by P. B. Shelley, Godwin, or society generally, her exclusive concern with women's issues, or a general hostility towards men.[5] These theses, however, remain unproven within the larger context of Mary Shelley's life and works. But the dream may be understood within Mary Shelley's conscious argument in *Frankenstein,* in which the mother-daughter sequence is as much Frankenstein's product as the Creature. In both instances, Frankenstein represents society's agent, and the roles of women and of men in Frankenstein's world, by extension, are ultimately societal constructs that are destructive to all.

In one circumstance in the novel in which we do see more deeply into Lavenza's interior world she functions as an overt expression of Mary Shelley's political agenda. When Lavenza "comes out" to defend the innocent Justine Moritz, she indicts both the prevailing judicial system as well as her own education, which had failed to prepare her for the world as it was.[6] Deeply affected by the unjust accusation that Moritz murdered William, Lavenza finds a voice that defies public and family opinion: she insists on Moritz's innocence while everyone else condemns her, underscoring the marginality of those who lack wealth and prestige. Lavenza wavers only when told that Moritz confessed, but her initial confidence is restored when Moritz explains to Lavenza that her confession was a lie: "Ever since I was condemned, my confessor has besieged me; he threatened and menaced, until I almost began to think that I was the monster that he said I was. He threatened excommunication and hell fire in my last moments, if I continued obdurate" (F 62). Again, the individual predicament serves to depict the societal condition.

The fact that Moritz and Lavenza, as women, do not possess the credibility to convince the jury of Moritz's innocence intensifies the book's condemnation of the judicial system and the predicament of women in the society. Furthermore, recognizing they are powerless, Lavenza councils Moritz—and herself:

> Yet heaven bless thee, my dearest Justine, with resignation, and a confidence elevated beyond this world. Oh! how I hate its shews and mockeries! when one creature is murdered, another is immediately deprived of life in a slow torturing manner; then the executioners, their hands yet reeking with the blood of innocence, believe that they have done a great deed. They call this retribution. Hateful name! When that word is pronounced, I know greater and more horrid punishments are going to be inflicted than the gloomiest tyrant has ever invented to satiate his utmost revenge. Yet this is not consolation for you, my Justine, unless indeed that you may glory in escaping from so miserable a den. Alas! I would I were in peace with my aunt and my lovely William, escaped from a world which is hateful to me, and the visages of men which I abhor. (F 62–63)

After Moritz is hanged, Lavenza's "sad and desponding" (*F* 69) mourning contrasts with her acquiescent response to her aunt's death. Frankenstein reports that Lavenza

> no longer took delight in her ordinary occupations; all pleasure seemed to her sacrilege toward the dead; eternal woe and tears she then thought was the just tribute she should pay to innocence so blasted and destroyed. She was no longer that happy creature, who in earlier youth wandered with me on the banks of the lake, and talked with ecstasy of our future prospects. She had become grave, and often conversed of the inconstancy of fortune, and the instability of human life.
>
> "When I reflect, my dear cousin," said she, "on the miserable death of Justine Moritz, I no longer see the world and its works as they before appeared to me. Before, I looked upon the accounts of vice and injustice, that I read in books or heard from others, as tales of ancient days, or imaginary evils; at least they were remote, and more familiar to reason than to the imagination; but now misery has come home, and men appear to me as monsters thirsting for each other's blood . . . . Alas! Victor, when falsehood can look so like the truth, who can assure themselves of certain happiness? I feel as if I were walking on the edge of a precipice, towards which thousands are crowding, and endeavouring to plunge me into the abyss." (*F* 69)

These passages, with Lavenza playing the central role, condemn organized justice and religion and concomitantly redefine the idea of "the monster." Moritz admits the threats and menaces of the priest almost made her believe "I was the monster that he said I was" (*F* 62). In this early example of brainwashing, Mary Shelley provides another lesson on the power of authority over the minds of its subjects. The second important redefinition of *monster* reverts to the subject of Elizabeth's education. Unprepared for a world in which "men appear . . . as monsters thirsting for each other's blood," the "vacancy of her mind" draws her towards the concept of the world as an abyss in which humanity perishes at its own hands.

Chastened, Lavenza retreats into character for the remainder of the novel, her brief dissent from the system suggesting a potential never developed, because she is, after all, a product of that system without the means or education to change her place within it. She placidly renounces her claim to marriage with Frankenstein if he has found another, but then she just as placidly accepts him. Shadowed by fear for their future happiness because of the past misfortunes, she simply refuses to "listen to such a sinister voice" (*F* 148). Her last actions in the novel circle back to her first. Once married, she lawfully belongs to Frankenstein, disposed of through a marriage contract reflective of the same legal code that had disposed of Moritz. When Lavenza observes Frankenstein's agitation on their wedding night, Frankenstein protects her from reality as one might a young child by not revealing the source of his own obvious fear. Egocentrically interpreting the Creature's threat, "I will be with you on your wedding night" (*F* 130), he entreats her to retire. Obediently, she does so. The rest, after a "shrill and dreadful scream" (*F* 150) is indeed silence. Elizabeth Lavenza last appears in *Frankenstein* as she was in the beginning, a figment of Frankenstein's mind, in his dreams, her sisterly soothing voice whispering in his ear.

Mary Shelley set her five novels following *Frankenstein* in varied locations and eras, spanning the fourteenth to the twenty-first centuries. Each represents its characters and events as analogs of larger societal values within a context that indicates her resistance to conventional norms. But the novels incrementally shift from the Frankensteinian landscape of male-autocracy, in which Mary Shelley's honored values of love (female and male), equality (female and male), nature, and expansive education are destructively suppressed. Instead, the later novels explore less-unidetermined landscapes in which those societally constructive values play an increasingly important role, often voiced through characters who, like Euthanasia in *Valperga* and Lionel in *The Last Man*, combine what Mary Shelley regards as the strengths of both genders. With *Falkner*, Mary Shelley represents another iteration of those combined strengths. She personifies them in the character of Elizabeth Raby, a young woman whose experiences are on a human scale, acted out in contemporary England, no doubt influenced by the irony of a society that had been gradually increasing the rights of its male citizenry while intensifying constraints on its female citizens.

Falkner's Elizabeth Raby, like *Frankenstein*'s Elizabeth Lavenza, is first introduced as a young child, though not through the filter of another character's voice as is Lavenza but through the narrator's, who proves to be a far more reliable commentator than Frankenstein. Briefly, Raby's father, Edwin Raby, defied his wealthy Catholic family — the oldest Catholic family in England — by marrying the non-Catholic Isabella and was disowned by "hardheartedness of the wealthy" (*Fa* 12). He struggles to earn a living for his beloved wife and child, but succumbs to consumption. Her mother struggles on, refusing to comply with Edwin's father's stipulation that he would support the child only if he were given complete custody, an experience directly drawn from Mary Shelley's early negotiations with P. B. Shelley's father. Four months later, Elizabeth Raby's mother, who had nursed her husband, also succumbs to consumption. We meet Raby, who is about six years old, not sheltered in some wealthy home but in a tattered dress in her usual place of retreat in a "thorny, stony-hearted world," at her mother's unmarked grave, where she took her picture books and her playthings, so she could talk to, and be blessed by, her Mama.

Mary Shelley drew the image of the child at her mother's grave and the grandfather's demand for complete possession of the child so directly from her own life that I wish to pause for a moment to comment on their significance, as well as on the other biographical allusions that she incorporated into her novels.[7] Students of the Romantics are fully aware that they all drew on and reworked their own histories as it fit the objectives of their works. Mary Shelley's commentary on this technique, written about Godwin, applies to her own writing as well: "Merely copying from our own hearts will no more form a first rate work of art, than will the most exquisite representation of mountains, water, wood, and glorious clouds, form a good painting, if none of the rules of grouping or coloring are followed."[8] The analogous rules of personal experiences, reshaped into the art of writing about larger societal issues in both *Frankenstein* and *Falkner,* speak to the author's self-confidence in projecting the microcosm of her own intellectual vision into the landscape of her art and obviate a reductive reading of the novel as *roman á clef,* an interpretation that invariably has critically circumscribed that vision.

The climax in *Frankenstein* occurs in that very dramatic moment when the scientist abandons his Creature, an event foreshadowed by the senior Frankenstein's abandonment of responsibility to educate his son away from the "train of . . . ideas" (F 25) that led to his ruin. *Falkner* contains an equally dramatic climax, but with significant modifications of role, intention, and outcome. Specifically, a short time before the book opens, Rupert John Falkner had forced his beloved Alithea Raby from her "selfish and contemptible" (Fa 94) husband, Sir Boyvill, whom she does not love, and her young son Gerald, whom she does. Though she loves Falkner—and had from youth, although wed at her father's will to the wealthy Boyvill—she attempts to return home out of love for her child and accidentally drowns. Falkner and his ally bury her in an unmarked grave, which he explains was the custom he had witnessed during his ten years in India, but also because of his ally's fears of being prosecuted for kidnapping or murder. Her complete disappearance convinces her husband she has willingly run off and he divorces her, forcing his son to bear witness against his mother in court. A distraught Falkner appears in Raby's churchyard, and attempts to commit suicide on the unmarked mound that is Raby's mother's resting place. However, when Falkner "drew the trigger, his arm was pulled; the ball whizzed harmlessly by his ear: but the shock of the sound, the unconsciousness that he had been touched at that moment—the belief that the mortal wound was given, made him fall back; and, as he himself said afterwards, he fancied that he had uttered the scream he heard, which had, indeed, proceeded from other lips" (*Fa* 19).

Rather than run from the scene, the young Elizabeth Raby takes action that symbolizes human responsibility. Elizabeth Lavenza's passive life ends with a scream, to Frankenstein a signal the Creature has bested *him*. Elizabeth Raby's scream—of warning and compassion—coalesces the lives of the girl and the man, who in the moment believes he "had uttered the scream." More than that, it presages what the remainder of the novel verifies: that Elizabeth Raby is the novel's hero.

When Falkner learns that Alithea Neville was Isabella Raby's dear friend, he puts aside his intended suicide to raise the child as his own daughter. In contrast to the world of the family Frankenstein, neither Falkner nor the young Elizabeth Raby envision their world as Edenic. Instead, Mary Shelley describes a world in which the father figure is guilt-ridden and often unreliable in judgment and action, while the child, innocent in herself, realizes from childhood that in her world good people die, have dark secrets, and at times conduct themselves inappropriately and even outright unconscionably.

The differences between Frankenstein and Falkner, Lavenza and Raby, inform us we have entered a new landscape. Frankenstein's hubris and egocentricity, bred of the privileges and blinders of his class, operate in an eighteenth-century world that engages the supernatural. Falkner, equally the victim of hubris and egocentricity, in his case bred from disdain and cruelty, lives very much in the real world. Lavenza's innocence is the outcome of overprotection and ignorance of the real world. Gaining experience only when the justice system hangs Justine Moritz, Lavenza remains class-bound and victimized. Raby, on the other hand, "the nursling of love and nature" (*Fa* 14) and also, significantly, having worldly experience and extended education, like the Creature, exchanges innocence for knowledge. But, unlike the Creature, she remains faithful to her values, even when faced with losing her beloved as well as a respected station in the world. As a result, even from early childhood she asserts her own will, able to deal with whatever events confront her.

Falkner's notion of raising the child for "the solace he needed" (*Fa* 28) parallels the Creature's need for companionship. At first Falkner provides Raby the kind of undemanding education that had molded the passive Lavenza. However, Falkner's idyll of dependency is disrupted when he hires a highly skilled governess for Raby, who encourages the girl's intellect: "from Miss Jervis she acquired the thoughts and experience of other men. Like all young and ardent minds, which are capable of enthusiasm, she found infinite delight in the pages of ancient history: she read biography, and speedily found models for herself, whereby she measured her own thoughts and conduct, rectifying her defects, and aiming at that honour and generosity which made her heart beat, and cheeks glow, when narrated of others" (*Fa* 39). Raby's relationship to her surrogate parent, unlike Lavenza's, changes over the course of time. Her better education, familial and formal, eventually empower her to become the decision maker oftentimes for both Falkner and herself.

Raby's independence leads her to befriend and then fall in love with Gerald Neville, who has dedicated his life to finding his mother and killing the man who abducted her so many years earlier. When Falkner realizes the situation, to set Raby free so she may marry Neville, he gives her a lengthy confessional letter that details the story of his love for Alithea and her death, as well as his sometimes ferocious nature. The letter tests Raby's independence and judgment, allowing Mary Shelley to use Raby's reaction to advocate a code of personal and public conduct in sharp contrast with the conventional power-based code that Falkner, Boyvill, and Frankenstein exemplify.

In *Frankenstein,* however, Mary Shelley uses the scientist to epitomize the sociopolitical power system but seldom allows him a glimpse of recognition into the hazards of that system or his role in it. The narrowness and privilege of his upbringing keep him victim and victimizer. In contrast, Mary Shelley delineates Falkner as a far more complex character. As a child, his father beats him cruelly, his first and unalterable lesson in life: "Oh, what a world this appeared to me! a war of the weak with the strong — and how I despised every thing except victory" (*Fa* 158). Later in childhood, the great kindness of Alithea Neville's mother opens his emotions to affection and solicitude. But his childhood wrongs doom him to "systematized insubordination" expressed by an "untameable nature" (*Fa* 171) particularly actuated at any instance of social or personal injustice.

The novel frequently structures Falkner's personal response into an overt political or social reproach. For example, Falkner's confession not only explains his actions but also functions in the novel as a commentary on poverty and suffering, largely the result of selfish fathers and selfish husbands who control society. So, too, his description of his ten years' service in India as an officer in "the Company's cavalry" gives Mary Shelley the opportunity to fault both the East India Company and the Indian rajahs: "I attached myself to several natives; that was a misdemeanor. I strove to inculcate European tastes and spirit, enlightened views, and liberal policy, to one or two native princes, whom, from some ill-luck, the English governors wished to keep in ignorance and darkness. I was for ever entangled in the intimacy, and driven to try to serve the oppressed; while the affection I excited was considered disaffection on my part to the rulers" (*Fa* 171–72).

These overtures sometimes drew "ingratitude and treachery" from those he tried to aid and distrust from his superiors. When he rescued an old rajahs's life and extricated "him from a difficulty in which the Europeans had purposely entangled him," suspicions that he "aspired to succeed to a native principality" led to his transfer to a different post. For his part, he admits, "My views were in diametrical opposition to the then Indian government. My conversation was heedless — my youthful imagination exalted by native magnificence; I own I often dreamt of the practicability of driving the merchant sovereigns from Hindostan" (*Fa* 172).

The most dramatic direct comparison — and variance — between *Frankenstein* and *Falkner* contrasts the systems of justice in both novels. In *Frankenstein*, Lavenza remains powerless to prevent her friend's murder at the hands of the law. Raby, on the other hand, faces a far more complicated situation. Though Falkner admits his kidnapping of Alithea directly led to her drowning, Raby reasons that Falkner is innocent of murder because "when he accused himself of murder, [he] spoke, as I thought, of a consequence, not an act; and if the chief principle of religion be true, that repentance washes away sin, he is pardoned, and the crime forgotten" (*Fa* 194). She takes on the responsibility of standing by him, teaching him her values, and in both, defying the conventional values of her society.

Falkner, reflecting on the injustice of the judicial and social system echoes the Creature's agony as an outcast: "Retribution or atonement—I am ready to pay it as it is demanded of me for Alithea's sake—but the injustice of man is not lessened on this account; henceforth I am to be stamped with ignominy—and yet in what am I worse than my fellows?—at least they shall not see that my spirit bends before them" (*Fa* 281). Through Raby's example, Falkner decides "to endure, and teach himself that resignation which is the noblest, and most unattainable temper of mind to which humanity may aspire" (*Fa* 198). His moral decision to endure reflects Mary Shelley's view of human nature as basically good but damaged by its interaction with a frequently hostile world.

Mary Shelley contrasts her condemnation of the justice system with an ideal of humane forgiveness. For example, Raby believes that Neville will also pardon Falkner after he has read Falkner's confessional letter and will disavow his pledge to kill his mother's abductor, echoing Prometheus' recantation of his own awful curse in P. B. Shelley's *Prometheus Unbound*. The question Neville faces includes both individual and societal considerations: "Can I take my mother's destroyer by the hand, and live with him on terms of intimacy and friendship? Such is the price I must pay for Elizabeth—can I—may I—so far forget the world's censure, and I may say the instigations of nature, as unreservedly to forgive?" (*Fa* 295). With some complex twists and turns, Neville, too, becomes Raby's pupil, and eventually fulfills this ideal.

Finally, Neville cedes to Raby the decision that he and Falkner both face if they choose to live as a family: "She alone can decide for us all, and teach us the right path to take. Do not mistake me, I know the road she will point out, and am ready to follow it. Do you think I could deceive her? Could I ask her to give me her dear self, and thus generously raise me to the very height of human happiness, with deception on my lips? I were indeed unworthy of her, if I were capable of such an act" (*Fa* 298).

Neville's defiance represents an advancement in his character rather than weakness or reversal, linking it to his own earlier defiance of his father and the world's condemnation of his mother. His final declaration not to separate Raby from Falkner echoes Raby's own defiance to remain with Falkner: "'If the world censure me,' he said, 'I am content; I am accustomed to its judgments, and never found them sway or annoy me. I do right for my own heart. It is a *godlike task* to reward the penitent. In religion and morality I know that I am justified: whether I am in the code

of worldly honour, I leave others to decide; and yet I believe that I am'"
(*Fa* 298).

His decision plays another important part in the presentation of female-male relationships in *Falkner* as compared with *Frankenstein*. Raby is not only the teacher in the story; teaching and learning are themselves shifting, communal roles, which further delineate the equality of the sexes rather than subservience on either part. Though at this point Raby is the teacher, earlier she had been Neville's pupil:

> The poetry of his nature suggested expressions and ideas at once varied and fascinating. He led her to new and delightful studies, by unfolding to her the pages of the poets of her native country, with which she was little conversant. Except Shakespeare and Milton, she knew nothing of English poetry. The volumes of Chaucer and Spenser, of ancient date; of Pope, Gray, and Burns; and, in addition, the writings of a younger, but divine race of poets, were all opened to her by him. In music, also, he became her teacher. She was a fine musician of the German school. He introduced her to the simpler graces of song; and brought her the melodies of Moore, so "married to immortal verse." (*Fa* 223)

Unlike the absence of female independence in *Frankenstein, Falkner* portrays the possibility of mutual interdependence.

Raby's tests are many, but she refuses

> to adopt a new system of conduct, become a timid, home-bred young lady, tied by the most frivolous rules, impeded by fictitious notions of propriety and false delicacy [?] Whether they were right, and she were wrong—whether indeed such submission to society—such useless, degrading dereliction of nobler duties, was adapted for feminine conduct, and whether she, despising such bonds, sought a bold and dangerous freedom, she could not tell; she only knew and felt, that for her, educated as she had been, beyond the narrow paling of boarding-school ideas, or the refinements of a lady's boudoir, that, where her benefactor was, there she ought to be; and that to prove her gratitude, to preserve her faithful attachment to him amidst dire adversity, was her sacred duty—a virtue, before which every minor moral faded and disappeared. (*Fa* 234)

To Neville's pleas that she not spend her days with Falkner in prison because it will harm her own health and spirit, Raby replies: "I think not . . .

I cannot believe that my spirit can be broken by injustice, or that it can quail while I perform a duty. It would indeed—spirit and heart would both break—were my conscience burtherned with the sin of deserting my father. In prison—amidst the hootings of the mob—if for such I am reserved, I shall be safe and well guarded by the approbation of my own mind" (*Fa* 238).

Falkner, then, has a genuine hero—and he is a she. Elizabeth Lavenza, the helpless victim, a character kept in a place of "omission" by the rules of society, is superseded by Elizabeth Raby, the paradigm of "commission," the product of education and experience. Tutored by Raby, both Neville and Falkner relinquish the power-based values to which they are accustomed. This growth filters to a degree even to Neville's father, whose deathbed kindness inspires Neville to observe: "His unwonted gentleness subdues my soul. Oh, who would rule by power, when so much more absolute a tyranny is established through love!" (*Fa* 275).

On November 8, 1835, Mary Shelley wrote, "as I grow older I look upon fidelity as the first of human virtues—& am going to write a novel to display my opinion."[9] *Falkner* displays a fidelity that goes beyond conventional loyalty to a father or a lover. Raby's primary fidelity is, in fact, to her own value system, one which questions, defies, and reeducates the world in which she lives, as did Helen in P. B. Shelley's *Rosalind and Helen*, which Mary Shelley quoted for her novel's epigraph.

Falkner's spotlight on this second Elizabeth remarkably annotates a major point of critical contention about her early masterpiece: the minimal role of women in *Frankenstein*. Mary Shelley constructed the power-driven value system of *Frankenstein* to symbolize the destruction of humanistic values. In the mitigating landscape of *Falkner*, however, she enfranchised those humanistic values, locating them within a framework that permitted change and choice for both women and men in contrast with the larger society and pioneered by a woman, one of the major symbols of the oppressed in *Frankenstein*.

Falkner's annotation of *Frankenstein* not incidentally extends also to the role of another woman in her society: the author herself. Both novels have had to contend with a critical reception that largely ignored the politics that are central to all of Mary Shelley's works because of the conventional belief that politics was not the province of women. Initially, *Frankenstein* defied this norm. Reviews, whether favorable or not, recognized the Godwinian reformist politics of the novel and assumed its author was male, occasionally naming P. B. Shelley. But by April 1818, the identity of the anonymous author had leaked out, and almost all the reviews of *Frankenstein* that followed revealed a singularly different infrastructure with a singularly different set of assumptions and guidelines. However ingenious the reviews found the novel, they critically transmuted it into the product of a "female author" and treated it within the Gothic genre, with allusions to politics and Godwin mentioned, if at all, in brief asides, relegated as tangential to the novel.

From this point, the contemporaneous critical reception of Mary Shelley's works largely eradicated her reformist sociopolitical agenda.[10] When *Falkner* was published, it was generally favorably reviewed as a romance, concerned with "thought and feeling, rather than manners and character."[11] A number of the reviews tied it to Godwin in its gloominess and its delineation of the human mind but not in its political agenda. In fact, even Godwin's politics were muted in these reviews: references were made to Sir Edward Mortimer, the leading character in George Colman the Younger's apolitical, unauthorized adaptation of Godwin's *Caleb Williams*.[12] When noticed, *Falkner*'s politics were either criticized for "constantly calling upon the reader's admiration and sympathy for a man who is morally a murderer" and for depicting a title character who is "acquitted though, in the romance of real life, a jury in such a case would be extremely apt to infer the worst, and to hang the prisoner" or praised for an "impressive" moral that demonstrates "the greatest punishment that a generous mind can endure is remorse" or as a story "of arresting power" in which the "chief criminal" is the hero and "engages the heart."[13] The last review, comparing Falkner to Sir Edward Mortimer (erroneously as the work of Godwin) absolves Mary Shelley of "inculcating that scepticism as to existence of human virtue and disinterested goodness, which her father's creations too potently taught. She seems also to have imbibed much of her husband's poetic temperament, its singular loveliness and delicacy, but to have shorn it of those extravagant visions and emotions which led him beyond the province of truth, and the dictates of a well-regulated judgment," a commentary that suggests as much a misreading of Godwin as of Mary Shelley. As another review plainly put the issue, "Mrs. Shelley wields a powerful pen for a female hand."[14]

Such apolitical misreadings have allowed reviewers to concentrate on Alithea Neville and Falkner rather than deal with the essentially defiant and independent Raby, who reshapes the world around her. The history of this critical bias continues into our own times, leading to modern assessments that judge *Falkner* to be a conventional Victorian romance and its author a resigned, conventional member of her society, whose Romantic ideology lies buried with her Romantic compeers.

But Elizabeth Raby's philosophic defiance in *Falkner* is very much at issue, just as Elizabeth Lavenza's passivity was in *Frankenstein*. Both women serve as generative metaphors for Mary Shelley's enlightenment conviction that the world could be bettered — the world just after the Napoleonic wars, when revolution seemed possible in Britain, as well as in the rapidly entrenching world of the Victorians. Mary Shelley shifted from the parable of *Frankenstein* to the more immediate, human-sized, albeit tamer, *Falkner* as a means of resisting, rather than conforming to, the values of the 1830s. Her reversioning reflects her judgment of her age. Parable would not serve, as she painfully learned with *The Last Man*. Rather, *Falkner* presents to her era not only the problem of systems based on power in the hands of the few but also, in the character of Elizabeth Raby and her influence on her circle, an accessible formula for interrogating and restructuring those values that lead to the destruction of the individual and the society.

Mary Shelley voices that interrogation in *Falkner* in a remarkable passage that directly glosses the Frankensteinian failure to revere and nurture the human soul. In the course of Falkner's moral "conversion," he observes:

> To the surgeon's eye, a human body sometimes presents itself merely as a mass of bones, muscles, and arteries — though that human body may contain a soul to emulate Shakespear — and thus there are moments when the wretched dissect the forms of life — and contemplating only the outward semblance of events, wonder how so much power of misery, or the reverse, resides in what is after all but sleeping or waking — walking here or walking there — seeing one fellow-creature instead of another. (*Fa* 280–81)

This commentary extends beyond the confines of a laboratory to the democratization of the value of the soul. In this vision of body and soul, of external and internal, Mary Shelley, who said of herself, "without a metaphor I cannot live,"[15] coalesced the metaphoric challenges that she unloosed in her first novel and then reassembled them to map the path towards remedy in her last.

2 : "To speak in Sanchean phrase"

Cervantes and the Politics of Mary Shelley's
History of a Six Weeks' Tour

JEANNE MOSKAL

In her 1826 review essay, "The English in Italy," Mary Shelley reflected on her elopement trip to the Continent in 1814, in these words: "But in those early days of migration, in the summer of 1814, every inconvenience was hailed as a new chapter in the romance of our travels; the worst annoyance of all, the Custom-house, was amusing as a novelty . . . it was acting a novel, being an incarnate romance."[1] In general, critics and scholars have taken this remark as an indication of the general lightheartedness of the Shelley party's endeavor, an approach that accords with their setting out apparently heedless of practical matters such as their own shortage of money and the dangers of encountering Napoleon's recently demobilized army.[2] However, in this chapter I take Mary Shelley at her word and ask, which novel were they enacting? Which romance were they incarnating?

Here I should like to consider Miguel de Cervantes' romance *Don Quixote* (1605, 1615) as one of the scripts for the journey she was "acting."[3] I argue that Mary Shelley, by identifying herself with Sancho Panza in *History of a Six Weeks' Tour*, situates her travel book within a matrix of political meanings, traceable through the associations of Cervantes, Don Quixote, and Spain with Godwinianism in the 1790s and with liberal politics in the 1810s. Moreover, her self-identification as Sancho in that travel book initiated a lifelong literary habit that enabled Mary Shelley to negotiate the gender politics of the nineteenth century by partly embracing and partly rejecting the "female Quixote" tradition associated with her mother, Mary Wollstonecraft. This approach thus contributes to the new scholarly emphasis on Mary Shelley as a lifelong reformer, deeply engaged in the liberal and feminist concerns of her day and scrupulous in thinking over their metaphorical underpinnings.[4]

Don Quixote and the Politics of Chivalry

Even before pen was put to paper, the elopement journey had its comic, quixotic elements. Once in France, P. B. Shelley and Mary Shelley resembled Cervantes' knight and his squire in several particulars. Their purchase of an ass that proves useless the next day (*TW* 19–20) suggests they were probably swindled, as Don Quixote frequently is (e.g. pt. 1, chap. 16).[5] P. B. Shelley's sprained ankle (*TW* 21) farcically echoes the beatings Don Quixote receives on his first quest. (However, the comparison conveniently ignores the impediment of P. B. Shelley's previous marriage and the presence of Claire Clairmont in the party.) Mary Shelley brought out the potential of the journey's quixotic elements when she crafted the journal into a travel book. The original 1814 journal for Tuesday, August 9, 1814, reads simply, in P. B. Shelley's hand, "we past thro Grosbois, Brie, & other villages" (*MWSJ* 11); Mary Shelley revised it to read: "[at Gros Bois] under the shade of trees, we ate our bread and fruit, and drank our wine, thinking of Don Quixote and Sancho" (*TW* 20), explicitly likening the travelers (two of them, at least) to the questing knight and his squire. Even though this is the sole mention of *Don Quixote* in *History of a Six Weeks' Tour*, the pattern of Mary Shelley's reading suggests its deliberateness: from October 7 to November 7, 1816, P. B. Shelley read *Don Quixote* out loud to Mary Shelley and Claire Clairmont in the evenings (*MWSJ* 139–45) as *History of a Six Weeks' Tour* metamorphosed from journey to travel book.

In reading *Don Quixote* during 1816, Mary Shelley was loyal to the literary taste of her father, William Godwin. Mary Shelley later quoted Godwin's praise of the book: "At twenty, I thought 'Don Quixote' laughable — at forty, I thought it clever — now, near sixty, I look upon it as the most admirable book in the world," [6] a remark that pinpoints Godwin's sixtieth year as the pinnacle of his admiration, exactly when Mary Shelley revised *History of a Six Weeks' Tour*. The previous year, Godwin had published at his own expense his *Lives of Edward and John Philips,* in which, writing of John Philips's adaptation of an earlier translation of *Quixote,* Godwin praised the original as an "incomparable monument of Spanish literature and genius."[7]

Not only did Mary Shelley share Godwin's reading, but, in likening herself to Sancho, she proclaimed herself, the literary traveler of *History of a Six Weeks' Tour,* a member of Cervantes' company, and implicitly, of

Godwin's. Since Godwin's literary taste for Cervantes had an unmistakable Jacobin political valence in the postwar period, Mary Shelley's declaration of loyalty to it also constituted a political statement on her part. As David Duff has explained, the revival of the genre of romance and the events of the French Revolution are intimately related, because "with the French Revolution, history itself seemed to enter the domain of the miraculous, and romance to offer a vivid and accurate language to describe what was happening."[8] In its conservative version, which is more familiar to us, Edmund Burke linked romance with the French Revolution by troping the *ancien régime* as a fairyland and lamenting that "the age of chivalry is gone,"[9] and Walter Scott evoked nostalgia for the feudal world in his immensely popular metrical romances and novels. In its liberal and Jacobin version, which is less familiar to us, writers created a "more fragmentary but no less vivid" revolutionary romance "that often employs the very same metaphors to opposite effect."[10] Indeed, Helen Maria Williams deliberately appropriated Burke's rhetoric by writing, "living in France at present, appears to me somewhat like living in a region of romance," where "events the most astonishing and marvellous are here the occurrences of the day."[11] As with the conservative version, there were two waves, one defined by Godwin in the 1790s and the second defined by P. B. Shelley, Leigh Hunt, Thomas Love Peacock, and others in the postwar period, forming "a radical cult of chivalry in the years 1815–1817."[12]

Godwin had forged the Jacobin link between romance and the French Revolution in his *Thoughts Occasioned by the Perusal of Dr. Parr's Spital Sermon* (1801), analyzing the apostasy of the Jacobin generation, especially Samuel Parr and James Mackintosh. Godwin writes, "the intercourse of the world has a powerful tendency to blunt in us the sentiments of enthusiasm, and *the spirit of romance;* and, whatever truth we may suppose there to be in the progressive nature of man, it is so far remote from the transactions of ordinary life . . . that it can with difficulty preserve its authority in the midst of so strong a contagion" (emphasis added).[13] Godwin's brave identification of his radical Jacobin idealism with "the spirit of romance," his linking of chivalry and revolution, became part of his permanent legacy when he expressed his desire that the *Reply to Parr* be included in all subsequent editions of his most famous work, *Political Justice.*[14] This legacy took a nasty turn in the hands of Godwin's enemies, such as Charles Lucas, whose blistering novel *The Infernal Quixote* (1801) — only one among dozens of novels, articles, and poems written from 1796 to 1802 excoriating Godwin[15]—blamed Godwin and his philosophy for undermining the British nation in various ways, from debauching women to fomenting the Irish Rebellion of 1798. Lest the reader miss the point, Lucas conveniently provides citations to *Political Justice* for his title character's suspect arguments.

Given Godwin's longstanding and notorious association with Don Quixote by 1817, Mary Shelley's evocation of Sancho as her double in *History of a Six Weeks' Tour* constituted a declaration of loyalty to Godwin's Jacobin "spirit of romance," a declaration of loyalty perhaps meant to soften the blow of her defiant elopement. At the same time, the embodiment of those radical ideals in Godwin's disciple P. B. Shelley enabled her to transfer the quixotic crown, and with it her primary loyalty, to a new wearer; she used the epithet to describe P. B. Shelley in his most idealistic moments. During the custody trial for his children, in 1817, she wrote him: "My sweet Love, You were born to be a don Quixote and if that celebrated personage had ever existed except in the brain of Cervantes I should certainly form a theory of transmigration to prove that you lived in Spain some hundred years before & fought with Windmills" (*MSWL* 1:27). And in 1820, Mary Shelley describes P. B. Shelley's intervention in a quarrel between a blacksmith's boy and a man chasing him with an umbrella: "Don Quixote did not like to leave the boy in thrall" (*MSWL* 1:132). Thus she makes explicit the similarity between this incident and Don Quixote's intervention on behalf of a child (pt. 1, chap. 4). By 1817, P. B. Shelley, not Godwin, has become her Quixote. The use of the Quixote metaphor in *History of a Six Weeks' Tour* simultaneously ratifies the meaning of the elopement as a radical transition from Godwin to P. B. Shelley and also makes clear that Mary Shelley's Jacobin commitments endure despite that change.

Despite P. B. Shelley's advent, the identification of Godwin as Quixote stuck. As late as the 1830s, Mary Shelley used the Cervantes biography to air some painful memories of the man who had been called "The Infernal Quixote." In addition to the memoir of her father as a public figure, which appeared anonymously in the Bentley's Standard Novels edition of *Caleb Williams* in 1831, Mary Shelley undertook a second memoir after his death, in 1836, in part to raise some money for the destitute Mrs. Godwin. As Pamela Clemit observes, she signed a contract with Henry Colburn for the memoir and began work by organizing Godwin's notes and letters and adding a biographical commentary.[16] By 1840, Mary Shelley appears to have abandoned the project, in part due to ill health. It is likely that ambivalence too played its part, an ambivalence registered in her use of multiple strategies (praise, explanation, and keeping silent), in alluding to Godwin's severity as a parent and in omitting any sensational material concerning her parents' courtship.[17]

Discreet but not silenced, Mary Shelley used the Cervantes biography for literary release. While pondering the second Godwin memoir, she began work, in January 1837, on the volume of Spanish and Portuguese *Lives* for Dr. Lardner's *Cabinet Cyclopedia*. Drawn by Cervantes, she singled out his biography to Leigh Hunt: "I am sure [the Life of Cervantes] will come home to you. Camoens [the Portuguese poet, in the same volume] was more unfortunate than he—but does not *come home to you* in the same manner" (*MWSL* 2:293; original emphasis). Cervantes seems to have "come home" to Mary Shelley in the fate he shared with Godwin: particularly his poverty and the excesses of his detractors. Mary Shelley's biography hammers away at the theme of Cervantes' poverty: "poverty in his native country hung like a heavy cloud over him" (*Lives, Italy* 3:143); "his poverty was the great and clinging evil of his life (3:153). Her insistence on this theme evokes Godwin's own chronic poverty and the fact that his own voracious need for money poisoned much of his relationship with his daughter and son-in-law.

Similarly, Mary Shelley's indignation in her discussion of Cervantes' detractors suggests that in this particular, too, Cervantes' life has "come home": "his very success excited the enmity of a variety of men of letters of his day, who could not endure that a man whose talents they had regarded with no consideration, should suddenly pass over the heads of all: a cloud of satires, epigrams, and criticism were levelled against his work. . . . But [Cervantes'] warm heart must have been pained at the falling off of some of his friends" (*Lives, Italy* 3:160–61). Again, the echo of her father's sorrows sounds in the account of Cervantes': the "cloud of satires, epigrams, and criticisms," we have seen, rained down on Godwin in novels like Lucas's *Infernal Quixote;* and Godwin too was "pained" in "the falling off of some of his friends," such as Mackintosh and Thomas Holcroft. Thus, in the Cervantes biography Mary Shelley gave literary form to some feelings raised by the unfinished memoir, relieved of the duty to account for Godwin as father and husband. In the late 1830s we see the resilience of the metaphor Mary Shelley invoked in *History of a Six Weeks' Tour,* of substituting the author of *Quixote* for the Infernal Quixote.

Don Quixote and Spanish Nationalism, 1810–1820

For Mary Shelley to speak of Cervantes in 1817 necessarily evoked thoughts of Spain, the recent events of the Peninsular War, and the current struggle for a constitutional monarchy.[18] Turning on one of his former allies, Napoleon sent French troops to Spain in 1807 on the pretense of enforcing Portugal's commitment to his Continental blockade. The Spanish Bourbon monarchy was in serious disarray, with the king, Charles IV (a cousin of Louis XVI of France), widely despised by his people, who thought that the country was ruled by the queen's lover, Manuel Godoy, and who fixed their affection and hope on the king's son Ferdinand, nicknamed "El Deseado," the Beloved. Napoleon installed his brother Joseph Bonaparte as King of Spain on June 6, 1808, and promulgated the Constitution of Bayonne, which was modeled after the French Constitution of 1791 and which provided for some minimal representative government, reform of the judiciary, and the promise of freedom of the press. Unlike its predecessor, however, it maintained Catholicism as the state religion. It was thus a considerable liberal advance over the absolutism that preceded it, even though it was instigated in a tyrannical fashion by a foreign power that had violated the idea of national sovereignty.

The Spaniards revolted, beginning with an uprising in Madrid in May 1808, when the Bourbons were removed from the capital. Joachim Murat, Napoleon's brother-in-law and military commander of Madrid, put down the insurrection mercilessly, immediately executing all citizens caught with weapons and carrying out the executions all night, events later immortalized in Francisco Goya's paintings. By early June, the revolt had spread, nobles and clergy joining the peasants in the cause of "King, Fatherland, and Religion" and calling for the reinstatement of "El Deseado," Ferdinand. The provinces turned to Britain for help, and the Peninsular War began.

The effect in Britain was profound. Napoleon's usurpation of power in Spain united conservatives, Whigs, and radicals in outrage: France was declared to be plainly in the wrong, Napoleon denounced as the devil.[19] Before 1808, many Whigs would have celebrated Napoleon as the destroyer of what William Wordsworth called the "detestable governments with which the nations have been afflicted," but after the events in Spain, even Whig politicians who had previously been sympathetic to Napoleon, such as Samuel Whitbread and Richard Brinsley Sheridan, now "saw him as a political aggressor for the first time and interpreted the war against Spain as one fought against a people rather than against princes."[20] Londoners gave a heroes' welcome to a deputation from the rebellious province of Asturia in Northern Spain: "Celebratory dinners were held in their honor, they were lionized by fashionable society, and when they went to the theatre the performance had to be suspended for an hour, such was the commotion."[21] The *Edinburgh Review* celebrated the uprising as reawakening the "liberty and patriotism which many have supposed were extinguished since the French Revolution."[22] Wordsworth, in his pamphlet *The Convention of Cintra* (1809), wrote an elevated account of the revivification of the Whig position as Whigs joined the nation's response to the uprising of 1808: "But, from the moment of the rising of the people of the Pyrenean peninsula, there was a mighty change; we were instantaneously animated; and, from that moment, the contest assumed the dignity, which it is not in the power of any thing but hope to bestow. . . . This sudden elevation was . . . welcome . . . inasmuch as it would give henceforward to our actions as a people, an origination and direction unquestionably moral."[23]

Wordsworth's deliberate reasoning about receiving "an origination and direction unquestionably moral" cannot disguise his observation that "we were instantaneously animated," a portrayal of the moment of 1808 shared by Samuel Taylor Coleridge, who wrote in *The Courier*, "It was the noble efforts of Spanish Patriotism that first restored us, without distinction of party, to our characteristic enthusiasm for *liberty*" (original emphasis).[24] One dissenting voice among the unity Coleridge describes was raised by travel writer Anne Plumptre, who in 1810 mocked the British about-face on Spain:

> We had been long accustomed to hear the Spanish character condemned for its cruelty, its jealousy, and its bigotry; to contemplate with horror and indignation the ravages and desolations made by the arms of Spain withersoever they were carried, whether among the mild and unoffending natives of America, or against her own subjects driven to revolt by oppressions which patience itself could endure no longer;—yet all on a sudden this country resounded with nothing but admiration of Spanish dignity, heroism, and magnanimity.[25]

Despite the difference in politics, Plumptre's "all on a sudden" confirms Wordsworth's sense of "instantaneous animation," and catches the spirit of the hour.

Given this nearly unanimous sentiment, it is no surprise that Spanish literary material became fashionable. Inaugurated in 1808 when Robert Southey translated *Chronicle of the Cid* and Felicia Browne (later Hemans) celebrated the alliance in her *England and Spain, or Valour and Patriotism,* it reached its peak with the publication in March 1812 of the first canto of *Childe Harold's Pilgrimage,* based on Lord Byron's visit to Iberia in 1809, and particularly memorable for its praise, in stanzas 54–57, of Augustina, the "Maid of Saragossa," who carried a gun at the Siege of Saragossa in 1808–9.[26] However, Mary Shelley's allusion to Cervantes in 1817 may well have caught the Spanish literary fashion after its peak, as suggested by Lady Morgan's novel *Florence Macarthy: An Irish Tale* (1818). Morgan capitalizes on the fashion in her half-Spanish, half-Irish, mantilla-wearing heroine, to whose guitar playing one character wearily responds: "Is she one of the '*Guitarie,*' the '*Tu mi chamas*' ladies, who thrum'd us to death, when Spain was in vogue?" (3:108).[27] Morgan's narrator defends the heroine's wardrobe by writing that "a black Spanish dress and mantillo [*sic*] . . . were then still in fashion, for whatever was *peninsular* in sentiment or habiliment had not yet fallen 'into the sear' of popularity" (original emphasis; 3:126). Lady Morgan's novel, then, usefully marks the Spanish vogue's connection to the Peninsular War, and registers that it had faded in some quarters by 1818.

The near-unanimity of public opinion in 1808, however, was built on shaky ground. Some liberals responded to the Spanish uprisings as a cleansed version of the French Revolution of 1789—a popular uprising against a despotic ruler, in this case, Napoleon; but others, more radical, were uneasy about the continued establishment of the Roman Catholic Church and about the popular desire to reinstate absolutism. The polarization between British liberals and conservatives, evidenced in *The Edinburgh Review*'s move to a more liberal position and the consequent founding of the reactionary Tory *Quarterly Review,*[28] was a response to the Spanish Constitution of 1812, also called the Constitution of Cádiz. This development sets up the matrix of political meanings Mary Shelley evoked. The Constitution of 1812 was written by the Cortes (parliament) while Ferdinand lived as Napoleon's prisoner in France. This constitution, like that of Bayonne, was modeled on the French Constitution of 1791. It provided for a strictly limited monarchy, holding that "the power to enact the laws resides in the Cortes together with the King" (Article 15). It established a parliament without special representation for the clergy or the nobles and made new administrative districts, including granting Spain's colonies representation in the Cortes. It also abolished the Inquisition. With this constitution, the liberal faction in Spain became visible, and British liberals and radicals could support their cause with a clearer conscience than they could that of peasants and priests calling for the restoration of Bourbon absolutism.

British conservatives, however, continued to support Ferdinand, who swept aside the Constitution of Cádiz at his restoration in 1814 by refusing to swear allegiance to it and relying on his popularity with the peasants instead. Ferdinand arrested and exiled the *liberales,* mostly drawn from the small middle class, reestablished the Inquisition and feudal rights for landlords, and abolished the freedom of the press, thus instituting "years of counterrevolutionary terror and black reaction." [29] After the war, patriotic Britons looked favorably on Spain and Ferdinand because many believed that the Peninsular War had been the decisive factor in weakening Napoleon and because Wellington's victories at Talavera (1809) and Vitoria (1813) had glorified the nation.[30] British conservatives' support for Ferdinand was lampooned in 1816 by diehard Bonapartist William Hazlitt: "Ferdinand . . . is an honest King. He is a tyrant both by profession and practice. He has but one idea in his head . . . that a king can do no wrong, and he acts up to it, as . . . Mr Coleridge cants up to it, or as Mr Southey rhymes up to it, or as Mr Wordsworth muses up to it." [31] Ferdinand's suspension of liberal values lasted until the Revolution of 1820, when the military, many of them liberalized, forced Ferdinand to accept the constitution. In response, P. B. Shelley wrote, "Liberty/From heart to heart, from tower to tower o'er Spain,/Scattering contagious fire into the sky,/Gleamed" ("Ode to Liberty," ll.2–5). The constitutional regime, in which all parties were discontent, lasted only until 1823, when Ferdinand summoned troops from France to help him oust the *liberales.* Byron mourned the ill success of the constitutional regime, writing, "Cervantes smiled Spain's Chivalry away;/. . . seldom since that day/Has Spain had heroes." [32] The meaning of *Spain,* then, shifted every few years with the fortunes of the king and constitution.

Among these shifts, the state of affairs between 1814 and Spain's Revolution of 1820 is definitive for Mary Shelley. At that time, British liberals looked to the Spain symbolized by the Constitution of 1812 as a remnant of the early heady days of liberty and the French Revolution, a remnant that, for the time being, was a victim of the forces of reaction that gripped

Europe after Waterloo. Hazlitt, writing in this interval, clearly linked the figure of Cervantes with a liberal political agenda: "nor perhaps is it too much to say, that, if ever the flame of Spanish liberty is destined to break forth, wrapping the tyrant and the tyranny in one consuming blaze, it is owing to Cervantes and his knight of La Mancha, that the spark of generous sentiment and romantic experience from which it must be kindled, has not been quite extinguished." [33] Hazlitt defines Cervantes as the preserver of "the flame of Spanish liberty" and links his cult in this interval between 1814 and 1820 with the cause of liberty and the constitution. Nearer the Shelleys after 1818, the flame was kept alive by their physician, Andrea Vaccà, a Cervantes enthusiast who had "assisted at the storming of the Bastille." [34]

Writing in that interval between 1814 and Spain's Revolution of 1820, Mary Shelley's comparing herself and P. B. Shelley to Sancho and Don Quixote had the political resonance of identifying with the Spanish liberals' constitution, which had just been quashed by the reaction in which the Bourbons and the Britons had participated. She identifies herself in *History of a Six Weeks' Tour* as one of those quixotic liberals who looked forward to the restoration of the constitution. True to her commitment, Mary Shelley eagerly followed events in Restoration Spain.

Her stepbrother Charles Clairmont, working as a tutor in Valencia in January 1819, witnessed and published an account of an event presaging the coming revolution. Insurgents had plotted to assassinate Ferdinand's Captain-General of Valencia, Francisco Elío. Discovering the conspiracy, Elío executed the conspirators, Ferdinand giving him a free hand. Charles Clairmont was brave — and imprudent — enough to publish his account of the executions in the *Morning Chronicle,* an action that might have proved "fatal" to him had he remained in Spain, but he moved to Vienna. [35] Mary Shelley responded avidly to this news item and other news from Spain (*MWSL* 1:86 and n). As the revolution succeeded in March 1820, Mary Shelley exulted at the triumph of parliament and constitution: "the Beloved Ferdinand has proclaimed the Constitution of 1812 & called the Cortes — The Inquisition is abolished — The dungeons opened & the Patriots pouring out — This is good. I shd like to be in Madrid now" (*MWSL* 1: 141). Mary Shelley here ironically echoes the epithet of the rebels of 1808, calling Ferdinand "the Beloved" only now that he has enacted some of the reforms of the Constitution of 1812, such as abolishing the Inquisition. Having declared her liberal loyalties by quixotic metaphor in *His-*

tory of a Six Weeks' Tour, Mary Shelley remained true to them, announcing here that she "shd like to be in Madrid" as the Revolution unfolded in Cervantes' homeland three years later. She repeated the sentiment in 1835 (*MWSL* 2:255). The Constitution of 1812 remained the touchstone of the loyalties that she declared in 1817 and that she held throughout her life.[36]

The Problem of the Female Quixote

The ancestral voices Mary Shelley heard in her incarnations of *Don Quixote* were not limited to William Godwin's. Her mother, Mary Wollstonecraft, mentioned Cervantes in her eloquent denunciation of the dangers to women of reading romance. Wollstonecraft anticipates the feminist insights of Catherine Belsey, who draws from Louis Althusser to argue that "not only [does] literature [represent] the myths and imaginary versions of real social relationships which constitute ideology, but also that classic realist fiction, the dominant literary form of the nineteenth century ... 'interpellates' the reader, addresses itself to him or her directly, offering the reader as the position from which the text is most 'obviously' intelligible, the position of the *subject in (and of) ideology*" (original emphasis).[37] In other words, literature forms a script—Mary Shelley said she was "acting a novel"—which the reader performs, in Althusser's and Belsey's view, unconsciously.

In the eighteenth century, Wollstonecraft and others were concerned not with classic realist fiction, as Belsey is, but with romances like the ones Cervantes satirized in *Don Quixote* and with which his was often grouped. For a woman reader, romances pose two obvious points of entry for such socialization: One interpellates her as a heroine or, for shorthand, a Dulcinea, after Don Quixote's mistress. Such an interpellation would maintain the feminine values of attractiveness to men and sexual virtue while offering women the limited but devious power over men available in a courtly system.[38] Or the woman reader can be interpellated as a hero, a Don Quixote, in hopes of attaining autonomy and intellectual scope, of being a full subject, at the cost of endangering her propriety by daring to cross gender lines. Thus romance implies a politics of gender in confronting women readers with two starkly opposed roles, neither one satisfactory.

Mary Shelley knew about this problem through Wollstonecraft's writings. The problem, for Wollstonecraft, was that women interpellated as heroines become blind to other models for their own behavior: "Women who are amused by the reveries of stupid novelists," writes Wollstonecraft, do so partly because, being "denied all political privileges . . . their attention [is] naturally drawn from the interest of the whole community to that of the minute parts," thus reinforcing the status quo. Since women readers this poorly educated cannot comprehend the general good, they are "confined to trifling employments," and "shamefully . . . neglect the duties of life." [39] As with Belsey, what concerns Wollstonecraft is the enforced passivity of "the subject in (and of) ideology" who seems to have herself freely chosen her limited lot in life. [40]

This attempt to conform to a truncated version of full subjectivity is reinforced by reading romances, as Wollstonecraft wrote in *Maria; or, the Wrongs of Woman*: "In many works of this species, the hero is allowed to be mortal, and to become wise and virtuous as well as happy, by a train of events and circumstances. The heroines, on the contrary, are to be born immaculate, and to act like goddesses of wisdom, just come forth highly finished Minervas from the head of Jove." [41] Wollstonecraft implies that any reader, male or female, would identify with a hero who "is allowed to be mortal" and who is shaped ("allowed . . . to become wise") by a process, "a train of events or circumstances." [42] The alternative, identifying with the "immaculate" heroines, is to accept confinement and stultification. Significantly, Wollstonecraft explicitly linked this problem with unseating Cervantes: "To speak disrespectfully of love is, I know, high treason against sentiment and fine feelings; but I wish to speak the simple language of truth, and rather to address the head than the heart. *To endeavour to reason love out of the world, would be to out Quixote Cervantes*" (emphasis added). [43] Wollstonecraft thus provides a clue that *Don Quixote,* its satiric purpose ignored, served as the touchstone for a politics of gender. Mary Shelley's tactic of casting herself as Sancho to P. B. Shelley's Quixote then also negotiates a politics of gender, as she avoids playing either the lead role, Quixote, or the role of Dulcinea, Don Quixote's mistress.

From the point of view of present-day feminists, Mary Shelley's identification with Sancho appears to be a capitulation to the process Judith Fetterley called "the *immasculation* of women by men." In this process, "as readers and teachers and scholars, women are taught to think as men, to identify with a male point of view, and to accept as normal and legitimate a male system of values, one of whose central principles is misogyny" (original emphasis). [44] Immasculated women readers dismiss women characters as trivial, identifying with males instead. While this perception may have some merit, from a historical point of view it is more important to recognize Mary Shelley's search for a life of significance and intellectual scope. Her search was conducted against a backdrop that began with Cervantes' domesticated Dulcinea but became more complex and trivializing of women as later novelists expanded on the Quixote theme.

Wollstonecraft probably used Cervantes as the touchstone for women interpellated as heroines because of the example of Charlotte Lennox's 1752 novel, *The Female Quixote*. Despite its title, which implies that Lennox's Arabella identifies with heroes or Quixotes, the plot's problem arises because Arabella is interpellated so severely as a heroine. She imagines, for example, that one of her suitors resembles Oroondates, the Prince of Scythia, a hero in *Cassandra, or the fam'd Romance* (1652), by Gauthier de Costes de la Calprenède, thus staying true to her feminine role as the object of affection. Like Cervantes' Quixote, however, she frequently misconstrues situations completely because of her books. Upon being educated out of her delusion, as part of the instruction that makes her marriageable, Arabella learns that "Love . . . is the Business, the sole Business of Ladies in Romances." [45] Lennox implies that "Ladies" in real life have other, more serious occupations, a conclusion that to some extent anticipates Wollstonecraft but ostensibly serves a more conservative agenda— making Arabella marriageable by reinstating her in a world of chastened dreams. What both Wollstonecraft and Lennox share is a fear of being trivialized because of interpellation as a heroine.

Mary Shelley's knowledge of these writers, and of their critique, can be inferred from her extensive reading of her mother's works, which she turned to frequently from 1814 to 1822 (*MWSJ* 684). The documentation for Lennox is sketchier. Mary Shelley alludes to Lennox in a letter of 1825, in which she refers to herself as "a female Quixote" (*MWSL* 1:499–500), although Lennox's novel does not appear on the Shelleys' Reading List. Yet Mary Shelley's own 1835 novel *Lodore,* discussed below, alludes to Lennox specifically in the remark that Ethel Lodore had "something of the Orondates' [*sic*] vein in her ideas" (*L* 25 and n). The dangers of interpellation as a heroine are clearly laid out: for Wollstonecraft, being trivialized and losing the chance at a life with intellectual scope; for Lennox, being trivialized and made unmarketable for marriage.

The romance posed for women readers the equal and opposite danger of interpellating them as heroes, as playing the part of Don Quixote himself, a danger articulated in the conservative rhetoric of the female Quixote, which had become inextricably tied to Wollstonecraft as an example of a woman who transgressed gender expectations by what she herself called asking "*men's* questions."[46] The Rev. Richard Polwhele, in *The Unsex'd Females* (1798), denounced Wollstonecraft as chief among "the female Quixotes."[47] While Polwhele was doubtless attacking, under the rubric of "quixotic," Wollstonecraft's Jacobin politics, his poem makes clear that the gender politics, the "unsex[ing]," bothers him just as much. The female Quixotes he denounces are also attacked as a "female band despising NATURE's law" (line 6) and as an "Amazonian band" (6 n). Clearly, then, a woman interpellated as a hero, Don Quixote, threatens the conservative ideal.

Following Polwhele, the motif of the female Quixote became a staple of anti-Jacobin and anti-Wollstonecraft rhetoric. Gary Kelly observes that numerous novels of the late 1790s "show the Quixote figure as an impractical dupe of 'Jacobin' intriguers, conspirators, and seducers. Accordingly, these novels usually gender the Quixote female, since 'woman' had long been a figure for the subvertible, seducible element in a social class and since the villain in anti-Jacobin novels aims to subvert the state by subverting 'domestic woman' and domesticity."[48] This subgenre of "female Quixote" novels makes its most pointed reference to the Godwin circle in Elizabeth Hamilton's *Memoirs of Modern Philosophers* (1800), a novel Mary Shelley read (*MWSJ* 651). There Hamilton satirizes Wollstonecraft's admirer Mary Hays as "Bridgetina Botherim." Bridgetina's pedigree, both Wollstonecraftian and quixotic, is clear from an early exchange between her mother, Mrs. Botherim, and Bridgetina in front of a Mr. Mapple:

"You will find, if you converse with her a little, that she is far too learned to trouble herself about doing any thing useful. Do, Bridgetina, my dear, talk to your cousin a little about the *cowsation,* and *perfebility,* and all them there things as Mr. Glib and you are so often upon. You have no ideer what a scholar she is . . . she has read every book in the circulating library, and Mr. Glib declares she knows them better than he does himself."

"Indeed, mamma, but I do no such thing," cried Bridgetina, pettishly: "do you think I would take the trouble of going through all the dry stuff in Mr. Glib's collection—history and travels, sermons and matters of fact? I hope I have a better taste! You know very well I never read anything but novels and metaphysics."[49]

Although Hamilton prefers the term "female philosophers" to "female Quixotes," Bridgetina's quixotic heritage is clear from her reading habits, in which new Godwinian metaphysics, like the novels of her predecessors, distance her from middle-class values. As Kelly notes, Bridgetina's Wollstonecraftian heritage is clear from her name, Bridgetina or Biddy, a diminutive of Bridget or Bride, "alluding to Bridewell, the house of correction for prostitutes," with which Wollstonecraft was famously equated.[50] Mary Shelley read Hamilton's novel in 1816, the year she was composing *History of a Six Weeks' Tour*. In the court of public opinion, even more than Wollstonecraft's disciple, Wollstonecraft's own daughter stood in greater peril of replicating her mother, of repeating "Bridget's" mistakes as a "Bridgetina."

That there still was a court of public opinion on the matter in the decade 1810–1820 is registered by another "female Quixote" novel, Eaton Stannard Barrett's *The Heroine; or the Adventures of a Fair Romance Reader* (1813), titled *The Heroine; or the Adventures of Cherubina* in its second edition (1814). Barrett reflects the fear of "unsex'd" women raised by the specter of Wollstonecraft, as Cherry, the heroine, imitates the male heroes of romance. At first content with the respectable enough fantasy that she will be rescued by a hero (echoing Lennox's Arabella), boredom forces Cherry to take the masculine part and declare, "I see plainly that if adventure does not come to me, I must go to adventure" (1:72).[51] She ventures into the masculine world of politics, preaching for parliamentary reform and even (as Barrett takes a cue from Lucas's *Infernal Quixote*), making common cause with the United Irishmen. When her speeches are well received, she declares: "I now found that a popular speech was not difficult, and I judged, from my performance that the same qualities which have made me a good Heroine would, if I were a man, have made me just as illustrious a Patriot" (3:128). In this quotation we see Barrett striking the equivalence between "Heroine" and "Patriot"; Cherry's declaration that "the same qualities" mark both roles reveals how closely the role of heroine or female Quixote resembled, for the conservatives, the political territory forbidden to women. Thus Barrett registers strongly the fear that women readers of romance will be interpellated as heroes, identify across gender lines, and by that very act enter politics. This fear of gender transgression is crystallized, for Barrett, in Cherry's decision that her "real" (i.e. chivalric) name is Cherubina—an echo of the name of Bridgetina, Hamilton's female Quixote, and also an allusion to the part of Cherubino in Mozart's *Marriage of Figaro* (1786), a "breeches-part" in which a woman cross-dresses as a man. Like Polwhele's "Amazonian band," "Cherubina" marks a transgression past acceptable gender boundaries.

The history of the "female Quixote" subgenre reveals two things. First, romances promise and threaten women readers with two equally unattractive choices—"bubbled" triviality if they identify with the heroine Dulcinea, "unsex'd" transgression if they identify with the hero Don Quixote. Second, the female Quixote by 1817 was inextricably linked to Wollstonecraft, her sexuality, her radical opinions, and her infamy. Faced with this cultural obstacle, Mary Shelley's choice of the role of Sancho permits her not only to avoid Dulcinea's triviality by venturing out with the hero Don Quixote but also to avoid the ridiculousness embodied in male Quixotes and the gender transgression embodied in female Quixotes.[52] Mary Shelley creates a gentler version of Wollstonecraft's heritage by identifying across gender lines as the squire, troping herself as a follower, not a replication, of Wollstonecraft's female Quixote. The empowerment involved in this compromise is revealed in the introduction to the 1831 edition of *Frankenstein*. Of the novel's origin, she writes: "Everything must have a beginning, to speak in Sanchean phrase; and that beginning must be linked to something that went before" (*F* 178), alluding to a remark by Sancho that in government "everything depends upon the beginning" (pt. 2, chap. 33; *F* 187 n). Near-silence and writer's block ("I was a devout but nearly silent listener"; *F* 179) had characterized the early stages of her participation in the ghost-story contest; her breakthrough comes in Sancho's persona, "speak[ing] in Sanchean phrase."[53]

The compromise worked by Mary Shelley is explored in greater depth in her novel *Lodore* (1835), in which the Cervantean vocabulary delineates the problems of interpellation in romance. This novel reworks material from the period of the quixotic elopement journey, as the characters Ethel and Edward Villiers try to evade bailiffs just as the Shelleys had done on returning to England.[54] Of *Lodore*, Mary Shelley wrote to Maria Gisborne, "did you recognize any of Shelley's and my early adventures—when we were in danger of being starved in Switzerland—& could get no dinner at an inn in London?" (*MWSL* 2:261), incidents shaped into fiction when

Ethel and Edward are refused service at an inn. Mary Shelley describes the Villiers' enchantment:

> [They] were so engrossed by the gladness of re-union, that had Cinderella's godmother transmuted their crazy vehicle for a golden coach, redolent of the perfumes of fairy land, they had scarcely been aware of the change. Their own hearts formed a more real fairy land, which accompanied them withersoever they went, and could as easily spread its enchantments over the shattered machine in which they now jumbled along, as amidst the cloth and gold of an eastern palace. (*L* 227–28)

While Mary Shelley chose the part of Sancho in *History of a Six Weeks' Tour,* Ethel chooses the Dulcinea part, saying, "we will play the incognito in such a style, that if our adventures were printed, they would compete with those of Don Quixote and the fair Dulcinea" (*L* 227). The narrator hints at the danger of looking trivial inherent in Ethel's choice, commenting: "There was something of the Orondates' vein in [Ethel's] ideas," an allusion to one of the more persistent textual delusions of Lennox's heroine Arabella (*L* 25 and n).

The novel goes on to explore the limitations inherent in Ethel's interpellation into Dulcinea's part. Ethel exults, "How much happier we are than all the heroes and heroines that ever lived or were imagined" (*L* 233), but the narrator suggests that her idealism cannot withstand too much reality: after her release from debtors' prison, "The sight of misery or vice . . . tarnished the holy fervour with which she would otherwise have made every sacrifice for Edward's sake. There is something in this world, which even while it gives an unknown grace to rough, and hard, and mean circumstances, contaminates the beauty and harmony of the noble and exalted" (*L* 275). Ethel is not reduced to the triviality of Lennox's Arabella, but she does seem to lack the fortitude Mary Shelley had, of necessity, embodied herself.

Lodore draws a contrast in Ethel's friend Fanny Derham, who chooses quite differently. Again, Mary Shelley uses Cervantes as a kind of shorthand: "Fanny's first principle was, that what she ought to do, that she could do, without hesitation or regard for obstacles. She had something Quixotic in her nature; or rather she would have had, if a clear head and some experience, even young as she was, had not stood in the way of her making any glaring mistakes, so that her enterprises were never ridiculous; and being usually successful, could not be called extravagant" (*L* 218–19).

Fanny, then, with the "something Quixotic in her nature," delineates a path for the woman reader of romance that is more sensible and more male-identified; her quixotic nature is tempered by being "never ridiculous." Fanny, however, remains a spinster at the novel's close, so this outcome could well be the lot of the woman reader of romance who takes not only the male role but the starring one.

In light of this dichotomy, in which Ethel traces one path as Dulcinea and Fanny another as Quixote, it makes sense that Mary Shelley consistently constructed her own role as that of Sancho, perhaps falling prey to the "immasculation" Fetterley fears by identifying against her sex but avoiding the Scylla and Charybdis of the self-deception shown by Ethel and the isolation that is Fanny Derham's lot. Mary Shelley clusters the traits of unconventionality in Fanny Derham while investing Ethel Lodore with more obviously feminine virtues. Ethel enacts the role of Dulcinea in her more domestic and proper sphere, accompanying her husband in the confines of prison — a husband who by his confinement is feminized — rather than ranging with him in the masculine world of journeys and jousts. *Lodore*, then, in its reworking of *Don Quixote*, presents a vindication of Mary Shelley's choice.

Curiously, it is upon concluding *Lodore* that Mary Shelley makes her sole unqualified identification with Don Quixote (unqualified by the term "female," that is, as in *MWSL* 1:499–500). *Lodore*'s printer lost a substantial section of volume three; since she had made no copy, Mary Shelley had to interrupt the Lardner *Lives* to rewrite the lost section. In the midst of this tangle, she wrote to Charles Ollier, who, with his brother James, had been P. B. Shelley's publisher from 1817 to 1822 and who now was working as chief literary advisor to Richard Bentley, the publisher of *Lodore*[55]: "You seem to think that you gave me an easy task in rewriting that unlucky MS — quite the contrary. . . . Give my compliments to Mr Bentl[e]y & tell him I am very sorry, that like Don Quixote, an Enchanter meddles with my affairs" (*MWSL* 2:206). Mary Shelley's allusion to Cervantes, recalling Don Quixote's standard excuse for befuddlement, that an enchanter was meddling in his affairs (e.g. pt. 1, chaps. 8 and 45), may well have been prompted by her previous association with Ollier, the copublisher, with Thomas Hookham, of *History of a Six Weeks' Tour*. Though an apparent departure from Mary Shelley's lifelong self-characterization as Sancho, this self-description as Don Quixote oddly accords with the pattern I have been describing, in that it associates Don Quixote with the experience of being silenced, of having lost one's manuscript, while the less ambitious course allows her to speak "in Sanchean phrase."

It is in *Rambles in Germany and Italy* that Mary Shelley offers a retrospective on her lifelong role as Sancho. As she returns to England from Lake Como, her son and his friends having gone ahead separately, she and her maid travel by *vetturino* with three Scotswomen. At Lago Maggiore, on a side trip to the Borromean island of Isola Bella, she writes:

> An island all to one's self is ever flattering to the imagination. No one to intrude unknown; the whole rule of the demesne in one's sovereign hands. . . . Taken all in all, I should like to live here; here to enjoy the aspect of grand scenery, the pleasures of elegant seclusion, and the advantages of civilization, joined to the independent delights of a solitude which we would hope to people, were it ours, with a few chosen spirits.
>
> Such reveries possessed me, as I fancied life spent here, and pictured English friends arriving down from the mighty Simplon, and Italians taking refuge in my halls from persecution and oppression—a little world of my own—a focus whence would emanate some light for the country around—a school for civilization, a refuge for the unhappy, a support for merit in adversity: from such a gorgeous dream I was awakened when my foot touched shore, and I was transformed from the Queen of Isola Bella into a poor traveller, humbly pursuing her route in an unpretending *vettura*. Such, for the most part, has been my life. Dreams of joy and good, which have lent me wings to leave the poverty and desolation of reality. How without such dreams I could have past [*sic*] long sad years, I know not. (*TW* 143)

Mary Shelley's fantasy of possessing "the whole rule of the demesne" forms an extended allusion to a crucial part of Sancho's story. Early on in their association, Don Quixote recruits Sancho as his squire by promising him the governorship of any island that he, Don Quixote, might conquer (pt. 1, chap. 7), an ambition that motivates Sancho's own activities and suggests that Sancho is somewhat autonomous in his service of chivalric ideals. Late in the sequel, Cervantes invents a group of malevolents who play an elaborate practical joke, apparently granting the squire his longstanding wish (pt. 2, chaps. 42–55). Sancho surprises everybody with his probity as a magistrate, but when the practical joke is revealed all of his ethical efforts prove ineffectual and ridiculous.

The Sanchean echo in Mary Shelley's abdication as "Queen of Isola

Bella" suggests that she too has renounced a dream of scope, offering political shelter to Britons and Italians from "persecution and oppression," a fusion of the domestic and political much like Euthanasia's in *Valperga*, in which "the world of [her] own" — a domestic space — would radiate "civilization" to the country around it, at that time in the full pursuit of national unity. Moreover, in a touching instance of symmetry, Mary Shelley was awakened "from such a gorgeous dream . . . when my foot first touched shore." Just as the teenaged travel-writer transformed herself into Sancho Panza by eloping, the mature travel-writer breaks the enchantment by returning to Italy, the scene where enchantment was most powerful, and then journeying home. We may conclude, then, that Mary Shelley's light Cervantean touch in *History of a Six Weeks' Tour* serves as a precocious declaration of lifelong political and filial loyalties and that the travel book as a whole functions much as an operatic overture, foreshadowing political and literary themes that sound as a leitmotif throughout her *oeuvre*.

3 : The Impact of *Frankenstein*

WILLIAM ST CLAIR

Literary and cultural history has traditionally been mainly concerned with authors and with texts. The printed writings of the past are presented as a march past of great names described from a commentator's box set high above the parade. Here we see the Augustans, followed by the Romantics, and then the Victorians. Early Modern gives way to the Enlightenment, and then the Revolutionary Age—or whichever other descriptive categories have been chosen.

We also have critical and hermeneutic models, nowadays applied to noncanonical as well as to canonical texts, which also give much weight to the chronological order of first composition. According to the conventions of these approaches, literary texts are believed somehow to catch the essence, or some essence, of the times that produced them or to reveal the discourses and ideologies with which the men and women of these times culturally constructed the historical situations in which they found themselves. And there are other text-based approaches that cut across time boundaries, for example, employing psychoanalytic theories to excavate a text's hidden meanings or applying theories of myth to help explain the enduring appeal of a story.

However, for answering the question that I wish to address here— What was the actual historical impact of *Frankenstein?*—none of these approaches is complete or satisfactory. All text-based and critical approaches, because they either ignore readers altogether or derive their readers from the texts, are caught in a closed system. Although they may help us to understand what meanings the readers of the past may have taken from a text, or ought to have taken if they were perceptive enough, they cannot, by themselves, without circularity, reveal the meanings they actually did take. They cannot take account of the fact that the impact of a text occurs at a time different from when it was first produced and often in different cultural circumstances. These approaches cannot therefore, by themselves, ever enable us to trace, let alone to quantify, wider cultural effects and cultural outcomes.

Reports of individual reactions to the reading of a text as recorded in, for example, letters, diaries, and other documents, can help us break out of the closed circle implicit in text-based approaches. But they too raise severe methodological problems. When the reports are as plentiful as they are in the case of *Frankenstein*, it is easy to slip into the belief that we have a reliable record of actual reception. Many commentators forget that however many such reports are found, even at best they can never be anything beyond a tiny, randomly surviving, and perhaps highly unrepresentative sample of the far larger total of individual acts of reception that were never even turned into words let alone recorded. The same methodological difficulties apply to the use of published reviews. Although useful for establishing horizons of expectations, published reviews cannot be assumed to be representative records of actual reception for anyone other than their authors, and often not even for them.[1]

How then can we trace the historical and cultural influence of *Frankenstein* without becoming presentist, determinist, circular, or anecdotal? How can we retrieve readerships? Counting the numbers of recorded editions, a commonly used surrogate for estimating readerships, is of only limited use. In the Romantic period the print runs of individual editions made from moveable type ranged from 500 or less to 10,000 or more. At the same time, many so-called editions were unsold sheets reissued with a new title page. With the adoption of stereotyping, the very notion of an "edition" makes little sense, as the example of *Frankenstein* vividly illustrates.

The approach to retrieving literary impact that I offer is to trace the text from the mind of the author, through the materiality of print, to the minds of readers. From book production figures, it is an easy step to book sales. I then use bibliographical information such as format, price, print runs, and lending and renting patterns to help to identify and, where possible, to quantify the readerships of the text at different times. Having identified the different constituencies of men and women who encountered the text in its different forms and attempted to assess or estimate the main cultural characteristics they brought to their experience, we have a more secure basis and a more systemic context on and within which to place and judge scattered empirical information of differing evidential value.

Authors, with few exceptions, want their books to be read. Without implying that texts consist of nothing more than authors' intentions, it is legitimate to begin with their own views. From the wealth of surviving material, we know a good deal about what the author Mary Shelley and her collaborator P. B. Shelley hoped for from the writing and publishing of *Frankenstein*. The preface, for example, which was drafted by P.B., explains that the story was not "a mere tale of spectres or enchantment" but "a point of view to the imagination for the delineating of human passions more comprehensive and commanding than any which the ordinary relations of existing events can yield." *Frankenstein*, the paratext declared, was a serious book with a serious purpose.

There is another resource of unique value. Nowadays it is considered unprofessional for authors to review books written by their friends, relatives, or lovers. In the Romantic period insider reviewing was easier, especially as reviews were invariably anonymous. Literary journals, which were each owned by the main book publishers, were not independent cultural institutions but an integral part of the network of horizontal and vertical property relationships which bound together the production, selling, and renting of books. Their editors seldom suffered Romantic agonies about preserving the creative freedom and artistic integrity of their contributors. The commonly held belief that journals could be bribed to give favorable reviews was, according to Hazlitt, himself a much bullied reviewer, quite untrue—a favorable notice, he says, could be obtained "through interest or to oblige a friend, but it must invariably be done for love, not money." [2]

One way of trading favors was for book publishers to supply review editors with readily written reviews. [3] P. B. Shelley prepared three such reviews in 1818, including one of *Frankenstein*. A passage from that review can be taken as an authoritative, explicit, and reliable statement of what he and Mary Shelley regarded as the main intended meaning and message of the work:

In this the direct moral of the book consists; and it is perhaps the most important, and of the most universal application of any moral that can be enforced by example. Treat a person ill, and he will become wicked.

Requite affection with scorn;—let one being be selected, for whatever cause, as the refuse of his kind—divide him, a social being, from society, and you impose upon him the irresistible obligations—malevolence and selfishness. It is thus that, too often in society, those who are best qualified to be its benefactors and its ornaments, are branded by some accident with scorn, and changed, by neglect and solitude of heart, into a scourge and a curse.[4]

Like virtually everything written by members of the Godwin and Shelley families, *Frankenstein* had a social, political, and ethical purpose. In accordance with the Godwinian theory of progress, in which the author and her collaborator both believed, *Frankenstein*, they hoped and intended, would help to change the perceptions, the knowledge, the understanding, and therefore ultimately the behavior, of those individuals who read or otherwise encountered it. Their book, they hoped, would contribute, in its small way, to the general intellectual and moral improvement of society in its slow, much interrupted, but cumulative progress towards perfection.

In making the publishing arrangements on Mary Shelley's behalf, P. B. Shelley told prospective publishers that he was acting for a friend who was abroad, a pretense that authors often adopted to protect themselves from disappointment. A phrase in the preface implies that the author was a man.[5] But if the publishers thought that P. B. Shelley was himself the author, that was no advantage in the negotiation. Both *Queen Mab* and *Alastor* had been printed "on commission," and the same would be true of *Laon and Cythna*, which was being turned down by another publisher at the same time he was negotiating for *Frankenstein*. In 1817 P. B. Shelley was just one of many unknown and unsuccessful authors whose books could only be published at his own expense and risk, if at all.[6] The notion that Mary Shelley was held back in the shadow of a famous and successful male author is an anachronistic casting back of modern presumptions.

Frankenstein was rejected by Murray and probably by Longman, the two leading publishers of the day.[7] Ollier, P. B. Shelley's own publisher, took only three days to say no. P. B. Shelley then turned to the outside firm of Lackington. Although they too declined to buy the copyright either in whole or in part, as P. B. Shelley had proposed, they offered to print the book at their expense, taking all profits, if there were any, from the first edition, the implication being that if the book did well, the author would benefit from a second edition. P. B. Shelley countered with an offer of half profits, and in August Lackington contracted to publish a single edition of 500 copies, dividing the net profits one-third to the author, two-thirds to the publisher.

Frankenstein, or, The Modern Prometheus, went on sale late in the year.[8] Like most novels of the time it was anonymous, in three volumes, and very expensive, a book intended to be sold primarily to commercial circulating libraries, with perhaps less than half the edition expected to go to individual buyers. The circulating libraries, which rented books to their members by the volume, liked the three-volume format since it allowed the same book to be out to more than one reader at a time. For circulating library readers, the effect was to require the story to be read as a serial in episodes, usually over three weeks. *Frankenstein* was only stretched to three volumes by printing few words to the line, few lines to the page, and few pages to the volume.

The plea in the preface for the book to be taken seriously was largely ignored when the book was reviewed in the literary press.[9] Lackington specialized in magic, pseudoscience, the illegitimate supernatural, and horror, a fact emphasized by their advertisements.[10] Although the advertisement pages were normally removed when books were bound, review copies remained unbound. For many purchasers or renters of the book, the advertisements therefore acted as an optional, disposable, extra paratext helping to preset their expectations as readers. In the case of *Frankenstein* the effect of this extra paratext was to offset the effect of the main paratext.

The book, it was noted by some reviewers, carried a dedication to Mary Shelley's father, the philosopher William Godwin. Despite the anonymity, the reviewers therefore correctly guessed that it was written by one of the Godwin circle—it was therefore likely to be objectionable. But on what grounds? The notion that the dead could be made to live again by manmade agency was, it was suggested, atheistical and blasphemous, a secret attack on a central tenet of the Christian religion. "These volumes have neither principle, object, nor moral," thundered the conservative *British Critic.* "The horror which abounds in them is too grotesque and *bizarre* ever to approach the sublime." The young Thomas Carlyle, who had only read a favorable review, reported that "Frankenstein, by Godwin's son in law, seems to be another unnatural disgusting fiction."[11] According to

William Beckford, the author of *Vathek,* another unusual and disturbing novel, *Frankenstein* was "perhaps the foulest Toadstool that has yet sprung from the reeking dunghill of present times."[12]

The whole edition of 500 copies was sold to the retail booksellers almost as soon as the copies were printed, so passing all the remaining sales risks to them, and the book reached its initial readers over the following months and years.[13] The total net profit declared to the author was more than the total declared cost of manufacturing, advertising, and selling the book. In 1818 Mary Shelley, with her third share, was commercially a far more successful author than P. B. Shelley. The first edition of *Frankenstein* had outsold all the works of her husband put together. It made more money than all P. B. Shelley's works would fetch in his lifetime. The gross rate of return to the publisher on his investment in *Frankenstein* cannot have been less than about 300 percent at an annual rate.

With such high and immediate profits on small sales and with plenty of publicity already obtained from advertising and reviews, it might have been expected that the publisher would have wanted to build on his success, especially as the possibility of a second edition had been discussed in the negotiations. But for Lackington, which had contracted for one edition only, the selling out of the first edition to the retailers was the end of the matter. In making this decision, Lackington was following the usual practice. Publishers' archives of the time record the publication of dozens of novels in three volumes in editions of 500 or 750, many without a spark of originality. The reason why *Frankenstein* had been turned down so decisively by the mainstream publishers probably had more to do with doubts about its subject matter than with any fears about its literary quality or commercial prospects. Publishers and circulating library owners were well aware that in the postwar decades, the narrow group of well-off readers upon whom their livelihoods depended was, for the most part, deeply conservative, indeed reactionary, in their political and religious opinions.

In 1823, five years after the first publication, Godwin wrote to tell his daughter that he had heard that a stage version was to be produced.[14] As the law stood then, the theater was able to adapt a novel without the need for permission either from the author or from the publisher. But if *Presumption, or the Fate of Frankenstein* and the rival stage versions that followed, were, we may say, legally pirated, they also helped to spread knowledge of the book. Godwin was able to negotiate for a second edition from another publisher which included some textual changes, this time in two volumes but still an unnecessarily extravagant format and still at a high retail price. Perhaps in an attempt to exploit the notoriety of the name which had now been publicly revealed, the second edition was advertised as by Mary Wollstonecraft Shelley.[15] Copies were still available at full price in the 1830s and probably later.[16] In 1831, however, again as a result of the interest caused by stage versions, Mary Shelley was able to sell the copyright to Richard Bentley for 600 shillings, the last financial benefit she or her family would ever receive from her work.[17]

Bentley, one of the most innovative publishers of the century, was among the first to realize the implications of the sharp increase in the price of three-volume novels, 'three deckers,' which the publishers had brought about in the previous decade.[18] In the late 1820s the owners of the copyrights of the Waverley novels had sharply reduced the prices and were rewarded with a huge surge in sales. Bentley realized that if he could buy the tail ends of copyrights of out-of-print novels cheaply, he could take a second tranche of profit from circulating libraries and from individuals who had not bought the first time round. Bentley insisted as a condition of buying a copyright that the author should correct errors and supply new material either in the text or as a preface or notes. Even if the changes were minimal, the revisions allowed him to claim a new copyright which, if not valid in law, would normally be respected within the mainstream book industry. If authors were reluctant or too busy to revise their texts, Bentley offered them the services of a professional reviser to do the work for them.

Mary Shelley was happy to comply. She made numerous changes to the text, some quite substantial, and added an autobiographical introduction explaining how and when the book came to be written. The new introduction, which was printed alongside the original 1817 preface, emphasized that in its essentials the story was unchanged and that the composition had been written in a collaboration with P. B. Shelley, but it said little further about the book's moral purpose. The *Bentley's Standard Novels* edition of *Frankenstein,* like most of the books in the series, was described as "Revised, Corrected, and Illustrated, with a New Introduction by the Author."

The initial list of *Bentley's Standard Novels* included works by many excellent recent authors whose works had become unavailable: Austen,

Beckford, Bulwer-Lytton, Burney, Edgeworth, Fenimore Cooper, Ferrier, Galt, Godwin, Marryat, Peacock, and others. With the exception of the Waverley novels, Bentley had made himself the owner of the copyrights of almost all the best fiction of the Romantic period. With a new title coming out every few weeks, *Bentley's Standard Novels* provided a carefully selected serial reading of most of the best fictional writing of the recent past. The books were tightly printed in one volume, already bound in cloth, so saving customers the usual further cost of rebinding, and included an engraved frontispiece. However, although they were less than a fifth of the price of new novels, they were not cheap by absolute terms. In the 1830s, a single *Bentley's Standard Novel* cost the equivalent of about half the weekly wage of a clerk or of a skilled manual worker. Bentley's novels were more expensive than Waverley novels, whose sales were far higher, and they were twice as expensive as reprints of out-of-copyright novels of similar length.[19] Within his chosen market, Bentley positioned himself as a monopolist as far upmarket as he could go.

The initial print run for the *Bentley's Standard Novels Frankenstein* was 3,500, with over 3,000 copies sold to the retailers in the first year.[20] Already the book showed a profit after all costs, capital, and current had been met, although at an amount well below Lackington's profit on the first 500. But having taken the second tranche of profit by offering the book at a reduced price, Bentley was in no hurry to take the third. That would only make commercial sense when the market at six shillings had been entirely exhausted.

When he bought the copyright of *Frankenstein*, Bentley could, as the law stood at the time, have expected to keep his monopoly until 1846 or, if the revised version was respected within the book industry, until 1859.[21] As events turned out, Mary Shelley was still alive at the time of the Copyright Act of 1842, which extended the copyright period to forty-eight years or the author's life plus seven, whichever was the longer. Bentley and his heirs thus found themselves windfall owners of a copyright monopoly on *Frankenstein*, which they could enjoy at least until 1866 and with luck until 1879.

Bentley's Standard Novels were printed using stereotype plates. Once the plates had been manufactured and used for the first printing, they could be put into storage to be brought out and used again later. Although over time the plates became worn, making the books printed later harder to read, they could, with the help of occasional repairs, continue to be reused again and again almost indefinitely as long as there was any demand.[22] Not only was Bentley therefore able to match his supply to a varying demand without the expense of resetting the book in moveable type, but he could also operate with smaller stocks than were needed when books were manufactured by moveable type technology. With all his capital costs on the copyright and on the manufacturing plant already paid for from sales from the first printing, his marginal manufacturing costs low and decreasing, and his working capital minimized, Bentley would have been highly competitive even without the protection of the lengthened copyright. For more than twenty years, he and his successors milked his properties, both the intellectual and the physical, accepting a steady fall in sales and working the increasingly obsolete plant, without replacement, until the books ceased to be sellable even at reduced prices.

In 1838, before the copyright change, William Hazlitt Junior, the essayist's son, asked Mary Shelley's permission to include *Frankenstein* in his series *The Romancist and Novelist's Library.* By this time, as a result of mechanization of manufacturing methods and reductions in the taxed price of paper, a new branch of the book industry had grown up, able to print fiction at prices far lower than had been possible even a few years before. *The Romancist and Novelist's Library* was cheap not only in relation to new three-volume novels and to Bentley's reprints but also in absolute terms in relation to incomes. "It is astonishing to me how much can be got for 2d [two pence, or one sixth of a shilling]," Mary Shelley replied. "I must have every Wednesday enlivened by your sheet."[23] But, having sold the copyright, Mary Shelley no longer had any rights over *Frankenstein*.

The copyright owners, protecting their high prices, said no, and they seem to have refused permission for any of the titles in *Bentley's Standard Novels* to be reprinted.[24] Other publishers of other copyrighted novels seem to have done the same. The sharp fall in the price of recently published books, which, had it not been for the copyright change of 1842, would have occurred in the 1840s, was postponed for a generation. Denied permission to reprint good modern English literature, Hazlitt and the other cheap fiction publishers turned to novels first published in America, France, and Germany; in the absence of international copyright, these could be freely reprinted and translated. The shops that sprang up near the new railway stations in the 1840s, it was noticed by those who feared the growth of reading, were filled with piracies of American books, "cheap French novels of the shadiest class," and other "positively injurious aliment for the hungry minds that sought refreshment on their feverish way," including Byron's *Don Juan*.[25]

Soon, with the establishment of international copyright, French, German, and other European fiction ceased to be available. With the lengthening of the British copyright regime, the amount of new British fiction entering the public domain slowed. W. H. Smith, who bought out virtually all the railway stalls to establish a monopoly, saw it as his mission to "purify" the business, only supplying the books produced by regular publishers at regular prices. As one source after another was closed off, the publishers of cheap fiction increasingly employed hack writers to produce the stories needed to fill their columns. As one retail outlet after another was denied them, such publishers were increasingly obliged to bypass the regular bookshops.

The *Bentley's Standard Novels Frankenstein* is found with four different title pages, dated 1831, 1832, 1839, and 1849. But, as the publishing and printing records show, this does not mean that there were four editions or four printings, as has always been assumed in previous writings about the book's publishing history. With *Frankenstein,* as with the other books in the series, Bentley's decisions on when to create a new title page were not timed to the selling out of previously printed stocks but to his general policies for occasionally relaunching and repricing and changing the binding style of *Bentley's Standard Novels* as a whole.[26]

By the mid 1850s, when the price of *Frankenstein* was down to 2.5 shillings, demand for all the *Bentley's Standard Novels* had fallen to a trickle and the series was allowed to die. Sometime before 1861, by which time most of the copyrights were expiring, all the stereotype plates from the series, except for those of Austen and Ferrier, which still had some commercial life left in them, were melted as scrap.[27]

With one exception, for most of the 1850s, 1860s, and 1870s, *Frankenstein* was out of print. It had also disappeared from the circulating libraries.[28] As a novel, as a text, as a piece of writing in fixed form in which a property right had been established by law, *Frankenstein* was condemned to a long period of catalepsy, neither quite dead nor quite alive. Unable to think of a way to profit from the property themselves, the copyright owners were determined, it would seem, like the dog in the manger, to deny others the opportunity to do so. While in copyright, *Frankenstein* was never issued as a yellow back or as a shilling shocker, never abridged, turned into a chapbook, or otherwise adapted for the huge numbers of lower-income readers who joined the reading nation in the middle of the nineteenth century.

The House of Lords' legal decision of 1774, which had declared that perpetual copyright was unlawful, had, by bringing about a drastic fall in the price of certain older books, transferred a huge quantum of purchasing power from publishers to book-buyers, leading to an explosion of reading in the Romantic period, a growth in the size of the reading nation, and a sharp rise in the quality of the national literature to which there was now cheaper and more plentiful access. The 1842 Copyright Act produced an exactly reciprocal effect. It handed over the copyright ownership of much of the literature of the Romantic period to private monopolists. A wide range of literary texts which had been just about to enter the public domain were, by Act of Parliament, converted into valuable windfall assets from which the lucky owners could extract a monopoly rent for many years. The change kept the prices of the reasonably modern English books several times higher than would otherwise have been the case, and it held back most of the nation's access to recent good literature for another generation. Victorian moralists often complained that their less-well-off countrymen read mostly rubbish, and they were right. It was the copyright regime they established in 1842 which brought about this result.

For the first fourteen years of its life as a novel, *Frankenstein* existed in about a thousand copies, far fewer than most of the works of Lord Byron and Sir Walter Scott sold on publication day. However, although the main facts and numbers about the book's early publishing history were published long ago, many currently available editions intended for students still spread the error that the book sold well from the beginning. James Rieger's edition (1974), for example, declares that "the novel was an instant success." Maurice Hindle's Penguin Classics edition (1985), says that *Frankenstein* "became an immediate best-seller." The Modern Library edition (1993), declares that it "immediately became a best seller." The Broadview edition (1994), says that *Frankenstein* was "an enormous success" from the beginning.[29] Other modern editions, without being so explicit, also give a misleading impression of the size of the early readership.

During the first forty years of *Frankenstein*, between seven and eight thousand copies were printed and sold, still fewer than Byron and Scott commonly sold in the first week. Although many copies were bought by circulating libraries, the total readership cannot have been large on such a small base.[30] The readership during the first fifty years of the book's existence was largely confined to a narrow slice of men and women at the topmost end of the income scale.

The main change occurred in late Victorian times. As soon as *Frankenstein* came incontrovertibly out of copyright in about 1880, the reprinting began. The huge demand that had been held back after 1842 could at last be satisfied. The price plummeted and the print runs soared (see appendix). In the first year, the first reprint of *Frankenstein* sold more copies than all of the previous editions put together. By the 1890s Routledge had sold 40,000 copies, and soon *Frankenstein* was available in a range of editions adapted to different groups of book buyers. One could buy it in full, with attractive illustrations, at 1 percent of the original price, and there were abridgements and arrangements for buying the book in parts, as well as a few more expensive versions. At the turn of the century, eighty years after its first entry into print culture, *Frankenstein* at last became accessible to the whole reading nation.

Some of the late-nineteenth-century reprints are books for the poor and the poorly educated, offered with well-intended condescension to men and women who had previously lived largely without books. *Routledge's World Library,* a paperback series, set out the publisher's aims and described the expected readership in an advertisement printed in each of its books:

> When I think of the long, gossiping, yawning, gambling hours of grooms, valets, coachmen, and cabmen; the railway stations conveniently provided with bookstalls, and crowded every morning and evening with workmen's trains—the winter evenings in thousands of villages, wayside cottages, and scattered hamlets—the brief, but not always well spent leisure of factory hands in the north—the armies of commercial and uncommercial travelers with spare half hours—the shop assistants—the city offices with their hangers on—the Board Schools—the village libraries—the Army and Navy—the barrack or the dockyard—again the vision of Routledge's World Library rises before me, and I say, "This, if not a complete cure for indolence and vice, may at least prove a powerful counter charm." [31]

Frankenstein was a borderline case for inclusion. "I issue 'Frankenstein' with some degree of hesitation," the editor, the Rev. H. R. Haweis, M.A., confessed, "but after mature reflection. The subject is somewhat revolting, the treatment of it is somewhat hideous."

In the Victorian higher literary culture too, attitudes were ambivalent. *Frankenstein* remained morally (and perhaps politically) suspect, and the book was seldom reprinted for a middle-class readership. The late-nineteenth-century feminists, suffragists, and reformers, who wanted to promote Mary Shelley as an example of a woman of achievement in her own right, found her book an embarrassment. "Everyone now knows the story of 'The Modern Prometheus,'" wrote Mrs Marshall in her biography of Mary Shelley in 1889, but she appears ashamed to admit that Mary Shelley wrote "the ghastly but powerful allegorical romance." "Surely no girl, before or since," she notes, before hurrying on to more congenial topics, "has imagined, and carried out to its pitiless conclusion, so grim an idea." [32] Lucy Maddox Rossetti, who wrote the Mary Wollstonecraft Shelley volume for the *Eminent Women* series, is also defensive and ambiguous. "Mary," she notes, "evidently wished to show what a being, with no naturally bad propensities, might sink to when under the influence of a false position— the education of Rousseau's natural man not being here possible, and . . . having visited some of the most interesting places in the world, with some of the most interesting people, she is saved from the dreary dullness of the dull." [33] Richard Church, who wrote the Mary Shelley volume for the *Representative Women* series, blames P. B. Shelley for not discouraging Mary Shelley's "girlish romanticism" and so allowing the book to be "marred very seriously by a certain haste, an indolence, a vagueness of construction." Mary Shelley, he remarks, who "was inclined to be a "wet blanket" both to herself and those around her," suffered from an "overtrained intellectual conscience." [34]

These attitudes seem to have continued for most of the first half of the twentieth century. Although, with this period too, it is frequently assumed that the book always sold well, the record shows quite a different picture. According to the recorded sales of the main available edition, that of *Everyman's Library*, the total annual sales for the whole British market, which included India, Australia, South Africa, New Zealand, and other English speaking countries overseas other than those in North America, only rarely went above 500 a year. At a time when the United Kingdom alone had a population of about 50 million and reading was still the main entertainment, these are very modest figures.

Reading the book, however, was only one of the ways in which *Franken-stein* exercised an influence on cultural attitudes. During most of the nineteenth century, it was not the book but stage adaptations of the story which kept *Frankenstein* alive in the culture. None of Mary Shelley's Victorian biographers, who were embarrassed by the book, even mentions that these versions existed.

In the 1820s, when the first adaptations were put on in London, theater managers did not have to ask permission from author or publisher, although they were encumbered with other restrictions. All theatrical performances needed a license from the Lord Chamberlain, which would not be granted if the text, which had to be submitted for clearance in advance, could not meet certain tight criteria. Only Covent Garden and Drury Lane were permitted to stage plays, whether new or old, and all adaptations had to include a good deal of music to pretend to be operas or pantomimes, not straight plays. The adaptations of *Frankenstein,* like most other adaptations, were, we can say, officially precensored not only to check that they were ideologically acceptable to the political and religious authorities but also to ensure that they were not legitimate drama. With the stage versions, as with the printed versions, the regulatory regime of intellectual property decisively influenced the nature of the actual cultural production.

In the novel the Creature comes into the world full of natural human sympathy, which is refined by his education, including his reading of Volney's *The Ruins of Empires.*[35] It is only when he is misjudged and mistreated by unfair, unenlightened human beings that he is corrupted and turns to violence. Treat other people as you would like them to treat you is the explicit message, a Christian as well as a humanist sentiment. The many stage versions that were put on after 1823 are also scarcely subversive — if they had been overtly subversive they would not have been licensed. The first, as its title, *Presumption, or the Fate of Frankenstein,* emphasized, saw the story as a warning against human pride. But, as had happened with the reviewers of the book, others feared something more sinister. The *Morning Post* led the attack: "To Lord Byron, the late Mr. Shelley, and philosophers of that stamp, it might appear a very fine thing to attack the Christian religion . . . and burlesque the resurrection of the dead . . . but we would prefer the comparatively noble assaults of VOLNEY, VOLTAIRE AND PAINE."[36]

Other reviews of the play linked it with the hated names of the two authors whose books, *Queen Mab* and *Don Juan,* were at that very time becoming available through cheap pirated editions to the same literate urban clerical and working classes whom conservatives most feared.[37] The play, according to the ultraconservative *John Bull,* was taken from the novel by "one of the coterie of that self-acknowledged Atheist Percy B. Shelley."[38] The *Theatrical Observer* reported that placards carrying the following message had been posted widely all over London.

TO THE PLAY-GOING PUBLIC
(For to no other part of the Community is this warning addressed)

Do not go to the Lyceum to see the monstrous Drama, founded on the improper work called *"Frankenstein."* Do not take your wives and families — the Novel itself is of a decidedly immoral tendency; it treats of a subject which in nature cannot occur. This subject is pregnant with mischief; and to prevent the ill-consequences which may result from the promulgation of such dangerous doctrines, a few zealous friends of morality, and promoters of this Posting-bill, (and who are ready to meet the consequences thereof) are using their strongest endeavours.[39]

Writers at the *Theatrical Observer* believed the placards represented a genuine protest, although they acknowledged the placards also helped the box office. During the first performances in London the audience was composed of "partisans and opponents," and quarrels between radicals and conservatives ensued.[40] By the time *Presumption* reached Birmingham in 1824, it had become part of the surrounding ritual of the performance that warning posters were circulated by self- appointed local upholders of public morality, denials were issued by the theater, and threats of legal action were thrown about by both sides.

The English Opera House, where *Presumption, or the Fate of Frankenstein* opened in 1823, was able to hold about 1,500 persons.[41] The Coburg Theatre, where *Frankenstein, or the Demon of Switzerland* opened shortly afterwards, held 3,800. Admission to the English Opera House cost five shillings for a box, three for the pit, two for the gallery, and one for the upper gallery; if the house was not full, the prices were drastically reduced.[42] The admission prices at the Coburg are likely to have been similar. Midweek was for "the better classes," Monday for "the higher working classes."[43] Every single night one of the Frankenstein plays was performed, it brought a version of the story to more men and women than the book had in ten or twenty years.

In the stage adaptations the setting was moved to wicked Venice, to icy Swiss forests, or to burning Sicilian mountains. Names, such as Manfred, were taken from more familiar stories, and characters like Ratzbaen, Tiddliwincz, and Captain Risotto were invented for laughs. The hunchback, who is not in the book, stole the show so often that he became indispensable to all later versions.[44] Turbans, veils, and turned-up slippers gave a hint of the East, and there were plenty of Italian banditti. Early in its stage life *Frankenstein* was frequently amalgamated with *The Vampyre,* not because that piece had been written on the same occasion in Switzerland in 1816, but as part of a general muddling of gothic, horror, and comedy.[45]

From the start, the stage Frankensteins mocked themselves. They are full of topical allusions and jokes, mostly probably now irretrievable. In the late Victorian version, for example, the Monster wore a hat which, by copying one worn in Gilbert and Sullivan's *Patience,* brought a laugh at the expense of Oscar Wilde. The story was cut, added to, transformed into pantomime or farce, combined with other stories, parodied, burlesqued, and reduced to cliché, tag, and catch phrase.

The playbills of the first 1823 version advertised *Presumption,* a new romance, with no mention of Frankenstein in the title.[46] But it soon became clear that the name itself was a magic word, a vital part of the appeal. In both of the two favorite early stage versions, the primary and secondary titles were soon reversed. *Presumption, or the Fate of Frankenstein* became *Frankenstein, or, The Danger of Presumption. The Man and the Monster* became *Frankenstein, or, The Monster.* By the 1830s, it was already common for the nameless monster to be called "Frankenstein," a deliberate confusion put about by the actors. By the end of the century the reversal of the names of the monster and the scientist had become so common that Fowler's *Modern English Usage* felt able to call it a "blunder . . . almost, but surely not quite, sanctioned by custom."

Comparing the dates of the books and the main stage and film adaptations, we can see how they interacted, conferring publicity and customers on one another (see appendix). In 1823 and again in 1831, the novel was revived by the stage versions. Likewise, the stage versions of the 1850s may have been stimulated by the Hodgson edition. In the 1880s, when its copyright expired, the reprinting of the novel led to a new play version, which in its turn stimulated more reprints. There was a surge in sales of the Everyman edition of the book in 1931–32 after the appearance of the 1931 James Whale film starring Boris Karloff. The performed versions form a continuous tradition from 1823 until the present day, slipping easily from stage to film and then to television and video. *Frankenstein* did not become part of popular culture with the cinema: the film industry picked it up from a culture where it was already a vigorous presence.

There is a moving scene in the 1931 classic where the as yet uncorrupted Creature plays happily with an innocent little girl, but such survivals of the original moral purpose are rare. The Frankenstein films in both Britain and the United States are as unstable as the stage versions. Continuing the tradition of their predecessors, they laughed at themselves and chased every passing fashion. Far into the twentieth century, Frankenstein and his monster continue to live largely independently of books.[47] Insofar as they have a printed or material existence at all, it has been in film posters, comics, and funny masks of Boris Karloff.

Almost all books published in the early nineteenth century that achieved any kind of popularity were adapted and transformed for the stage. The stage versions of stories in verse and prose by Scott, Byron, Moore, Campbell, Southey, Dickens, and others lived (and many soon died) alongside the printed texts of the original works, most of which continued to be readily available and to be widely read. The printed texts stood like fixed beacons, circumscribing the limits of possible mutation and ready at all times to draw audiences back to the originals. In the case of *Frankenstein,* on the other hand, with long periods in which there was no easily accessible book to act as beacon, there was more freedom. New stage versions tended to mutate from other earlier mutations rather than directly from the original. Parodies parodied parodies, moving in any direction that the moment made promising. Refused a life in the reasonably stable culture of print and reading, *Frankenstein* survived in a free-floating popular oral and visual culture, with only the central episode of the scientist making the Creature holding it tenuously to its original.

In Victorian times, even when *Frankenstein* was not in print and when there was no play on the stage, the story was alive in the nation's memory. All through the nineteenth century we find references and allusions in literature, journalism, and politics. Scholarly books, drawing on such allusions, have used hermeneutic and psychoanalytical techniques to explore the Frankenstein monsters lurking in deep recesses of the Victorian mind.[48] Such allusions are, it is suggested, the occasional visible manifestations of deeper myths pervading Victorian society. No doubt the Victorians suffered from monsters, like everybody else. But such claims rest on assumptions that the novel was being read or that its text had somehow infiltrated the collective subconscious and stayed there, and that the collective unconscious can be recovered by modern critical reading of texts. In fact, most of those who used, heard, and understood Frankenstein expressions in Victorian times were unlikely to have read the book, and if they saw a stage version, they could only have had only the sketchiest idea of the rich layers of meaning of the book. The Frankenstein phrases of Victorian times do not come laden with hidden meanings or evoke the riches of the literary text. They mean less, not more, than meets the eye.

The word *Frankenstein* in Victorian culture is a cliché, a convenient tag for those who feared change: Do not free the slaves, do not reform Parliament, do not give votes to the working class, do not give independence to the Irish. If you do, you will create a Frankenstein monster that will turn and destroy you. Already by 1824, within a year of the first stage version, that had become the single, simple, unvaried meaning of *Frankenstein*—a Creature that turns on its creator. By the end of the century, the simplicities of the stage versions had defeated the complexities of the literary text. Anyone who took a different meaning was reading against the grain and against the norm. So universal was this accepted meaning that the editor of the Penny Novels abridgement dropped the authors' preface and provided a preface of his own to ram home the perverse interpretation (see appendix).

Frankenstein thus stands in contrast to P. B. Shelley's *Queen Mab* and Byron's *Don Juan*. In the 1820s, 1830s, and for many years afterwards, there was a clear demand for access to all three books, particularly by readers for whom all books were expensive and largely inaccessible but who often went to the theater. But whereas, owing to a quirk in the copyright law, *Queen Mab* and *Don Juan* were freed from private copyright ownership, their price plummeted, their readerships soared, and the cultural influence of both books grew enormously, the original *Frankenstein*, as a result of another quirk in the copyright regime, was held back from most of its potential readers. A gripping tale with a reformist moral message, the book might have taken its place alongside *Queen Mab*, *Don Juan*, Volney's *Ruins*, Paine's *Rights of Man*, and the other famous works of the radical canon that helped to shape a new skeptical, reformist, urban culture.

As events turned out, the Frankenstein story, for most of those who encountered it, conveyed a central message that was contrary to the plain meaning of the original book. The impact has been, for the most part, the direct opposite of what the author and her collaborator hoped for and intended.

Appendix

Summary Publishing History, prices in shillings

		Copies Printed[1]	Price
1818	Lackington, 3 volumes[2]	500	16.5 unbound 24 bound
1823	Whittaker, 2 volumes[3]	?500	14. unbound 19. bound
1831	Bentley's Standard Novels, 1 volume	3,500	6.
1832	Bentley, new impression 3,170 copies sold to retail booksellers in the first year[4]	500	
1836	Bentley, new impression[5]	500	
1838	[*Romancist Library* offer refused] Dates uncertain, price reduced to		[0.17] 5. and later 3.5
1839	Bentley, new impression[6]	750	—
1847	Price reduced to		2.5
1849	Bentley, new impression[7]	1,000	

1. The main editions of *Frankenstein* are noted in W. H. Lyles, *Mary Shelley: An Annotated Bibliography* (New York: Garland Publishing, 1975) to which my list adds several others not previously recorded. The figures exclude "overcopies," the extra copies not always included in the publisher's accounts, which were normally run off allegedly as an insurance against spoilage. The two accounts transcribed in *Shelley and His Circle* (Cambridge: Harvard Univ. Press, 1961–), 5: 397, for example, imply a few overcopies. Bentley took twenty overcopies on his initial two impressions of 4,000.

2. Typical standard binding prices in advertisement, signed W. Bent, dated October 16, 1818 in *The Modern Catalogue of Books* (London, 1818).

3. This edition is not made from the same standing types as the first, as suggested by Lyles, but is a complete reprint in moveable type that includes some changes to the text.

4. Strahan / Spottiswoode Archives, British Library.

5. Ibid.

6. Ibid.

7. Ibid.

		Copies Printed	Price
1855	Hodgson's "Parlour Library" edition, perhaps pirated, includes 1817 preface and 1831 introduction		
	bound version	n.a.	1.5
	paper version	n.a.	1.

1850s through 1870s   Mostly out of print but protected by copyright

1879	Book becomes free of all copyright restrictions		

1882 to 1899	Routledge[8]	40,000	
	one version		1.
	bound version		0.5
	paper version		0.25
	Most Routledge editions contain both the 1817 preface and 1831 introduction, but the *Routledge World Library* edition omits both, substituting a preface by the editor of the series, which describes the book's moral purpose as "vague and indeterminate"		

?1880s	Milner's *Cottage Library*[9]	n.a.	1.

1883	Dicks's *English Library of Standard Works*[10] in four weekly parts, with paper covers	n.a.	0.2
	as part of a volume paper covers, containing six other novels and forty-eight short stories	n.a.	1.5
	Dicks's editions, which contained the 1817 preface and 1831 introduction, probably sold in tens or hundreds of thousands of copies[11]		

---

8. Routledge Archives, University College, London.

9. No copy found, but advertised in Milner's lists over many years.

10. The existence of this huge edition has not previously been noted as far as I can tell, probably because, having been printed on frail paper, only a few copies have survived. *Frankenstein* was serialized in parts 18 to 23, and forms part of vol. 3.

11. Estimate based on the known sales of some of his other reprints.

1893   *Masterpiece Library*
        "Penny Popular Novels" abridged   n.a.   0.08
        Omits both the 1817 preface and 1831 in-
        troduction, substituting a preface by the
        editor, W. T. Stead, which offers the, by
        now, conventional warning of the dan-
        gers of creating monsters that destroy
        their creators:

> *Everybody has heard of* Frankenstein.
> *But comparatively few have read the*
> *weird and powerful novel which made*
> *the name of Frankenstein one of the sym-*
> *bol words of the language . . .*
>
> *Who is there, especially among those of us*
> *who are of a strong and virile character,*
> *who has not had cause to shudder at the*
> *consequences of his creative imagination?*

1897   Gibbings, art nouveau design and illus-
        trations, published in partnership with
        J. B. Lippincott in Philadelphia; con-
        tains the 1817 preface and 1831
        introduction   n.a.   3.5

ca. 1897 Downey's *Sixpenny Library*[12]   n.a.   0.5

1909–10 Routledge sells about 1,000 copies

1910–14 Routledge sells about 200 to 300 copies
        a year

1912   *Everyman's Library*[13]   n.a., but probably 8,500   1.0
        Contains the 1817 preface and 1831 in-
        troduction. Over 8,000 sold by 1918

1919–21 Out of print

---

12. No copy found, but advertised in *The Vicar of Wakefield*, n.d. but ca. 1897. This series was well printed on poor, easily perishable paper, and it is not surprising that no copy
has been found.

13. Figures kindly supplied from the Dent archives at Chapel Hill by Mark Reed. I am
most grateful to Professor Reed for his help in this and other matters. The dates given refer to dates of publication given on the title pages and referred to on later reprints. The
production figures are usually noted in the accounts of the previous years. In general,
about a third of the Everyman production was exported to the United States as part of
the Dent-Dutton partnership.

1922	New impression	n.a., but probably 4,000	
1927	New impression	4,000	
1930	New impression	4,000	

Over 3,000 sold in 1931–32, time of the
first release of the Whale film starring
Boris Karloff.

| 1933 | New impression | 4,000 | |
| 1939 | New impression | 4,000 | |

From 1912 to 1940 sales to the retailers
in the British market were typically
well below 500 copies a year. The exceptions were 1912, the year of publication (2,250), 1930 and 1931 (1,000 and
750), 1932 (2,000), and 1933 (600).[14]
The years of largest sales in the American market were 1913 (1,000) and 1922
(1,500). The surge in 1932 (600) is far
less marked than in the British market.

Some Nineteenth-century Stage Versions

(Summarized from Steven Earl Forry, *Hideous Progenies: Dramatizations of Frankenstein from the Nineteenth Century to the Present* [Philadelphia: Univ. of Pennsylvania
Press, 1990]. This list is reasonably complete in regard to performances in London.
The extent of performances elsewhere cannot be estimated, but they were always
numerous.)

Early Favorites

1823 *Presumption, or The Fate of Frankenstein,* later renamed *Frankenstein, or, The
Danger of Presumption;* played thirty-seven times in its first season and frequently afterwards until the 1850s[15]

1826 *The Man and the Monster,* later retitled *Frankenstein, or, The Monster,* "a peculiar romantic, melo-dramatic pantomimic spectacle"; played frequently until
1840s

1826 Text of *The Man and the Monster* printed

---

14. Rounded.

15. Forry gives a figure of 37. A 1824 Birmingham playbill declares that the piece had
drawn "109 full houses last year at the English Opera House." Forry, *Hideous Progenies,* 9.

Others

1823   *Another Piece of Presumption* (burlesque)
1823   *Humgumption; or, Dr Frankenstein and the Hobgoblin of Hoxton* (burlesque)
1824   *Frank-in Steam; or, The Modern Promise to Pay* (burlesque)
1826   *The Monster and the Magician, or, The Fate of Frankenstein* ("melodramatic romance")

Victorian

1849   *Frankenstein, or The Model Man* (dramatization); fifty-four performances in London's West End
1850s   *The Man and the Monster* revived in Birmingham, Edinburgh, and perhaps elsewhere
1865   Text of *Presumption, or the Fate of Frankenstein* printed; kept in print for many years at 0.08 shillings, for use by amateur dramatic societies
1867   Text of *The Man and the Monster* reprinted
1887   *Frankenstein, or, The Vampire's Victim*; 106 performances in London's West End

Frankenstein as a Popular Expression in the Nineteenth Century

(I have added to the examples summarized in Chris Baldick, *In Frankenstein's Shadow* [Oxford: Oxford Univ. Press, 1987]. This list, I emphasize, is not a selection aimed at arguing a point but a collection of those reports I have encountered in reading. Although they are a randomly surviving sample, the number is sufficiently large to regard their near unanimity as likely to be representative. I include source references only for the additions.)

1824   Canning in the House of Commons: To emancipate West Indian slaves "would be to raise up a creature resembling the splendid fiction of a recent romance"
1830   *Fraser's Magazine*: A state without religion is "a Frankenstein monster"
1832   Reform Bill: At least three cartoons titled "The Political Frankenstein"
1837   De Quincey: Godwin's philosophy is "a monster created by Frankenstein"
1837   Carlyle, *French Revolution*:[16] "France is 'a monstrous Galvanic Mass.'"
1838   Gladstone notes in his diary that Sicilian mules "really seem like Frankensteins of the animal creation"[17]
1843   *Punch* cartoon. "The Irish Frankenstein"

---

16. Baldick shows, with numerous precise quotations, how deeply the Frankenstein story permeated Carlyle's descriptions of the French Revolution. The book is not named directly, although in Carlyle's *German Romance*, he speaks of the "gory profundities of Frankenstein."

17. Quoted in Forry, *Hideous Progenies*, 36. Gladstone read the book in 1835.

1848 Mrs. Gaskell, *Mary Barton*: "the actions of the uneducated seem to me typified in those of Frankenstein, that monster of many human qualities ungifted with a soul"

1854 *Punch* cartoon: "The Russian Frankenstein"

1866 *Punch* cartoon: "The Brummagen [working class] Frankenstein"

1866 Included in Wheeler's *Dictionary of Noted Names*

1869 Cartoon: "The Irish Frankenstein"

1870 Included in Brewer's *Dictionary of Phrase and Fable*

1871 Included in Tyndall's *Fragments of Science for Unscientific People*; *Punch*: "Frankenstein's Chemistry"[18]

1872 John Ruskin: "I have had indirect influence on nearly every cheap villa builder between this [house] and Bromley; and there is scarcely a public house near the Crystal Palace but sells its gin and bitters under pseudo-Venetian capitals. . . . One of my principal notions for leaving my present house is that it is surrounded by Frankenstein monsters of indirectly my own making." From a letter to the *Pall Mall Gazette*, on the influence of *The Stones of Venice* on English architecture[19]

1882 Phoenix Park murders; *Punch* cartoon of Parnell: "The Irish Frankenstein"

Some Film Versions to 1974

(Summarized from Donald F. Glut, *The Frankenstein Legend* [Metuchen, N.J.: Scarecrow Press, 1973].)

1910 Edison's version

1915 *Life without Soul*, lost

1931 *Frankenstein*, dir. James Whale, Universal, with Boris Karloff

1935 *The Bride of Frankenstein*, starring Karloff

1939 *Son of Frankenstein*, starring Karloff

1942 *Ghost of Frankenstein*

1943 *Frankenstein Meets the Wolf Man*

1945 *House of Frankenstein*, starring Karloff

1945 *House of Dracula*

1948 *Abbot and Costello Meet Frankenstein*

1957 *I Was a Teenage Frankenstein*

1957 *Curse of Frankenstein*, Hammer horror starring Peter Cushing

1948 *Revenge of Frankenstein*, Hammer, starring Cushing

1958 *Frankenstein—1970*, starring Karloff

1958 *Frankenstein's Daughter*

1962 *The House on Bare Mountain* (mildly pornographic)

---

18. Quoted ibid.

19. E. T. Cook and Alexander Wedderburn, eds., *The Collected Works of John Ruskin* (London: Allen, 1903–12), 10:459.

1964 *Evil of Frankenstein*, Hammer
1965 *Jesse James Meets Frankenstein's Daughter*
1967 *Frankenstein Created Woman*, Hammer
1967 *Mad Monster Party*, cartoon with voice of Karloff
1969 *Frankenstein Must Be Destroyed*, Hammer
1970 *Horror of Frankenstein*, Hammer
1970 *Dr. Frankenstein on Campus*
1971 *Dracula vs. Frankenstein*
1973 *Frankenstein and the Monster from Hell*, Hammer
1974 *Young Frankenstein*, dir. Mel Brooks.

4 : From *The Fields of Fancy* to *Matilda*

Mary Shelley's Changing Conception of Her Novella

PAMELA CLEMIT

Though *Matilda* remained unpublished during Mary Shelley's lifetime, it is now probably her best-known work after *Frankenstein*. Since 1990, three editions of *Matilda* have appeared, all of which are based on the fair copy transcribed by Elizabeth Nitchie in 1959.[1] Following Nitchie, most critics have read this story of incestuous love between father and daughter as an uncontrolled expression of private anxieties concerning Mary Shelley's relationships with her father, William Godwin, and her husband, Percy Bysshe Shelley.[2] Those critics who have claimed to offer something other than psychobiography have focused on Mary Shelley's assault on the ideology of the bourgeois family, but this view still assumes her fundamental antipathy to the two most powerful men in her own family.[3]

My experience examining the manuscript of *Matilda* together with the rough draft, *The Fields of Fancy* (published in full in the recent Pickering and Chatto *Novels and Selected Works of Mary Shelley*), has led me to different conclusions.[4] To read *Matilda* solely as an expression of psychic crisis is to underestimate Mary Shelley's achievement as a self-conscious artist. Far from being an uncontrolled "outburst" or "therapeutic purge," *Matilda* is a carefully crafted work employing many of the conventions of the fictional model that Godwin originated in *Caleb Williams* and that was developed in several other novels of the period, notably *Frankenstein*.[5] Moreover, the original conception of the novella turns out to have been strikingly different from the finished work, on which all current readings are based. Whatever her personal feelings, Mary Shelley's changing conception of her novella shows her experimentation with and revaluation of literary themes and techniques shared with Godwin and P. B. Shelley.

In both *The Fields of Fancy* and *Matilda*, the narrative centers on Mathilda's first-person account of her ambivalent relationships with two men of different generations. The first half focuses on Mathilda's interaction with her father. Having abandoned her after the death of her mother in childbirth, he returns after an absence of sixteen years and becomes her constant companion. A few months later he confesses his incestuous love for her (which she in part reciprocates) and commits suicide. In the second half, attention shifts to her encounter with a young Shelleyan poet-figure (variously named Welford, Herbert, Lovel, and finally Woodville[6]): He tries to rescue her from introspective withdrawal after her father's death but is unable to meet her needs, and she eventually dies alone. While this set of relations offers an oblique commentary on the two most intense relationships of Mary Shelley's life, the novella as a whole exceeds its biographical interest. It was composed during the melancholy period following the deaths of the Shelleys' two young children, Clara, in September 1818, and William, in June 1819;[7] even so, as Mary Shelley later remarked in her journal, "when I wrote Matilda, miserable as I was, the *inspiration* was sufficient to quell my wretchedness temporarily" (*MWSJ* 442).

The period of emotional distance between Mary Shelley and her husband after their double bereavement was also one of creative interaction, even collaboration. *The Fields of Fancy,* written between August 4 and September 12, 1819, shows a return to the shared projects and reading matter of the previous summer, which supports Betty Bennett's view that the work began as "an act towards reconciliation."[8] Three main areas of this period of literary interchange bear directly on *The Fields of Fancy:* the Shelleys' joint interest in Plato's *Symposium,* their mutual encouragement to write drama, and their shared fascination with the topic of incest. Mary Shelley's independent development of these shared concerns calls into question the frequent assertion that the novella lacks artistry.[9]

For example, Mary Shelley creatively adapts several features of the *Symposium*. In a letter to John and Maria Gisborne of July 10, 1818, P. B. Shelley wrote that he was translating Plato's *Symposium* "only as an exercise or perhaps to give Mary some idea of the manners & feelings of the Athenians" (*PBSL* 2:20).[10] Though he may have envisaged the *Symposium* as a work that would educate Mary Shelley, she herself used it as a mode of instruction in *The Fields of Fancy.* In Chapter 1 she sets up an intricate narrative frame that is indebted to Platonic and Dantean allegories of the soul's journey through earthly suffering to union with the divine.[11] Though this frame was dismissed by Nitchie as "largely irrelevant" and has been overlooked by critics until very recently,[12] it is central to Mary Shelley's original conception of the novella as a cautionary tale of excessive passion. An unnamed first-person narrator, mourning the loss of her loved ones, is conducted by Fantasia (an allegorical figure) to the Elysian Fields, where the narrator overhears Mathilda, who is now immortal, telling her tale of earthly sufferings to the prophetess Diotima, the instructress of Socrates in the *Symposium*.[13]

A frequently cited source for the title and opening of *The Fields of Fancy* is Mary Wollstonecraft's "The Cave of Fancy,"[14] and certainly there are broad parallels between the start of *The Fields of Fancy* and Chapter 3 of Wollstonecraft's unfinished tale. In the latter, the child Sagesta visits the Cave of Fancy and is educated by a spirit who presents the story of her earthly life as a "useful lesson": married to a man she did not love while loving someone else, she resisted her adulterous passion and found consolation in a life "enlivened by active benevolence."[15] In *The Fields of Fancy* Mary Shelley adopts a similar didactic structure, except that it is not the suffering Mathilda but the detached onlooker Diotima who adopts an instructive role.

Diotima's discourse offers a revision of the reported debate between Socrates and Diotima in the *Symposium*. Following Diotima's speech there, which includes an account of the ascent of the lover of wisdom from the world of sensible objects to the contemplation of eternal beauty, Diotima in *The Fields of Fancy* describes examples of beauty in the sensible world. However, unlike Socrates' instructress, Mary Shelley's Diotima also catalogs instances of man-made evils: during her earthly life, she recalls, she found "that spirit of union with love & beauty which formed my happiness & pride degraded into superstition . . . cruelty — & intolerance & hard tyranny was grafted on its trunk & from it sprung fruit suitable to such grafts" (*M* 356). And when Diotima resolves to teach others to seek in their own hearts the source of the love of beauty, her aspiration is couched in terms reminiscent of Godwin's gradualist theory of political progress, in which individual moral improvement is a prerequisite to collective reform: "if I can teach but one other mind what is the beauty which they ought to love — and what is the sympathy to which they ought to aspire . . . then shall I be satisfied" (*M* 357).[16] That "one other mind" turns out to be Mathilda's, whom Diotima addresses in overtly didactic terms: "It is by the acqiurement [*sic*] of wisdom and the loss of the selfishness that is now attatched [*sic*] to the sole feeling that possesses you that you will at last mingle in that universal world of which we all now make a divided part" (*M* 407).

Yet at the end of her narrative Mathilda substitutes for Diotima's goal of collective wisdom a wish for individual reunion with her father: "I am here not with my father but listening to lessons of Wisdom which will one day bring me to him when we shall never part" (*M* 405). This discrepancy between the instructive tenor of the frame and the wish-fulfilment of the inset narrative highlights the unreliability of Mathilda's first-person account and invites us to read her story as a warning of the dangers of selfish passion, designed to educate the listening narrator. Such overt didacticism is absent from *Matilda,* where the narrative frame is abandoned and the story is presented as Mathilda's written memoir.

While *The Fields of Fancy* is rooted in the literary interests Mary Shelley shared with P. B. Shelley, *Matilda* shifts towards Godwinian themes and techniques. Contrary to the opinion of Jane Blumberg and others that "publication was not a serious original consideration,"[17] there is evidence that Mary Shelley planned to publish *Matilda* for Godwin's benefit. The fair copy is dated November 9, 1819, indicating that Mary Shelley began rewriting *The Fields of Fancy* as *Matilda* on the very day she heard that Godwin had lost a lawsuit concerning his house in Skinner Street and was required to pay back rent of £1500.[18] *Matilda* was probably completed in February 1820, and in May of that year Mary Shelley gave the manuscript to Maria Gisborne to take to Godwin in England.[19] Godwin, however, no doubt mindful of previous allegations of incest between P. B. Shelley, Mary Shelley, and Claire Clairmont during their Continental tour of 1816, did not publish it.[20]

This is not to suggest that Mary Shelley revised the novella along Godwinian lines simply because she planned to send it to him, but to challenge the prevailing view that *Matilda* is "devoid of the professionalism which characterizes Shelley's important novels."[21] The terms of Godwin's criticism of the manuscript, far from merely revealing his unacknowledged private feelings, as Terence Harpold has conjectured,[22] show a recognition that it was based on the fictional model he himself had pioneered. According to Maria Gisborne's journal entry for August 8, 1820:

The pursuit . . . he [Godwin] thinks the finest part of the whole novel. The subject he says is disgusting and detestable; and there ought to be, at least if [it] is ever published, a preface to prepare the minds of the readers, and to prevent them from being tormented by the apprehension from moment to moment of the fall of the heroine; it is true (he says) that this difficulty is in some measure obviated, by Mathildas protestation at the beginning of the book, that she has not to reproach herself with any guilt; but, yet, in proceeding one is apt to lose sight of that protestation; besides (he added with animation) one cannot exactly trust to what an author of the modern school may deem guilt. (*MGJL* 44)

Godwin's invocation of "the modern school," together with his praise for the pursuit and his focus on the issue of guilt, clearly indicates that he read *Matilda* in terms of the themes and conventions associated with his own school of fiction.

Placing the novella in the Godwinian genre sheds light on several changes of structure and emphasis in *Matilda*. For one thing, the tale is now told by Mathilda on her deathbed and addressed to Woodville: Mary Shelley abandons the Elysian framework of *The Fields of Fancy*, substituting a confessional account of traumatic experience in the manner of Godwin's novels from *Caleb Williams* to *Mandeville*. Just as Godwin's use of the unreliable narrator invites the reader to play an active interpretative role, so the ambiguity of Mathilda's narrative assigns to the reader the task of evaluating her guilt or innocence. For example, Mathilda's remark to her father that she thinks *Myrrha* — a play based on the story of Myrrha's incestuous love for her father Cinyras in Ovid's *Metamorphoses* — "the best of Alfieri's tragedies" (*M* 20) is open to dual interpretation.[23] Taken at face value, it is no more than an innocent observation Mathilda "chanced to say" (*M* 20), a reading supported by the fact that she is expressing a common literary preference of the day.[24] On closer inspection, though, the remark suggests her secret complicity with, even encouragement of, her father's passion: it occurs shortly after Mathilda has described the visits of a young and agreeable suitor as "obnoxious" (*M* 19); it alludes to a play in which the daughter harbours incestuous feelings towards her father; and it is accompanied by a quotation from John Fletcher's play *The Captain*, in which the heroine unwittingly tries to seduce her father. Ambiguous moments like this suggest the hidden psychological impulses of a flawed narrator, not a distressed author unaware of the full implications of what she is saying.

Again, Mary Shelley follows Godwinian precedents in structuring *Matilda* as a fall narrative, a motif that remains latent in *The Fields of Fancy*, further refuting charges of a lack of authorial control. Mathilda's narrative is crafted around two scenes of temptation and/or fall. These are placed on either side of the highly charged central pair of chapters dealing, respectively, with her prophetic dream of her father's death and with the pursuit leading to her discovery of his actual death. In the first temptation sequence, Mathilda (successfully) persuades her father to reveal the secret of his mysterious, brooding behavior; in the second, she (unsuccessfully) tempts Woodville to commit suicide by drinking laudanum. Yet the coherence of this two-part narrative is not merely a matter of structural symmetry: it also reflects the troubled psychology of the protagonist. Cheated by her father's suicide of the deathly union she might have chosen, Mathilda tries to achieve the same outcome with Woodville instead.

In addition to this new coherence of design, Mary Shelley makes numerous small changes that, as in other Godwinian novels, establish competing frameworks for the interpretation of events. To begin with, she emphasizes Mathilda's deterministic outlook. For example, at the start of her narrative, Mathilda now declares: "My fate has been governed by necessity, a hideous necessity" (M 6). Rather than evincing a collapse into autobiographical transparency, as some critics have argued, this new emphasis on necessity signals Mathilda's affinity with earlier Godwinian protagonists, who cast themselves as victims of forces beyond their control.[25] Again, at the end of the novella, Mary Shelley highlights Mathilda's shaping of her past experience into a sequential pattern: "It was May, four years ago, that I first saw my beloved father; it was in May, three years ago, that my folly destroyed the only being I was doomed to love. May is returned, and I die" (M 67). Though these insistent repetitions suggest that Mary Shelley's revisions are not always stylistic improvements — there is a loss of the lyric intensity of The Fields of Fancy's ending[26] — such an emphasis on the conscious construction of the past reinforces Mathilda's perception of herself as no longer having choices.

Mary Shelley also gives a fuller account than previously of the early life of Mathilda's father, which offers a causal explanation for his later, otherwise unaccountable, failure to take responsibility for his dependent child. In keeping with Godwin's view of character as the product of circumstances,[27] Mary Shelley highlights the indulgent, aristocratic education that made Mathilda's father unable to moderate his passions in adulthood: "He was nurtured in prosperity and attended by all its advantages; every one loved him and wished to gratify him" (M 7). Similarly, the all-consuming nature of his passion for his early love, Mathilda's mother, Diana, makes his extreme reaction after her death more plausible, while the social isolation of the couple — "they were never seperate [sic] and seldom admitted a third to their society" (M 9) — sets up the pattern he attempts to recreate with the adult Mathilda: "I dared say to myself," he later confesses, "Diana died to give her birth . . . she ought to be as Diana to me" (M 35). Again, Mary Shelley develops her earlier account of Mathilda's loveless childhood so that, as Mathilda says, "it may be apparent how when one hope failed all life was to me a blank" (M 11). For example, the new episode of Mathilda's abandonment at the age of seven by her much-loved nurse, which replicates her father's disappearance, helps to explain her enchantment by "the voice of affection . . . so new to me" (M 16) when he returns. Such developments in characterization, by establishing knowable causes for irrational-seeming behavior, tend to support Mathilda's view of herself as the victim of unfavorable circumstances.

Other changes, however, highlight the ambiguities of Mathilda's narrative, encouraging a more open-ended interpretation. Building on literary allusions already present in The Fields of Fancy and adding new ones, Mary Shelley establishes a second framework for the interpretation of events, calling upon mythic analogues and literary allusions that, as in Frankenstein, introduce the possibility of multiple, contradictory meanings.[28]

The first two chapters of Matilda establish two mythic and literary frames of reference bearing on the central issue that so worried Godwin, the guilt or innocence of the heroine: the Sophoclean drama of the Oedipus story, newly added here,[29] and the Christian ascent of Dante's Purgatorio, here given a more prominent role than in The Fields of Fancy. Each of these frames of reference presents Mathilda in a different light. On the one hand, Mathilda's opening invocation of Oedipus at Colonus signals a new consciousness of herself as a protagonist in a "tragic history": previously unable to divulge the "sacred horror" of her tale, she declares, "now about to die I pollute its mystic terrors. It is as the wood of the Eumenides none but the dying may enter; and Oedipus is about to die" (M 5). Significantly she casts herself as the ancient, guilt-ridden Oedipus rather than as his daughter Antigone, who attends him to his death; this prepares for her subsequent self-characterization as a seeker after forbidden knowledge. On the other hand, there are several allusions to Dante's encounter with Matelda in the Purgatorio.[30] Like Matelda, who draws Dante through the waters of Lethe to purify him in preparation for his meeting with Beatrice,

Mathilda in her youthful exuberance in the Scottish countryside, "gathering flower after flower . . . singing as [she] might the wild melodies of the country" (*M* 12–13), is seen as a figure of purity. This notion is reinforced by her identification with Proserpine, with whom Dante's Matelda is also associated, while Mathilda's father imagines her as a heavenly guide resembling Beatrice.[31] Such allusions prepare for Mathilda's imaginary rewriting of the episode in which Dante awaits the descent of Beatrice: now assuming Dante's role, she yearns "to see the car of light descend with my long lost parent to be restored to me" (*M* 62–63).

This dual representation of Mathilda as both guilt-ridden and innocent, both sexual transgressor and sexually pure, gains further resonance from Mary Shelley's invocation of the Christian myth of transgression in *Comus* and *Paradise Lost,* a staple source for the destabilization of mythic referents in the Godwinian novel.[32] Though Mathilda presents herself as guilty of a mistaken desire for knowledge, she also depicts herself as blameless. As a child she imagines playing the part of the guileless Lady in *Comus* and appropriately gets lost in a wood on the way to meet her aristocratic father — who, with his enchanting discourse, turns out to resemble the evil tempter Comus rather than the Earl of Bridgewater. Again, Mary Shelley rewrites an earlier passage describing Mathilda's conversations with her father in prelapsarian terms to highlight the heroine's blame of her father: "I lament now, I must ever lament, those few short months of Paradisaical bliss," says Mathilda: "I disobeyed no command, I ate no apple. . . . Alas! my companion did, and I was precipitated in his fall" (*M* 17).[33]

Here Mathilda presents a partial, ironic reversal of the roles of Adam and Eve, casting herself as an entirely innocent Adam — who, unlike Milton's Adam, does not even taste the apple — and casting her father as Eve. This view of her father as tempter is one he himself comes to share. At the moment when he reveals his love for her, he speaks of himself as a "fallen archangel . . . devil as I am become," a satanic transformation to which Mathilda assents in her expression of physical distaste: "I spurned him with my foot. I felt as if stung by a serpent" (*M* 28). Yet Mathilda herself is by no means exempt from satanic transformation. In her self-consciously literary temptation of Woodville to suicide by holding out a "pleasant potion" in the manner of Comus, she echoes Satan's persuasion of Eve — "we are about to become Gods: spirits free and happy as gods" — and cites the words of Spenser's Despair, who tempts the Redcrosse knight of Holiness to kill himself (*M* 58 and n.).[34]

Yet Mary Shelley's rewriting of *The Fields of Fancy* as *Matilda* involves more than this new formal and thematic complexity. Like her other works in the Godwinian genre, at the heart of the novella is a critical reappraisal of a specific set of intellectual concerns. In particular, Mary Shelley calls into question Godwin's emphasis on the unrestrained exercise of private judgment, the basis of the theory of gradual social amelioration set out in *An Enquiry Concerning Political Justice,* a theory her husband had come to share.[35] If this revaluation of Godwin's social theory reflects Mary Shelley's personal situation — certainly both Godwin and P. B. Shelley appeared to maintain a disconcerting philosophical detachment from her grief in the summer of 1819 [36] — it is also a product of aesthetic distance and control. Mary Shelley's primary concern is not so much with family personalities as with family writings.

Indeed, the first half of *Matilda* is closely modeled on the central scenes of Godwin's most celebrated narrative of revolutionary change, *Caleb Williams.* Like the inscrutable aristocrat Ferdinando Falkland, whose position is based on the lie of his own perfection, Mathilda's father maintains a dignified public reserve but suffers secret paroxysms of frenzy. Like Caleb conjecturing the source of his master's agonies, Mathilda is fascinated by "the diseased yet incomprehensible state of [her father's] mind" (*M* 20) and determined to seek out the cause. After listening to the account of her father's behavior by his servant, which, like the tale of Falkland's steward, Collins, testifies to a lifetime of devoted service, she wonders, "Could there be guilt in it?," directly echoing Caleb's conjecture about Falkland's suffering: "Is this the fruit of conscious guilt?" (*M* 24, *CW* 101). Just as Caleb is hurried on by a "fatal impulse," Mathilda declares, "I hardly know what feelings resis[t]lessly impelled me"; while her father's criticism of her "frantic curiosity" resembles Falkland's castigation of Caleb's "foolish inquisitive humour" (*CW* 110, *M* 27, *CW* 123).

In the scene when she confronts her father and demands the truth, Mathilda employs the familiar language of Godwinian gradualism. "Let him receive sympathy . . . Let him confide his misery" (*M* 25), she says to herself before meeting him, invoking the values extolled in Godwin's notional vision of transformed human relations at the end of *Caleb Williams.*[37] When she first addresses her father, she claims to speak "although with the tender affection of a daughter, yet also with the freedom of a friend and equal" (*M* 26), gesturing towards that erosion of parent/child distinctions Godwin saw as an essential preliminary to wider social change.[38]

"Permit me to gain your confidence," she continues, alluding to "the forbearance that man is entitled to claim from man" (*E* 134) that Godwin argued should be exercised towards all men and women as a means of fostering moral autonomy and that Caleb and Falkland fail to exercise towards each other.[39] When her father continues to resist her entreaties, she exclaims, "You do not treat me with candour," invoking the prime Dissenting virtue of candor that underpins Godwin's emphasis on the duty of private judgment.[40]

Yet Mathilda's trenchant advocacy of frankness and sincerity leads to disaster. Like Caleb in his search for the truth about his master's guilt, and Frankenstein in his quest for the origins of life, Mathilda starts out with benevolent intentions but ends up unleashing forces beyond her control. Rather than leading to a new egalitarian partnership, as imagined, her father's revelation of his incestuous feelings leads to the breakdown of community and, finally, to death. "A mighty revolution had taken place with regard to me," she says, "the natural work of years had been transacted since the morning" (*M* 30). In the reversal that follows, both parties flee from the intimacy they formerly sought. Though initially it is Mathilda's father who assumes the role of Godwinian social outcast — "I must expiate these crimes," he says, "in the solitude I shall seek I alone shall breathe of human kind" (*M* 32, 35) — after his death Mathilda too takes on this role. In the second half of the novella she replicates her father's early mysterious behavior, only this time the story of disabling guilt, like Caleb's, is told from the inside.

Yet other elements in the second half of the tale suggest Mary Shelley's critical engagement with a new generation of family writings, this time those of P. B. Shelley. At first glance, Mathilda's rejection of Woodville's consolation looks like a repudiation of the utopian vision of human potentiality articulated in *Prometheus Unbound* in favor of the darker vision of *The Cenci,* the fifth act of which was praised by Mary Shelley in her 1839 "Note" to that work as "the finest thing [Shelley] ever wrote" (*M* 286).[41] Certainly Woodville, the spokesman for Shelleyan optimism, is ambivalently portrayed. On the one hand he is an ideal poet-figure compared to Plato, the "poet of old whom the muses had crowned in his cradle, and on whose lips bees had fed," and displaying Christlike qualities: "As he walked among other men he seemed encompassed with a heavenly halo" (*M* 47). At the same time, he is morally naive: "He seemed incapable of conceiving of the full extent of the power that selfishness & vice possesses in the world" (*M* 48). To some extent he appears as a figure of admonishment, since he too, like both Mathilda and her father, has suffered the premature loss of a loved one — his fiancée Elinor — but, unlike them, he is consoled by his Godwinian faith in gradual progress. Yet for all his visionary insight into human ordering schemes, like Diotima in *The Fields of Fancy*,[42] he is unable to respond to individual human need.

The clash between Woodville's idealizing temperament and Mathilda's experience of "dreary reality" (*M* 56) is most evident in the scene in which she tries to persuade him to join her in a suicide pact. In an effort to counteract Mathilda's despair, Woodville puts forward an argument based on Godwin's belief in the individual's duty to exercise his or her talents in pursuit of the general good.[43] Though Woodville recognizes that the attainment of general happiness is a distant prospect, he stresses the value of each individual contribution to that goal, echoing Diotima's account of her instructive role: "if I can influence but a hundred, but ten, but one solitary individual, so as in any way to lead him from ill to good, that will be a joy to repay me for all my sufferings" (*M* 59). Again, he makes a distinction between individuals actively committed to public good, such as himself, and others who have countless opportunities to forward the progress of mind in everyday life, such as Mathilda: "if you can bestow happiness on another; if you can give one other person only one hour of joy ought you not to live to do it?" (*M* 60).[44] Woodville's optimistic arguments are called into question, however, by the context in which they occur. Though his lessons momentarily buoy up Mathilda, they also provoke her most extreme expression of social alienation: adopting the language of monstrosity previously associated with her father,[45] she describes herself as "this outcast from human feeling; this monster with whom none might mingle in converse and love . . . a marked creature, a pariah, only fit for death" (*M* 61).

While the interaction between Woodville and Mathilda suggests the limitations of utopian social theories when faced with individual suffering, it also raises the question of whether Mathilda is beyond all help. As well as expressing scepticism concerning the visionary idealism of *Prometheus Unbound,* Mary Shelley offers a critical response to P. B. Shelley's version of "sad reality" (*PBSPP* 237) in *The Cenci.* Though in the preface to that play P. B. Shelley sketches an ideal outcome to Beatrice's story that evades the problem of her suffering, in the play itself he presents a convincing dramatic portrait of a character "violently thwarted from her nature by the necessity of circumstance and opinion" (*PBSPP* 238). However, the role of "circumstance and opinion" in Mathilda's story is by no means clear-cut. Mary Shelley explores the nature of suffering from the inside, focusing on the disabling ambiguities of the heroine's experience. Though Mathilda's experience centers on incestuous feelings rather than the physical act of incest,[46] it is nevertheless one from which she does not recover: "say not to the lily laid prostrate by the storm arise, and bloom as before. My heart was bleeding from its death's wound; I could live no otherwise" (*M* 45). It is this state of psychological arrest that sets her apart from Woodville, and, she feels, from all humanity, making her unable to respond to new experiences. Each time Woodville leaves her, "despair returned; the work of consolation was ever to begin anew" (*M* 55).

Rather than betraying authorial alienation, this disquieting emphasis on the traumatic nature of suffering confirms Mary Shelley's self-conscious literary affiliation with Godwin. That affiliation is not so much with the author of the 1790s but with the creator of the 1817 novel *Mandeville*, which she praised in her 1831 "Memoirs of William Godwin" as superior to all his works in "forcible developement of human feeling" (*M* 250).[47] It is no accident that Godwin shared Mary Shelley's preference for *The Cenci* over *Prometheus Unbound*, or that he later praised her portrait of Beatrice, a figure disabled by successive calamities, as the "jewel" of *Valperga*,[48] since he had taken as the subject of his most recent novel a protagonist traumatized by past experiences of loss and betrayal. In *Mandeville*, Godwin pursues his characteristic analysis of the disjunction between society as it is and subjective experience to a new extreme. He concedes that the individual could be undone as much by psychological impulse—in this case, the repressed passion of sibling incest—as by external circumstances. Mary Shelley's assimilation of this dark vision in *Matilda* reaffirms the significance of her novella as a carefully wrought work of fiction in the Godwinian tradition.

5 : Mathilda as Dramatic Actress

CHARLES E. ROBINSON

Mary Shelley's *Matilda*,[1] arguably her second most important text and only now receiving the attention it is due, was ignored for so many years because it was not available for critical analysis until Elizabeth Nitchie published it in 1959,[2] one hundred forty years after it was written. Mary Shelley began this novella shortly after her son, William, died in June 1819: she drafted it first as *The Fields of Fancy*, a complicated frame tale that introduced Mathilda's first-person narrative about her life; Mary Shelley then abandoned the frame and redrafted the entire novella entirely from Mathilda's point of view. The full text of the earlier "Fields of Fancy," now published for the first time in the new Pickering and Chatto edition of Mary Shelley's works, provides evidence for a radical reinterpretation of the theme and characters of this story—one that emphasizes Mary Shelley's sophisticated use of a histrionic and hysterical persona as the narrator of her novella.

Until recently, most critics have approached *Matilda* as some form of autobiography or psychobiography, too hastily conflating or equating the first-person narrator Mathilda with the author Mary Shelley. Elizabeth Nitchie started this process by claiming that "many elements in [the novella] are drawn from reality. The three main characters are clearly Mary Shelley herself [= Mathilda], William Godwin [= Mathilda's unnamed father], and P. B. Shelley [= the poet Woodville], and their relations can easily be reassorted to correspond with actuality" (vii). I offer a radically different reading of the novella and assert that Mary Shelley is an artist who more frequently than not created sophisticated narrators quite different from herself. Certainly, the frame tale of *Frankenstein*, in which

Mary Shelley created distinct narrative voices in the persons of Walton, Victor, and the monster, should point us in that direction — as should *The Last Man,* in which we encounter Lionel Verney as the main narrator. For further evidence of Mary Shelley's narrative distancing, consider her "Recollections of Italy," in which she constructs an outside narrator who dislikes Italy only to introduce the Anglo-Italian (and Shelleyan) Malville in defense of things Italian.

This is not to say, of course, that Mary Shelley is not "figured" in her fiction, but that presence is more often a modest or indirect one: in *Frankenstein,* for example, we find at least glimpses of her in the character MWS (that is, Margaret Walton Saville), who receives Walton's letters — and if we pronounce Saville (from the outermost frame tale) as a French name, then the homophonic Safie (from the innermost tale) might yield us another MWS impersonation.[3] In *The Last Man,* we sense Mary Shelley not far from the outside narrator who discovers and assembles the Sibylline leaves that become the narrative of Lionel; and in the first novella about Mathilda, we find Mary Shelley prominently figured in the grieving outside narrator of *The Fields of Fancy.*

Before considering *The Fields of Fancy* and its relations to *Matilda,* however, I first wish to focus on the character of Mathilda in the received text and to suggest that Mary Shelley did not much like her eponymous protagonist. If "dislike" is too extreme a word in this context, I suggest at least that Mary Shelley distanced herself from Mathilda and that Mathilda is a substantially flawed character. In 1990, I tried to move Mary Shelley scholarship in this direction when Betty Bennett and I published *The Mary Shelley Reader*; in the brief preface, I wrote that in Mathilda "the reader will encounter a complicated persona who, 'in a strange state of mind,' struggles as a self-conscious tragic actress in a drama about the taboo subject of incest" (*MSR* vii). This statement has influenced at least Charlene Bunnell, who in 1997 published an excellent article on the entire *theatrum mundi* motif in *Matilda,* in which she proves that Mary Shelley should not be confused with her narrator.[4] Three additional 1997 essays on *Matilda* have also subordinated Mary Shelley biography in order to concentrate on more substantial and objective matters in the narrative. The best of these, by Audra Dibert Himes, argues that Mathilda was consumed by a transgressive desire for her own father and that she cloistered "her emotional and physical desire by turning life into art — into discourse."[5] Although this "art" refers to Mathilda's act of confessional writing, Himes is keenly aware of how much the art of drama, especially of Alfieri's tragedy of *Myrrha*, determined Mathilda's construction of her own character.

It is surprising that critics have until recently overlooked the *theatrum mundi* motif and the overwhelming evidence that Mathilda conceives of herself as a tragic actress who has played a dramatic role not only in her life but also in the very narrative that she constructs for Woodville and thus for her audience. As part of that audience, we overhear a dramatic monologue or at least a monologue that deals with the dramatic—and in either case, we are asked to question the reliability (and integrity) of the narrator and, therefore, to argue that Mary Shelley is no more Mathilda than Browning is the Duke of Ferrara.

Mary Shelley's novella opens in the month of March, with Mathilda "in a strange state of mind" as she "begin[s] to write [her] tragic history" (*M* 5); and at the very end of the narrative, three months later in May, she exclaims: "Again and again I have passed over in my remembrance the different scenes of my short life: if the world is a stage and I merely an actor on it my part has been strange, and, alas! tragical. . . . This was the drama of my life which I have now depicted upon paper. . . . Woodville, I close my work; the last that I shall perform" (*M* 66). It is significant that these and other *theatrum mundi* metaphors were added to the narrative late in the textual history—that is, while Mary Shelley was transforming *The Fields of Fancy* into *Matilda* and making explicit Mathilda's self-consciousness as an actress, performer, and (possibly) dissembler.

Once we realize that Mathilda is an actress with a propensity for playing roles, the entire narrative can be viewed in a different light. Consider another addition Mary Shelley made in the process of transforming *The Fields of Fancy* into *Matilda:* "I was a solitary being, and from my infant years, ever since my dear nurse left me, I had been a dreamer. I brought Rosalind and Miranda and the lady of Comus to life to be my companions, or on my isle acted over their parts imagining myself to be in their situations" (*M* 13). Here the solitary Mathilda revealed that she would sometimes lose herself in female dramatic roles, specifically from Shakespeare's *As You Like It* and *The Tempest* and from Milton's *Comus*. Acting these parts encouraged another kind of dreaming: "Then I wandered from the fancies of others [i.e., the dramas] and formed affections and intimacies with the aerial creations of my own brain." In her youth, at least, she distinguished these imaginary dreams (and, apparently, her dramatic role playing) from reality: "but still clinging to reality I gave a name to these conceptions and nursed them in the hope of realization" (*M* 13–14). As a child, after she had been abandoned by her "nurse," Mathilda nursed her own childish dreams without much danger; as a young adult, however, one of her dreams became a reality in the form of her father, thereby validating the world of dream and encouraging Mathilda to undertake even more roles.

What Mathilda as a child most dreamed about—or imagined, or nursed, or dramatized—was what she hoped to realize—namely, a reunion with her father: he was the "idol of [her] imagination. [She] bestowed on him all [her] affections." She gazed "continually" on his miniature; "again and again" she read his last letter about his desire to return and "claim" his daughter. Accordingly, for Mathilda,

> My favourite vision was that when I grew up I would leave my aunt . . . and disguised like a boy I would seek my father through the world. My imagination hung upon the scene of recognition; . . . I imaged the moment to my mind a thousand and a thousand times, perpetually varying the circumstances. Sometimes it would be in a desart; in a populous city; at a ball; we should perhaps meet in a vessel; and his first words constantly were, "My daughter, I love thee"! (*M* 14)

The "scene of recognition" is but one of dozens of dramatic phrases that punctuate Mathilda's narrative, each drawing attention to her self-conscious role-playing in her relationships with others. In some cases, what Mathilda imagines, Mathilda gets: her imagined ideal of "My daughter, I love thee" is made painfully real when she provokes her father to confess his incestuous desire for his daughter with, "My daughter, I love you!" (*M* 28).

The dramatic and the incestuous, like the dream and the reality, are frequently intertwined in this narrative. For example, just after unsettling her father with a reference to Alfieri's incest drama, *Myrrha,* Mathilda comments on the "new scene" and the "sad scenes" (*M* 21) that led up to her own catastrophe. After her father's declaration of his love for her threw her into despair, Mathilda histrionically acted out her disgust for her father: "I tore my hair; I raved aloud; at one moment in pity for his sufferings I would have clasped my father in my arms; and then starting back with horror I spurned him with my foot. I felt as if stung by a serpent" (*M* 28). When she recovered from this state of near "madness" and "ceased to weep," she "began to reflect . . . how it became [her] to act" (*M* 29, 30) and even considered putting on the habits of a nun. Later, after her father delivered his confessional letter to her and after she found his dead body, she in fact opts for the habits of a nun so she "might feign death"—she repeats that she "would feign to die," declaring that her "plan must be laid with art," and regretting that she "who had before clothed [her]self in the bright garb of sincerity must now borrow one of divers colours: it might sit awkwardly at first, but use would enable [her] to place it in elegant folds, to lie with grace." Alluding to the "grief [that] might change Constance" in Shakespeare's *King John*, she looks "back with disgust at [her] artifices and contrivances" by which she had gained the solitude that she so much desired: "In solitude only shall I be myself; in solitude I shall be thine," that is, her father's (*M* 41, 42).

Mathilda's desire to be alone, to be, as it were, the only one on stage, is thwarted by the appearance of the poet Woodville in her retreat, and Woodville makes her aware of at least some of her selfishness, her unreasonableness, her arrogance, and her peevishness—all words that she uses to define herself. But Mathilda experiences no anagnorisis with this partial self-knowledge—her long life of acting and deceit continues to determine her unsocialized behavior with Woodville. As she explains at the end of Chapter 10: "I am, I thought, a tragedy; a character that he comes to see act: now and then he gives me my cue that I may make a speech more to his purpose: . . . I am a farce and play to him, but to me this is all dreary reality" (*M* 56). Here Mathilda is imposing her own view of life on Woodville—it is she who casts Woodville as dramatist; she (not Woodville) controls the play and the metaphors of *theatrum mundi* in *Matilda*. That control is soon put to the test when Mathilda selfishly plans "the whole scene" of her own and Woodville's suicides: "I procured Laudanum and placing it in two glasses on the table, filled my room with flowers and decorated the last scene of my tragedy with the nicest care" (*M* 57).

Woodville, however, will not play the scene that Mathilda stages—instead, he tries to redeem her: "Come, as you have played Despair with me I will play the part of Una with you and bring you hurtless from his dark cavern" (59). That Woodville fails to redeem her is made clear by the death scene, what Mathilda calls "the last scene of [her] tragedy" (64) and "the last scene of [her] life" (65), in which, as in the entire narrative, she still plays a part: "I take a pleasure in arranging all the little details which will occur when I shall no longer be. In truth I am in love with death; no maiden ever took more pleasure in the contemplation of her bridal attire than I in fancying my limbs already enwrapt in their shroud: is it not my marriage dress? Alone it will unite me to my father when in an eternal mental union we shall never part" (65). As Mathilda explains it in her final words, "the turf will soon be green on my grave; and the violets will bloom on it. *There* is my hope and expectation" (67).

When the curtain closes on these last words of Mathilda's dramatic monologue, we as the audience are asked to interpret her performance — and to do so without invoking the life of Mary Shelley. It is not Mary Shelley who created a persona of herself in Mathilda; rather, it is Mathilda who wore the mask: she creates a persona who simultaneously disguises and reveals her character. We know that she "feigned" death, donned costumes, misrepresented the truth, lied, played roles, acted — and, I suggest, overacted the role she constructed for herself. The words "My daughter, I love you" should not have prompted such an extreme reaction from someone who not only sought that love but also loved her father passionately in return. Even Mathilda tells us that she overreacted: "I was doomed while in life to grieve, and to the natural sorrow of my father's death and its most terrific cause, immagination [sic] added a tenfold weight of woe. I *believed* myself to be polluted by the unnatural love I had inspired" (*M* 60, emphasis added). If we compare this to P. B. Shelley's similar statement on behalf of Beatrice Cenci, who "*considered* [the rape] a perpetual contamination both of body and mind" (*PBSPP* 238, emphasis added), we find that both Shelleys in 1819 were dramatizing casuistical responses by victims of incest — and in both cases, the flawed tragic heroines lack self-knowledge and never achieve an anagnorisis in the course of their dramas.

Although P. B. Shelley used his preface to *The Cenci* to define Beatrice Cenci's character flaws, Mary Shelley had no such overt means to define the flaws of Mathilda. However, Mary Shelley did guide the reader in the first version of her narrative, *The Fields of Fancy*, in which the reader is invited to read Mathilda's narrative as the product of the same kind of intellectual and moral blindness that P. B. Shelley represented in the character of Beatrice. In the original frame tale, we find that the Mary Shelleyan narrator together with Diotima and Mathilda herself all emphasized Mathilda's flaws: at her death, Mathilda was "a soul longing for knowledge & pining at its narrow conceptions" (*M* 353); after she died and passed to the Elysian fields, she still lacked and needed "to acquire knowledge & virtue" and "intellectual improvement" because her heart had "been shut through suffering from knowledge" (*M* 353, 354). She could not yet be reunited with her father in death because of her "ignorance" (354); in life, when she had been "unthinking or misconducted in the pursuit of knowledge," she was in need of "lessons," but "the only words of wisdom to which she had ever listened" (354, 355) were the ones of Diotima in the Elysian Fields. Once she realized that knowledge was the end of her being, she confessed "how wayward a course did [she] pursue on earth," when her "passions & feelings . . . hurrie[d her] from wisdom to selfconcentrated misery & narrow selfish feeling" (358). Finally, Diotima told the dead Mathilda that she was "yet unfit" to be reunited with her father and that her redemption could be accomplished only "by the acqiurement [sic] of wisdom and the loss of . . . selfishness" (*M* 407, appendix 1).

There are two conclusions to be drawn from this litany about Mathilda in *The Fields of Fancy,* the first of which is that Mary Shelley obviously took pains in the original frame tale to characterize Mathilda as a narrator who lacked knowledge and virtue — someone in need of redemptive self-knowledge. When she abandoned the frame that had informed the reader about Mathilda's self-deception, she then was forced to add to Mathilda's monologue many more references to life as a tragedy — making Mathilda all the more a heroine of extreme sensibility who lived art more than life. That Mary Shelley originally distinguished herself from this flawed and overly dramatic character is made evident from there being a separate narrator in the original frame tale, a narrator with whom Mary Shelley obviously did identify. The parallels are very persuasive: Mary Shelley had suffered the loss of her daughter, Clara, in Venice in September 1818 and of her son, William, in Rome in June 1819; and the unnamed narrator began *The Fields of Fancy* with an announcement that "it was in Rome . . . that I suffered a misfortune that reduced me to misery & despair." This narrator then encountered the "lovely spirit" Fantasia, a self-representation of the very imagination that Mary Shelley had "ever worshiped & who tried to repay my adoration by diverting my mind from the hideous memories that racked it" (*M* 351) — in almost identical terms, Mary Shelley explained in 1822 that when she "wrote Matilda, miserable as [she] was, the *inspiration* [i.e., Fantasia] was sufficient to quell [her] wretchedness temporarily" (*MWSJ* 442). But Fantasia, or imagination, could accomplish only so much in addressing the misery and despair of Mathilda: "You mourn for the loss of those you love. They are gone for ever & great as my power is I cannot recall them to you" (*M* 351).

Nevertheless, writing fiction, Mary Shelley seems to be telling us, is at least somewhat therapeutic—providing a temporary means to escape the pains of life. Living fiction, on the other hand—as Mathilda did—merely compounds the lie and leads to even more pain. So we should not be too hasty to equate Mary Shelley writing *Matilda* with Mathilda writing *Matilda*: although Mary Shelley said she "ought to have died" that summer of 1819 when she was writing the fiction about Mathilda (see *MWSL* 1: 108), the very writing sustained her life; however, Mathilda did die after she wrote her narrative, one that fictionalized her life by dramatic excesses, even including the feigning of her own death. Again, Mathilda's fault seems to be in her self-deception: she lived not in the real world but in the world of make-believe, feigning her life as well as her death, until her self-confessed tragedy closes with the realization of her dreams and desires—her own death.

Mathilda's ability to feign life and death takes me to my second and more provocative conclusion: that the dissembler Mathilda might have feigned her own narrative and that we, as readers, might be able to lift the veil, remove her mask, and see her more as victimizer than victim in this incest drama. If we see her as playing a role and doubt her credibility, it is possible to argue that she, rather than her father, initiates the incest or that she at least misrepresents her own sexual desire for her father, whom she hopes to meet "at a ball"; or "perhaps . . . in a vessel" (*M* 14).[6] There is undoubtedly a crafty actress at work in the text of *Matilda*. There is an equal craftiness in the artistry of Mary Shelley, who embedded in Mathilda's narrative a number of allusions to other incest texts, some of which emphasize the daughter as the sexual aggressor.

The evidence of *Matilda* suggests that Mary Shelley as artist used an elaborate set of allusions in order to contextualize her study of incest. Most readers stumble upon the introductory reference to Oedipus just after Mathilda announces the "sacred horror in [her] tale that rendered it unfit for utterance" (*M* 5), but many are not aware that Mary Shelley alludes to another instance of mother-son incest when Mathilda quotes from John Fletcher's *Cupid's Revenge* in *The Fields of Fancy* (*M* 388). More to the point, however, is Mathilda's later comparison of herself to the daughter Sigismunda, who was so loved by her father, Tancred, that he killed her lover Guiscardo: "I did not wring my hands, or tear my hair, or utter wild exclamations, but as Boccacio describes the intense and quiet grief [of] Sigismunda over the heart of Guiscardo, I sat with my hands folded, silently letting fall a perpetual stream from my eyes" (*M* 29 and n). Although Mary Shelley had read this story about "Ghismonda" in Boccaccio's *The Decameron* (4.1) in May 1819 (*MWSJ* 262–64), she called the heroine "Sigismunda," the name suggesting that she had also read Dryden's erotically charged version of the same tale in "Sigismonda and Guiscardo, from Boccace" in his *Fables Ancient and Modern*.[7] But Mary Shelley might have misappropriated the name "Sigismunda" from Cervantes's strange novel *Persiles and Sigismunda*, which she was also reading in late May 1819 (*MWSJ* 264–65), just before she began *Matilda*. If she did read Dryden's *Fables*, she could also have encountered there the story of Cinyras and Myrrha, another incest story (from Ovid's *Metamorphoses*) detailing the love of a daughter for her father. If she did not read Dryden, then she could have encountered a variant of the Myrrha story in the Cervantes novel as well.[8] Either way, the love of a daughter for a father is signaled — just as it is when Mathilda later in her narrative reacts to her father's coldness by quoting Lelia's speech from Fletcher's comedy, *The Captain*:

> for what should I do here,
> Like a decaying flower, still withering
> Under his bitter words, whose kindly heat
> Should give my poor heart life? (*M* 20)

Lelia, it turns out, returns the heat: she later propositions her father and argues that "'tis not against nature/For us to lye together; if you have/An Arrow of the same Tree with your Bow,/Is't more unnatural to shoot it there/Than in another?"[9]

Of course, the most persuasive evidence of a daughter's complicity is Mathilda telling her father that Alfieri's *Myrrha* is her favorite play. Those who do not recall the specifics of the story of Myrrha in Ovid's *Metamorphoses* may be surprised to learn that the daughter is the one who desires and confesses her love for her father, the father being outraged by the sexual impropriety. Those who do know the Ovid and Alfieri texts have usually assumed that Mary Shelley merely (and cleverly) reversed the position of seducer and seduced — but Mary Shelley may have been even more clever — she only appeared to reverse the positions, and the allusions confirm that Mathilda had repressed or rewritten the narrative of her own passionate love for her father.

In both Ovid's and Alfieri's narratives, a crucial figure in the relation between father and daughter is the nurse: in Ovid (and in Dryden's version of the tale in *Fables Ancient and Modern*), the nurse negotiates the incest bed for daughter and father; in Alfieri, where the daughter desires but does not sleep with the father, the nurse attempts to minister to a Myrrha whose obsessive love for her father prompts thoughts of flight and suicide. The common denominator in these narratives is that the nurse attempts to elicit the secret love from the daughter, hoping that voicing the secret would be therapeutic. But there is neither therapy nor recuperation in the Myrrha stories; and in Mary Shelley's *Matilda,* there is neither nurse nor recuperation. As Mathilda herself remarks, "from my infant years, ever since my dear nurse left me, I had been a dreamer" and "I . . . nursed [my dreams and conceptions] in the hope of realization" (*M* 13, 14).

Mathilda, self-nursed, was all the more vulnerable to her own fanciful representations of reality. Denied the companionship and friendship of others by her aunt, she comforted herself "by pleasant day dreams": she loved "all the changes of Nature" as well as all of Nature's trees, animals, and other "inanimate objects." Her "books in some degree supplied the place of human intercourse," and she even "addressed [her harp] as [her] only friend": "I could pour forth to it my hopes and loves, and I fancied that its sweet accents answered me" (*M* 11–13). When her father's letter arrives on her sixteenth birthday, she again "read and re-read his letter," retreated into the "solitude of the woods [to] imagine the moment of [their] meeting," where she "indulged in wild dreams," and lost her way "in the intricacies of the woods" (*M* 15). When her father starts to shun Mathilda, her "wandering fancy brought by its various images now consolation and now aggravation of grief to [her] heart," and she compares herself to "Proserpine who was gaily and heedlessly gathering flowers on the sweet plains of Enna, when the King of Hell snatched her away to the abodes of death and misery" (*M* 19-20). These and other statements by Mathilda make evident that she was unaccustomed to dealing with or confronting the realities of life and that she preferred to live in worlds that she created from her own imagination — worlds of dream or illusion.

These imagined worlds become all the more necessary for Mathilda to cope after her father's declaration of love for his daughter. When he faints during that confession, the overcome Mathilda gazes down at his "deathly pale" face, asserting that she will never speak to him again and imagining he is in "his grave" (*M* 29). After retiring to her chamber, she indicates that she "awoke to life as from a dream," but she still feels as if her father "with white hairs were laid in his coffin." A few minutes later, she offers her father a reprieve by constructing an elaborate narrative in which he could be punished and purified prior to their next reunion: she imagines that he would "spend another sixteen years of desolate wandering" and "undergo fearful danger and soul-quelling hardships: let the hot sun of the south again burn his passion worn cheeks and the cold night rains fall on him and chill his blood":

> To this life, miserable father, I devote thee! — Go! — Be thy days passed with savages, and thy nights under the cope of heaven! Be thy limbs worn and thy heart chilled, and all youth be dead within thee! Let thy hairs be as snow. . . . Let the liquid lustre of thine eyes be quenched; and then return to me, return to thy Mathilda, thy child, who may then be clasped in thy loved arms, while thy heart beats with sinless emotion. Go, Devoted One, and return thus! — This is my curse, a daughter's curse: go, and return pure to thy child, who will never love aught but thee. (*M* 30)

That same evening, just after midnight, Mathilda constructs another fanciful narrative after she feels threatened by her father's footsteps pausing at the door of her chamber. Apparently giving up on her hope to purify her father, she reverts to her earlier conviction (or desire) to never again see her father. By dawn, she is "weary with watching" and "sought for repose" even though she "knew [she] should be pursued by dreams." Her dream, however, is more like a nightmare that would prevent her from ever seeing her father again: she pursued her "deadlily pale" father to the edge of a precipice where he appeared ready to commit suicide (*M* 31). When that dream is transformed into an even darker reality as Mathilda actually pursues her father to the sea in the midst of a thunderstorm, she is seized by a "strange idea" by which she links the fate of her father to the condition of an oak tree that might be struck by the next flash of lightning: "for in that state, the mind working unrestrained by the will makes strange and fanciful combinations with outward circumstances and weaves the chances and changes of nature into an immediate connexion with the event they dread" (*M* 38). In the next instant, lightning did in fact destroy the oak — and signals that Mathilda's father will also not survive.

By acknowledging that her mind "makes strange and fanciful combinations with outward circumstances," Mathilda does what she does best, blur the boundaries between fact and fiction and, in so doing, make the reader suspect that she may not be a very reliable narrator. That suspicion is confirmed in the final chapter, in which Mathilda constructs her eloquent apostrophe to Nature, confessing her propensity for the world of dream and illusion, her peopling of Nature with "wild fancies of [her] own creation":

> For it will be the same with thee, who art called our Universal Mother, when I am gone. I have loved thee; and in my days both of happiness and sorrow I have peopled your solitudes with wild fancies of my own creation. The woods, and lakes, and mountains which I have loved, have for me a thousand associations; and thou, oh, Sun! hast smiled upon, and borne your part in many imaginations that sprung to life in my soul alone, and which will die with me. Your solitudes, sweet land, your trees and waters will still exist, . . . though what I have felt about ye, and all my dreams which have often strangely deformed thee, will die with me. (*M* 65)

What I am proposing is that Mathilda has peopled her own incest narrative with even wilder "fancies of [her] own creation." Her solitary years of living fictions led her to fictionalize the last years of her life and to color the narrative in such a way that she represses or denies her own sexual desire for her father. If, as she confesses, her "dreams . . . strangely deformed" Nature, then it is likely that these same dreams deformed or at least misinformed her text and her narration about her incestuous relationship with her father.

If we fail to recognize the falsifying effect of Mathilda's dreams and instead believe the fiction that Mathilda consciously or unconsciously presents in defense of her having been victimized by her father, then we the readers are complicitous. But if we decode the text (primarily by means of the allusions to the incest narratives of Boccaccio, Ovid, Fletcher, and Dryden) and see Mathilda for the splendid but flawed actress that she is, then we discover a new meaning to this novella, one in which the narrator presents a fictional text designed to delude her audience and possibly herself. At the same time, we also discover just how clever Mary Shelley was as a writer of fiction: she was able artistically to transform her own personal grief into the misinforming musings of a narrator who creates her own persona, a created character who is not to be confused with Mary Shelley the author.

6 : Between Romance and History

Possibility and Contingency in Godwin, Leibniz,
and Mary Shelley's *Valperga*

TILOTTAMA RAJAN

Mary Shelley's choice of prose is often seen in gendered opposition to her husband's poetry. Mary Favret, discussing Mary Shelley's portrayal of Percy as an ineffectual angel in the notes to his poems, sees her as setting the novel against poetry, realism against idealism, so as to model the "definition of genres for the rest of the nineteenth century."[1] Mary Shelley may indeed have used the "story of particular facts" to disfigure what her husband's poetry had made beautiful (*PBSPP* 485). Yet her novels also bear a complex, symbiotic relationship to the discourse of imagination and ambition associated with her male colleagues, while narrativity is the form of her engagement with this discourse.

Mary Shelley was particularly drawn to an intergenre I have called *autonarration,* in which characters and episodes from the author's life are reworked into fictional form.[2] Autonarration allowed her to think through the cultural and emotional configurations in which she was inscribed by transposing them onto the mirror-stage of a virtual reality projected into the past, the future, or the fantastic. Mary Shelley's texts can thus be seen as an autometaphoric record of her relationship to a Romanticism that she displaces between fictional equivalents of Byron, Godwin, P. B. Shelley, and herself, so as to defer reaching any prematurely negative conclusions about it. The correspondences between real and fictional characters in any one text are as important as the differences in the ways the fictional is mapped onto the real *between* texts and the consequent splitting and recombining of relationships between traits and the characters to which they are attached. In *Matilda* Mary Shelley idealizes and abjects her husband as Woodville, while in *Valperga* she protects him by dividing the traits of Prometheanism between the Byronic Castruccio and the androgynously

Shelleyan Euthanasia. Then again, if the lost republican moment meta-phorized through Euthanasia is defeated by the hegemony of Castruccio, in *The Last Man* it is equivocally salvaged through a Godwinian contin-gency that allows the Shelleyan Adrian to survive Raymond within the unchangeable necessity of the plague.

As a process of constant intertextual revisioning, narrative is the frame-work for Mary Shelley's ongoing dialog with Romanticism. Moreover, any gendering of genres between the Shelleys is complicated by the fact that Godwin too wrote novels. In the 1790s, Godwin deployed the *novel*—a term he used synonymously with *romance*—not against poetry but as a form of skeptical utopianism in which political desire is exposed, through the "experiment" of fiction, to its own unconscious. In this chapter, then, I deal with Mary Shelley's most darkly utopian romance, *Valperga,* in re-lation to a textual family that includes not only P. B. Shelley's *Prometheus Unbound* but also, more importantly, Godwin's *St. Leon,* his essay "Of His-tory and Romance," and his *Life of Cromwell.*

Valperga is the history of the medieval prince Castruccio, whose hege-mony emerges on the cusp between the republican commune and the *signoria,* a compromise that gives local autonomy a stay of execution while also preparing the way for the despotic city-states of the Italian Renais-sance and the protonation states of France and Germany. However, Ca-struccio's history also contains the lost story of the two women whose desire provides him with narrative legitimacy. Euthanasia is the character most like P. B. Shelley, figuring the "knowledge," "virtue," and "liberty" he associated with the epipsyche (*PBSPP* 74), but Euthanasia is denied Promethean power because of her gender. As a woman never economized within the marriage circuit who never gives up her public role for domes-ticity, Mary Shelley's heroine recapitulates Mary Wollstonecraft's ideal of the rational feminist, along with Godwin's hope for a "euthanasia of gov-ernment" in self-government.[3] Beatrice, daughter of two feminist heretics, is briefly elevated by the people's belief in her prophetic power, but she is driven into hysteria when Castruccio abandons her to unsuccessfully at-tempt to return to Euthanasia, whose ideals he has betrayed. Though the text struggles to show Beatrice's power as deluded, finally depicting her as the victim of the witch Mandragola, her identity as a prophetess remains a metaphor (as in Godwin's *Lives of the Necromancers* [1834]) for a possible synergy between feminism and the masculine modes of imagination and ambition. The novel's most compelling segments concern Euthanasia's relationship to Beatrice, to whom she gives a home, whose deep dejection she can palliate but not cure, and through whom Mary Shelley rethinks her relationship not only to her own dejection, evidenced in *Matilda,* but also to her mother's unsustained rationalism and rejection of Romantic imagination.

As a partly fictitious history, Mary Shelley's novel recalls Sophia Lee's *The Recess* (1785), which also combines heroic romance with the sentimental novel. Lee's counterfactual history boldly gives Mary Queen of Scots two daughters, constructing a lost female genealogy. She anticipates Hans Kellner's argument that history is based on the destruction or forgetting of information and his unusual claim that the category should include not only what is "unrecorded" but also "information non-existent in time and space."[4] Similarly, while Mary Shelley begins by acknowledging the "public histories" of five male historians, at the end she claims that her history is based on "the private chronicles" of Euthanasia — chronicles that no more exist than the character herself, whose very "name [has] perished" (*V* 322). Yet *Valperga* is not a romance in the same sense as *The Recess,* which is full of flagrant violations of probability, such as the representation of an eternally youthful Leicester, who is Mary Queen of Scot's lover and years later her daughter's husband. Indeed, Mary Shelley considered her novel a history and spent hours researching a period that her contemporary Henry Hallam described as "a labyrinth of petty facts so . . . incapable of classification as to leave only confusion to the memory."[5] As important, then, as Lee's fiction is Godwin's essay "Of History and Romance" — a theory of the counterfactual that sets up a more negative and recursive dialectic between romance and history.

Godwin's essay begins as a theory of possibility opened up by a critique of the universal or probabilistic history favored by the Scottish historians and generates a version of the historical novel distinct from the work of their literary executor, Walter Scott. For if Scott begins the gendered colonization of romance by history, Godwin provocatively reverses this priority by arguing that "the writer of romance is to be considered the writer of real history."[6] Godwin uses the term *romance* synonymously with *novel* in a revealing syncresis of imagination and realism. He attributes to the novelist a unique power of penetration into the human psyche that allows him to see "what it is of which social man is capable" (*HR* 363). If the historian oversees the necessary laws of things as they are, the novelist's focus on individuals introduces an element of variability into these laws. Jon

Klancher has aptly described this variability as "contingency."[7] This contingency is the source of an unpredictable possibility in which the novelist sees "conjunctures and combinations [which] . . . though they have never yet occurred, are within the capacities of our nature" (*HR* 363).

Godwin's privileging of "individual" over "general" history and of romance over fact (*HR* 361–62) makes possible Mary Shelley's claim to have composed her history from the "chronicles" of an invented character. For although there is a certain sobriety to the paradoxes of Godwin's essay (with its emphasis on "scrutinis[ing] the nature of man," *HR* 362), the transgressiveness of his argument is played out in his own experiment with his theory in *St. Leon.* This work is the history of an aristocratic gambler who chances upon the secrets of alchemy, thereby prolonging his life and acquiring infinite wealth. Realistic rather than fantastic except in the one detail of St. Leon's powers, Godwin's novel makes magic (and thus imagination) both the subject of his novel and the mechanism by which its plot unfolds. He plays fact against romance so as to transpose history from the actual into a potential or experimental space midway between things as they are and things as they ought to be. This experiment, like the introduction of Euthanasia into an otherwise "historical" narrative, allows the reader to play with a "counterfactual history": a history that might have happened instead of the one that actually occurred. In neither the essay nor the novel does Godwin simply substitute romance for history, magic for realism. Instead the two poles are metaphors, between which history emerges as what Jameson calls the "political unconscious." This perhaps is why Godwin never mentions Lee, whom he knew personally but whom he may have seen as prematurely replacing realism with romance, only to have desire unravel into actuality.

Although Klancher takes *contingency* to be a postmodern term, the word has an extensive earlier provenance, having been used by Joseph Priestley and, most importantly, by the seventeenth-century philosopher Gottfried Wilhelm Leibniz.[8] Godwin's essay, I suggest, is strongly influenced by Leibniz, who in the course of the Romantic period came to be associated less with optimism than with a conjunction of imagination, necessity, and freedom within the framework of a uniquely idealistic materialism.[9] Leibniz helps us to understand several elements in the Godwinian theory of possibility that subtends *Valperga.* To begin with, there is the coexistence of possibility and necessity. Unlike Lee, who represents the impossible as fictionally happening, Mary Shelley never transgresses the necessity of things as they are. She does not provide a mimesis of feminist history but intimates it only as a thought experiment made fictionally possible by the fact that Euthanasia, an "unreal" character, occupies the same diegetic space as the historical Castruccio. Euthanasian possibility thus exists only as a virtual countermovement within the necessary reality of Castruccio's career. But secondly, insofar as the real finally precludes the possible, the real itself is contingently transformable. This potentiality has to do with Leibniz's theory of the subject as an aggregation of "monads" that are strictly necessitated and yet "infinitely divisible" into unexplored possibilities (M 65).[10] It accounts, in turn, for Mary Shelley's attraction to Byronic characters seemingly antithetical to feminist desire and for Godwin's similar fascination with St. Leon and Cromwell. It explains as more than just fatalism her decision to place the romance of Euthanasia inside the history of Castruccio, as well as Godwin's emphasis on Cromwell rather than on the republicans as a site of political desire.

Godwin's familiarity with Leibniz is suggested by the critique of optimism in the fourth book of *Political Justice*. Though Godwin mentions neither Leibniz nor Voltaire's well-known parody of him, that he may have Leibniz in mind is suggested by his coordination of several Leibnizian motifs in this section: the notion of necessity itself as the connection "between all things in the universe," the notion of possible worlds, and the link between necessity and optimism (*PJ* 1:449–55). At this stage, Godwin is critical both of optimism and of the view that "necessity" does not preclude liberty. But these objections do not necessarily constitute a rejection of Leibniz, which may be why he is not named. For one thing, Godwin attacks only the synchrony of necessity and optimism, or the view that the world chosen by God is necessarily the best one possible. In the second prong of his critique, Godwin soon modifies his position, supplementing the mechanist notion of a necessity that makes the universe systematically predictable (evident in Priestley's *Doctrine*) with the idea of a radical contingency, figured as the "grain of sand" that might have altered the entire course of the universe (*HR* 372).

Godwin's later arguments for the complementarity of necessity and contingency bring him very close to the Leibnizian position, and he does sometimes use the word *contingency* (at least once) in a Leibnizian sense.[11] Leibniz's notion that "the individual concept of each person includes once and for all everything that can ever happen to him" (*D* 19) is identical to "necessity," except that for the more empiricist Godwin the individual is programmed by circumstances rather than by his concept. At the same time Leibniz does not subscribe unequivocally to necessity, arguing that God's foreknowledge of "future contingencies" does not entail a predestination that precludes "human liberty" (D 20). The bridge between necessity and contingency is, briefly, the idea of possible worlds. Unlike geometrical truths (which are true in all conceivable worlds), human events are contingent if they could have happened otherwise in another world in which the predicates of the subject — say, Caesar — or the circumstances affecting him are different (D 22). These other worlds are not "existent," but they need only be free from internal contradiction to be real in possibility (M 43). Possible worlds thus have an existence in logic, or as Gilles Deleuze puts it, they are not impossible but simply in*com*possible:[12] they do not belong to the same set or series as do things as they are. As a result, though things are as they are, this does not lead to a theory of fatality, since "nothing is necessitated whose opposite is possible" (D 22).

Just as important, Leibnizian possibility (unlike contemporary possible worlds theory) has its origins not only in logic but also in a dynamic physics that, as Margaret Wilson points out, is elusively linked to a metaphysics interested in "immaterial forms, entelechies, or souls as the real . . . basis of phenomena."[13] Leibniz grants possible worlds a virtual reality by eliding the difference between essence and existence through the figure of God as the ultimate possibility. Thus the reality of possible worlds is founded in the "existence of the necessary Being in whom essence includes existence or in whom possibility is sufficient to produce actuality" (M 44). Two things follow from the attribution of possible worlds to God. First, these worlds are not just logical entities, "substances purely possible," which will never exist and are therefore "chimeras" (C 97). Second, insofar as it is the existence of a "Necessary Being" that makes possibility "actual," necessity paradoxically guarantees possibility and contingency. And although Leibniz is careful to say that God brings into being only the best of all possible worlds, he also argues against such limitations by claiming, almost Romantically, that the "supreme substance . . . must be incapable of limitation and must contain as much reality as possible" (M 40).

If logic and metaphysics are imaginatively confused, the theory of monads also materializes metaphysics as physics while idealizing matter as spirit. Indeed it is the symbiosis of metaphysics with physics that makes Leibniz's interest in souls and entelechies preidealist as well as post-theological. *The Monadology* is Leibniz's most suggestive experiment with a physics of possibility—its fragmentary form being itself a form of possibility.[14] From the theory of monads we can extrapolate both an account of possible worlds—of other monads with their own principle of development—and a theory of the subject, its determination, and its growth. Indeed it is the latter that makes Leibniz influential for Romantics such as Friedrich Schelling, by allowing the transmigration of possibility from the spatial discourse of logic into the temporal discourse of "freedom."

Briefly, the figure of monads allows Leibniz to think of the subject as simple yet possessed of infinite potentiality, as a unity that is infinitely self-differing. Monads are simple substances, like atoms, capable of no further division, and like matter they are neither generated nor extinguished. But what is theoretically simple is always experientially complex, as Leibniz suggests using the analogy of thoughts and, elsewhere, of motives: we "experience multiplicity in a simple substance when we find that the most trifling thought of which we are conscious involves [*enveloppe*] a variety in the object" (*M* 16). Hence, although Leibniz initially describes a monad as without "parts," he very soon recognizes it as microscopically divisible, so that every "portion of matter is like a garden full of plants and like a pond full of fish" (*M* 1, 67). The monad, moreover, is "a manifoldness which changes," (*M* 12), its divisibility making such changes contingent and unpredictable. "Each portion of matter" can be "divided without end, every part into other parts, each one of which has its own proper motion" (*M* 65).

Insofar as each monad contains other monads, the notion of entelechy that makes an individual's development deducible from his "concept," becomes infinitely subvertible by the individual entelechies of the parts that comprise this concept. As simplicity becomes complexity, so too necessity becomes contingency and even freedom, Leibniz's very terms being monads that are infinitely complex and transformable. As for subjects or bodies, Leibniz sees them as "aggregation[s]" of monads, which themselves are infinitely divisible (*C* 244). The subject on one level would then contain "the law of the continuous progression of its own workings," as a principle of development that is at once its necessity and its integrity. On another level, as compounds of substances each with their own "soul," subjects are "diversely" rather than predictably "transformable" (*C* 244). Or, in other words, their determination is a kind of freedom, bearing in mind Schelling's postulate that freedom does not belong to the individual; rather man is "the property of freedom."[15]

Leibniz's unique syncresis of necessity, possibility, and contingency is important in several ways for Godwin and Mary Shelley, who do not so much seek the utopia of romance as explore the space opened up by the dialectic between historical necessity and Romantic possibility. Monadology allows for the coexistence of the possible alongside the actual as a virtual reality. Godwin could not agree with Leibniz that God had chosen the best of all possible worlds—if indeed Leibniz himself was sure on this count.[16] Nevertheless, it is the theory of possible worlds as rationally coherent rather than fantastical that allows for a magic realism in which the thought experiments of alchemy or feminist history can actually happen. Further, Leibniz permits Godwin, and through him Mary Shelley, to retain a necessitarian concept of character without allowing necessity to foreclose possibility. Characters such as St. Leon and Castruccio are flat characters who are entirely predictable, so that "everything which is to happen" in their histories is already "virtually included in . . . [their] concept" (C 20). Yet a different world in which republican ideals might acquire agency in a marriage of Euthanasian desire with Promethean will is not impossible but only in*com*possible with things as they are (which is how Godwin could write two noncompossible endings to Caleb Williams). Thus, Leibniz's God can "produce different substances according to the different views which [she] has of the world" (C 23), as an author produces different characters so as to include in the universe of Castruccio the possible world of Euthanasia and Beatrice. Moreover, even simple characters such as Castruccio are "diversely transformable," as Godwin suggests when he too uses the metaphor of molecular aggregation to describe first the simple necessity by which a character "acts under successive circumstances" and then the contingent and unpredictable ways in which these very circumstances allow a character to "increase and assimilate new substances to its own" (HR 372).[17]

The microscopic penetration into character that discloses the simple as complex is specifically the prerogative of the novelist or romancer. Indeed, we might well be reading Godwin when we examine how Leibniz applies his principle of the infinite divisibility and differentiation of unity to the analysis of motives,[18] writing of the "infinity of figures and of movements, present and past" that enter into any action, as well as of the way such analysis can be "continued into greater detail without limit" (*M* 36). The novelist captures the minute particulars—or, as Leibniz says, the ever "more detailed contingencies" (*M* 37)—that elude the historian's overview. In doing so, she sees a space for possibility within law, or difference within the same.

Yet this very use of contingency to open up necessity into freedom is itself subject to a necessary contingency, and here too Leibniz's paradoxical coordination of terms proves relevant. For Godwin ends his alchemizing of history as romance with a curious caution, pointing to the unreadability of those details that allow the romancer to imagine between the lines of things as they are. To conceive new characters is easy enough; but to say how "such a person would act" in situations modified by "minute shades in a character" leaves the romancer "straining at a foresight" too great "for the powers of man." The historian, by contrast, admits that "events are taken out of his hands" and "determined by the system of the universe" (*HR* 372). In the end, then, Godwin returns to history, though only as a difference from romance that inscribes it in a negative dialectic rather than in a linear and teleological development. This return mirrors the recantation at the end of *St. Leon*, where the protagonist renounces "ambitious and comprehensive schemes" (435) in an unsatisfyingly corrective turn to the domestic.[19]

Historical romance was for Mary Shelley a way of rethinking Promethean potential within a dialectic that Godwin himself had difficulty mediating. Possibility obviously enters *Valperga* through Euthanasia and Beatrice, both unfinished characters who must be imagined and reimagined in a mutually supplementary relationship. But Castruccio is as important; he most embodies the irresistible power of necessity, both in his necessary subjection to the logic of his career and in the way this career becomes the necessity within which Euthanasia's and Beatrice's lives are lived. Mary Shelley's encryption of feminist possibility within this larger cycle is no less puzzling than Godwin's later reticence about the republican period of Vane and his concluding emphasis on Cromwell as the Commonwealth's only example of individual rather than general history. Godwin, it seems, would rather focus on a "usurper" than on the "virtuous and perhaps magnanimous men" who made the "visionary attempt to establish a republic in England."[20] In pursuing political desire through histories excentric to it (as Godwin also does in *Mandeville*), both writers compel idealism to work with material that profoundly resists it. Yet Mary Shelley is also fascinated by Castruccio—a fascination inherited from Godwin, who locates contingency not in the republicans but in a Napoleonic necessity first fictionalized in his own *St. Leon.*

Beginning with the interlude in England, where Castruccio is the still-empty object of the King's desire, *Valperga* generates a curious attraction towards him, having to do with his elusive potentiality. Mary Shelley advances the date of Castruccio's birth by eight years, both intensifying the sense of waste when he dies at only thirty-nine (rather than forty-seven) and making him younger and more impressionable than he actually was during the family's expulsion from Lucca. She dwells on his adolescence as a polymorphous and unstable period during which his character is still malleable enough for him to side first with the barons and then with Gavaston and even to love someone from the opposite party. Not that there is any doubt as to his development, which already has been written in history. But drawing on Godwin's discussion of the monadic programming of princely character (*PJ* 2.5–30), Mary Shelley adopts a causality according to which the necessity that rules his career is entirely contingent, a product of rank, circumstances, and historical period rather than of anything innate.

That Castruccio could not have been different given his context does not reduce his responsibility for what he does, but it makes him culpable as a type rather than as an individual. Moreover, given the text's hybrid identity as a historical *romance,* it allows us to imagine other possible Castruccios, just as for Leibniz there are other Adams who might have existed in other worlds. In a significant redundancy, Mary Shelley repeatedly advances the turning point at which Castruccio's "character" is once and for all "formed" (*V* 288) in a negative direction—as if deferring the moment when possibility is narrowed into destiny.[21] She departs from history to leave him unmarried and thus never fully contained within existing structures. Castruccio's attraction can be approached in terms of what Georges Bataille calls the "psychological structure" of fascism as an "affective formation" prevalent in Italy, where the more "homogeneous" form of monarchy had been weakened. For fascism, in Bataille's analysis, combines the homogeneity of "discipline" and "obedience" with an "essential *heterogeneity*" associated with "imperative violence, and the positioning of the chief as the transcendent object of collective affectivity."[22] It is this subversive, yet repressive, "sovereignty" that draws Beatrice to Castruccio. In fact she herself, as a prophetess, embodies a different kind of heterogeneity in the form of what Bataille calls "the sacred,"[23] thereby differing radically from Euthanasia, whom P. B. Shelley describes in terms of the homogeneity of "a feudal countess [whose] castle is the scene of knightly manners of the time" (*PBSL* 2:353).

Significantly, Beatrice never ceases to love Castruccio and even reproaches Euthanasia for deserting "this glorious being." Dismissing his Machiavellian politics as "mere forms," she echoes Asia's description of Prometheus when she insists on the transcendental ideality of Castruccio: "He remained, and was not that every thing?" (*PBSPP* 162; *V* 250). Beatrice's fate warns us against being seduced by romance, and the fallen prophetess is the vehicle of the novel's most bitter diatribe against "imagination" (*V* 244). But Euthanasia also continues to love Castruccio, although she disciplines herself to renounce him. When Castruccio asks her to care for Beatrice, Euthanasia is drawn to her not only out of female solidarity but also because Beatrice is a part of Castruccio that he has loved, wounded, and cast off. As long as Euthanasia is with Beatrice, she is able to keep Castruccio at a distance, because she *is* caring for him through Beatrice, "repair[ing his] work" (*V* 240) and, at the level of the text's libidinal economy, re-forming him into what he should be. Beatrice is also in a sense the feminine, and thus safely defeated, version of Castruccian power. When Beatrice dies, Euthanasia once more becomes concerned with Castruccio, as she fatally reenters the political fray to save him from himself. Indeed, her fantasies about remaking Castruccio in defeat and reading philosophy with him on a Shelleyan island (*V* 293, 302), recall Beatrice's more passionate pronouncements on how she wants her lover to be a monster so that she can "shade him as the flowering shrub invests the ruin" (*V* 250). The text does not completely disallow these fantasies. For although Castruccio disappoints us *ideologically,* he has no further sexual entanglements after his betrayal of the two women, protecting the reader from further *romantic* disappointment.

The possibilities attached to Castruccio are undefined, but while Sismondi celebrates the prosperity of Florence after his death,[24] Mary Shelley leaves us with a sense of waste and abrupt termination. We can nevertheless trace these possibilities through other texts, including the reworking of Castruccio in *The Last Man,* in which the militaristic Raymond also engages in various constructive civic projects. Within an arc that leads from regionalism to hegemony, *Valperga* is set in an unstable period between local state-forms such as the bishoprics and the communes, nation-states such as the German Empire and the papacy, and local tyrannies (such as that of Castruccio) that both prefigured and sought to forestall national hegemonies. Therefore Romantic historians, though lamenting the chaotic history of Italy, also found the Middle Ages rich in political experimentation. Hallam, for instance, saw in the Lombard League the unrealized promise of a "permanent federal union of small republics," while Sismondi saw Italian history as a dialectic in which the defeat of liberty led the citizenry to seek new outlets in political forms that were by no means limited to republicanism.[25] The period of Castruccio presented more obscure possibilities than others, being characterized by a micropolitics so like a "labyrinth"[26] as to resist simple binaries of Guelph and Ghibelline, papacy and Empire, or localism and hegemony. Still, insofar as this period, like the Commonwealth period of Godwin's *Mandeville,* was one of tactical rather than ideological alliances, its history too opened up detailed contingencies within the larger inevitability of a movement from local to national state-forms.

These contingencies are Godwin's concern in his *The Life of Cromwell,* published the year after *Valperga* as the fourth volume of his *History of the Commonwealth.* Indeed, at the time Mary Shelley and Godwin were involved in a complex dialog over the recoverability of a lost republican moment at the parallel sites of the Commonwealth and the Italian Middle Ages. In *Mandeville* (1817), Godwin finds nothing but trauma: he focuses on royalists rather than republicans and on the story of a psychically disfigured individual who never really enters history. If *Mandeville* is the pretext for the violence and factionalism of *Valperga,* in *The Life of Cromwell* Godwin returns to the possibilities of the commonwealth in ways enabled by his daughter's historical romance. *The Life*'s end is remarkably reminiscent of *Valperga,* where the abrupt termination by epidemic of Castruccio's career "in the maturity of his glory" (*HC* 4:324) leaves the sense of a meteoric and unconsolidated energy. As Cromwell's projects "were antiquated and annihilated . . . as soon as they were deprived of his energies to maintain them" (*HC* 4:607–8), so too Castruccio had no successors and was a singular individual after whose death Lucca fell back into "primitive insignificance" (*V* 325). Earlier, Godwin praises Cromwell for "the fertility of his conceptions [which], like the intrepidity of his spirit, was incapable of being exhausted," and he adds,"we seek in romance for characters, with qualities enabling them to achieve incredible adventures . . . [but Cromwell was] a real personage" (*HC* 4:vii).

Recalling his own statement on how "character increases and assimilates new substances into its own, and how it decays, together with the catastrophe into which by its own gravity it naturally declines" (*HR* 372), Godwin questions the view that Cromwell's death coincided with the term of his abilities. Like St. Leon, whose life was mobilized by "experiments," Cromwell's was a "government of experiments" (*HC* 4:603), proceeding according to a principle of perfectibility, or "perfectihabies" as Leibniz says in describing the logic of entelechies or souls (*M* 48). Had he lived ten years longer, Godwin suggests, Cromwell might well have achieved a "permanent settlement of England under a system of rational liberty" (*HC* 4:597).

There is little sense of specifically political possibility in *Valperga,* except for Euthanasia's early reference to Castruccio's "romantic conception of future union among the Italian states" (*V* 168). Instead, the political romance of Castruccio stems from the inadequacy of Euthanasia, whose "liberty" often seems transcendentally aestheticized. Yet Castruccio exists only as what Mary Shelley—like Kant and Plato—calls an "idea" (*V* 181). We can speculate that she was drawn to a certain power of will in him, to an individuality which, like an accident, temporarily changed the course of history. She might have agreed with his most recent biographer, Louis Green, that the enigma of Castruccio lay in the way his career followed "the seemingly destined curve of his fortunes from nadir to nadir through an arc of irresistible advance." According to Green, Castruccio's career was a "near miss" whose value lay in the way *failure* had interrupted an otherwise predictable history. As a failure, Castruccio's life laid the ground for innovations that "develop slowly" from "unsuccessful [adaptations] which, by falling short of or overreaching what is demanded of them, gradually define the limits of tolerance [they] seek to master." [27]

One of Castruccio's failures is Euthanasia, whose life is also both a near miss and a contingency unforeseen in official histories. Euthanasia functions effectively as long as she practices a local and domestic form of government, but she knows her territory must eventually be absorbed by a larger state (*V* 100). Ironically, she is defeated when she assumes political as well as social agency, thus confusing good and the means of good in the conspiracy against Castruccio. Mary Shelley knows that her character's republicanism and idealism are at odds with modernity, which is why the text finally sets Euthanasia aside. Yet, as a female ruler who never marries, she is an exception to political and literary rules. In her relationship with Beatrice, she also shows an adaptability that she is not permitted to develop in public life. In a clear allusion to Godwin's concept of "perfectibility," Mary Shelley writes that her "character was always improving, always adding some new acquirements" (*V* 297). Euthanasia may be a nostalgic figure like Guinigi or Marguerite—the character in *St. Leon* modeled on Wollstonecraft—but she is also one of the shadows that futurity casts on the present.

It is hard to say by the end whether Euthanasia's relationship with Castruccio is a failure or a near miss, whether she lived too late or too early. Her life does not change the course of events. On the other hand, it is precisely this measurement of history in terms of "events" that the novel questions. Mary Shelley's own re-vision of history is reflected in the fact that the male writers identified in the preface as sources are replaced by the end with the "private chronicles" of Euthanasia, as the novel ends with her death rather than relying for Castruccio's life on "public histories" (*V* 5, 323). That this life contains feelings unrecorded by "history" is a fact of which we are aware, as in Castruccio's last, poignant interview with Euthanasia; indeed the narrator more than once draws attention to the *historiographical* need for recording such feelings (*V* 204, 323–24). From this need grows the recognition of Godwin and later feminist historians that the personal is the public;[28] in this sense, "Euthanasia" is not without impact on history.

Euthanasia's effect on political rather than historiographical justice is less certain. But she does not die, she is "lost" and "never heard of more." She becomes a phantasm in the political unconscious who "sleeps in the oozy cavern of the ocean" (*V* 316, 322), like Panthea in the arms of Ione (*PBSPP* 161). The last chapter resonates with echoes from P. B. Shelley's work and anticipations of Byron's *The Island* (1823), where the lost lovers also survive in a cave in the sea. The darker romance of Euthanasia's disappearance returns her from the possible to the virtual, a term that may better describe potentiality in *Valperga*. In *Bergsonism*, Gilles Deleuze distinguishes the *virtual* and its *actualization* from the less cautious pairing of the *possible* and its *realization*. Realization "involves a limitation by which some possibles" are set aside, in a process by which the real is "in the image . . . of the [single] possible that it realizes." Whereas the possible is an idea to be realized, the virtual is a network of possibilities that are *actualized* (or imaginatively developed) along lines of "difference," "divergence," or "creation."[29] Possibility is what Godwin plays with when he foresees

Cromwell's future with "a sagacity scarcely less than divine" (*HR* 372). But virtuality is all Mary Shelley allows us when she lets us create different scenarios for her characters, whose detailed contingencies may well unravel their promise. Euthanasia survives her end as a virtual character, and, as Godwin says, "we never know any man's character" (*HR* 371), thus we cannot know the possible world in which she might have prevailed. Yet virtuality, as the site of imagination, may be that space between romance and history that escaped Godwin in his false return to domesticity in *St. Leon* and to things as they are in the essay on romance and history.

7 : Future Uncertain

The Republican Tradition and Its Destiny in *Valperga*

𝓜ICHAEL 𝓡OSSINGTON

Valperga: The Republican Ideal Beyond Time

Accounts of the republican city-states of medieval Italy, gleaned from a variety of historical and literary sources, had a special significance not only for the Shelleys but for Byron, Hazlitt, Hunt, Keats, and many other English Romantic writers.[1] Yet the attraction of such political and poetical consciousnesses, literally or imaginatively in exile from contemporary England, to narratives of the Italian republican tradition, typically took the form neither of nostalgia nor of vicarious pleasure. Rather, no doubt much influenced by their reading of Dante, these writers seem to have been absorbed by the disillusion and frustration of political ideals and fascinated by the refusal of time to supply the story they wanted to hear and to tell.

This chapter focuses on the awareness displayed in the Shelleys' work of the vulnerability of the republican ideal of self-governing communes based on principles of civic liberty and the eschewal of self-interest to corruption and abuse. Such is the clarity of this awareness that it amounts to a kind of reading of history as tragedy in which the fallen hero or heroine is the "type" of the ideal republic. To the Shelleys, the past betrays the fragility of this ideal, its susceptibility to destruction even as it is actualized. What remains is a pretext for the hope of recovery that remains just that, a construct, a notion, an idea. The past itself, in the sense of what is called *history,* becomes an imaginative investment whose returns are never realized, always deferred. The republic is often, so to speak, the tragic protagonist in the second-generation Romantics' fictionalized histories or dramas, its destruction redeemed by what can be extracted from the past for the future. Art, in the form of the idea of "the Poet" and "Poetry" in P. B. Shelley's work, or of the highly educated, self-consciously "literary" heroines of Mary Shelley's novels, such as Euthanasia in *Valperga,* is to be seen, not without a measure of ironical self-awareness, as what might just be able to achieve such redemption.

I take as my starting point P. B. Shelley's letter of September 1821 to Charles Ollier, his publisher, in which he describes Mary Shelley's second novel: "The romance is called *Castruccio, Prince of Lucca,* and is founded (not upon the novel of Macchiavelli under that name, which substitutes a childish fiction for the far more romantic truth of history, but) upon the actual story of his life" (*PBSL* 2:353). Since the idea of there being a "truth" to history that poetry and fiction are uniquely equipped to communicate is, of course, central to the work of P. B. Shelley, the reading of *Valperga* intimated in this letter is, in one sense, unremarkable. It is telling that "romance" is not simply to be seen as a literary effect, the generic packaging in which the past, particularly the medieval period for Romantic writers, can be appropriately wrapped, but rather as the most suitable way in which "the truth of history" may be expressed. *Valperga* can be seen, in these terms, as offering an alternative to the idea that history is to be understood simply — or even at all — as a narrated record of past events.

In important ways, *Valperga* seems to resist, as much as be accommodated by, the generic label *historical novel* that literary history has attached to it. It not only tells us about the past and about the relationship of the past to the present and the future, it also alerts us to the dynamic and constantly shifting relationship among all these temporal realms, both within the time of the novel and between that time and the time of its reception in the 1820s and beyond. It is suffused by a sense of the fluidity of time, or perhaps, more precisely, of distinct but sometimes overlapping temporal planes or zones (the Dantesque image of circles seems especially appropriate). Moreover, the variety of perspectives afforded by these different temporalities becomes the means by which the politics of the novel is articulated. Its idealism, in the face of one aesthetically compelling version of the story of republicanism in Italy in the middle ages, a setting that we would characterize as charged with despotism and violence, is instead seen from a vantage point above and beyond the repugnant yet engrossing agents of "history," as it is conventionally understood.[2]

Beatrice, through her heretical, Manichean genealogy and supposed powers of prophecy, represents a dramatic example of the way in which a critique of the time of the novel—which is, or at first sight appears to be, Castruccio's lifetime—is performed. But I am primarily interested here in Mary Shelley's construction of the figure of Euthanasia as a means through which the temporal world, both past and present, can be set apart, criticized, and imaginatively overcome. Whereas Castruccio's political designs and actions are part of a comfortably familiar, well-documented narrative of events called *history*, Euthanasia can be seen as literally outside time, detached in Mary Shelley's invented realm of "Valperga." Indeed, as has been pointed out, the word *or* in the title Godwin is said to have given the manuscript, *Valperga: or, the Life and Adventures of Castruccio, Prince of Lucca*, is no mere grammatical nicety.[3] It highlights the space given to Euthanasia in the novel as a refuge from, and an alternative to, the destructive and exhausting march of recorded events that attach to Castruccio's "Life and Adventures." In Euthanasia's carnivalesque court at the end of volume 1 (*V* 104–17), Valperga suggests itself as a means of subverting temporality, a space above and beyond time. But Euthanasia's displacement of the temporal is at its most consummate in the absorbing account of her disappearance, "lost" at sea, as the chapter heading has it (*V* 316), in an episode that testifies fittingly to the mutability that is her credo:

> Earth felt no change when she died; and men forgot her. Yet a lovelier spirit never ceased to breathe, nor was a lovelier form ever destroyed amidst the many it brings forth. Endless tears might well have been shed at her loss; yet for her none wept, save the piteous skies, which deplored the mischief they had themselves committed;—none moaned except the sea-birds that flapped their heavy wings above the ocean-cave wherein she lay;—and the muttering thunder alone tolled her passing bell, as she quitted a life, which for her had been replete with change and sorrow. (*V* 322)[4]

There are no human testimonies of grief ("for her none wept"). Instead, nature is eloquently elegiac and thus reciprocates the "change and sorrow" characteristic of her life. That "men forgot her" suggests that culture is guilty of failing to accommodate what Euthanasia represents. Her republican ideals constitute a politics that could not, by definition, be achieved in time.

Valperga then questions the way that history is to be made and written, exposing its reliance on the necessarily artificial strategies of narrative that, from Aristotle onwards, account for the genre's uneasy relations with fiction. A clue to Euthanasia's instrumental role in this questioning comes in the opening sentences of the conclusion of the novel (which follows on directly from the passage quoted above): "The private chronicles, from which the foregoing relation has been collected, end with the death of Euthanasia. It is therefore in public histories alone that we find an account of the last years of the life of Castruccio" (*V* 323). These sentences have a disconcerting effect. They announce that, in retrospect, the time of the novel should be seen as Euthanasia's rather than Castruccio's. In so doing, they function not just as an acknowledgment of the fiction of the "history" we have been reading but of the dependence of the narrative on Euthanasia's existence. The reference to "private chronicles" here is not simply the deployment of a well-known novelistic device of inventing sources either to lend credibility to what is confessedly a fiction or, more likely, self-consciously to invoke generic, fictional strategies to a knowing readership. At issue here, rather, is the way that alternatives to so-called public history may be presented.

In this respect, Lockhart's review of *Valperga* in *Blackwood's* is one of the novel's most acute readings and instructive criticisms. Lockhart reverses the terms of the polarity between "history" and "fiction" offered by P. B. Shelley in the letter to Ollier cited above. Whereas he dismisses the opportunistic substitution of "a childish fiction for the far more romantic truth of history" in Machiavelli's *Life of Castruccio Castracani*,[5] Lockhart, thoroughly approving of the "glowing and energetic sketch" it provides, and implicitly endorsing its historical veracity, laments that "Mrs Shelley has not done justice to the character of Castruccio."[6] Furthermore, in his comment that "Mrs Shelley's book has no inspiration, but that of a certain *school,* which is certainly a very modern, as well as a very mischievous one, and which ought never, of all things, to have numbered ladies among its disciples," Lockhart seems to identify the novel's ideology as at once Godwinian and effeminate: "The attempt, whether successful or not, certainly is made to depict the slow and gradual formation of a crafty and bloody Italian tyrant of the middle ages, out of an innocent, open-hearted and deeply-feeling youth. We suspect, that in the whole of this portraiture, far too much reliance has been laid on thoughts and feelings, not only modern, but modern and feminine at once."[7]

Such "modern and feminine . . . thoughts and feelings" are at odds with Lockhart's implicit endorsement of Machiavelli's encomium to Castruccio's masculinism: "He used to say that men ought to try everything, not to be afraid of anything; and that God is a lover of strong men, because we see that he always punishes the powerless by means of the powerful."[8] Insofar as it associates the novel's artistic failings with the (gendered) politics of the school from which it issues, Lockhart's critique, wilfully immune to Euthanasia's alternative model of a republican polity, cannot help but make one recall Hazlitt's essay on *Coriolanus*. Hazlitt's essay constitutes a challenge, if not a threat, to a Godwinian, antiauthoritarian politics in its assertion that "The language of poetry naturally falls in with the language of power" and in its provocative politicization of the imagination and understanding as "The one . . . an aristocratical, the other a republican faculty."[9] But such an equivalence of aesthetic and abusive political power is precisely what *Valperga* seeks to question. Indeed, *Valperga* can be seen to function as a revisionary, feminist critique of the kind of overtly masculine politics and rhetoric of Lockhart's review, Hazlitt's essay, and, a ghostly precursor, Machiavelli's *The Prince*.

The Prince focuses on, amongst other things, an ethical issue central to *Valperga*, the relationship between a politically engaged individual's private life and public life: "And many writers have imagined for themselves republics and principalities that have never been seen nor known to exist in reality; for there is such a gap between how one lives and how one ought to live that anyone who abandons what is done for what ought to be done learns his ruin rather than his preservation: for a man who wishes to profess goodness at all times will come to ruin among so many who are not good."[10] The works of the Shelleys are exercised perpetually by the "conflicting demands of public power and private morality" addressed here.[11] Euthanasia offers hope in overcoming the "gap" between "how one lives and how one ought to live" by symbolizing a heroic, in some respects invincible, combination of an ideal political morality (with reference to Machiavelli, above, perhaps an "imagined" republic), on the one hand, and a poetic sensibility, on the other. Before this can be examined, however, it is necessary to trace, albeit briefly and selectively, a genealogy of Euthanasia's symbolic function. I refer to two poems of 1818 by P. B. Shelley that demonstrate the difficulty of discovering a fully achieved, ideal moment in the history of the Italian republics and to three early works by Mary Shelley that entertain an ironical and self-conscious perspective on the vagaries of republican history.

The Elusiveness of Republican Ideals: Percy Shelley's "Mazenghi" and "Lines written among the Euganean Hills"

Mary Shelley includes a portion of "Mazenghi" in the "Fragments" section of her edition of *Posthumous Poems,* accompanied by a note: "This fragment refers to an event, told in Sismodi's [sic] Histoire des Republiques Italiennes, which occurred during the war when Florence finally subdued Pisa, and reduced it to a province. The opening stanzas are addressed to the conquering city." [12] The episode to which the Swiss historian refers took place in 1405:

> The Florentines hardly thought it possible to breach the walls of Pisa, so they decided to destroy the city by starving it, while their army attacked successively the various castles in the territory. The Pisans, for their part, strove to provide themselves with supplies; they sent some galleys to get provisions from Sicily, one of them, surprised on its return by vessels the Florentines had had armed at Genoa, took refuge under the tower of Vado. A Florentine called Pierre Marenghi, who wandered far from his native land, on whom a death sentence hung, seized this opportunity to render his fellow citizens a conspicuously brave act. He flung himself from the shore, a torch in his hand, and swam to the galley, in spite of arrows being shot at him. Wounded in three places, he continued for a long time to cling to the ship's prow, holding up the torch, until the fire had caught the enemy galley in such a way as it could not be extinguished. It burned opposite the tower of Vado, while Pierre Marenghi returned to the shore. He was remembered afterwards with honor in his homeland. [my translation] [13]

The tragic irony of Sismondi's account is that in banishing Pietro Marenghi, the Florentines had exiled a heroically loyal citizen. But P. B. Shelley's rendition of Marenghi's story (in which he changes the protagonist's name to "Albert Mazenghi," hence the poem's title) tells of a different kind of tragedy that befalls the hero.[14] He is wrongfully excommunicated from the once exemplary but now corrupt Florentine republic, having succumbed to what a line in a stanza recently conjectured to belong to "Mazenghi" calls a "love . . . misdirected,"[15] that is, patriotism. The poem suggests that Mazenghi can only fulfill the truly communal ideals of a republic while in exile, in the company of amphibians, reptiles, and birds: "He had tamed every newt and snake and toad,/And every seagull" (*OSA* lines 106–7). Physically isolated in the dangerous and inhospitable marshland around the tower of Vado on the Tuscan coast[16]—off which "the Sicilian vessel which bore Euthanasia" is wrecked by a storm (*V* 322)—like other Shelleyan heroes, he appears most at ease outside human society, beyond the reach of time.

Nevertheless, "The thought of his own kind" (*OSA* line 159), that is, his sympathy for the starving Pisans, is eventually overwhelmed by "The thought of his own country" (*OSA* line 161).[17] The defining moment, and tragic fall, of the hero lies in his assumption of a political identity, where previously the scene had been remarkable precisely because it had been empty of the possibility of any humanly defined identity whatsoever. Both in its suggestion that there is no praxis that is not corrupt and its acknowledgment that "good and ill like vines entangled are" (*OSA* line 49), "Mazenghi" displays, in albeit cryptic, fragmentary form, a melancholy rather than (as elsewhere in P. B. Shelley's oeuvre) celebratory admission of a ceaselessly dynamic Manicheism. As in *Valperga,* in which Euthanasia's loyalty to her Guelph ancestors compels her to mobilize her subjects and allies for the siege of Valperga by Castruccio even as she recognizes her implication in a type of politics she refuses,[18] "how one ought to live" in an ideal republican society is bleakly remote from political actualities.

"Mazenghi" is set at the point when Florence itself, venerated by Sismondi as the most democratic of the Tuscan city-states in the middle ages, has become corrupted by aggressive, imperial ambition. It suggests that P. B. Shelley was drawn to that moment when, within one influential model of Enlightenment historiography, the trajectory of republican history from decline to fall is precipitated.[19] Such a model of inevitable decline can apparently only be resisted, as in "Lines written among the Euganean Hills," by the poet's speculative attempts to create the past anew by refashioning its relationship to the present. But in "Lines" the poetic venture of shaping in space and time a chain of unity in another rich repository of the Italian republican tradition, the "plain of Lombardy . . . Islanded by cities fair" (lines 91, 93), is knowingly exposed as hazardous if not delusory. Venice ("thy towers . . . Quivering through aerial gold," lines 142–43) may emit a magical aura from the distant peaks of the Euganean Hills (where Castruccio resides with Guinigi, *V* 24–29), but in situ its materiality is repulsive, its towers, "Sepulchres, where human forms,/Like pollution-nourished worms,/To the corpse of greatness cling,/Murdered, and now mouldering" (lines 146–49)—a description resembling that of England in the later sonnet, "England in 1819." There is no unequivocal faith here or elsewhere in P. B. Shelley's work in a Hegelian world-spirit realizing itself, no belief in a teleological imperative that is magically going to bring things right in time. If the fusion of what is valuable about the republican tradition with a renewed political morality cannot be achieved, then the poet resigns himself to the fact that memories of Venice and its neighbouring city-republics will vanish:

> But if Freedom should awake
> In her omnipotence, and shake
> From the Celtic Anarch's hold
> All the keys of dungeons cold,
> Where a hundred cities lie
> Chained like thee, ingloriously,
> Thou and all thy sister band
> Might adorn this sunny land,
> Twining memories of old time
> With new virtues more sublime;
> If not, perish thou and they!—
> Clouds which stain truth's rising day
> By her sun consumed away—
> Earth can spare ye: while like flowers,
> In the waste of years and hours,
> From your dust new nations spring
> With more kindly blossoming.
> (lines 150–66)

Here temporal waste (line 164), on an analogy with the cycles of destruction and creation in the time of the physical world, may ultimately yield a "kindly blossoming" (line 166). But such an oblique way of expressing hope, through allowing that sheer mutability may, in time, redress despair at the present state of things, places the onus of intervening in history on the poet's imagination rather than on individual actors. Thus it is not statesmen or military strategists (to whom agency is usually attributed by historians) who can unblock the impasse these beleagured cities have reached, but poets.

Allegory and Irony in *History of a Six Weeks' Tour* (1817), *Frankenstein* (1818), and "Giovanni Villani" (1823)

P. B. Shelley's description of Castruccio to Ollier as "a little Napoleon . . . [who,] with a dukedom instead of an empire for his theatre, brought upon the same all the passions and the errors of his antitype" (*PBSL* 2:353) anticipates Lockhart's weary complaint that in *Valperga* "we find Mrs Shelley flinging over the grey surtout and cocked hat of the great captain of France, the blazoned mantle of a fierce *Condottiere* of Lucca."[20] With, one feels, a disingenuity verging on bathos, an afterthought to Ollier, "I ought to tell you that the novel has not the smallest tincture of any peculiar theories in politics or religion" (*PBSL* 2:355), pronounces even as it tries to defuse its allegorical potential. However, "Sismondi's delightful publication, *Histoire des Republiques Italiennes de l'Age Moyen* [*sic*]" (*V* 5), to which the reader is referred in the preface to *Valperga*, afforded an exemplary model of a critique of contemporary European experiments with republicanism.[21] An influential mediation of the first Paris edition of *Histoire* to an English audience,[22] an essay in the *Quarterly Review* of June 1812 registering that "the work is prohibited at Paris," suggests that a survey of the democratic city-states of medieval Italy serves as a reminder of an alternative precedent to Napoleon's brand of republicanism: "the quality which most forcibly characterizes his [Sismondi's] history, is the zeal which it displays in the cause of national independence, the abhorrence of tyranny and of the lust of dominion."[23]

Euthanasia, who sees her first duty as "to resist the incroachments of Castruccio, and to preserve the independence of her subjects" (*V* 212), seems to reinforce the barely veiled critique of Napoleonic imperial aggression Sismondi provided with what Hazlitt called "the genuine feelings of an enlightened reasoner."[24] Furthermore, *Valperga*'s plot can be seen as urgently relevant to the worryingly "enslaved state" of England during the time of the novel's most intense composition (1820–21) and to the quest for Italian freedom from Austrian domination in the (failed) revolutions in Piedmont, Naples, and Sicily.[25] The Shelleys were profoundly aware of efforts to liberate Italy from the domination of competing powers—the papacy, the Holy Roman Empire, Napoleon, and now Austria, all of which had, at different times, held sway since the era of Dante, in which *Valperga* is set.[26]

Yet if the contemporary urgency of libertarian struggle is evident in the composition and reception of *Valperga,* it is also worth registering the origins of the novel's equally acute sense of the ironies of republican history. In the second of the "Letters Written During a Residence of Three Months in the Environs of Geneva, in the Summer of the Year 1816" (published in *History of a Six Weeks' Tour,* in 1817), Mary Shelley's description of the Plainpalais refers to the Geneva revolution of 1792, in which democrats sympathetic to the French Revolution overthrew the magistracy and substituted a revolutionary government that itself only lasted until 1795 before being put down, ironically in the name of the French Republic, by Napoleon[27]:

> Here a small obelisk is erected to the glory of Rousseau, and here (such is the mutability of human life) the magistrates, the successors of those who exiled him from his native country, were shot by the populace during that revolution, which his writings mainly contributed to mature, and which, notwithstanding the temporary bloodshed and injustice with which it was polluted, has produced enduring benefits to mankind, which all the chicanery of statesmen, nor even the great conspiracy of kings, can entirely render vain. From respect to the memory of their predecessors none of the present magistrates ever walk in Plainpalais. (*TW* 46)

The cool eye cast on the vagaries of revolutionary politics in this passage suggests that there is a certain poetic justice in the inheritors of Rousseau's revolutionary views revenging themselves on the heirs of the republican magistracy that had banished him. But there is also an acknowledgment that the genuinely revolutionary climate of the 1790's itself succumbed to corruption and that tyranny in the name of republicanism was, through Napoleon, substituted for the political ideals articulated by Rousseau and embraced by the Genevan democrats. The "Restoration Settlement" of 1815 is consolidated in the idea that the present magistrates are able to perpetuate their antipopular, anti-Rousseauist sentiments by boycotting the park. The monument to the citizen of Geneva serves as a means of remembering and upholding their traditional resistance to him, and the Pickering and Chatto edition refers the reader to perhaps the greatest expression of such ironies in a note that records Byron's reported comment on the bust of Rousseau: "it was probably built of some of the stones with which they pelted him" (*TW* 46 n. a).[28]

In *Frankenstein,* in a replay of the revenge of the populace on the magistrates, little William, brother of Victor and son of a Geneva magistrate, is murdered by the Creature in the Plainpalais (*F* 51; *F* 51 n. a; *TW* 46 n. b) after uttering the words, "My papa is a Syndic—he is M. Frankenstein—he would punish you" (*F* 106). Again the finely attuned, original annotation of the Pickering and Chatto edition suggests that "M. Frankenstein's long period of public service may be imagined as encompassing the condemnation of Jean-Jacques Rousseau by the syndics (1762)" (*F* 21 n. a). Thus the significance of the locale of William's murder would seem to support those interpretations of *Frankenstein* that, among other symbolic associations, see the Creature as embodying the downtrodden masses repressed by a supposedly enlightened but in fact reactionary republican patriarchy.[29] Suspicions of how republican ideals may be betrayed, perhaps unwittingly, by self-interest, are evident at the opening of Victor's narrative:

> I am by birth a Genevese; and my family is one of the most distinguished of that republic. My ancestors had been for many years counsellors and syndics; and my father had filled several public situations with honour and reputation. He was respected by all who knew him for his integrity and indefatigable attention to public business. He passed his younger days perpetually occupied by the affairs of his country; and it was not until the decline of life that he thought of marrying, and bestowing on the state sons who might carry his virtues and his name down to posterity. (*F* 21)

While this passage tries to persuade the listener, Robert Walton, that the speaker's father saw parenthood as subsumed within the greater good of public duty, there lurks here an ominously self-regarding dynastic ambition that prefigures Victor's. The idea of "the state" as constituting, in certain influential traditions of republican political thought, the only legitimate framework through which an individual's desires and passions may be articulated, is severely rebuked by Euthanasia in *Valperga*:

> It is strange, that man, born to suffering, and often writhing beneath it, should wantonly inflict pain on his fellows; but however cruel an individual may be, no one is so remorseless as a ruler; for he loses even within himself the idea of his own individuality, and fancies that, in pampering his inclinations, and revenging his injuries, he is supporting the state; the state, a fiction, which sacrifices that which constitutes it, to the support of its mere name. (*V* 176)

The idealism of Victor's father, then, like that of Castruccio, turns out to be sinisterly self-interested and preoccupied with perpetuating power over time in order to make a mark on history. Such critical appraisals of republican history align Euthanasia's role as political conscience in the novel with Dante's works.

Jean de Palacio established long ago that *Valperga* is suffused with "la pensée dantesque,"[30] but, in addition to pervasive literary indebtedness, we need to register that English literary figures like Hunt sought to co-opt Dante, and Italian literature generally, to the liberal cause in English politics and that in Italy "Dante and the other great poets of the past were elevated to the status of patron saints in the national revolutionary cult."[31] From this perspective, Mary Shelley's essay "Giovanni Villani," on the Florentine historian whose *Croniche* (covering the period up to his, and Dante's, lifetimes) provided much of her novel's circumstantial detail, is educative in its sympathetic treatment of partisanship in historical writing. Given the audience of Hunt's *The Liberal,* in which the essay was published in 1823,[32] Mary Shelley is aware of performing "a thankless office" (*M* 132) in seeking to elevate the personalized historical method of "a violent party-man" (*M* 137) to an exemplary status.

Villani's ferocious loyalty to the papacy and his hostility to the house of Swabia are heavily foregrounded in *Croniche* at every turn. Thus Charles of Anjou (1227–85), glossed by Mary Shelley as "a cruel, faithless, but heroic tyrant," is portrayed by Villani "with the partiality of a partizan" (*M* 135), whereas Manfred (1232–66), for Mary Shelley "the noblest king and the most accomplished cavalier that ever existed" (*M* 136), is gratuitously slandered.[33] There is nothing remarkable, perhaps, in Mary Shelley, like some latter-day new historicist, finding Villani interesting because of, not in spite of, the way his interpretation of the past is shaped so saliently by a religious and political outlook to which she is antipathetic. But "Giovanni Villani" also demonstrates the author's recognition that the necessity of being implicated in political life afflicts the corruptible as much as the incorruptible, such as Euthanasia, and that the former are objects as worthy of study or even of sympathy as the latter. As such, it shows her to be compelled by prototypes of Castruccio, that is, to repeat her gloss on those like Charles of Anjou, "heroic tyrants," who seem to anticipate Marx's famous dictum that "Men make their own history, but not of their own free will; not under circumstances they themselves have chosen but under the given and inherited circumstances with which they are directly confronted."[34]

Mary Shelley might also have been receptive to the application of Marx's words to Dante himself as well as to Villani's view of Dante. Since Dante's theodicy, as expounded in *Monarchia,* was not beyond being understood by Italian nationalists in the Romantic period as a political manifesto for a united Italy ruled by a single emperor, Castruccio's unpleasant methods in *Valperga* could be seen to represent an attempt, albeit thwarted, to fulfil a version of Dante's goal. But Dante's implication in contemporary Florentine politics, precipitating the events that arguably motivated the *Divine Comedy,* in no way disqualifies his unique gifts as a poet, as his ideological opponent Villani admits in a passage that Mary Shelley uses to speak for itself at the end of "Giovanni Villani":

> This Dante, on account of his knowledge, was somewhat presumptuous, satirical, and contemptuous. He was uncourteous, as it were, after the manner of philosophers; nor did he well know how to converse with laymen. But on account of his other virtues, his science, and his merit as a citizen, it appeared just to give him perpetual memorial in this our Chronicle, although his great works left in writing bestow on him a true testimony, and an honourable fame on our city. (*M* 139)

Villani's censure here is only half-hearted, and what seems to draw Mary Shelley to celebrate Villani's *Croniche* is its acknowledgment, in spite of his partisan tenor, that Dante's poetry is capable of transcending the specifity of its cultural moment. One thinks immediately of a similar moment of recognition in *A Defence of Poetry,* when in the course of "observing a most heretical caprice in his [Dante's] distribution of rewards and punishments," P. B. Shelley remarks that *Paradise Lost* "contains within itself a philosophical refutation of that system of which, by a strange and natural antithesis, it has been a chief popular support" (*PBSPP,* 498). In the following passage, Euthanasia's reading of Dante mirrors the sense in both "Giovanni Villani" and *A Defence* that he has helped later generations to see that genuine freedom is to be identified with contestation:

> Florence was free, and Dante was a Florentine; none but a freeman could have poured forth the poetry and eloquence to which I listened: what though he were banished from his native city, and had espoused a party that seemed to support tyranny; the essence of freedom is that clash and struggle which awaken the energies of our nature, and that operation of the elements of our mind, which as it were gives us the force and power

that hinder us from degenerating, as they say all things earthly do when
not regenerated by change. (*V* 81–82)

Dante's politics may itself be tainted by his partisan loyalties, but his
poetry releases a vital energy which Euthanasia, like the poet himself in
the *Divine Comedy,* internalizes within what can be seen as the poetic conscience of *Valperga.* As in *A Defence,* poetry in *Valperga* (as symbolized by
Euthanasia) is the means through which freedom can be achieved, and the
example of Dante is shown to guide her, and thus the reader of the novel,
towards a critical vigilance beyond the confining aridity of the present.

Euthanasia: The Art of Dying Well

Euthanasia's understanding of freedom in terms of dynamic change in *Valperga* may be seen to correspond to the idea in *A Defence* that the poet
is uniquely gifted with an ability to understand the necessarily unstable
yet potentially liberating relationship between past, present, and future.
In both cases, death in some sense is the fulfilment, or ultimate poetic recognition, of such freedom, and in both cases the aesthetic force of this
idea appears to be connected to the political goals it serves.[35] Castruccio,
on the other hand, who is interested in pursuing a narrowly delimited
fixity in a foreseeable future when he will have control, is acknowledged
to be defeated by time through the inscription on his tombstone, "BREVI
MEMORES VOS MORITUROS" (*V* 326).[36] Where Castruccio's preserve is
an impoverished sense of amoral expediency — "the principle of decision
was always with him, that which would most conduce to the fulfilment of
his projects, seldom that of good or evil which affected others" (*V* 101) —
Euthanasia, by contrast, inherits from her father a richly discerning awareness of temporal significance: "I learned from him to look upon events as
being of consequence only through the feelings which they excited, and
to believe that content of mind, love, and benevolent feeling ought to be
the elements of our existence; while those accidents of fortune or fame,
which to the majority make up the sum of their existence, were as the dust
of the balance" (*V* 82). The most sustained evocation of Euthanasia's far-
seeing emphasis on "mind, love, and benevolent feeling" may be found in
the Dantesque soliloquy she delivers as Valperga falls under siege:

> "The earth is a wide sea," she cried, "and we its passing bubbles; it is
> a changeful heaven, and we its smallest and swiftest driven vapours;

all changes, all passes—nothing is stable, nothing for one moment the same. But, if it be so, oh my God! if in Eternity all the years that man has numbered on this green earth be but a point, and we but the minutest speck in the great whole, why is the present moment every thing to us? Why do our minds, grasping all, feel as if eternity and immeasurable space were kernelled up in one instantaneous sensation? We look back to times past, and we mass them together, and say in such a year such and such events took place, such wars occupied that year, and during the next there was peace. Yet each year was then divided into weeks, days, minutes, and slow-moving seconds, during which there were human minds to note and distinguish them, as now. We think of a small motion of the dial as of an eternity; yet ages have past, and they are but hours; the present moment will soon be only a memory, an unseen atom in the night of by-gone time. A hundred years hence, and young and old we shall all be gathered to the dust, and I shall no longer feel the coil that is at work in my heart, or any longer struggle within the inextricable bonds of fate. I know this; but yet this moment, this point of time, during which the sun makes but one round amidst the many millions it has made, and the many millions it will make, this moment is all to me. Most willingly, nay, most earnestly, do I pray that I may die this night, and that all contention may cease with the beatings of my heart. Yet, if I live, shall I submit? Is all that we prize but a shadow? Are tyranny, and cruelty, and liberty, and virtue only names? Or, are they not rather the misery or joy, that makes our hearts the abode of storms, or as a smiling, flower-covered isle? Oh! I will no longer question my purpose, or waver where necessity ought to inspire me with courage. One heart is too weak to contain so overwhelming a contention." (*V* 212–13)

Transience and material flux are here seen as the very essence of time in which all activity necessarily takes place, but this extraordinary passage refuses to testify to mutability as overpowering human will. Euthanasia's words acknowledge a multitude of reflections on the temporal, including: the likelihood that ultimately (i.e., in time) human actions may not be able to be understood; that our sense of the past is profoundly selective and necessarily full of distortions, forgetful in that what seem to us to be mere interstices between significant, recognizable events are in fact moments as full as any others; that the present is always by definition on the verge of becoming the past and that it may soon not be remembered at all. Yet Euthanasia's consciousness of the overwhelming nature of memory, of the impossibility of quantifying either time or remembrance, of the endless, energetic losses and makings of time in which all human and natural activity takes place, leads her to a gesture of defiance rather than surrender. Instead of her temporal awareness inducing collapse or willing her towards amnesia, she is galvanized by the knowledge that "this moment is all to" her. This sentence and those that follow identify her utterly with Hamlet, another tragic, heroic figure afflicted by an awareness of the moral and political dangers of ignoring time's presences and pasts.

Euthanasia's emphasis on the primacy of feeling, love, and poetry offers an alternative, nonauthoritarian view of governance, a political ideal that is perhaps closest to an ideal Godwinian anarchism. Of course she is a fiction, and she is acknowledged as such within the distinction between "private chronicles" and "public histories" (*V* 323) discussed above. As such, her destiny is to fall out of the historical picture just as she had been artificially inserted into it. But she is indestructible too, "lost," not killed. In a text that foregrounds disenfranchised and abused women, Euthanasia's gender accentuates her difference, but it does so in terms of a strong alternative to patriarchal republicanism. As in the poems by P. B. Shelley concerning republican history and the memories of Rousseau recalled by the visit to the Plainpalais in *History of a Six Weeks' Tour*, in *Valperga* the good are not losers, though they may appear defeated and their efforts forgotten. Far from being a model of stoical feminine resignation, a displaced version of one (rather unhelpful) biographical model of Mary Shelley herself, Euthanasia, as her name suggests, represents that heroism in destruction towards which both Shelleys seem to be drawn. She is a means through which a negotiation can be made between a recalcitrant present and the ideals of the past and future, and, as such, her function is partly that of a provocative anachronism. The word *tragedy,* which I invoked earlier to situate Euthanasia's role within other English Romantic writing about republican history, is intended to imply not capitulation but, on the contrary, resilience.[37] Her name, which translated literally from the Greek means "good death," suggests not only that her nobility is consummated in death but also that her death is not a moment of closure or finality. Her artistic function is to die well and lastingly. And this sense of a moral truth surviving beyond an actuality that seems to have defeated it is presumably what P. B. Shelley meant in describing *Valperga* as expressing "the . . . romantic truth of history."

8 : Reading the End of the World

The Last Man, History, and the Agency
of Romantic Authorship

SAMANTHA WEBB

Is not the catastrophe [in Valperga*] strangely prophetic[?] But
it seems to me that in what I have hitherto written I have done
nothing but prophecy what has arrived to. Matilda foretells even
many small circumstances most truly — & the whole of it is a
monument of what now is.* — Mary Shelley to Maria Gisborne,
May 3 [May 6], 1823 (*MWSL* 1:336)

It is easy to understand why Mary Shelley would have felt herself to be
something of a prophet in May 1823. *Valperga,* written in 1820, had just
been published, less than a year after her husband's drowning, and Mary
Shelley had a chance to look back over her years with the poet and examine the connections, often profound and unconscious, between her art
and her life. In *Valperga* (1823) and in *Matilda* (1959), she had represented
the drowning deaths of central characters several years before that of her
husband in July 1822. In a letter, Mary Shelley even describes her frantic journey to Pisa for news of P. B. Shelley in terms of Mathilda's futile
attempts to prevent her father's suicide in the sea. Small wonder, then,
that critics have moved to biography to explain some of the most interesting aspects of her fourth novel, *The Last Man* (1826). The novel is surely
a "monument" to a past time, and it is organized around the figure of
a prophetess, the Sibyl of Cumaea. The novel's loving portraits of P. B.
Shelley and Lord Byron, its relentless apocalyptic theme, the often-quoted
journal entry in which Mary Shelley explicitly identifies with her lonely
protagonist,[1] and the opening "Author's Introduction" that locates the
story within the Shelleys' own 1818 visit to Naples all point to its deeply
autobiographical roots. Such biographical readings are confirmed in her

journal, where Mary Shelley so frequently and so sadly apostrophizes the dead P. B. Shelley. "I write—and thou seest not what I write" (*MWSJ* 441) seems to be a pervasive theme for the period during which she was composing this novel.

As her first major work after P. B. Shelley's death, *The Last Man* has frequently been positioned as the transitional work in her career. Some critics argue that in it, Mary Shelley was able to put to rest her major ideological conflicts with the politics of her husband, as well as the oppressive guilt his memory placed on her.[2] In her later works, it is argued, Mary Shelley retreats into a (questionably termed) "Victorianism," represented both in an increasingly conservative social vision and in the adoption of an omniscient narrative voice. But these readings tend to downplay the complexities of Mary Shelley's post-*Frankenstein* work. Furthermore, casting Mary Shelley as the quintessential child of Romanticism who rather disappointingly became a Victorian implicitly places her later work outside the Romantic canon and amounts to a political indictment whose yardstick is the men in her life, William Godwin and P. B. Shelley. Mary Shelley is certainly critical of the radical politics we have come to associate with a particular brand of Romanticism; she is, further, working out new ways of achieving self-identity as an author in the wake of the personal loss of her primary audience. However, in *The Last Man* she is also grappling with one of the central dilemmas of authorship in the Romantic period: What is the authority of the author and of writing in a culture of mass, anonymous readership?

The Last Man explores this issue by presenting an author without readers, a lost Sibylline prophecy, and an editor who seems curiously ambivalent about the narrative of future devastation she reconstructs.[3] What I want to do is situate *The Last Man* within the larger novelistic practice of the frame narrative in order to position Mary Shelley's later work within, rather than against, the varied discourses of Romanticism and to expand beyond biography the critical frame of reference for this very rich novel. In its frame structure, *The Last Man* foregrounds the dynamic exchange that occurs between writers and readers, questions the rhetoric that claims an ultimate cultural authority for authors, and develops new models for authorship, for composition, and for authority that go beyond notions of power.

The frame is an integral part of the novel and contributes significantly to the range of its themes. There is an implicit parallel between the plague and the scattered Sibylline text, in that both demand interpretation and a mediating figure to facilitate that interpretation. Both the plague and the fragmented text that writes of it are alien, their authorship unaccountable. They beg to be assimilated into an epistemology, to be made intelligible, to be "framed"; and it is that process of interpretation that Mary Shelley's novel explores.

Lionel Verney is the only survivor of a plague that has wiped out the earth's population in the late twenty-first century. He writes his autobiography and leaves the manuscript in Rome as a "monument" to human history. The story tells of England's peaceful transition to a republic in the year 2073 and Lionel's early, transformative friendship with Adrian, the Earl of Windsor and would-be heir to the throne. Through his association with Adrian, Lionel and his sister, Perdita, establish a domestic circle close to the center of power in England, he through his marriage to Adrian's sister and she by marrying the Byronic Lord Raymond, who eventually becomes Lord Protector. Romantic trials soon put their domestic felicity at risk as Raymond begins an affair with the Greek princess Evadne and Perdita, always extreme in her affections, cannot forgive him. In shame, Raymond gives up the Protectorship and rushes off to fight in Constantinople, where he is killed. Perdita drowns herself in guilt and despair. The collapse of the domestic world prefigures the collapse of the entire human world, and the rest of the novel is taken up with describing the plague, its relentless movement towards England, and the social consequences of its advance: international trade stops, class distinctions collapse, social organization breaks down, and colonized peoples "invade" England. Adrian eventually becomes Lord Protector, but it is only to lead the few surviving English to Europe, ultimately to die. Adrian himself, along with his niece, is eventually drowned in a storm at sea, and Lionel is left alone in the world to write his autobiography for no one to read. The frame of the novel, the "Author's Introduction," marks a temporal displacement: Lionel's story has somehow been recuperated into antiquity by the Sibyl of Cumaea and is later found as "piles of leaves, fragments of bark, and a white filmy substance" (*LM* 1:7) by an editor in the year 1818. The editor, with a "companion" who has since died, reconstructs and publishes from the Sibyl's leaves the story told by Lionel Verney.

Thus, the novel deploys the "found manuscript" device, a common, frequently playful narrative strategy, particularly in the eighteenth century. It participates in the long tradition of the epistolary and the fragment and focuses on an editor-figure, invested with the authority to make pronouncements about the text without taking any authorial responsibility for it. Examples of editorial frame narratives include Jonathan Swift's *Tale of a Tub* (1704), Henry McKenzie's *The Man of Feeling* (1765), and Horace Walpole's *The Castle of Otranto* (1765). In all these cases and many others, the framing editor highlights a suspicion of the grounds of reception, acting as a guide — even if negatively — for "right" reading. The presence of an editor, however transparently fictional and ironic, implies that the internal text and the voice that speaks it are in need of a mediator, an authoritative presence who will preserve the integrity of either the text or the reader. We see this latter type of frame in *Pamela* (1740–41), when the "editor" steps in and reveals the morals that young people should draw from the story. The former type of editor appears in works like McPherson's Ossian poems and Walter Scott's ballad collections, in which the editor guarantees the authenticity of the manuscript text.[4]

During the Romantic period, the found manuscript device becomes more symbolically loaded, and it does so for fairly specific reasons. As Jon Klancher observes, the Romantics are the first group to become "radically uncertain of their readers,"[5] and the editorial frame absorbs and textualizes this uncertainty by attempting to predict, to regulate, or to undermine the work's own reception. In the early nineteenth century, the expansion of the literary marketplace, the professionalization of authorship, the practice of authorial anonymity, and the explosion of periodical publishing all contributed to the dispersal of authority in the public sphere. The literary authority accorded to, and contested in, periodicals like the *Edinburgh,* the *Quarterly,* and *Blackwood's* contributes to an emerging iconography of the critic/editor, satirized most pointedly in James Hogg's *Confessions of a Justified Sinner* (1824). The framing editor frequently represents a specific literary institution or is a professional literary man — for example, an antiquarian, a scholar, or a journalist–who is empowered through that institution to make pronouncements about the text. This type of appropriation of the manuscript erects a mediating, corrective discourse that usurps the narrative authority of the internal narrator and locates that authority within an institutional discourse. As he or she reads and writes over the text, the editor "reframes" it — makes it "intelligible" — according to the terms of a discourse outside the purview of the original narrator.

The most elaborate use of this type of frame device was made by Walter Scott, who exploited it with great dexterity throughout his long and prolific career.[6] In his historical novels, multiple frame narrators overwrite each other as a way to guarantee their own authority and to set the terms of the text's reception. As the frame narrators overwrite, criticize, and quibble with one another's texts, the question arises as to who has the authority to become the "filter" through which the story can be told. For example, *Old Mortality* (1816), part of the first installment of the four-part *Tales of My Landlord* series, is triply framed: the internal narrator is the religious fanatic, Old Mortality, who tells his version of the bloody conflict over the Scottish Covenant; Peter Pattieson, the secondary narrator, meets Old Mortality, verifies and rewrites the story in an authoritative version that can be taken as historically accurate; and Jedediah Cleishbotham, Peter's executor, appropriates the late Pattieson's manuscripts and reminds readers of his commercial interests in the publication.

These framing figures highlight a competition for narrative authority by developing different, frequently opposing narrative points. Old Mortality is the last survivor of a violent conflict and has made it his life's work to reinscribe the epitaphs on the gravestones of Covenant "martyrs," an act that seeks to set in stone a particular version of history. His purpose for doing so is "to warn future generations to defend their religion even unto blood."[7] He believes Peter will faithfully inscribe the same purpose when he writes the story down. In contrast, Peter, with a preservationist antiquarian zeal, gathers the tale in order to write an "authoritative" national history, not simply to repeat local lore as it is told to him by a presumably biased narrator. Since his goal is to move beyond the antagonisms of history, he refuses to be bound by Old Mortality's version of history. Peter therefore distances himself from the title character, supplementing that version with other views in order to construct a history considered "accurate," "unbiased," and "authoritative": "My readers will of course understand, that in embodying into one compressed narrative many of the anecdotes which I had the advantage of deriving from Old Mortality, I have been far from adopting either his style, his opinions, or even his facts, so far as they appear to have been distorted by party prejudice. I have endeavoured to correct or verify them from the most authentic sources of tradition" (65). As a historian, Peter Pattieson feels himself in no way bound by the terms of the original storyteller. In fact, to accept them would be to reinscribe all the violence, prejudice, and bloodshed of that period into the present.

But Peter's manuscripts themselves are not immune from modification. Despite Peter's conscientious disclosure of supplementary sources and his declared aims of writing an "authoritative" version of Old Mortality's story, Jedediah Cleishbotham, the external narrator, criticizes him for his lack of fidelity to the original source. He dismantles the historical authority Peter claims over the tale and claims his own authority on commercial grounds. He accuses Peter of inventing some incidents "for the mere grace of his plots" (56) and claims the primary place himself as surrogate-author simply because he is the agent of the story's publication. In this way, the outer frame of the novel recasts Peter's history as a work of fiction and shifts the grounds of its authority from the discipline of history to the practice of novel-writing, which is where Peter's narrative fails. Furthermore, Jedediah's preface relocates the site of the book's circulation from a scholarly field to the commercial literary marketplace.

For Scott, then, the multiple narrative frames function to organize the inner story, endlessly reinterpreting and recirculating it. They also function to point out the power of the reader to create the terms of the story, to accord or withhold narrative authority from the author, and to mark the outer limits of any interpretive framework. The exchange that occurs between an author and a reader has been theorized by Ross Chambers, who, in *Story and Situation,* defines narrative as a "transactional phenomenon" and shows the central role of the reader in generating meaning and according authority to the narrator: "Transactional in that it mediates *exchanges* that produce historical change, [narrative] is transactional, too, in that this functioning is itself dependent on an initial *contract,* an understanding between the participants in the exchange as to the purposes served by the narrative function, its 'point.'"[8] In *The Last Man,* the odd temporal displacement of readers into the past troubles the question of authorial authority from the outset. Lionel's authorship is in crisis precisely because he has no readers to participate in his narrative "transaction" or to accord him authority; his "point" fails him when his isolated situation recalls itself. Thus, the rhetoric that undergoes a crisis in *The Last Man* is one that equates becoming an author with social agency and the need to affect a community of readers.

For the young Lionel, an early belief in the agency of books and education undergirds his own authorial practice. Authorship becomes a substitute for "an active career," offering no less a possibility for social agency than would a place in politics. Books are identified with culture and "civilization," and they come to separate Lionel's early savage "wilderness" from the domestic "paradise" (*LM* 1:122) of Windsor Castle, or, rather, books are used as the means of exchanging the one state for the other. He describes his attitude towards his own authorship: "I found another and a valuable link to enchain me to my fellow-creatures; my point of sight was extended, and the inclinations and capacities of all human beings became deeply interesting to me. Kings have been called the fathers of their people. Suddenly I became as it were the father of all mankind. Posterity became my heirs. My thoughts were gems to enrich the treasure house of man's intellectual possessions; each sentiment was a precious gift I bestowed on them" (*LM* 1:122).

Certainly, there is a touch of irony in these youthful extravagant claims for authorial power. However, Lionel expresses here the view of authorship as a powerful socializing force. He views his position as an author as offering no less a possibility for social agency than do the politically active roles assumed by Lord Raymond, Ryland, and Adrian, each of whom represents different models of political power. Authorship is figured through institutions that guarantee individual and social continuity — paternity and royalty. But Lionel deliberately positions his authorial persona beyond nationality ("I became the father of all mankind"), beyond the particularities of culture and history. This is a powerful position of authority that certainly recalls P. B. Shelley's claims for poets in the *Defence of Poetry* (1821).

This view of the cultural authority of authors becomes one of many models of power posited in the novel. Lionel's first meeting with Adrian gains its transformative power because of Adrian's knowledge of and appeal to a literary tradition, which accords him not only individual authority but also cultural and political authority. Lionel exclaims, "This . . . is power! Not to be strong of limb, hard of heart, ferocious and daring; but kind, compassionate and soft" (*LM* 1:26). Literary knowledge, embodied by Adrian, thus becomes precisely an empowering, transformative means of exchange. Lionel's transformation from "an unlettered savage" (*LM* 1:27) is couched in the powerful language of conversion:

> We sat in [Adrian's] library, and he spoke of the old Greek sages, and of the power which they had acquired over the minds of men, through the force of love and wisdom only . . . . As he spoke, I felt subject to him; and all my boasted pride and strength were subdued by the honeyed accents of this blue-eyed boy. The trim and paled demesne of civilization, which I had before regarded from my wild jungle as inaccessible, had

its wicket opened by him; I stepped within, and felt, as I entered, that I trod my native soil. (*LM* 1:24)

Adrian enters Lionel's life as the bearer of an intellectual tradition, indeed as a gatekeeper of (Western) civilization; he is, furthermore, literally an "unacknowledged legislator," since his father, the King, had abdicated the throne in 2073 when England became a republic. This passage emphasizes Adrian's knowledge as an irresistible rhetoric, which ultimately initiates Lionel into that "sacred boundary which divides the intellectual and moral nature of man from that which characterizes animals" (*LM* 1:26). Lionel's "soul threw off the burthen of past sin to commence a new career in innocence and love" (*LM* 1:26). He is in a position very much like that of Victor Frankenstein's Creature, finding himself the construction of another being and fundamentally re-created by the encounter. But rather than being alienated and excluded from the social realm in that re-creation, Lionel actually becomes "human" (*LM* 1:26) under Adrian's tutelage. The literary tradition, then, acts as a force for social integration and community. Lionel's use of such extravagant language is not merely an overblown rhetorical flourish, nor can it be accounted for as Mary Shelley's retrospective deification of her dead husband, who was the model for the Adrian character.[9] Through the language of conversion, Mary Shelley indicates the powerful agency of books and "literary" education and the transformative potential of literary and cultural knowledge.

No sooner is this figurative power established, however, than it is thrown into question. Lionel's sanguine view of the near-limitless power of books is belied by their ineffectiveness at "curing" Perdita of her grief over Raymond's betrayal. Noting that she had remained, even after her marriage to Raymond, "to a great degree uneducated" (*LM* 1:121), Lionel explicitly uses literary knowledge as a means of expanding her vision and taking her out of her own sufferings. "My schooling first impelled her towards books; and, if music had been the food of sorrow, the productions of the wise became its medicine" (*LM* 1:123). Lionel's goal in educating his sister is to reintegrate her into the domestic circle at Windsor, to bring her "to a saner view of her own situation" (*LM* 1:121). However, for Perdita, books only allow a partial consolation, and she refuses the domestic integration offered by Lionel. So fiercely does she reject such integration that Lionel and Adrian resort to drugging her — literally medicating her — in order to bring her away from Constantinople. Perdita's refusal to receive literary education on the terms Lionel sets out, her rejection of his "point," marks the limits of that educational process and denies him the authority he needs to succeed in his project. In this way, Mary Shelley calls into question any totalizing process or epistemology that offers a "panacea" for individual or social ills, be it education, "civilization," domesticity, or love.

The second half of the novel focuses more closely on the plague and the powerful control it exerts on the world. Many critics have read this plague as Mary Shelley's ultimate critique of the brand of revolutionary Romanticism espoused by P. B. Shelley and have sought to identify it with various revolutionary ideals: the French Revolution,[10] the repressed female,[11] and democracy or egalitarianism.[12] However, such identifications tend to conflate the *effects* of the plague — the return to England of repressed cultures, the leveling of class structures, the erection of false prophets, anarchy — with its *causes,* which remain mysterious and unexplained in the novel. The plague is ambiguous; it is and is not all of these things. More than being a symbol, it is a fulcrum on which to scrutinize the act of interpretation itself, the ways in which humanity makes sense of an Other and the consequences of those interpretations. It is important that at no point does Lionel use his story as a warning to an anticipated "post-pestilential" society, an audience he at times projects and invokes. In fact, Lionel resists any attempt to "make sense" of the plague or to give it a "point." He describes, but does not privilege, the ways in which the population grapples with the plague's effects, attempting to construct epistemologies that will contain or account for them: "Philosophers opposed their principles, as barriers to the inundation of profligacy and despair, and the only ramparts to protect the invaded territory of human life; the religious, hoping now for their reward, clung fast to their creeds, as the rafts and planks which over the tempest-vexed sea of suffering, would bear them in safety to the harbor of the Unknown Continent" (*LM* 2:213).

The epistemological barriers are essentially the ways in which the intellectual tradition, so crucial for Lionel's sense of himself, attempts to interpret the plague. But the novel settles on none of these as the explanation for the plague's sway over the earth. While the plague elicits agonized questionings of Promethean proportions, Lionel deliberately avoids ascribing any kind of intentionality to it. Invoking the doctrine of Necessity, he says: "If my human mind cannot acknowledge that all that is, is right; yet since what is, must be, I will sit amidst the ruins and smile. Truly we were not born to enjoy, but to submit, and to hope" (*LM* 3:310). Not only is Lionel's neutral perspective "anti-political and anti-ideological," as Anne Mellor and Jane Blumberg suggest,[13] but it is also a statement against intentionality, or at least against attributing intentionality to any supernatural force. To resist according an otherworldly agency or intentionality to the devastating plague is, to some extent, to resist its power to circumscribe human life. Lionel's interest is not to determine *what* the plague "means"—a divine judgement of some sort or the end of a foretold prophecy—but to create an epistemology that will withstand its organizing force.

After Clara and Adrian are drowned at sea, Lionel attempts to use writing as a signal to other survivors, essentially to write himself into a community, literally to "enchain" himself to others. He scrawls on the walls of towns between Ravenna and Rome, " 'Friend, come! I wait for thee!' " (*LM* 3:353). But the fact that Lionel continues to narrate his story until his departure from Rome—and indeed that he chooses to go on living— suggests that he has found a mode of being in the world beyond community as well as a way of writing beyond audience. "I had used," he says about halfway through the story, "this history as an opiate; while it described my beloved friends, fresh with life and glowing with hope, active assistants on the scene, I was soothed; there will be a more melancholy pleasure in painting the end of all" (*LM* 2:209). Clearly, composition can perform a function independent of readers; it has value independent of the "transaction" that takes place between an author and a reader. In this context of presumed lastness, writing thus becomes an anterior activity, a memorialization of the past, not an exchange with or a "gift" to posterity. The model that Lionel discovers is writing as consolation and the written manuscript as a memorial or monument.

Critics have pointed out that Lionel's dedication to the dead ironically calls up William Godwin's *Essay on Sepulchres* (1810), in which he proposes the establishment of memorials to the "Illustrious Dead in all ages." [14] These memorials would take the form of simple, white, wooden crosses, placed at the burial spots of influential people. Arguing that it is because death claims the world's great minds that civilization remains "in its infancy" (8), Godwin illustrates how such memorials would preserve to public memory all the worth of the deceased and thus help to advance the general good by inculcating a kind of reverence for the past. He mourns the fact that "we cut ourselves off from the inheritance of our ancestors; we seem to conspire from time to time to cancel old scores, and begin the affairs of the human species afresh" (14). The memorials would be a testament to the progress that had taken place since their subjects' deaths, and they would remind viewers of the subjects' role in that progress. What Godwin was seeking through such a project is a sense of generational and cultural continuity that would preempt attempts at radical breaks with the past. He assumes that progress is impossible without memory and that memory is most usefully accessed through the immediacy of the public memorial, placed at the very burial spot. The memorials, in a very real sense, serve as links in the chain of posterity.

It is precisely this disconnection from history that Lionel's memorializing narrative attempts to prevent. Imagining a "post-pestilential" race who will begin human history anew, Lionel rationalizes his urge to write through the now-obsolete paradigm of "enchainment.": "Yet, will this world not be re-peopled, and the children of a saved pair of lovers, in some to me unknown and unattainable seclusion, wandering to these prodigious relics of the ante-pestilential race, seek to learn how beings so wondrous in their achievements, with imaginations infinite, and powers godlike, had departed from their home to an unknown country?" (*LM* 3: 362). While he lacks the immediate authorial authority that comes only from an exchange with readers, he gains the historical authority of the witness. His first impulse is to see himself as the sole remaining link to posterity. As such, he becomes the sole source of past, the one who speaks history for an imagined, but by no means guaranteed, future generation.

Inherently, this is a powerful position of authority and, as we saw with Walter Scott, it carries with it many ideological pitfalls. Just as Old Mortality, the last remaining witness in the Covenanters' rebellion, charges himself with reinscribing the epitaphs of the Covenant "martyrs" on their tombstones, Lionel Verney becomes the last witness and recorder of the epidemic, indeed of the last historical event. But, unlike the Scottish "fanatic," Lionel rejects any kind of ideological position to frame either the epidemic or his survival of it. Old Mortality's moral was for "future generations to defend their religion even unto blood," a moral that attempts to forestall other interpretations of the epitaphs, to reinscribe a bloody conflict into the present. By comparison, Lionel's goals are much more modest, his memorial being merely to "the *existence* of Verney" (emphasis mine) and his manuscript simply "a record of these things."

This offers a key, I think, to Mary Shelley's political commitments and to the peculiar position she has traditionally occupied within Romanticism. As Jane Blumberg shows in her study of Mary Shelley's early novels, Mary Shelley was wary of any revolutionary cause that called for violence.[15] Consequently, it is easy to accuse her of political quietism, especially if her reservations are compared with the hopefulness of her husband. However, her resistance to violence and to totalizing epistemologies suggests no less a "Romantic" worldview than that assumed for her contemporaries. Lionel's writing has a public function, and, although his "reading public" is inaccessible, he is mindful of the possible uses which a "misreading" (or an "over-reading") of the plague by some future finder of his manuscript may have. Because of the possibility of misinterpretation, inherent in any act of reading, in his own narrative he avoids investing the plague with any kind of intentionality that may exert a "false" epistemological control over some future civilization.

This position is illustrated in the final parts of the novel, when the remaining English exiles, on their way to Switzerland, encounter the denizens of the "impostor-prophet." This man is the only political figure in the novel to gain Lionel's unambiguous censure, and presumably Mary Shelley's as well. The impostor-prophet demands absolute allegiance on the grounds that only he can save his followers, and only his followers will be saved. Lionel describes him:

> instigated by ambition, he desired to rule over these last stragglers from the fold of death; his projects went so far as to cause him to calculate that, if, from these crushed remains, a few survived, so that a new race should spring up, he, by holding tight the reins of belief, might be remembered by the post-pestilential race as a patriarch, a prophet, nay a deity; such as of old among the post-diluvians were Jupiter the conqueror, Serapis the lawgiver, and Vishnou the preserver. (*LM* 3:301)

The impostor-prophet desires the power to dictate human belief, to be himself the epistemological center of the post-pestilential world. He claims, in other words, the ultimate cultural authority, the power to "authorize" culture. On one hand, the impostor-prophet can be read as the ironic undercutting of Lionel's own early associations of authorship with royalty and paternity. Just as the collapse of real culture exposes the rhetoric of culture, the impostor-prophet exposes the social consequences of any extravagant claims for cultural authority: an "alliance of fraud" (*LM* 3: 301) or a kind of intellectual enslavement. On the other hand, Lionel's strong indictment of this man offers a clue as to his own authorial prac-tice and assumptions. Because of the dangers involved in leaving a writ-ten "record of these things," Lionel avoids equating his authorship of his manuscript with a more figurative authorship of a "post-pestilential race." He refuses the authoritative and authorial positions that are a consequence of his lastness.

Part of Mary Shelley's critique in *The Last Man,* then, is of those who would organize the social realm around the sign of their own author-ship—those, in other words, who would become the ultimate agents of culture, the "unacknowledged legislators of the world." The contrast be-tween Adrian and the impostor-prophet represents the use and misuse of power and the potential consequences of claiming "legislatorship" of the world. While Adrian clearly represents the positive side of power ("kind, compassionate and soft" [*LM* 1:26]), the imposter-prophet represents its dangerous underside, which involves manipulation and absolute power.

With his departure from Rome, Lionel Verney writes himself out of human history, only to be reinscribed into it by the voice of the Cumaean Sibyl and recuperated *as* history by the 1818 editor. It is significant that his writing is recuperated into a context that he could not have imagined or projected. This foregrounds his own lack of authorial control over how his text is received. In contrast to Walter Scott's Peter Pattieson, who is decidedly unconcerned that he is altering the narrative of Old Mortality, Mary Shelley's editor wonders whether she has unduly altered the story and speculates that in doing so she may have diminished the text. What is striking about Shelley's editorial frame is that the editor's reaction to the story is so muted. Rather than showing the editor is disturbed or fright-ened by the apocalyptic narrative, as one would expect, her framing nar-rative seems to indicate she is engaged in a solipsistic exercise in personal nostalgia: "My labours have cheered long hours of solitude, and taken me out of a world, which has averted its once benignant face from me, to one glowing with imagination and power" (*LM* 1:8). Her focus of identifica-tion with the text is ultimately private and personal. The editor offers an apology for her feelings, explaining them as a kind of escapist consolation:

Will my readers ask how I could find solace from the narration of misery and woeful change? . . . Such is human nature, that the excitement of mind was dear to me, and that the imagination, painter of tempest and earthquake, or, worse, the stormy and ruin-fraught passions of man, softened my real sorrows and endless regrets, by clothing these fictitious ones in that ideality, which take the mortal sting from pain. (*LM* 1:8)

She views Lionel's story as fictional. The editor's reaction parallels Lionel's attitude towards his own writing in that both use narrative as consolation rather than as exchange. The story allows each of them to remember their dead companions, substituting a textual presence for a bodily one and substituting fictional writing for real life. Rather than framing the Sibylline text as a warning and as a prophesy, the editor frames it through its gathering and assimilates it to a personalized past rather than to a terrifying generalized future. Like Scott's framing figures, Mary Shelley's reject the terms of the original authors: it is a resistance to using this text *as* prophesy, a refusal to frame the text as powerful, divinely inspired, and authoritative. No longer the living voice of the Cumaean Sibyl, the text in its recuperated nineteenth-century context is simply "piles of leaves, fragments of bark" (*LM* 1:7) — artifacts found in a cave. This refusal to interpret or to frame serves as a thematic counterpoint to Lionel's reluctance to attribute any kind of intentionality to the plague itself.

The reason for this blunting of interpretive authority can be located in the historical gap that exists between the Sibyl and the 1818 editor. The Sibyl represents a specific type of cultural authority that links authorship to the public, political realm. (And indeed, this would have been the only authority publicly accorded to women in antiquity.) In a literary context, Mary Shelley's immediate source for the Cumaean Sibyl figure is Book 6 of Virgil's *Aeneid,* in which the Cumaean Sibyl guides Aeneas through the underworld. Mary Shelley would, moreover, have been aware of other famous Sibyls, particularly Cassandra, the Trojan prophetess cursed by Apollo to have her prophesies forever disbelieved.[16] The Roman Senate turned to Sibylline prophesies in times of crisis and to make important decisions, and thus the Sibyl herself carried great political authority.[17] For the nineteenth-century English reading public, however, the Sibyl does not carry the prophetic authority she once did. Therefore the editor, as the figure who grounds the frame of reference for this novel in the contemporary world, receives the Sibylline text as an artifact, a historical curiosity from a bygone era, which achieves its value as a rare object, not as a prophetic warning. Like the antiquarian Peter Pattieson, who reworks Old Mortality's biased history into an "authoritative" one, the editor here refuses to appropriate the scattered Sibyl's leaves for the prophetic purpose they would have carried in ancient Rome—as a kind of revelatory sacred document that inscribes the end of the world by merely describing it.

By having Lionel's apocalyptic narrative recuperated as Sibylline leaves in the year 1818, Mary Shelley historicizes both authorship and readership. These distinct historical contexts point to the different ways in which texts and authors function as agents of change in a culture's public sphere. In Lionel's postapocalyptic, posthuman world, writing (and narrative and even language) is obsolete for all but the most self-reflexive purposes. In antiquity, by contrast, the divinely inspired written word of the Sibyl was an indispensable part of the nation's public life, her oracles having a direct influence on her culture. In nineteenth-century England, of course, the Sibyl's authority no longer holds; her religious authority has been supplanted by Christianity, her political context in the Roman Empire has yielded to the British Empire, and her medium of communication has been replaced by print technology. The nineteenth-century editor foregrounds these latter contexts, which mark the profession of authorship in her time. In contrast to the role of authors in the ancient world, the authority of the author in the culture of mass, anonymous readership is, to a great extent, blunted.

While Mary Shelley certainly believes in the agency of authorship and in the power of writing to change the world, she also believes in the equal agency of readership and is suspicious of the ways texts can be made to function in society. Her critique is certainly located in contemporary debates about the social function of writing; it also proceeds from a sense of alienation from her own audience, surely a uniquely contemporary dilemma for Romantic period authors. In many ways, Mary Shelley's frame in The Last Man completes the work of the eighteenth-century frame narrative. It does so by reaching outside its own frame to explain the physical book in our hands. However, rather than attempting to regulate the reader's reception of the text, Mary Shelley suggests that an author's attempt to fix meaning will always escape the frame, which is ultimately bounded by the reader.

9 : *Kindertotenlieder*

Mary Shelley and the Art of Losing

CONSTANCE WALKER

In December of 1820, a package arrived for the Shelleys in Pisa from Leigh Hunt; in it, he enclosed several recent copies of the *Indicator,* including the issue from the previous April featuring his essay "Deaths of Little Children." Hunt's essay, which subsequently would be widely reprinted and anthologized, suggested that pleasant memories of one's children will eventually overtake the painful memories of their deaths; moreover, parents "who have lost an infant are never, as it were, without an infant child. . . . This one alone is rendered an immortal child. Death has arrested it with his kindly harshness, and blessed it into an eternal image of youth and innocence." [1] Mary Shelley, an unwilling authority on the subject after losing her first three children, responded to Hunt with some asperity:

> That one upon the death of young children was a piece of as fine writing
> & of as exquisite feeling as I ever read—To us you know it must have
> been particularly affecting—Yet there is one thing well apparent—You,
> my dear Hunt, never lost a child or the ideal immortality wd not suffice
> to your immagination [sic] as it naturally does thinking only of those
> whom you loved more from the overflowing of affection, than from their
> being the hope, the rest, the purpose, the support, and the recompense
> of life. (*MWSL* 1:170–71)

When Mary Shelley herself wrote of death in her journals, letters, and fiction, she offered a more harrowing, honest, and profound version of grief as real and as essentially inconsolable than did Hunt or indeed most of her contemporaries. The first of my aims in this chapter is to explore some of those differences, surely accountable in part to the succession of losses in her tragic life. While clearly her novels address large social, political, and philosophical concerns, I argue that they are also fantasies that spoke of and to her very real psychic needs in the face of a series of devastating losses. On a basic structural level, *Frankenstein, Matilda,* and *The Last Man* all tell the same story of abandonment and mourning: like Mary Shelley herself, the eponymous characters progressively lose almost everyone dear to them to violent death or fatal illness and end up utterly alone, anticipating only their own deaths as a release from misery. They are tales that return obsessively to loss and hauntingly reproduce the circumstances of her own children's deaths. In depicting the death of William in *Frankenstein* and that of Evelyn in *The Last Man,* for instance, she clearly draws upon the deaths of her premature daughter, in 1815, of Clara Everina, in 1818, and of William, in 1819, to provide the terrible details of what it is like to find one's child dead or to watch helplessly at the bedside of a dying child.[2] My second aim, then, is to explore why she returned to such painful material at all and to examine the manifold uses she makes of it in *The Last Man,* a novel that is better understood in the context of maternal bereavement and mourning.

Virtually every commentator, beginning with Mary Shelley herself, has drawn parallels between *The Last Man* and the author's own personal circumstances. Mary Poovey, Anne Mellor, and Fiona Stafford all discuss the novel as a projection of grief, usefully focusing upon the ways in which the novel mirrors and facilitates Mary Shelley's mourning, primarily for P. B. Shelley.[3] More recently, Mary Jacobus describes *The Last Man* as "suffused with maternal mourning as well as survivor guilt." But whereas Jacobus's reading invokes Kristevan melancholia, mine focuses upon Kleinian mourning, specifically upon Melanie Klein's theory of the recapitulation of the infantile depressive position in mourning and in creativity.[4] For in psychoanalytic terms, *The Last Man* may be seen as an expression of destructive fantasies deeply and specifically rooted in Mary Shelley's traumatic experiences of maternal loss from its epigraph onwards: "Let no man seek/Henceforth to be foretold what shall befall/Him or his children."

Before turning to Klein, however, I would like to consider briefly some modern perspectives on maternal bereavement that may offer some insight into the terrible depression that Mary Shelley suffered in the summer of 1819 and the significance of the series of maternal losses she suffered from 1816 through her near-fatal miscarriage in 1822. Those around her at the time perceived her grief as excessive, none more so than her father, as evidenced in his almost unbelievably obtuse letter of September 9, 1819, reproaching her: "You have all the goods of fortune, all the means of being useful to others. . . . [But] all is nothing, because a child of three years old is dead."[5] From a sociological standpoint, Clare Gittings argues that the improvement of life expectancy of infants towards the end of the eighteenth century "led to much closer familial ties being sundered when a child died. If the child was past infancy . . . the suffering which parents experienced could be devastating."[6] And modern studies in bereavement similarly identify the loss of a child as "the most distressing and long-lasting of all griefs."[7] As Irving Leon states, "probably the most painful and overwhelming grief — usually more debilitating than even the death of a spouse — is the death of one's child. . . . The depth and complexity of the [parent-child] relationship makes this object loss intolerable. In fact, the guilt, depression and rage are usually . . . crushing, unbearable, and ultimately traumatizing." Intrapsychically, Leon notes, such losses entail not simply the loss of one's child but also of one's identity, one's emotional sustenance, one's connection to the future, and one's sense of invulnerability: as he puts it, "a sense of power, of having defeated death, is extinguished by the occurrence of death when it is least expected."[8]

Moreover, cross-cultural studies indicate gender differences in mourning, finding that women generally mourn the deaths of their children longer and more intensely than do men.[9] Acute, chronic grief and depression have been associated with those who have previously experienced important losses, in particular the "early loss of the mother, especially if accompanied by disruption and lack of care"[10] as well as with those who have experienced "several losses within a short space in time,"[11] all factors in Mary Shelley's particularly complicated and intense grief for her children. And intense it was, as we know from her own accounts as well as those of her companions: as she wrote to Thomas Jefferson Hogg in February 1823, "the pangs I endured when those events happened were so terrible, that even now, inured as I am to mental pain — I look back with affright to those periods of agony" (*MWSL* 1:317).

Mary Shelley was by no means the only woman to lose her children or to write about her loss. There are numerous nineteenth-century elegies written by mothers for their children; others were written for children of their acquaintances or were perhaps simply inspired by the pathos of the subject, such as John Clare's "Impromptu Suggested While Viewing an Infant Grave" or Louisa Shore's "A Requiem. On reading some verses about a poor woman seen carrying the coffin of her infant in her arms to the burial."[12] Felicia Hemans's "Dirge of a Child," Lady Stuart-Wortley's "An Infant's Funeral," Amelia Opie's "On the Death of a Child," Caroline Bowles Southey's "To a Dying Infant," and Charlotte Elliott's "From a Mother to her Departed Babe" are but a few examples of such *Kindertotenlieder,* elegies that differ from Mary Shelley's representations of maternal loss in several important ways. Their elegiac form is in and of itself significant, given the elegy's typical "lyric reversal from grief and despair to joy and assurance":[13] the great majority of these poems understandably seek meaning and consolation in the face of deaths that seem particularly wrong and difficult to bear.

The very severity of that pain encourages denials both of the deaths themselves and of the need to mourn them. For instance, the title of Elliott's "From a Mother to her Departed Babe" is roundly denied by the poem's chorus of "Thou art not gone!; We cannot part."[14] Children who have died are commonly portrayed as not dead but merely resting, sleeping, veiled from sight. And when children are actually acknowledged as being gone, they are gone to a brighter, happier home. Moreover, it is only a temporary and not an eternal separation: as Caroline Bowles Southey writes in "To a Dying Infant,"

> And when the hour arrives,
> From flesh that sets me free,
> Thy spirit may await
> The first at heaven's gate
> To meet and welcome me.
> (lines 106–10)[15]

These poems thus seek to deny or at least to mitigate eternal separation by imagining eternal union or reunion. In the early nineteenth century, women were customarily encouraged not to attend burials but only funeral services, and their poems too focus less on the materiality of the loss than on a deathless spiritual bond.

Other such elegies for children seek to deny not so much the deaths themselves as the need for grief and mourning. The imagery of the poems is remarkably uniform: children are routinely described not as human beings but as idealized flowers, dewdrops, evanescent phenomena of the natural world. "A bud their lifetime and a flower their close" John Clare says of infants ("Graves of Infants," l. 5), and Felicia Hemans similarly writes in "Dirge of a Child," "Fragrance and flowers and dews must be/ The only emblems meet for thee" (lines 29–30).[16] If children are seen as lovely but ephemeral, their deaths make more sense and one need not mourn their promise, which has already been fulfilled. Indeed, many of the elegies assert that it is actually better for the children's sake in the Christian scheme of things that they have died: by dying young, they have preserved the innocence of their souls; they will never be tainted by sin or guilt or the passions of the evil world. As Mary Masters puts it in an elegy of 1755,

> But now by Death she's kindly freed
> From the unequal, cruel Strife,
> Blest be the Pow'r that has decreed
> A Period to this wretched life.
> (17–20)[17]

John Clare takes this dynamic a step further in the grotesque "On an Infant Killed by Lightning":

> O woman! The dread storm was given
> To each to be a friend;
> It took thy infant pure to heaven,
> Left thee behind to mend.
> (17–20)[18]

Life is an enemy, and death is transformed into a friend, a gift, and, most paradoxically of all, into the very answer to a mother's prayers in Amelia Opie's "On the Death of a Child":

> But He, that God who "heareth prayer,"
> To hers a favouring answer gave:
> And sav'd her child from every snare,
> By—precious gift!—an early grave.
> (13–16)[19]

The very extremity of these religious rationalizations suggest how powerfully these elegists need to deny death; as Freud noted in *The Future of an Illusion*, "a religion's technique consists in depressing the value of life."[20] If life is misery and sin, there is no need to mourn anyone's death, least of all a child's.

I include these elegies with their psychological strategies of denial and rationalization as background because they provide a useful comparison and contrast to the ways in which Mary Shelley writes about death, particularly the death of children. Given the extent of her losses, one might well expect to find an even greater need for mitigation and solace. And in fact there are clearly places where she too depends upon the conventional iconography of death and denies its finality, particularly in "The Choice," a poem mourning not just P. B. Shelley but also her children, to whom a third of the poem's lines are devoted: there, for example, Clara's death is mitigated to sleep, as if the girl had been enchanted by the Lilac Fairy in "The Sleeping Beauty": "First my sweet girl—whose face resembled *His*/ Slept on bleak Lido, near Venetian seas" (*MWSJ* 492; 63–64). There too, William does not simply die but instead meets Death's "caress" (84). She seems to be substituting gentler ends for her children than those they actually met, and in a sense she is keeping them alive, another example of the desire for psychic prolongation so manifest in the other elegies.

Yet elegiac forms and formulas ultimately suited neither her talents as a writer nor her real emotional needs. It is precisely the *lack* of continuity represented by a child's death, as she stresses in her response to Hunt's essay, that invalidates conventional elegiac consolations. Accordingly, *The Last Man,* her fuller treatment of grief, eschews such euphemisms in favor of a remarkable analogue for maternal despair. Instead of focusing upon consolation and denying the need for mourning, here Mary Shelley creates a starkly painful narrative of repeated trauma and devastating loss. The specific attributes of mourning for the death of a child, that most debilitating of blows—the sense of wrongness, unnaturalness, and untimeliness, of rage, guilt, and suicidal despair, of bitter severance from the past and the future—are writ large here in terms of the book's conception, tone, rhythms, and narrative patterns as well as its explicit themes.

That *The Last Man* is centrally concerned with grief is plainly evident in the novel's subject and plot: it is an apocalyptic story of abandonment in which Lionel Verney is left utterly and irrevocably deserted. Even more pertinent, it is a story of human vulnerability and helplessness in the face of what is described as "virulent, immedicable disease," strongly reminiscent of the typhoid and malaria responsible for the deaths of Mary Shelley's own children—"Mal'aria, the famous caterer for death" (*LM* 363), as she bitterly notes.[21] The plague is, significantly, a disease originating in the south, which calls to mind Mary Shelley's letter of June 29, 1819, to Marianne Hunt blaming her children's deaths on the unhealthy Italian climate:

We came to Italy thinking to do Shelley's health good—but the Climate is not any means warm enough to be of benefit to him & yet it is that that has destroyed my two children—We went from England comparatively prosperous & happy—I should return broken hearted & miserable—I never know one moments ease from the wretchedness & despair that possesses me—May you my dear Marianne never know what it is to loose [sic] two only & lovely children in one year—to watch their dying moments—& then at last to be left childless & for ever miserable[.] (*MWSL* 1:101)

The agent of destruction, similar in life and art, becomes in the novel a force that eradicates not only all that is precious in life but human life itself, the scale of the desolation an imaginative and apt analogue for the maternal grief Mary Shelley describes in her letters.

The plot of gradual abandonment is accompanied by the pervasive tone of anxiety and dread that permeates the book, particularly in volumes 2 and 3. As the plague claims more and more victims, Lionel and Idris become increasingly absorbed in fears for their children's lives. Lionel notes that Idris's loss of her second child

dashed the triumphant and rapturous emotions of maternity with grief and fear. Before this event, the little beings, sprung from herself, the young heirs of her transient life, seemed to have a sure lease of existence; now she dreaded that the pitiless destroyer might snatch her remaining darlings . . . The least illness caused throes of terror; she was miserable if she were at all absent from them; her treasure of happiness she had garnered in their fragile being, and kept forever on the watch. (178)

He speaks in similar terms of his own growing apprehension: "The thought of danger to them possessed my whole being with fear . . . no labour too great, no scheme too wild, if it promised life to them" (195–96). Such concerns are shared by all of the surviving parents; a performance of *Macbeth* in plague-ravaged London is brought to a halt by the scene in which Macduff learns of the death of his children, at which "A pang of tameless grief wrenched every heart, a burst of despair was echoed from every lip" (221).

Inevitably the Verneys' own worst fears are realized, over and over and over, as all three of their children die. The book is remarkable for the sheer number of anxious, agonizing vigils at sickbeds and deathbeds it contains (the *Literary Gazette*'s description of the book as a "sickening repetition of horrors" [*LM* xiv] is exact); but again, I would suggest that their presence in the novel is dictated by Mary Shelley's own traumatic experience of helplessly watching her own children die. Fittingly, the most painful of such scenes is that of five-year-old Evelyn's death. This is presented unflinchingly, with the narrator focusing upon the child's illness and the agonies of those attending him. Instead of emphasizing the glories of the afterlife, Verney describes all that will be lost with Evelyn:

> For a whole fortnight we unceasingly watched beside the poor child, as his life declined under the ravages of a virulent typhus. His little form and tiny lineaments encaged the embryo of the world-spanning mind of man. Man's nature, brimful of passions and affections, would have had an home in that little heart, whose swift pulsations hurried towards their close. His small hand's fine mechanism, now flaccid and unbent, would in the growth of sinew and muscle, have achieved works of beauty or of strength[.] His tender rosy feet would have trod in firm manhood the bowers and glades of earth — these reflections were now of little use: he lay, thought and strength suspended, waiting unresisting the final blow. (337)

Evelyn is no flower or dewdrop one would expect to live only briefly, but rather "the world-spanning mind of man" in "embryo," an image that rather suggests enormous human potentiality and perhaps the Shelleys' hopes for their own children. Unlike Clare and Hemans, who emphasize the desirability of dying as a child, before one's soul is tainted by passion, Verney mourns his child's lost opportunities to fulfill "man's nature." Where Evelyn might have gone, what he might have made, what he might have been is lost, and the loss is not rationalized by imagining his soul gamboling in paradise.

Unlike the bathetic deaths of Little Nell and Paul Dombey or the death-bed sermons preached by other children of Victorian fiction (clear examples of rationalization, in imagining that the children themselves really wish to die and go to heaven) Evelyn's death is simply and sparely recounted: "At length the moment of his death came: the blood paused in its flow — his eyes opened, and then closed again: without convulsion or sigh, the frail tenement was left vacant of its spiritual inhabitant" (337). The simple description focuses upon the fact of mortality rather than immortality, and Verney's elegiac words for his child bleakly offer an unresolved choice between the rationalization of the *Kindertotenlieder* and introjection: "thou, sweet child, amiable and beloved boy, either thy spirit has sought a fitter dwelling, or, shrined in my heart, thou livest while it lives" (338). The circumstances of Evelyn's death inevitably suggest the death of William Shelley, who also suffered for precisely two weeks before succumbing to his fatal illness, and the importance of Evelyn's loss in the narrative suggests the importance of William's loss for Mary Shelley. "After my William's death," she wrote in her journal entry of October 10, 1822, "this world seemed only a quicksand, sinking beneath me." And Evelyn's death is followed swiftly, almost anticlimactically in the novel by the deaths of Clara and Adrian, completing the collapse of the human world.

What we have, then, in the early Victorian *Kindertotenlieder* and *The Last Man*, are two very different depictions of responses to loss: in the former, the loss is minimized and mitigated if not outright denied; in the latter, the loss is painfully recreated and reexperienced. Psychologically, what might account for this latter response? Here I turn to Melanie Klein's distinction between normal and abnormal mourning as set forth in her paper "Mourning and Its Relation to Manic-Depressive States," written in 1940, after the death of her oldest son. After an initial stage of denial (as depicted in the *Kindertotenlieder*), "the characteristic feature of normal mourning is the individual's reinstating the lost loved object inside himself." Abnormal mourning, on the other hand, is the inability to do so. Klein argues that those who fail in the work of mourning "have been unable in early childhood to establish their internal 'good' objects and to feel secure in their inner world." [22]

Such insecurity results from the frustrations of earliest infancy: according to Klein, the infant's experiences of frustration when deprived of the mother's breast and "all it has come to stand for: namely, love, goodness, and security," lead to the earliest fantasies of aggression and destruction aimed against the mother and the breast; when the mother disappears, even temporarily, the infant then feels as if she has destroyed her mother, and the ensuing guilt and despair "awaken the wish to restore and recreate her" by means of reparative fantasies in the stage Klein calls the infantile depressive position. According to Klein, such positive and negative fantasies function in the creation of the infant's inner world—good objects are introjected, bad objects projected outward—and also as defense mechanisms to protect the ego. Normally, the "reappearance of the mother makes [the infant] more aware of the resilience of his external objects and less frightened of the omnipotent attacks he makes on them in phantasy," and thus leads to the resolution of the infantile depressive position. But given the loss of her mother and the instability of her early care, the infant Mary Shelley would have had far fewer resources in reality with which to combat such unconscious fantasies of rage and guilt.[23]

Reparative and destructive fantasies continue to inform adult psychic life, and they play an important role in the processes of mourning and creativity. In mourning, the inner world is transformed into "disharmonious chaos."[24] Mourning "is a reliving of the early depressive anxieties; not only is the present object in the external world felt to be lost, but also the early objects, the parents."[25] Melanie Klein continues, "these too are felt . . . to be destroyed whenever the loss of a loved person is experienced. Thereupon the early depressive situation, and with it anxieties, guilt, and feelings of loss and grief derived from the breast situation . . . are reactivated." Again, the relevance to Mary Shelley is plain: the real loss of her mother was arguably embedded in each of her subsequent losses, increasing her grief exponentially.[26] And the "disharmonious chaos" that typifies the inner world in mourning is reflected perfectly in the apocalyptic vision of *The Last Man*. Such chaos is normally surmounted by the introjection and reinstatement of the good inner objects and the rebuilding of the ruined inner world.

Klein's student, Hanna Segal, has further postulated that all fantasy, conscious as well as unconscious, is essentially reparative and that "all creation is really a re-creation of a once loved and once whole, but now lost and ruined object, a ruined internal world and self." Accordingly, she interprets *A la recherche du temps perdu* as Proust's massive attempt to recreate lost inner and external worlds; as she puts it, "What Proust describes corresponds to a situation of mourning: he sees that his loved objects are dying or dead. Writing a book is for him like the work of mourning in that gradually the external objects are given up, they are reinstated in the ego, and re-created in the book."[27] Such introjection of the lost good object is apparent in "The Choice," in which Mary Shelley's uncharacteristic decision to use verse suggests her desperate desire to keep P. B. Shelley alive by incorporating him and becoming a poet herself. This desire is also apparent in the first part of *The Last Man*, which recreates her lost circle of intimates and, in Kleinian terms, rebuilds her inner world. But what psychic needs drive the second half of the book, in which chaos predominates and the recreated good objects are once again ruthlessly destroyed?

Just as Mary Shelley was not the only mother to lose her children, so she was not the only person to create fantasies of total abandonment, and it may be instructive to compare the universal destruction depicted in *The Last Man* with another such apocalyptic vision. In 1893, Dr. Daniel Schreber, later diagnosed by Freud as suffering from paranoia, believed quite literally in an imminent world catastrophe, described by Freud as follows:

> At the climax of his illness, under the influence of visions which were "partly of a terrifying character, but partly, too, of an indescribable grandeur," Schreber became convinced of the imminence of a great catastrophe, of the end of the world. Voices told him that . . . the earth's allotted span was only 212 years more; and during the last part of his stay in Fleschsig's clinic he believed that that period had already elapsed. He himself was "the only real man left alive," and the few human shapes that he still saw—the doctor, the attendants, the other patients—he explained as being "miracled up, cursorily improvised men." [28]

Both Klein and Freud "agreed that Schreber's 'end of the world' delusion represented 'the projection of . . . [an] internal catastrophe.'" [29] And although Mary Shelley did not believe her apocalyptic scenario to be literally true, as Schreber did, there are nevertheless clear similarities in the content of Schreber's vision and *The Last Man*. The novel can be regarded as the projection of an internal catastrophe, the collapse of not merely Mary Shelley's external world but her Kleinian inner world as well. Her representation of that world is driven not only by reparative urges but also by guilt and persecutory anxiety.

Such anxieties and guilt return even to those who have successfully resolved the infantile depressive position, something I believe Mary Shelley may not have been able to do. As Klein notes, "If, for instance, a mother loses her child through death, along with sorrow and pain her early dread of being robbed by a 'bad' retaliating mother is reactivated and confirmed" (321), reawakening persecutory feelings that the mother "had died in order to inflict punishment and deprivation upon [her]" (323). The fears and guilt of the motherless child may well have informed the mature fantasies of the childless mother. According to Klein's theory, "at an unconscious level the death and destruction of a beloved object is seen as a result of one's own hatred and aggression. Unconsciously, mourning is experienced as punishment—living in an empty world—for having destroyed what was good in it."[30] Mary Shelley's unconscious guilt for the deaths of P. B. Shelley, her children, and, most fundamentally, her mother, coupled with her persecutory anxiety and her unconscious rage at her abandonment, all emerge in her depiction of a world disintegrating irreversibly into chaos: her ruined inner world is transposed into an apocalyptic external one. The extent of the psychic devastation precludes the defensive strategies of normal mourning, which find expression in the elegiac mode; the series of deaths in Mary Shelley's life did nothing to check or belie the guilt stemming from earlier destructive fantasies.

Lacking the basis to recreate a secure world, she instead creates a representation of chaos, much as the creature does in *Frankenstein*. *The Last Man* is a portrait of "the phantasies belonging to the earliest depressive position, where all the objects are destroyed."[31] Tellingly, Mary Shelley projects all that is destructive into the ravaging plague, which is itself annihilated, interpretable in terms of Kleinian defense mechanisms as an attempt to protect her ego from the knowledge of its darker impulses. Yet her unconscious guilt for the series of deaths is too strong to be wholly displaced by means of projection, and Lionel Verney's utter solitude at the end of the novel correlates perfectly with Klein's view of mourning as the punishment of living in an empty world. Seen thus, the book is driven not simply by reparative urges but by a need for self-punishment, all the more poignant in the face of such very real losses. In a way, the 1826 *London Magazine* review got it exactly right: "bad enough to read—horrible to write" (*LM* xiv).

Yet the novel's final chapter tells a story not simply of despair but of survival, of the art of losing: Verney's attempts to find solace and rebuild the semblance of a life as the sole inhabitant of Rome are analogous to what may have been Mary Shelley's own attempts at reconstructing her internal world. By means of the novel she has once again destroyed all her loved objects, yet she can face the ruins and survive, albeit in a much diminished way. As Klein notes, the process of mourning is never definitively over, and Mary Shelley's letters, journals, and late fiction attest to her ongoing mourning for her children.[32] That she recognized at least in part the profound connections between her fiction and her traumas is evident in a journal entry written on June 7, 1836, the seventeenth anniversary of William's death: "Others write—my Father did—in peace of heart—the imagination at work alone—some warmth imparted to them by the strong conjuring up of fictitious woes—but tranquil in their own bosoms—But I!

O my God — what a lot is mine — marked by tragedy & death — tracked by disappointment & unutterable wretchedness — blow after blow — my heart dies within me" (*MWSJ* 548).

Her remarks imply a strong, manifest, and lasting connection between writing and trauma, trauma too deep-seated to be mitigated by normal defensive strategies or depicted by conventional elegiac means. Even as her writing preserves and perpetuates loss, it also may have served to a certain extent to recreate, appease, and perpetuate her lost objects. Like the locks of Clara's and William's hair she carefully preserved in her writing desk for thirty years, her fantasies — articulated and published — preserve her children even as they attest to their loss. Fittingly enough, in a passage from *Falkner* they inform a metaphor of the resurgence of the past into eternity itself: "It is a singular law of human life, that the past, which apparently no longer forms a part of our existence, never dies; new shoots, as it were, spring up at different intervals and places, all bearing the indelible characteristics of the parent stalk; the circular emblem of eternity is suggested by this meeting and recurrence of the broken ends of our life" (*Fa* 43).

10 : Politicizing the Personal

Mary Wollstonecraft, Mary Shelley,
and the Coterie Novel

GARY KELLY

Both Mary Wollstonecraft and Mary Shelley have been read as autobio-graphical and expressive or confessional novelists, in themselves and in the relation between them as mother and daughter.[1] Some critics have seen this autobiographical content, whether conscious or unconscious, as the site of the political element in Wollstonecraft's and Mary Shelley's novels.[2] There has, however, been increasing emphasis on seeing Wollstonecraft and Mary Shelley as politically motivated self-conscious artists interested in using the novel to intervene in their respective worlds.[3] In this chapter, I argue that Wollstonecraft's and Mary Shelley's use of autobiography may be understood, perhaps best understood, as a conscious and deliberate device in their original and significant development of a particular form of the novel of their time, which I will call the coterie novel. In putting forth this argument, I reinterpret what I and others have examined as the English Jacobin or Godwinian novel,[4] and so I propose adding the coterie novel to my earlier taxonomy of late eighteenth- and early nineteenth-century fiction.[5]

The coterie novel was derived from forms that had long been in use but that underwent rapid elaboration and intense application during the Revolution debate of the late eighteenth and early nineteenth century, es-pecially in the circles to which Wollstonecraft and Mary Shelley belonged. The coterie novel was designed not only to serve the political and asso-ciated programs of such self-conscious political avant-gardes but also, at the same time, to express, reflect, or embody the character of these avant-gardes. It was intended to promote the political and cultural authority of the coterie that produced it, during critical periods in the struggle for leadership among the revolutionary middle classes. In order to show how

Wollstonecraft and Mary Shelley developed the coterie novel for their own ends, and in different but connected historical conditions, I'll describe first the kind of coteries in which they each participated, then the novels produced by members of these coteries and some of their associates, and finally some central traits of the novels produced by these two coteries, including the novels of Mary Wollstonecraft and Mary Shelley.

In general, the coterie was characteristic of the rise of civil society in late eighteenth-century European countries and their colonies and ex-colonies. The term *coterie* describes a group of personally acquainted individuals, meeting informally and corresponding with each other, who advance certain shared social, cultural, and political interests. A coterie may have included salons, or more or less regular, semiformal meetings, but by the late eighteenth century the salon as such was perhaps associated more with fashionable and influential ranks in society than with the more avant-garde, oppositional, professional, and especially intellectual groups who formed coteries. There were coteries of many kinds, but political-literary coteries seem to have proliferated and had a particular character during the Revolutionary and Romantic periods.

These groups were organized to lead and manage scattered political movements in a revolutionary, or potentially revolutionary, situation at a time when party organization was still relatively undeveloped. For example, during the early phase of the French Revolution, the Girondins, with whom British Revolutionary sympathizers had most in common, were a dominant grouping but did not constitute a political party in the modern sense. They were a diverse and scattered group of individuals, some of whom were closely, indeed personally and intimately connected, especially in the coterie led by Marie Roland and her husband, who was for a time head of the Revolutionary government.[6] In fact, this kind of connection was part of their broadly Rousseauist and sentimental social and political philosophy. The Girondin coterie, led by the Rolands, had a strong interest in literature and print as vehicles for leading and sustaining a nationwide movement.

Mary Wollstonecraft went to Paris in December 1792 to join this coterie, though in fact she became involved in another coterie, one of British, American, and Continental European expatriates who had gathered around Thomas Christie and his friends.[7] They too had a strong interest in making the coterie a scene for avant-garde forms of revolutionary conjugality and friendship, as well as professional and business relationships and literary projects promoting their idealized self-image and interests. Members of this coterie may have intended not only to support the Girondin Revolution and the Roland coterie, with which they were associated, but also perhaps eventually to transfer their activities to a position of revolutionary leadership in Britain. After members of the Jacobin coup d'état and the Terror arrested and executed leading Girondins and dispersed the Christie coterie, Wollstonecraft returned to England. Here she soon associated with the Godwin coterie, a leading group of the so-called "English Jacobins" who are more accurately described in terms of ideology and program as "English (or British) Girondins." Unlike the Roland coterie, the circle of William Godwin and his friends did not control a revolutionary government, but (perhaps as a consequence) they were decidedly intent on achieving revolution through writing and print, and their coterie had a distinctly and sharply focused literary-political character. Like the Roland and Christie coteries, however, members of the Godwin coterie also attempted to live out their revolutionary principles in daily conjugal, domestic, and private social life. The same was true of the Godwins' successor coterie, that of the Shelleys, in the post-Napoleonic 1810s and 1820s.

The politicized and consciously avant-garde domesticity and private social life and culture of the Godwin and Shelley coteries became represented in various ways in their novels, and their political lifestyle was seized on eagerly by hostile counterrevolutionary writers in the late 1790s and the 1820s. For their vision of revolutionary theory (which they called *philosophy*) and practice depended on a particular relationship between the two, informed by a version of certain elements from enlightenment materialism, sociology, and political theory. They argued that individual subjectivity and social identity and relations are constructed, for better or worse — usually worse — by the form of government, very broadly defined, under which people lived. Corrupt government, as in the court monarchies of the *anciens régimes,* inevitably construct corrupt individuals and corrupt social relations. Thus individual subjectivity and social relations, even at the level of private domestic life (including sexuality), reflect and in turn reproduce the prevailing system of government. This argument encounters a problem, however: if government maintains and reproduces itself in its social order and the consciousness of its subjects, how is this fact to be recognized, let alone lead to revolutionary transformation (or even abolition) of government? The English Jacobins of the Godwin coterie, followed by the Shelley circle, answered this problem by proposing that "enlightened" individuals, working in a political coterie or revolutionary vanguard, provide the necessary revolutionary leadership. Not surprisingly, they cast themselves in this historic role.

This vanguard was formed of a shifting personnel of disaffected or socially marginalized intellectuals of various kinds, some in frequent contact and some merely corresponding members, some from outside the professional middle class (e.g., Thomas Holcroft and Tom Paine), some from marginalized social-religious communities (e.g., William Godwin, Anna Laetitia Barbauld, and Mary Hays), some from politicized provincial Enlightenments (e.g., Robert Bage and Amelia Alderson, later Opie), and some feminists (e.g., Mary Wollstonecraft and Mary Hays). They saw their intended revolution as primarily a revolution in individual consciousness, achieved by vanguard intellectuals such as themselves. This would occur mainly through a dialectic between their experience and certain kinds of reading, especially their brand of philosophy, which could include anything from novels to argumentative and analytical discourse of historic and conventional kinds. Reading such "philosophy," be it a novel or a treatise, induces critical reflection on experience, which reveals that experience to be shaped by systemic injustice and oppression rather than by individual misfortune or criminality. This dialectic is represented again and again in novels of the Godwin coterie. Individuals revolutionized in this way would form avant-garde coteries in order to maintain and promote enlightenment.

Another important way to spread their message, however, would be by producing more philosophy, eventually achieving a socially universal revolution. To accomplish their revolution through literature, members of the Godwin and Shelley coteries, more perhaps than any others active in their day, planned and published works in a deliberately wide range of forms, styles, genres, and discourses. There was, though infrequent, the philosophical treatise such as Godwin's *Political Justice.* There was more historiography, ranging from Holcroft's projected histories of court government through Wollstonecraft's history of the early French Revolution to Godwin's later literary and cultural histories. There were familiar essays on a range of subjects, such as Godwin's *Enquirer.* There were education manuals, ranging from Wollstonecraft's earlier work to her second *Vindication,* including a work by Hays and her sister. There were polemical tracts, such as those of Hays, Barbauld, Holcroft, and Godwin in the mid-1790s, variously addressing different levels and sections of the reading public from "the people" to the political class, and including middle-class women. There was the occasional political travelogue such as Wollstonecraft's *Letters* from Scandinavia. There were translations of various kinds, such as Holcroft's and Wollstonecraft's earlier work. There were the plays of Elizabeth Inchbald, Holcroft, and Godwin, including tragedy, comedy, and melodrama. Members of the Shelley coterie also wrote and published, or at least projected, a similar range of works, though the circle was most notable for its political and mythological poems and verse dramas, perhaps marking a shift in the later period away from directly engaged forms of polemical writing, predominantly prose. Foremost in both the Godwin and Shelley coteries, however, was the novel.

These coteries were especially interested in the novel partly for the obvious reason that the novel was the most widely read form of print, besides newspapers and magazines, among the middle-class reading public. This was the public these coteries, like most politically motivated novelists of the time, wished to reach and to politicize in certain ways. The coterie novel was designed with two principal functions: it communicated a shared discourse among the coterie itself, sustaining their coherence and impetus; and it represented the coterie's culture and politics in such a way as to constitute its wider readership as virtual members of the coterie. The coterie novel was intended to interpellate its readers in a particular way, drawing them, directly or by extension, within the coterie's culture and consciousness, constructing them as subjects of a certain kind and thus subjecting them to the leadership of the coterie that produced these particular novels.

Such interpellation was accomplished through novelistic construction of certain themes and formal devices, which addressed the coterie and the wider public in different but overlapping ways. For the coterie members and their associates, the interpellation was through a shared code of textual signs and their references to the coterie and its interests; for the wider reading public, the interpellation was through the textual construction itself and also through a sense, communicated by textual signs and supplemented by extratextual information, such as public notoriety of the coterie, that the text was a coterie text, a form of secret communication. In this respect, counterrevolutionary critics and parodists were justified in representing the Godwin and Shelley coteries as versions of secret societies, like the Freemasons and the Illuminati, who were supposed to have conspired to overturn the established order through ideological and cultural subversion.

Certainly the circles to which Mary Wollstonecraft and Mary Shelley belonged were the leading producers of coterie novels in Britain during their respective periods. Writers in the Godwin circle may be said to have developed the coterie novel of the political vanguard at this time. The Godwin coterie included the novelists Holcroft, Godwin, Wollstonecraft, Inchbald, Hays, and Eliza Fenwick. Associated with or admired by these writers were others who produced versions of the coterie novel. One was Robert Bage, whose novels represent the interests and even the personnel of the coterie at the center of the Midlands Enlightenment. Another associate was Dr. John Moore, whose novels represent the interests and some characters from an interconnected set of circles that included elements of the Scottish Enlightenment, the English Nonconformist Enlightenment, and the circle of the leading writer of Sensibility, Helen Maria Williams. Amelia Alderson (later Opie) was closely associated with both the Godwin circle and the Norwich provincial and Nonconformist Enlightenment, which had strong literary interests of their own. Later she became the most prolific fiction writer of the group, though *Adeline Mowbray* (1804) is partly critical in its representation of key figures of the Godwin coterie, especially Godwin and Wollstonecraft.

Then there were a number of writers who had more or less tenuous associations with the Godwin circle and whose novels represented, sometimes critically, that circle's interests, leading figures, and novelistic practice. For example, Charles Lloyd was associated with both the Godwin circle and the Wordsworth-Coleridge circle, from which he later distanced himself and which he represented critically in his novel *Edmund Oliver* (1798). Charlotte (King) Dacre may have been indirectly connected with the Godwin circle through her father; certainly her novel *Zofloya* (1806) opens with a précis of Godwin's political sociology and attempts to meld the erotic Gothic romance with the Godwin circle's novelistic practice of psychopolitical analysis of character. Dacre's novel also provides a literary link between the Godwin and Shelley circles: it was closely imitated by P. B. Shelley in his two early Gothic romances, *Zastrozzi* and *St. Irvyne*. A later associate of Godwin's, if not a member of his circle, and a literary link between their novels and those of the Shelley circle, was Lady Caroline Lamb, whose *Glenarvon* (1816) is a politicized *roman à clef* attempting to combine elements similar to those found in Dacre's novel. It would be possible to extend exploration of variously tenuous and indirect developments of the Godwin circle's coterie novels.

Poets were more prominent in the Shelleys' circle than in Godwin's, but the Shelley coterie also planned or produced a large number of novels, many of which have the thematic and formal traits of the Godwinian coterie novel, led by the novels of Mary Shelley herself. In many ways Mary Shelley was a product of the political coterie culture of her day. She spent most of her early years in her father's later circle, she was imbued with the writings of her mother and father and their coterie of the 1790s, and she and P. B. Shelley later read many works produced by members of the Rolands' Girondin coterie. Furthermore, for much of its existence, the Shelley circle was in self-imposed exile in Switzerland and Italy and must have become aware of the impact made by the expatriate coterie of Germaine de Staël-Holstein, whose *Corinne* (1807) was the most influential European novel of the Napoleonic period. The book could also be seen as a form of coterie novel used to spread the protoliberal ideology and politics of Staël's circle, and this in itself would have interested the Shelley circle.

P. B. Shelley published no novels after his youthful Gothic extravaganzas, but he did plan or start several novel projects and took a close interest in Mary Shelley's novel writing. Besides her, Thomas Love Peacock was the most prolific novelist associated with the Shelley circle. His partly burlesque, partly sympathetic representations of the Shelley coterie, their ideas, and their literary practices use elements of the earlier anti-Jacobin novels that attacked the Godwin circle and their fiction. Other writers associated at some point or other with the Shelley circle, such as Thomas Jefferson Hogg, John Polidori, and Edward Trelawny, also published novels that resembled the Shelley's coterie novels in some respects. At a further remove but linked to both the Godwin and Shelley circles and their novelistic practice was Edward Bulwer, later Bulwer Lytton, who did not produce coterie novels as such but developed the form of the Godwin-Shelley coterie novel to become the most influential early Victorian novelist of social protest and reform. This literary development could be extended to at least some novels by Dickens, the Brontës, and George Eliot.

It is well established that writers in the Godwin and Shelley coteries thought carefully about adapting the novel form to the task of disseminating their ideas to a wide reading public, but it should be emphasized that in doing so they also aimed to establish their vanguard role as political coteries with that reading public, which constituted the potentially revolutionary class at that time in Britain. They designed their novels to exhibit certain similar characteristics, recognizable as such not only to close associates with inside knowledge but also to a significant portion of the reading public at large, so that each novel would evoke for those readers the identity of the coterie and their novelistic *oeuvre* as a whole and as a continuing project. Certainly the character and personnel of these coteries and the formal and thematic characteristics of their novels were recognizable enough to be publicly criticized and burlesqued by sympathizers and opponents alike. Most novels by writers in the Godwin and Shelley coteries, including those of Wollstonecraft and Mary Shelley, were intended to be read as instances of a historically and culturally specific genre. By *genre* here I mean a set of writing practices designed for particular purposes and certain rhetorical effects and recognizable as such to most readers in a particular time and place. Much scholarship and criticism has already been devoted to describing those practices, especially in the novels from the Godwin coterie, and there is neither space nor need to describe those practices again in full here. It will be useful, however, to show how three central elements of this form of coterie novel, elements that have autobiographical and collective group resonance, help constitute the Godwin-Shelley coterie novel as such and themselves acquire new significance by being read in terms of the coterie novel as a historically particular genre.

One such distinctive element, seen clearly in the novels of Wollstonecraft and Mary Shelley, is the handling of narrative form. Many novels from the Godwin and Shelley coteries are written in first-person narrative, specifically the confessional or autobiographical mode, with explicit reflection on the relation between the narrator's experience and the prevailing social and political order. This was intended to be the appropriate form for authoritative representation of systemic oppression experienced at the personal level, by both narrator-protagonist and implied author. The form is employed not only to engage the reader's political sympathy for the narrator but also to show the reader how reflection on experience produces politicized awareness—implicitly the first step toward reform of or revolution against the prevailing order. The narration is often framed as an address to a particular person, and in some instances narration forms an element in the plot, in which storytelling affects subsequent action. So Caleb's narration in Godwin's *Things as They Are; or, The Adventures of Caleb Williams* (1794) eventually moves Caleb's persecutor to confess, and Maria's life story converts Jemima from prison guard to helper in Wollstonecraft's *The Wrongs of Woman; or, Maria* (1798). Significantly, the intratextual narrative relationships in *Frankenstein* (1818) or Mary Shelley's other novels do not sustain change in action; these novels seem to have a more pessimistic view of the conversionary effect of self-narration on others. On the other hand, this apparent failure is staged in such a way as to imply that the primary address is in fact beyond the text's bounds, effecting politicization and conversion there, as in Mary Hays's *The Victim of Prejudice* (1799) or Mary Shelley's *The Last Man* (1826).

Many Godwin and Shelley coterie novels do use omniscient third-person narration, but they do so in a way distinct from that of conservative novelists like Austen and Scott. In coterie novels, the omniscient third-person narrator retains some traits of a first-person narrator, empathizing with the suffering protagonists, engaging in autobiographical asides and references, using a lyrical style, and embodying a model avant-garde consciousness that parallels that of the represented protagonists. This is the kind of third-person narration found in Inchbald's *A Simple Story* (1792) and *Nature and Art* (1796) and in such novels of Mary Shelley's as *Valperga* (1823).

Such use of narrative form, whether first-person or third-person, reflects the belief of the Godwin and Shelley circles in the "spread of truth," or enlightenment through nonviolent and interpersonal means. This staging of politicizing narration implicitly enacts the personal exchange within the politicized coterie and invites the reader to an indirect participation in the coterie. This process may be envisaged as the formation and enlargement of a coterie intended eventually to constitute a revolutionized civil society. Public notoriety could actually assist the coterie novelist here, lending to the fictional representation what was culturally accepted as the superior authority of the "real," or actual, experience. Even when the reader had no direct knowledge of the coterie, however, both the confessional first-person form and the sympathetic and expressive third-person form could invite a reading in which presumed autobiographical authenticity underwrites the fiction.

A second, related element in these coterie novels is their characterology, or selection, arrangement, and use of character, including coded or allusive names. These novelists construct character deliberately as versions of the authors themselves and other members of the coterie. The inquiring plebeian Caleb Williams can obviously stand for the book's author, who was also already famous as the author of a philosophical inquiry into the nature of political justice when the adventures of Caleb Williams were published. Wollstonecraft's Maria is also its author, Mary, but she is generalized politically and historically through references and allusions to Marie Roland, victim of the masculine Jacobin Terror, and Mary Queen of Scots, victim of masculine court politics in a previous era of revolutionary change. Hays used actual letters, as well as character resemblances, between herself and Godwin in *Memoirs of Emma Courtney,* arranged in a framework known to resemble her thwarted love for William Frend. More critical portraits of members of the Godwin circle appear in Charles Lloyd's *Edmund Oliver* and Amelia Opie's *Adeline Mowbray,* while Peacock's *Nightmare Abbey* and other novels offer versions of figures in the Shelley circle. Lamb's *Glenarvon* was widely read as (merely) a *roman à clef* about her affair with Byron, but, like the novels of Wollstonecraft, Hays, and Opie, it resembles the Godwin and Shelley coterie novels in generalizing autobiography to an explicitly political critique of contemporary society. Shelley's *The Last Man* is widely regarded as a portrait of the Shelley circle and its intrarelationships, but it, too, generalizes these in a post-Napoleonic critique of masculine history implicitly set against the failure of European liberal revolts of the early 1820s.

This effect of generalized and politicized autobiography is reinforced by these novels' construction of the subjectivity and personal relations of their protagonists as the afflicted sites of internalized and domesticated social conflict. Individual subjectivity in excess, alienated from or by society, especially when the protagonist is ostensibly motivated by desire for social progress, was a continuing theme in cultural politics from the Revolution debate of the 1790s to the emergence of liberal ideology in the 1820s. Its most familiar novelistic representation for modern readers is in *Frankenstein,* but it was found in many kinds of cultural representation at that time, frequently in texts of the Shelley coterie, especially the poems of P. B. Shelley and Byron. This focus on vanguard individuality and individualism was used by counterrevolutionary critics to portray the Godwin and Shelley circles as at best impractical extremists and at worst egotistical enemies of social convention and stability, as in the public condemnation of Wollstonecraft following Godwin's *Memoir* of her or the scandal of supposed sexual irregularities in the Shelley circle.

Nevertheless, character so deployed functions with the dual address typical of these coterie novels. To readers in the coterie or its extended networks or to readers informed by reviews or even gossip, the novels would acquire an additional dimension of political authority (or scandal) through known, advertised, or surmised relations between fictional characters and members of the author's coterie. Many members of the wider reading public were accustomed by reviews, newspapers, and the general tenor of contemporary public debate to relate politics to personality. Such readers would readily suppose, for better or worse, that the author and his or her views, experience, and associates were represented in the novel. In either case, a reader's recognizing a particular text as belonging to the coterie novel form would invite that reader to adopt a sympathetic position in relation to the implied or actual coterie in and behind the novel.

This invitation is reinforced by these novels' handling of dialogue to construct a version of the coterie's practice of argument and debate, thereby calling upon the reader as an implied participant in the coterie's ideology, culture, and politics. Earlier coterie novels, such as Holcroft's *Anna St. Ives,* Godwin's *Things as They Are,* and Wollstonecraft's *The Wrongs of Woman,* make significant use of dialogue in the plot by including debates and scenes of judgment staged as public or semi-public tribunals. In such cases the protagonist often validates his or her political views with autobiographical discourse that is both expressive and reflective, confessional and forensic. Such handling of dialogue is designed to have greater rhetorical force on auditors or readers within the novel as well as the readers outside the novel. At the same time, such dialogue also implicitly models the free intellectual exchange promoted and ostensibly practiced by the coterie in real life. As the reader follows such dialogue, he or she becomes implicated in its process and thereby, again, in the coterie's ideology, culture, and politics.

In such novels, the dialogical scene of judgment is also an implied analogy to both the Revolutionary tribunals in France and the treason trials in Britain. The implied contrast between dialogue as free intellectual exchange — as coterie culture — and dialogue staged in a public tribunal suggests that the actual existing state, monarchic or popular, is unable to render justice, let alone accomplish the spread of truth. Presumably, a revolution may be necessary to extend coterie dialogism into the state and the public political sphere. Novelists of the Shelley circle are less interested in using dialogue in debate or tribunal, however, than in using it to represent a subjectivity and an intersubjective relations suited to emergent liberal ideology. According to this ideology, the state should be founded on the sovereign self-aware subject and sustained through social relations stemming from such subjectivity. Dialogue used in this way responds to the widespread desire of the period to subsume the conflicts and confrontations of the Revolutionary and Napoleonic periods in a new formation of political ideology and culture. In this respect, *Frankenstein* and its successors mark the sublation of the Godwinian in the Shelleyan coterie and that of Revolutionary English Jacobin discourse in Romantic liberalism.

The third, and perhaps the most obvious, element of the Godwin and Shelley coterie novel, however, is its handling of reference and allusion, especially in the embedded revolutionary reading list, naming of people and places, and certain settings. The embedded reading list includes references to particular texts and authors, such as Rousseau's *La Nouvelle Héloïse* in *The Wrongs of Woman*, Helvétius in *Emma Courtney*, and Volney, Plutarch, and Milton in *Frankenstein;* or there is the opening invitation to read *Valperga* against the *Histoire des républiques italiennes du moyen âge* by J. C. L. Sismondi, liberal historiographer and member of Staël's traveling coterie. Sometimes these works are designated as means of self-politicization by enabling critical reflection on personal experience. *Frankenstein* offers perhaps the most striking instance of references to works of the coterie itself, in its quotations from P. B. Shelley and Byron.

Politically significant allusion through the naming of characters is another aspect of characterization that usually has historical resonance, as with the well-known example of Falkland in *Things as They Are* — an allusion to the chivalric figure of the English Civil War. Naming of places and the use of certain settings also invoke a range of politically significant historical reference, as in Victor Frankenstein's Genevan home or the places visited by Reginald de St Leon in his traversal of historic sites of resistance, reformation, and revolution — places that would be familiar not only within Godwin's own coterie but also in liberal English dissenting circles and later revolutionary ones. Such use of references and allusion again functions in the double-address characteristic of these coterie novels. It invokes what can be considered a field of common knowledge within the coterie while promoting emancipatory reading for the public beyond the coterie and inviting vicarious participation in the coterie's culture.

As already suggested, despite the similarities between the coterie novels of the Godwin and Shelley circles, they were situated in and addressed different literary and political conditions; consequently and necessarily they had different emphases and configurations. Other important issues remain to be examined: for example, the different inflection that Wollstonecraft and Mary Shelley, as a Revolutionary feminist and a Romantic feminist, respectively, gave to their use of the coterie novel form, distinguishing their work within the genre, creating perhaps a third direction of address — to women readers both within their different coteries and among their wider reading publics. Another issue deserving consideration is the way in which the Godwin coterie's novel form, designed to address first the Revolution debate of the 1790s and then the Revolutionary aftermath, was subsumed into Mary Shelley's novels, in particular those that were designed to address the Napoleonic aftermath and emergent liberal politics and revolt. A further issue is the way in which novels of both the Godwin and the Shelley coteries presented themselves as politically and artistically avant-garde work against what Pierre Bourdieu would call the consecrated, or more widely accepted, avant-gardes of Sensibility and Romanticism, respectively.[8] Investigation of these and other questions requires further research, and I would hope future scholars may be assisted by this essay's consideration of the politics of reading and writing in the novels of Mary Wollstonecraft's and Mary Shelley's coteries.

11 : Mary Wollstonecraft Godwin Shelley

The Female Author between Public and Private Spheres

MITZI MYERS

> Binary distinctions are an analytic procedure, but their usefulness does not guarantee that existence divides like that. We should look with suspicion on anyone who declared that there are two kinds of people, or two kinds of reality or process.

To no binarism is this warning by Mary Douglas more applicable than with a priori commitments to the publicity of men's sphere and the privacy of women's,[1] yet two decades after the distinguished anthropologist's caveat, binary assumptions still trouble literary histories and cultural studies of the Romantic period.[2] Elsewhere I survey how much recent theoretical and historical scholarship currently understands, misreads, and interrogates gendered public and private spheres in the Habermasian sense (which is quite different from the conduct-book binarisms noted below) and consider what a framework that takes seriously a literary bourgeois public sphere as contextualized in British culture might offer in re-thinking women's writing. Here I want to complicate, or to simplify, these already vexed and hardworking terms by teasing out conjunctions of the public and private as they apply more specifically to Mary Shelley's work and to writings about her.[3] I must especially note the endlessly proliferating readings (many of them brilliant) of private history as public fiction, what one might call the "Percy's-wife" or "daddy's-girl" approach to Mary Shelley, perhaps a manifestation of the more general taste in late Enlightenment and Romantic literary culture and in its modern academic heirs for privileging the confessional, finding out about us while gossiping about the Romantics.[4] Here, too, Mary Shelley is, as so often, an exemplary case.

The larger question always in mind is, of course, where do we "place" within public and private categories (however diversely or overlappingly our terms are defined) a woman writer labeled Mary Wollstonecraft Godwin Shelley, whose very name encodes a multiplicity of heritages and identities, a heavy freight to carry up the authorial "staircase I am climbing," as a letter of 1823 puts it (*MWSL* 1:361). Where does she fit? How are we reading her? Do we still literalize Mary Shelley's own remark that her "chief merit must always be derived," without sufficiently considering the public ambition simultaneously encoded in the 1827 letter in which this phrase occurs?[5] Are there better or fuller ways to read her that might also help us with other women writers of her time?[6] Does her name irresistibly elicit critical family romances, however variant and nuanced these may be? In precisely what ways is she (or is she at all) a *Romantic*, if we dare define that term?[7]

Once upon a time, not so very long ago, feminist critics confidently mapped what they thought of as two "spheres," or spaces — the "public" and the "private." In the venerable terms of old conduct books, freshly spiffed up as the standard late-twentieth-century paradigm for placing the female author as "proper lady" or "domestic woman," feminist critics opposed the man's world "out there" to the feminine locale *not* "out there." Although many of us are no longer quite so sure that those paper maps provide accurate guides to historical actualities or that those notoriously slippery terms can be stabilized to determinate meanings, critical exegesis predicated on the same old spheres still regularly issues from university presses, quite as if this framework were set in stone instead of constituting a verbal trope for ordering messy realities, quite as if the warnings about mistaking official prescriptions for past behaviors and rhetorics that social historians have issued for two decades had never existed.

Jay Mechling, for example, interrogated any causal connection between "official advice and actual practice" in 1975, pointing out that female readers most exposed to such advice were least likely to follow it, that actual behavior and women's perceptions of their behavior demonstrated striking disparities.[8] As a social historian searching for evidentiary solidity, Mechling is concerned about taking normative advice for scientific truth. A feminist critic and literary historian must be more intrigued by the female respondents' skillful manipulations of official rhetoric for their own purposes in his samplings. As William Hazlitt observed to James Northcote of prescription in general: "Those doctrines are *established* which need propping up, as men place beams against falling houses. It does not require an act of parliament to persuade mathematicians to agree with Euclid, or painters to admire Raphael." [9] Far from taking official spherist ideologies of masculine "public" manhood and femininized "private" ladydom as handy cribs for literary criticism, we might better, so the social historians say, "make problematic the very *existence*" of behavioral manuals and predictably gendered rhetorics. [10]

For the most part, we still do not. Despite the recent efflorescence of academic interest in Habermas's bourgeois public sphere and its possible implications for female authorship in late Enlightenment and Romantic literary history, many critics still prefer their literary subjects constrained and confined, mad, bad, or even dead. For an example of the pervasive binarism of public and private spheres in relation to Mary Shelley, we might consider Johanna M. Smith's " 'Cooped Up': Feminine Domesticity in *Frankenstein*." Billed as "A Feminist Perspective on *Frankenstein*" in Smith's 1992 teaching text, a volume in the Bedford series of Case Studies in Contemporary Criticism, Smith's essay will surely generate numerous student clones. If she editorially argues for a true genealogy of *Frankenstein* criticism as an example of how critical histories and authors are continually constructed and reconstructed, Smith nevertheless reproduces in her own contribution the staid spherist framework that inevitably inscribes her text's author as somebody's daughter, somebody's wife — not to mention a one-book writer. Paralyzingly insecure about her potential for public authorship, Smith's fearful subject, the victim of an "ideology of dependent femininity" who is thus "*conditioned* to think she needed a man's help" to brave the literary marketplace, is victimized by a conjugal collaboration that is tantamount to "a kind of rape." Meek and vulnerable, the aspiring author as transparent register of "debilitating femininity" just like her tale's "oppressively feminine" women, Mary Shelley needs her husband's (and before him, her father's) help to "straddle the line between public and private," thus rendering complementary the enculturated "gender difference between feminine passivity and masculine activity." [11]

Although Smith duly notes *Frankenstein*'s ubiquitous presence in popular culture, she does not notice one striking manifestation thereof: the tale's frequent inclusion in course syllabi for young adults, a story not only taught in high schools and universities but actively sought out by apprentice readers on their own. [12] After all, not many adolescents — and Mary Godwin was but sixteen when she ran away from home — write a tale that enduringly mesmerizes their cohorts, the coming-of-age audience. Indeed, what even younger child doesn't know *Frankenstein,* even if she or he confuses the maker and the monster (not much of a slip, in light of the fact that the general public is similarly inclined and academics more learnedly debate just which character *is* the monster — and on what grounds).[13] From this perspective, the authoress of *Frankenstein* might be read not as daddy's girl, mamma's unknowing murderess and insufficiently feminist daughter, or the great canonical poet's wife, but as a shocking and shockingly successful teenage author, a girl who makes a name for herself in the history of popular culture not by daydreaming pubescent pap, vapid love stories like today's *Sweet Valley High* series, but by grappling with tough issues and taking as her topic the bad boy, the social rebel.

Rather than the anxious lady writer or the serious Romantic stamped with the academic seal of approval (witness the many 1997 conferences commemorating her birth), Mary Wollstonecraft Godwin Shelley might be figured as an early nineteenth-century S. E. Hinton, the girl who made herself famous in young adult literature with *The Outsiders* (1967) and other gritty novels of marginal guys and murderous gang clashes, of rumbles, knives, and guilt. Written when she was a junior in high school and published two years later, with initials in place of "Susan Eloise," Hinton's first-person apprentice novel got right inside Ponyboy and uncompromisingly faced the outcast loner's tough choices. No one could believe that so young and supposedly sheltered a woman could write so convincingly and philosophically about sensitive male protagonists and their often violent struggles between reality and idealism. Nor did Hinton stop: decades later, like Mary Shelley, she is still going strong, unrepentantly tackling topics that many women writers would not touch and successfully doing so in an impressive series of social-problem novels.[14] Adolescent writers who successfully write for adolescents are almost as rare as child authors — and surely none has had so huge and continuing an impact or seemed less "cooped up" in their far-flung appeal and ongoing reincarnations as *Frankenstein*'s creator.[15]

If the young author's bold first book quickly outpaced Percy Shelley's poems to date, rendering her the early public success that he was not, the later author, so Mary Poovey and similarly distinguished critics have argued, stages a "retreat from unorthodoxy," one she believes is "evident even in the supposedly unorthodox 1818 *Frankenstein.*" In Mary Shelley's career, Poovey's influential chapters suggest, the proper private lady equals the authorial schizophrenic: "the differences between her first novels and her last three are so marked that the seven novels could almost have been written by two different persons. Shelley's contemporaries noted this . . . [and] recorded their conviction that she was, in some sense, simply not what she seemed to be." Notable among them is Edward John Trelawny, complaining to Claire Claremont in the 1870s that "Mary was the most conventional slave I have ever met . . . she was devoid of imagination and Poetry . . . she did not understand or appreciate" P. B. Shelley. Poovey is quoting from Elizabeth Nitchie's 1953 study, *Mary Shelley: Author of "Frankenstein,"* but Poovey does not cite what Nitchie had to say even then about Trelawny's spitefully personalized cavils as a serious misrepresentation of an important and undervalued woman writer's public career.[16] Forty years ago, Nitchie censured "mere identity-hunting" and urged more scholarly attention to Mary Shelley's contradictions. Yet the Nitchie who disparages equating a text and the real woman on one page unequivocally pronounces that "Mathilda is certainly Mary herself" on another.[17]

From the beginning of her career, indeed, the writing woman has posed a problem in somehow being "not what she seemed to be." If the household manager can (quite erroneously, it now seems) be thought of as confined within, the author is, by virtue of writing, transgressively outside — going public with the private.[18] And if she is a Romantic author, as Mary Wollstonecraft Godwin Shelley is conventionally defined, that private material intended for publication is often very private indeed, however decorously disguised as somebody else's "tragic history" replete with "sacred horror" and "mystic terrors."[19]

It is true that William Godwin, himself notorious for publicly exposing his dead wife's traumas and amours, balked at a daughter's tale about paternal incest as a bit much for public consumption, even if said fiction was intended to line his always empty pockets, even if the physical deed was not actually committed.[20] But the author herself apparently meant to publish her story — and went to considerable trouble to retrieve her manuscript from her foot-dragging father. Already, within this essay, within this one paragraph, multiple meanings of *public* and *private* circulate confusingly. And perhaps lewdly: only imagine what the Reverend Richard Polwhele would make of *Matilda* — bold girls who "point the prostitution of a plant" and "dissect its organ of unhallow'd lust" or even Amazonian Wollstonecraft's taking the breeches part would not hold a candle to the bad dad who wants his daughter's body, especially when the daughter herself planned to tell the world of a father approaching his child's "sacred" chamber like "an unlaid ghost" who "find[s] no quiet from the burning hell that consumed his heart," of a very young first-person narrator whose desperate pursuit of that fleeing parent ends in the discovery of "something stiff and straight" covered on a cottage bed and in her own fixation on an emulative suicide, driven by the "withering fear that I was in truth a marked creature, a pariah, only fit for death" (205, 239).[21] Mathilda's self-dramatizing (and physically virginal) despair outdoes Ovid's sexually knowing (and hugely pregnant) Myrrha, the guilty seductress of her father turned into a weeping tree when the gods bless her petition for escape.[22]

Why Shelley's adolescent protagonist feels so guilty and how her tale should be read are currently hotly contested and certain to become more so now that both versions are available in the 1996 annotated edition. But Godwin's worries over a voyeuristic public's almost certain spectacularization of a tale whose subject he thought "disgusting and detestable" are not negligible, and his incongruous and belated efforts to keep the lid on family scandals (such as the 1816 suicide of Wollstonecraft's natural daughter Fanny) may be matched by numerous passages in his daughter's own letters: she who can be read as shrinking proper lady can also be situated as shrewd public author, assessing the apposite time and format for publishing the private.[23] Paradoxically, perhaps Mary Shelley herself— with her eloquent espousal of self-reference in art, what she calls in the essay "Giovanni Villani" the "habit of self-analysation and display," and her own production of "works where the individual feeling of the author embues the whole subject with a peculiar hue," taking the "human heart as an undiscovered country"—might be held responsible for the determinedly personal readings of her work, with Matilda fast becoming the competitor of Frankenstein as overdetermined family romance (331).[24]

Paradoxically, too, as this essay argues and briefly exemplifies, perhaps the only way out of this personalist thematization is to delve further into the private: to move Mary Shelley's letters from behind-the-scenes snippets to public context and to scrutinize very carefully unnuanced identifications of character and creator (as in Nitchie's "Mathilda is certainly Mary herself") and untenable assumptions about authorship that rely more on familial dynamics than on the larger literary and cultural matrices. Just like us, Mary Shelley could know her mother solely through the maternal printed words and the paternal widower's subjective (and intertextually allusive) accounts. Ironically, although I can do no more than gesture toward these conclusions here, reconsidering Mary Shelley as the public *literary* daughter of two major writers, alluding to and rewriting the works of those parents (who were themselves heirs of multiple literary genealogies), can help us resituate not only one female author, redefine not only the vexed traditional assumptions about gendered citizenship and active political agency, but may also guide us in rethinking our conceptualizations of "the Enlightenment" and "Romanticism" and of what constitutes generic categories like "fiction" and "history" as well. Only when we move as deeply into the writer's private sphere as carefully annotated editions make possible will we be able to make viable larger pronouncements about female authorship and the dynamics of the literary public sphere.[25]

If, as Frederick L. Jones, editor of the now superseded 1944 edition of Mary Shelley's letters once noted, "it is as the wife of Shelley that she excites our interest and arouses our desire to know as much about her as we can," that Romantic desire to know the inside story seems to be turning toward another chapter, one enduringly relevant for more women writers than this essay's subject (xxix; quoted in *MWSL* 1:xi). There is, it seems, no escape for daddy's girl, still the definitive construct within which we read women writers, whether figuratively, as in the classic formulation of Sandra M. Gilbert and Susan Gubar's literary patriarchs and the madwomen in the attic whom they engender, or literally, as in the cases of Hannah More, Frances Burney, Maria Edgeworth, Sydney Owenson (Lady Morgan), Elizabeth Barrett Browning, Anne Thackeray Ritchie, Virginia Woolf, and of course Mary Wollstonecraft Godwin Shelley.[26] There is, apparently, no escape for *Frankenstein*'s mother either. Despite the huge body of meticulously edited letters and journals, despite the increasing focus on other writings (as in teaching texts of *Matilda, Valperga, The Last Man,* and *Lodore*), readers that reprint alternative works, and the recent critical anthology pointedly entitled *The Other Mary Shelley: Beyond Frankenstein*), Mary Wollstonecraft's and William Godwin's daughter and Percy Bysshe Shelley's wife cannot seem to escape her "hideous progeny" or her titillating family history.[27]

Less distant from the anti-Jacobin voyeurs transfixed by what Robert Southey called Godwin's "stripping his dead wife naked" in his 1798 exhibition of her sexual liaisons and suicide attempts than we choose to think, modern literary critics still hyperventilate over the intellectual incest and erotics of authorship embodied in the Godwin and Shelley households.[28]

If our discourse is different from the generous indignation of Southey or the lip-smacking righteousness of Richard Polwhele and the reactionary press, we also fixate on primal scenes, mortified female flesh, matricide, and, in several recent essays and Katherine Hill-Miller's 1995 book, incest and patricide. Gender, as we have all long known, is an essential category of literary and historical analysis, but in the case of the Godwins and Shelleys, nothing sells like down-and-dirty sex. Despite the merits of Hill-Miller's *"My Hideous Progeny": Mary Shelley, William Godwin, and the Father-Daughter Relationship,* the reader occasionally longs for attention to the feminist, radical, and marketplace politics that also inform and environ Mary Shelley's writings. Whatever their fixations, literary daughters are not wholly explicable in paternal terms; there is always an excess in the daughters' narratives.[29] Every woman writer is somebody's daughter, but that's not all she is, nor is daughterhood a unitary experience.

Frankenstein, it would seem, has already been probed from every conceivable (pun intended) familial angle, with mothers, fathers, husbands, and children variously (and sometimes contradictorily) aligned with the significant others of Mary Shelley's life. Even before the pathbreaking 1979 anthology *The Endurance of Frankenstein,* which reprinted Ellen Moers's "Female Gothic" and includes U. C. Knoepflmacher's still-provocative "Thoughts on the Aggression of Daughters," the family romances embedded in Shelley's first-born novel already had set the terms for analytic discussion. It is difficult for most critics to give fair play to the whole family, and, like Pamela Clemit's recent overview of *The Godwinian Novel,* Hill-Miller's study emphasizes the surviving father over the dead mother. Maggie Kilgour's 1995 *The Rise of the Gothic Novel* somewhat atypically aligns the tales of father, mother, *and* daughter, but her generic genealogy is not Hill-Miller's more literal genealogical aim.[30] Given the murderous themes she finds in the fiction, Hill-Miller's introduction sets out the father-daughter dynamic with commendable clarity and compassion. Although Godwin's emotional awkwardness is never shirked, Hill-Miller gives the ambitious father the credit he deserves for his daughter's admirably developed intellect. Her portrayal is moving, tragic, and accessibly written, a useful overview for students as well as Romanticists who want to move beyond *Frankenstein.* It is thoughtful on the relationship of the father's fictions to those of the daughter, as well as on the more strictly biographical nexus. It is also notably free of psychoanalytic jargon and deftly weaves the analysis with plot summary so that even readers unfamiliar with some of the novels can follow the argument.[31] The discursive footnotes provide a useful guide to studies of Shelley's fiction, although, like the creature, the criticism runs faster than any pursuing bibliography.

Hill-Miller has written well on other literary fathers and daughters (she is especially good on Thackeray and Ritchie), and, given her psychological preoccupations, she capably and tastefully handles Shelley's longer tales and integrates those she considers into a coherent and often persuasive explanatory framework.[32] Hers is a narrative about the intricate and repetitive literary relations produced by Shelley's childhood veneration of Godwin as her "God"; despite its title, however, this is not a study of Mary Shelley's whole literary output in conjunction to her celebrated father.[33] Instead, Hill-Miller opens with "The Biography of a Relationship" between the two and then closely analyzes *Frankenstein, Matilda, Lodore,* and *Falkner.* She occasionally mentions other work, but within this conceptualization of Shelley's authorship, Daddy matters most; when he dies or his progeny kills him off, Mary Shelley no longer needs fiction. Rather than focalizing *Frankenstein,* as is usually the case in Mary Shelley studies, Hill-Miller makes *Matilda* her primal text. Although she manages to find new familial resonances in the most-worked-over of Shelley's family fictions (Hill-Miller suggests that Frankenstein's creature's repulsive "straight black lips" align him with the "livid" lips of his creator's dream about Elizabeth and thus with incestuous desire, the lips being both dead and labial), the most interesting of her chapters is that on *Matilda,* surely one of the oddest gifts a daughter ever bestowed on a needy parent (65). Even the eternally bankrupt Godwin would not pay off his debts with that shocking story of paternal passion, and the author found herself debarred from her own manuscript. If *Frankenstein,* the endlessly adaptable Swiss-army knife of Romantic fictions, can be put to almost any use in addition to the familiarities of the psychoanalyzed household,[34] *Matilda*'s claustrophobic sexuality still retains the power to stun — and to baffle interpretations that would relate the story to its literary lineages or to Mary Shelley's reformist politics.

The novella, Hill-Miller urges, illuminates not only Mary Shelley's fiction but also the mythologies of Western culture. When we see more clearly what Mary Shelley is up to in loving, hating, and symbolically murdering her father, we are also understanding what it means to be daughters within a broader context. Like others who have tackled *Matilda,* Hill-Miller draws from current work on incest that understands the involvement (whether physical or merely psychic) not as aberrant but integral to the father-daughter relationship.[35] Mary Shelley's romances are thus important for their message about the daughter's destiny in patriarchal society and their exemplification of the literary strategies through which one daughter wrote herself free of her fixations. The impressive roster of fiction discussed here matters because it sensitively explores tensions inherent to the daughter's ambiguous positioning in the family romance we take for granted in Western culture. Resentful at the disappointing legacy her much-adored father allots her, Mary Shelley uses her first two novels to work through intersecting themes of maternity and incest. Daughters and their surrogates in *Frankenstein* and *Matilda* are doomed by guilty paternal attraction, compelled to see themselves as filthy and sinful matter, and linked in a dance of death with the father figure. In the last two fictions, in contrast, Mary Shelley deploys her favored themes of maternity and incest to liberatory effect. While still demonstrating the incestuous currents that shape the father-daughter relationship, *Lodore* and *Falkner* nevertheless allow the daughter to move beyond the father's orbit, into the "liberating but equivocal power" of motherhood.[36]

Thus the figure of the monstrous daughter vanishes from the later tales, having become instead a daughter at once protecting and punitive, a latent feminist who is as much her mother's child as daddy's girl. Selected for the dust jackets of both Anne K. Mellor's and Emily W. Sunstein's studies of Shelley, as well as the cover of the 1997 *Keats-Shelley Review*, Richard Rothwell's familiar 1840 painting (now in the National Portrait Gallery) eerily reproduces William Godwin's face in his daughter's feminine features: in material as well as textual form, Mary Wollstonecraft's daughter is also (although not only) daddy's girl. One might have thought that Hill-Miller's study would remain the definitive investigation of Mary Shelley's father-daughter fictions, but, given the fascinations of the family's multiple guilty sexualities, *Matilda* will no doubt prove as fertile as *Frankenstein*. Caroline Gonda's *Reading Daughters' Fictions 1709–1834: Novels and Society from Manley to Edgeworth* interprets Shelley through it; Terence Harpold explicates *Matilda* as a "profoundly autobiographical" seduction fantasy complexly imbricated in life circumstances; Tilottama Rajan analyzes *Matilda*'s intertextuality as a replay of the mother's work as well as a quasifictionalization of the daughter's desires and revenges, an "abjected" narrative too close to life to qualify as art, a weird work that cannot be fully appreciated—or indeed read—without reference to authorial biography;

Margaret Davenport Garrett argues that Shelley's writing and rewriting of the incest myth mirrors not only authorial experience but also Everywoman's problem of love "when it takes place in a cultural environment in which the woman thinks of herself as morally inferior and knows that society expects her to be protected by a male."[37]

One occasionally wonders if it is Mary Shelley who is sexually fixated or academic Romanticism. No wonder "Valerius: The Reanimated Roman" sardonically observes that "in modern times, domestic circumstances appear to be that part of a man's history most worth enquiring into."[38] Perhaps signifying a paradigm shift in *Matilda* criticism, Charleen E. Bunnell argues for a split between the deluded heroine, a solipsistic tragic dramatist, and the author, who constructs *Matilda*'s egotistic revelations in a deliberately hyperbolic style. Bunnell makes a strong case for a theatricalized reading, a girl steeped in sensibility gone bad, "a debilitating subjectivity devoid of reason and altruism."[39] She makes much of the daughter's delusionary concept of her life as a literary construct and notices that the equally egocentric father indulged the proverbial young girl's taste for novels until he was cured by the superior mother, Diana. Curiously, however, she never connects Shelley's irresponsible parent with the late eighteenth-century English and early Romantic French heroes of feeling whose male maladies—impotence as disguised power—have been ably diagnosed by Claudia L. Johnson and Margaret Waller.[40] Moreover, Bunnell never addresses the question of the reader, left guideless when the original frame, which "placed" the heroine's experience within a learning context and provided a narrator other than Mathilda herself as well as the instructive spirit Fantasia and the philosopher Diotima, was set aside. Because the tale never went public in Shelley's lifetime, no one can say definitively what the nineteenth-century audience would have read had "Papa" actually published and profited from his absent daughter's manuscript, as was the case with *Valperga*.[41] Surely, however, those readers would have been conditioned to move beyond our set of incestuous relations (Romanticists commenting on one another) to the sociocultural and political import of the incest motif.

Like the even more neglected Enlightenment Oriental-tale lineage of *Matilda,* the eighteenth-century Gothic tradition gets brief mention in recent writing, but earlier audiences most likely would have noticed the public (and political) resonance of incest instead of idealizing it as "Romantic Symbol," as in one classic essay, or, as Percy Bysshe Shelley puts it, "like many other in*correct* things a very poetical circumstance." After all, the late eighteenth century's imagined illicit familial carnality both influenced and reflected the period's personal and political concerns, operating metaphorically for perceived or threatened catastrophic social and state conditions. Just like *Frankenstein,* the incest motif purveys serious social commentary as well as cheap thrills and private family romances.[42]

Certainly there are many continuities between private lives and public texts, but, paradoxically, as private letters attest, these may be more ambiguous and crafty than we are accustomed to think. Consider for example a self-description that has been noted before (and usually excerpted). It is worth reading as a whole precisely because it so richly demonstrates the nuances and interplay between public and private that it is so easy to elide in citing snippets for an argument. It is Mary Shelley's self-depiction in response to Edward John Trelawny's 1829 request for anecdotes toward a projected life of her dead husband:

> I have often thought—often done more than think on the subject There is nothing I shrink from more fearfully than publicity—I have too much of it—& what is worse I am forced by my hard situation to meet it in a thousand ways—Could you write my husband's life, without naming me it were something—but even then I should be terrified at the rouzing the slumbering voice of the public—each critique, each mention of your work, might drag me forward—Nor indeed is it possible to write Shelley's life in that way. . . . You know me—or you do not, in which case I will tell you what I am—a silly goose—who far from wishing to stand forward to assert myself in any way, now than [sic] I am alone in the world, have but the desire to wrap night and the obscurity of insignificance around me. This is weakness—but I cannot help it—to be in print—the subject of *men's* observations—of the bitter hard world's commentaries, to be attacked or defended!—this ill becomes one who knows how little she possesses worthy to attract attention—and whose chief merit—if it be one—is a love of that privacy which no woman can emerge from without regret—Shelley's life must be written—I hope one day to do it myself, but it must not be published now—There are too many concerned to speak against him—it is still too sore a subject— Your tribute of praise, in a way that cannot do harm, can be introduced into your own life—But remember, I pray for omission—for it is not that you will not be too kind too eager to do me more than justice—But I only seek to be forgotten. (*MWSL* 2:72)

And again on July 27, 1829, she recurs to the same themes:

> Your recollections of our Lost One will be precious as a record of his Merit—but I am averse to having those mingled with a history which will be the subject of cavill. I hope one day to write his Life myself— not to be published in my lifetime or even my childs. Meanwhile we neither desire the pity nor justice of the few attended as they would be by the barking and railing of his enemies and the misjudgement of the multitude. (*MWSL* 2:82–83)

Bennett's notes on this passage situate it, as it must be read, within the public context. The full text here, with its deftly tailored effacement for the intended reader and its buried ambition to do a life herself, might be usefully compared with the messy and much more revealing text of the 1838 journal entry Mary Poovey cites from Jones's edition as a "defense of [Shelley's] refusal to speak out for liberal political causes." [43] In the long sequence of entries (*MWSJ* 2:552 ff.), complete with annotations, from the Feldman and Scott-Kilvert edition, the oscillations and nuances provide a very different feel from the cleaned-up text that Jones produced, which enables Poovey's deprecatory reading. Perhaps it is only when the private is fully public that it makes the female author make sense, not just as a daughter or a wife but as a writer imbricated within the sociopolitical and literary cultures of her time as well as within her family of nativity.

12 : Poetry as Souvenir

Mary Shelley in the Annuals

$\mathcal{J}$UDITH $\mathcal{P}$ASCOE

In 1828, Charles Heath set out with Frederick Mansel Reynolds on a collecting tour of northern England and Scotland, stopping in the Lake Dis-
trict and Edinburgh to add specimens to his collection. The geographic
sweep of Heath's pursuit conjures up a tourist's enterprise, the modern-
day traveler's gathering of tea towels from vacation spots, but Heath's
pursuit centered on the gathering of poets for his fledgling annual, the
Keepsake. Although he was seeking poems from individuals with serious
literary aspirations, for example, Sir Walter Scott, William Wordsworth,
and Robert Southey, Heath astutely appealed to these writers' pocket-
books. Scott was offered £800 to edit the *Keepsake* and another £400 to
contribute 70 to 100 pages of text; Southey reported being offered fifty
guineas for "anything which I would supply him [Heath]."[1] A year earlier,
William Harrison Ainsworth, the first editor of Heath's *Keepsake* project,
had found fault with the annual's title, claiming it "savour[ed] of a gift
from Tunbridge Wells."[2] Ainsworth's comment, with its allusion to Tunbridge Wells's status as a popular tourist spot and royal watering hole,
furthers the association of poem with souvenir implicit in Heath's mode
of collecting.

The word *souvenir* makes its first recorded appearance in English in
1775, when Horace Walpole wrote obsequiously to a female friend, "You
have always been so good to me, Madam, and I am so grateful that if my
souvenirs were marked with cups, there would be many more than mile
stones from hence to Ampthill" (*OED*). Walpole uses the word in its sense
as "a remembrance, a memory," but in just a few years (if not sooner), the
word would be used in the more material sense in which we know it today,

as "something (usually a small article of some value bestowed as a gift) which reminds one of some person, place or event" (*OED*). Maria Edgeworth, in 1803, attributes to a character the desire to "offer souvenirs to her English friends." The word's French origin (*subvenire*—"to come into the mind") recalls the more ephemeral, first definition of the word ("a memory"), but by the time the commonplace books I discuss here were being compiled, the word had taken on the equivocality inherent in a material reminder of a past experience or state of mind. The word *keepsake* also has its origins in the Romantic period; 1790 and 1794 passages from Frances Burney and Ann Radcliffe are listed by the compilers of the *Oxford English Dictionary* as the earliest citings of this word.

I want to focus here on what I call a souvenir ethos that dominates the pages of both private albums or commonplace books and the commercial annuals that evolved from these personal anthologies. This souvenir ethos, most fully articulated in the annuals, is intricately caught up in their editors' efforts to downplay the frankly commercial nature of their undertakings.[3] I begin by summarizing briefly my conclusions regarding the annuals before focusing on Mary Shelley's contributions to the 1831 *Keepsake* and the way in which the memorialization of P. B. Shelley is enlisted in the service of the annuals' nostalgic sensibility.[4]

Two important features of the private albums anticipate the commercially produced annuals: the way poems find their ways into albums and the type of poem preferred by album compilers. The commonplace book inscriber plucks a particular poem from the vast array of poems available to her in a variety of venues—newspapers, literary journals, published volumes—and places her own mark on it through (1) her act of selection, (2) the act of inscribing it in her own handwriting, and (3) the writing of her own name beside that of the author. The album owner who becomes the eventual reader of this poem experiences the poem not primarily as a representation of a particular poet but rather as an embodiment of the aesthetic taste or thematic interests of her friend (or of the friend's projection of the gift recipient's literary preferences). The new meaning the poem takes on as part of a "private" compilation completes the poem's trajectory from the realm of public discourse to the realm of personal feeling. Read by the targeted single reader (the album's owner), the poem is a reflection of its inscriber. But read by this reader as part of an anthology devoted to poems judged to please her, the poem becomes a mark of a particular moment in its owner's life and the particular nexus of relationships that sustained her at this point in time. The poem thus makes possible a narrative of its possessor, not of itself.[5]

Although the standard fare of the albums does include such frivolous diversions as charades and enigmas, popular word games and riddles, they almost all share a preoccupation with death that is materialized in the albums in a number of different guises. There are poems about people who have died, poems whose commonplace book status is attributable to the fact that they were written by someone who has since died, poems about dead infants, and, in the ultimate amplification of this mortality motif, poems about dead infant twins. The poems gathered in commonplace books organize themselves around loss rather than literary reputation; they serve as tokens of sorrow rather than marks of artistic genius. The annuals and gift books strove to capitalize upon this mourning aspect of private collections, appropriating the keepsake aesthetic that was characteristic of private albums.

The notion of the poem as souvenir can be juxtaposed with a Romantic concern for the authenticity and originality of poetic endeavor, evidenced most notably by Wordsworth's erasure of poetic lineage in his description of the imagination as an "unfathered vapour" in book six of *The Prelude*. Susan Stewart characterizes the souvenir as "reaching only 'behind,' spiraling in a continually inward movement rather than outward toward the future." In Stewart's analysis, "the souvenir displaces the point of authenticity as it itself becomes the point of origin for narratives."[6] The keepsake or souvenir recalls a lost love or now distanced experience, one that can never be recovered. The material reminder of some once-visited place or emotional attachment replaces one history (the experience of that place or love) with another (the experience of the souvenir, handled and regarded through the passage of the years). The word *keepsake,* the title of the annual to which William Wordsworth and Mary Shelley, among other illustrious Romantic era writers, contributed, recalls the souvenir's palliative or aggravating capacity (does it soften the loss or serve as a constant reminder of loss?) quite deliberately and, in so doing, participates in the cultural appropriation of the poem as commemorative object.

A list of the titles assigned to annuals and gift books demonstrates their publishers' desire to position the books as gifts of friendship. Titles such as *Forget-me-not, Friendship's Offering, Pledge of Friendship, Remembrance, Literary Souvenir,* and *Anniversary* make the volumes markers of the enduring power of affectionate relationships. Bradford Allen Booth refers to titles like *Remember Me, May You Like It, The Nosegay,* and *Love's Offering* as evidence that these productions "could have interested only the most mawkishly sentimental and exotically romantic," but the proliferation of gift books with such titles suggests a broad audience of mawkish consumers.[7] Although William Harrison Ainsworth objected to the *Keepsake*'s title as smacking too much of touristic experience, the preface to the first volume of the annual carried out a spirited defense of the name: "It is a good English word; cordial, unpremeditated, concise; extremely to the purpose; and, though plain, implies a value. It also sets us reflecting on keepsakes in general, and on the givers of them; and these are pleasant thoughts."[8] The exact terms of this defense are revealing for the way they anticipate the criticism that would get heaped on the annuals as an excessively ornate and theatrically emotive genre. Anticipating these charges of foreignness and femininity, the preface writer emphasizes Englishness, frank sincerity, and plainness. A keepsake, he continues, "implies something very intimate and cordial," something that is "above . . . ceremonious niceties."[9]

Arjun Appadurai's discussion of gifts in his introduction to *The Social Life of Things* helps to explain the annuals' flagging of their gift status. As Appadurai reminds us, gifts are associated with reciprocity, sociability, and spontaneity; they are starkly opposed to "the profit-oriented, self-centered, and calculated spirit that fires circulation and commodities." Gifts "link things to persons" and "embed the flow of things in the flow of social relations." In contrast, commodities are typically held to "represent the drive of goods for one another."[10] Depending on title and contents to intimate a book's gift status, the annual editors worked to situate these volumes in the private space of the home and the intimate realm of sororal affection rather than in the public market for luxury goods. Contemporary commentators on the gift books advanced this effort to domesticate the annuals by describing them as furniture for the most intimate private spaces. An 1829 advertisement for the *Amulet* excerpts this comment from *Blackwood's Edinburgh Magazine:* " 'The Amulet' may lie on the couch of the room where friends meet in health and cheerfulness, or below the pillow of the room where sickness lies afar from sorrow, and the patient feels that no medicine is better for the weakness of the body than that which soothes and tranquillizes the soul."[11] The *Amulet,* situated on the couch or below the pillow, becomes a necessary accouterment of affectionate relationships. The purchaser of the annual, according to this promotional piece, does not experience it in the solitude we associate with scholarship or connoisseurship but rather in the midst of heartfelt associations.

A title like the *Keepsake,* as well as gesturing toward such associations, also underscores the need for preservation, further removing the volumes from the realm of commodity exchange. Frederick Winthrop Faxon, in his survey of literary annuals and gift books, quotes an 1893 *Atlantic Monthly* commentator who recalls this function of the annuals: "These books were not to be resold; a last year's Annual was not to be thought of as a present however attractive in itself. Its dates betrayed it. They were gifts, and often treasured up as the faded rose and the ivory Malbone miniature of her bridal days are treasured in the matron's cabinet, because they were haunted with the secret and subtle fragrance of bygone memories."[12] This passage implies that the annuals were lacking in resale value because any value they possessed resided in their souvenir status, their association with past moments and memories unique to the possessor. It also, however, allies the books, which were, of course, commercially produced, to more idiosyncratic tokens of affection, such as the faded rose preserved in a "matron's cabinet."

Commodification would seem to homogenize value and might be set in opposition to a discriminating culture that ensures some things remain unambiguously singular (for instance, a painting by Picasso). But Igor Kopytoff recognizes the symbiotic vacillation between singularization and commodification as part of what he calls the cultural biographies of things. The singularity of a work of art is "confirmed . . . by intermittent forays into the commodity sphere, quickly followed by reentries into the closed sphere of singular art."[13] The annuals' self-representation as cherished or collectible items relies on a similar strategy of singularization.

The annual editors used steel-plate engravings, featured prominently in nearly every advertisement or review of these volumes, to enhance their products' claim to uniqueness. Southey's derogatory reference to the gift books as "picture-books for grown children" assumes the reader will find in less frivolous literary offerings the preeminence of text over picture or, at least, a clear distinction between text and illustration.[14] But Romantic era poets traded heavily in illustrations of themselves, counting on particular portraits to shape public perception and increase the audience for their poems. Wordsworth cooperated with a series of portrait painters who immortalized his figure in poses of rural solitude. *Wordsworth on Helvellyn,* the solitary poet seeking his inspiration in nature, supplanted a more sociable Wordsworth, who dictated poems to family members.[15] Richard Holmes notes the way Byron's publisher saw to it that the engraved versions of his portraits, used on the frontispieces to editions of his poetry, were "improved" to satisfy popular expectations. Holmes writes, "In the second version of Westall's 1813 portrait, Byron's eyes were raised apocalyptically to heaven, his hair quiffed and tinted, his brow blanched, his throat swollen with passion, and even his decorative collarpin altered from a gentleman's cameo to a large, glassy lover's keepsake."[16]

That ostentatious lover's keepsake marks the extent to which the souvenir ethos that dominates gift book editing is present as well in the marketing of volumes of poetry that are credited with greater aesthetic value than the annuals. The gift books and annuals share a souvenir impulse not only with the commonplace books that predated them but also with the offerings of poets like Byron and P. B. Shelley. As Mary Shelley's contributions to the *Keepsake* effectively demonstrate, annual aesthetics and Romantic aesthetics are entangled to such an extent that it is impossible to discern where one leaves off and the other begins.

Two recent studies of Mary Shelley's work help to coalesce the issues at stake in a discussion of her contributions to the *Keepsake*. Sonia Hofkosh sees Mary Shelley's participation in the annuals as a disfiguring process, citing the length restraints on her stories and the economic necessity of her employment as evidence for a view of the stories as enactments of disempowerment. She calls Mary Shelley a "proficient cosmetologist, practiced as a writer of abbreviated tales that appeal especially to 'feminine readers' " of gift books "famous for their lavish formats and expensive, original engravings."[17] Hofkosh reinscribes the conventional view of the gift books as showy female commodities undeserving of the contributions of a serious artist like Mary Shelley.

Writing on *Frankenstein,* Judith Pike distances Mary Shelley from the sentimentalization of death, which is an essential aspect not only of the gift books but also of early nineteenth-century culture at large. Pike claims that Mary Shelley debunks the "conventionalized portrayal of death and the cult of mourning by presenting the reader with the terror of the unsublimated dead body."[18] While Pike does not make specific reference to the gift books or annuals, the fetishization of the dead body which she claims Mary Shelley counters in her most famous novel was a constitutive feature of the annuals in which she published short stories and poems. Both Pike and Hofkosh situate Mary Shelley at a distance from the more superficial or corporeal preoccupations of her culture, preoccupations upon which the annuals overtly capitalize.

Mary Shelley's letters suggest that she had a far less tortured relationship to the annuals than these critics might assume. She wrote in 1835 to Maria Gisborne in praise of a story she had received from her husband and pondered how it might procure the publication it deserved — in an annual:

> I am anxious to thank S.G. [Signor Giovanni, John Gisborne] for the pleasure I have received from his tale of Italy a tale of all Italy — breathing of the land I love — the descriptions are beautiful — & he has shed a great charm round the concentrated & undemonstrative person of his gentle heroine. . . . It is difficult however to judge how to procure for it the publication it deserves. I have no personal acquaintance with the Editors of any of the Annuals — I had with that of the Keepsake — but that is now in Mrs Norton's hands — & she has not asked me to write — so I know nothing about it. (*MWSL* 2:245)

Mary Shelley does fret about the length constraints the annuals placed on her work. She notes, "When I write for them, I am worried to death to make my things shorter & shorter — till I fancy people think ideas can be conveyed by intuition — and that it is a superstition to consider words necessary for their expression" (*MWSL* 2:245). But the fact that she enthuses about Gisborne's story and then refers to the annuals as suitable sites of publication for it suggests that she had no automatic or philosophical objection to the aesthetic cultivated by these volumes.

Mary Shelley's letters to the editor of the *Keepsake* concenter most often on the issue of payment; clearly publication in these volumes held foremost importance for the opportunity it provided of earning money. She wrote Frederick Mansel Reynolds in December of 1832, concerned that Heath was withholding payment for one of her stories he had in hand until he actually published it: "I do not see why he should be so cross — I had no idea of an objection & and have counted on it — or I should not be so troublesome — and he need not be so stingy — it is very unamiable" (*MWSL* 2:178). In the same month, the exact terms of her financial distress are laid out in a letter to John Gregson, whom she petitions to speak on her behalf to her father-in-law, Sir Timothy Shelley. After describing her urgent need for more money to cover little Percy's school bills, Mary Shelley writes: "It is impossible to say how excessively anxious I feel. To know that there is a debt I am unable to pay, is very painful, but the idea of any injury arising to Percy in the course of his education, is ten times worse" (*MWSL* 2:178).

We should acknowledge Mary Shelley's pressing financial motivation for publishing in the *Keepsake* without equating that need with aesthetic indifference. Mary Shelley clearly did not limit her annual publications to the sweepings of her desk but rather published work there that she counted as her very best. In a letter Betty Bennett dated to 1835, Mary Shelley copies her poem published in the 1831 *Keepsake* for Maria Gisborne, calling it "the best thing [she] ever wrote." Intended to be set to music, "The Dirge," as the poem is titled, is a lyrical lament for the death of P. B. Shelley which incorporates details of his demise: a "gallant bark," a storm at sea, an ocean grave. She writes, in the second of the poem's three verses:

> Thou liest upon the shore, Love,
> Beside the knelling surge;
> But sea-nymphs ever more, Love,
> Shall sadly chaunt thy dirge.
>
> O come, O come — O Come!
> Ye spirits of the deep!
> While near his sea-weed pillow
> My lonely watch I keep.
> (*MWSL* 2:247)

The poem trades on the facts of P. B. Shelley's sensationalized death, as Mary Shelley immerses herself (and her reader) in aestheticized sorrow. In the same letter to Maria Gisborne, she wrote: "I can never write verses except under the influence of a strong sentiment & seldom even then" (*MWSL* 2:246). Her poem produces strong sentiment in her readers by conjuring up P. B. Shelley's drowned body in aestheticized form, pillowed on seaweed with sea nymphs chanting his dirge. If, as Judith Pike suggests, Mary Shelley debunks the conventionalized portrayal of death in *Franken-stein*, here she seems to participate in the cult of mourning endemic to the annuals. P. B. Shelley's death haunts any reading of his wife's dirge.

Mary Shelley's "Dirge" follows an engraving in the *Keepsake* entitled "The Use of Tears," which portrays a young woman with eyes downcast and bedclothes in dishabille, tended by an older woman who wears a veil, summoning associations with religious suffering. The engraving accompanies a poem of the same title by Lord Morpeth (George Howard, sixth

Earl of Carlisle), which was presumably solicited as a companion piece. There is nothing fresh or novel about Lord Morpeth's treatment of tears. His poem concludes:

Tears at each pure emotion flow:
They wait on Pity's gentle claim,
On Admiration's fervid glow,
On Piety's seraphic flame.

'Tis only when it mourns and fears
The loaded spirit feels forgiven,
And through the mist of falling tears
We catch the clearest glimpse of heaven.[19]

No very obvious connection exists between the poem and the engraving it complements; one can imagine any number of different poems or stories that might equally account for the bedridden girl and her companion. But almost any poem *will* do so long as it allows the reader to identify with sadness, loss, or generalized strong feeling. Vagueness allows appropriation.

Mary Shelley's poem, arguably more musical in meter and evocative in imagery, serves a similar, although not identical, function. The well-known details of P. B. Shelley's death pin the poem to a specific grief-inducing episode. To use her "Dirge" in reference to one's own grief would serve to heighten the significance of a more "ordinary" person's death. Still, Mary Shelley's grief can be tapped for readers' individual purposes; the point of her poem in the vehicle provided by the *Keepsake* is not so much art for art's sake but art for sorrow's sake.

Mary Shelley's *Keepsake* "Dirge" bears comparison with a poem she wrote in response to Wordsworth's "Elegiac Stanzas, Suggested by a Picture of Peele Castle in a Storm, Painted by Sir George Beaumont." Mary Shelley's 1825 poem, entitled "On Reading Wordsworth's Lines on Peele Castle," anticipates her later dirge in its rhyme scheme and imagery. She writes:

The gentlest rustling of the deep
Is but the dirge of him I lost,
And when waves raise their furrows steep,
And bring foam in which is tossed.

A voice I hear upon the wind
Which bids me haste to join him there,
And woo the tempest's breath unkind
Which gives to me a kindred bier.
. . . .
Then wildly to the beach I rush,
And fain would seize the frailest boat,
And from dull earth the slight hull push,
On dancing waves towards him to float.[20]

The provenance of Mary Shelley's poem—the fact that it is a poem inspired by a poem inspired by a painting—recalls the infinite regress of the souvenir in Susan Stewart's description, its constant turning back to a point of origin supplanted by the souvenir itself. Mary Shelley's poem is the product of a grief stung into presence by Wordsworth's poem, which was inspired by the loss of his brother. Wordsworth's memorialization of his brother becomes a mode of access for Mary Shelley's memorialization of her husband. The companion poems enact the same kind of commerce in grief upon which the annuals ultimately capitalize. Wordsworth's poem is appropriated by Mary Shelley just as the ubiquitous poems about death in the annuals allow (indeed, invite) appropriation and individuation by the annuals' readers.

Mary Shelley's two poems commemorating her husband are also noteworthy for the way in which she rewrites the scene of P. B. Shelley's death, inserting herself into the aftermath of the boating accident and the recovery of P. B. Shelley's body, scenes at which she was not historically present. In "Dirge," the narrator describes herself keeping a "lonely watch" near her love's "sea-weed pillow," and in "On Reading Wordsworth's Lines," the narrator imagines herself rushing to the beach and seizing "the frailest boat" in order to float toward her beloved.

Bette London calls attention to the way in which Mary Shelley is similarly inserted into Louis-Edouard Fournier's 1889 painting, *Funeral of Shelley*, in which she appears as a kneeling figure at the margin of a representation of P. B. Shelley's cremation, in London's words, "barely distinguishable from a shadowy mass of nameless observers, while the standing figures of the privileged mourners (the poet's friends and literary compatriots Byron, Hunt, and Trelawny) command visual attention."[21] London reads Fournier's painting and Henry Weekes's monument to P. B. Shelley and Mary Wollstonecraft Shelley–in which Mary Shelley and P. B. Shelley assume the position of Madonna and Christ in Michelangelo's *Pietà*—as inscriptions of the spectacle of masculinity in which Mary Shelley serves primarily to support scenes of male self-display.[22] But in Mary Shelley's inscriptions of herself at the scene of her husband's death, P. B. Shelley is largely dematerialized; "A Dirge" focuses on free-floating expressions of grief: "Ah, woe! ah, woe! ah, woe!"

A generalized sense of the dead P. B. Shelley rather than a materially de-tailed version of him animates these poems; it is "the poor heart's fond pic-turing" that sends the narrator of "On Reading Wordsworth's Lines" rush-ing to the beach. This phrase also shifts attention from the dead person to the speaker—and then, presumably, to the reader, as she conflates the speaker's loss with her own—and the speaker's and reader's feelings. Mary Shelley paraphrases a stanza of Wordsworth's poem only to emphasize her point of disagreement with his depiction of his own sorrow. "The feeling of my loss will ne'er be old—," Wordsworth writes, "This, which I know, I speak with mind serene." In Mary Shelley's redaction, the lines become: " 'My bitter grief will n'er grow old, / Nor say I this with mind serene.' "[23] Mary Shelley enlists Wordsworth's poem in the self-perpetuating sorrow that is the most consistent register of gift book aesthetics. The structure of feeling the gift books enact is one of continuously memorialized loss, loss sharpened by a hundred literary and pictorial reminders.

Clearly, given her loss of three children and the drowning of her hus-band, Mary Shelley was uniquely credentialed as a spokesperson for hu-man grief and suffering. A sample passage from her journal, dated Novem-ber 1822, reminds us of the emotional aftermath of her husband's death and also of a mode of being that, I think, is quite foreign to us now, one that involves living through and in tragedy rather than drawing oneself up and walking away and beyond. Mary Shelley writes:

It is better to grieve than not to grieve. Grief at least tells me that I was not always what I am now. I was once selected for happiness—let the memory of that abide by me. You pass by an old ruined house in a deso-late lane & do not heed it—but if you hear that that house is haunted by a wild & beautiful spirit, it acquires an interest & beauty of its own. So may it be said of me that I am nothing, but I was something and still I cling to what I was. When for an instant the vulture grief does not loosen his grasp, that he never does, but sleeps upon its prey—I feel myself sink to a lethargy worse than despair. (*MWSJ* 443)

It is easy to characterize the annuals as empty commercial ventures, all show and no substance, devoid of aesthetic merit. But I would argue, instead, that the annuals trade in poems and pictures that can be appropriated by the reader to serve as tokens of grief and mourning, that the annuals' luxe bindings coincide with stark enactments of death, that Mary Shelley's immersion in the annuals underscores the interdependencies of individual suffering and commercial art. Finally, I would suggest that the transition from private albums to commercial annuals enacts the changing connotations of the word *souvenir* in Romantic era culture. The album compiler inscribes a poem to aid memory. The annual purchaser buys a book as a remembrance of friendship. The souvenir as mode of memory becomes the souvenir as marketable object. However, the line between these two meanings does not really divide. As the annuals persist in reminding us, the Romantic era poem participates in both the constitution and commodification of memory.

13 : "Trying to make it as good as I can"

Mary Shelley's Editing of P. B. Shelley's Poetry and Prose

MICHAEL O'NEILL

The vexed question of the nature and value of Mary Shelley's editing of P. B. Shelley's work is the subject of stimulating recent analyses by Neil Fraistat, Mary Favret, Susan Wolfson, and Lisa Vargo.[1] These pieces dwell on Mary Shelley's editorial "construction" of P. B. Shelley.[2] They veer between commentary on (shading into censure of) her alleged suppressions and, in Favret's and, to a lesser degree, Wolfson's case, approval of her supposedly canny appropriations, as when Favret sees Mary Shelley offering through her Notes in her 1839 editions "a defense of prose" that "establishes poetry as an exercise in vanity."[3]

So far as the moments of censure are concerned, these essays are colored — more, perhaps, than their authors realize — by Trelawny's wittily calumniating account of Mary Shelley in his *Records of Shelley, Byron, and the Author* (1878). This work creates a myth of Mary Shelley as an orthodox, bourgeois figure, with little sympathy for her husband's work and radical opinions. As Emily W. Sunstein observes, "*Records* has reverberated from that day to this."[4] So far as the praise for Mary Shelley's canny appropriations is concerned, the mainspring is evidently our own culture's fraught politics of gender. But both censure and praise may tell us more about the critic's views than about Mary Shelley, and in either case gender assumptions may result in prejudgement. Here, I seek to qualify uncritical acceptance of contemporary materialist and feminist readings of Mary Shelley's editing. The two isms interlock, but the second section of this chapter focuses on materialist readings. The first section looks at the potentially problematic nature of gender-based accounts of Mary Shelley's editing before offering, through consideration of a test case, an alternative model of interpretation.

Gender-based readings of Mary Shelley's editing often subscribe to the contestable assumptions underlying this sentence from the Introduction to *The Other Mary Shelley:* "What these essays discern is a writer whose resistance to Romanticism from within the discursive field we call 'Romantic' is in many ways continuous with the insights of contemporary feminist analysis."[5] Despite the hint of qualification in the phrase "in many ways," "continuous with" closes a shade too quickly the gap between Mary Shelley and "contemporary feminist analysis." In its application to Mary Shelley's editing, this mode of analysis can be provocatively partisan. Favret's Mary Shelley, cast by the critic as anticipating recent critiques of "masculine" Romanticism, "tells us that [P. B. Shelley's] poetry is not all that *impressive*" and locates "'truth' and 'reality' apart from poetic imagination." Favret may be right to argue that women such as Mary Shelley "were trying to claim a type of influence . . . as their own,"[6] but her view that Mary Shelley sought such influence by denigrating her husband's work is unpersuasive. Drawing on my study of Mary Shelley's editing of P. B. Shelley,[7] I argue that Mary Shelley's labors represent a heroic attempt to undertake a virtually impossible task to the best of her abilities. She herself suggests terms in which her editing might be praised when she writes to Leigh Hunt in December 1838 that "The edition [Shelley's *Poetical Works* in four volumes] will be mine—& though I feel my incompetencey—yet trying to make it as good as I can, I must hope the best" (*MWSL* 2:305). "Trying to make it as good as I can," in the face of formidable obstacles, serves as a fitting description of an impressive editorial enterprise.

Even while she was writing her despairing and moving "Journal of Sorrow" in the aftermath of P. B. Shelley's untimely death, Mary Shelley was showing a grasp of the difficulties of her self-imposed editorial task that it seems appropriate to call "professional." Writing to Maria Gisborne, she says: "now I am convinced there is nothing perfect and I wish all to be sent to me without delay. . . . Pray let all Mss. of whatever kind—letters &c be sent to me immediately" (*MWSL* 1:292). For Susan Wolfson, Mary Shelley's desire to edit P. B. Shelley began as therapy and turned artfully—in the Notes to the four volumes of P. B. Shelley's poetry in 1839—"into a public discourse of her privilege as [Shelley's] reader."[8] But the obvious comfort that Mary Shelley derived from editing P. B. Shelley's work should not lead us to underrate her evident desire to do a good job.

A fundamental virtue of Mary Shelley's editorial practice is her archival scrupulousness. In general, she, at the very least, merits the late E. B. Murray's affecting tribute in the first volume of *The Prose Works of Percy Bysshe Shelley.*[9] After P. B. Shelley's death she made every effort to collect any manuscripts in the possession of such people as the poet's publisher, Charles Ollier, and his unofficial literary agent, Thomas Love Peacock, in order to carry out her design of "republishing S's works as well as the writings he has left be[hind]" (*MWSL* 1:261). In her republishing and fresh bringing forth of P. B. Shelley's works there are imperfections, shortcomings, and errors. It would be miraculous if there were not. But justice demands that judgements of her work should be put into appropriate historical contexts. Indeed, as Betty T. Bennett points out, "Mary Shelley's letters reveal that her editorial principles, stated or implied, stand up well even by modern standards that undertake to preserve all of a writer's works and present them as much as possible as the author wished."[10]

The essays already mentioned are distinguished by considerable argumentative nuance and scholarship, and they perform the great service of making us think hard about Mary Shelley's editorial practice. So Lisa Vargo remarks that in reading *The Triumph of Life* we must beware of "an unwitting acceptance of Mary Shelley's decision to edit out Jane Williams's role in the textual condition of the poem." Vargo has in mind the fact that the conversation between Rousseau and the poet is interrupted by drafts of "To Jane" ("The Keen Stars Were Twinkling") and "Lines Written in the Bay of Lerici." "Does the textual aside," asks Vargo, "illuminate Shelley's simultaneous acceptance and condemnation of Rousseau, which he connects with his own experience in the lyrics to Jane Williams?"[11] However, "aside" begs a question through its concealed theatrical metaphor; it makes the lyrics part of a drama centered on the composition of *The Triumph of Life.*

Vargo writes thoughtfully about the implications of Mary Shelley's "versioning" of the poem (remarking, for example, that Mary Shelley is the only editor to point out the presence of what in *Posthumous Poems* she calls "a chasm . . . in the MS. which it is impossible to fill up").[12] But the notion that Mary Shelley excludes from her version of *The Triumph of Life* reference to the lyrics to Jane Williams because they "present a disruption to her textual pleasure" is debatable.[13] One might and should praise Mary Shelley for picking her way round extraneous material and following the tangled thread of the composition of *The Triumph of Life.* Given the relative expense and scarcity of paper, it is unsurprising that P. B. Shelley should break off from drafting a long poem to compose a shorter poem on available sheets.

Exercised, like other critics, by the supposition of a sexual subtext beneath Mary Shelley's textual endeavors, Vargo takes as her starting point Jerome J. McGann's notion of "elective affinities between love and textuality."[14] She is not alone in her assumption that Mary Shelley's approach to editing P. B. Shelley's works lends itself to psychoanalytical interpretation. Often what is seen to govern this Mary Shelley is the need to sustain a ghostly, self-vindicating relationship with P. B. Shelley. Here a gender-based approach joins forces with psychologizing speculation. It is as difficult to rebut as to prove the argument that unconscious or semi-conscious motives are significantly at work in Mary Shelley's editing. Such an argument depends less on evidence than on the adoption of a particular interpretative mode. But Mary Shelley's description of what she tried to do in editing the manuscript of *The Triumph of Life* warrants attention. On the poem's first publication (in *Posthumous Poems* [1824]), Mary Shelley writes in the preface that the poem "was left in so unfinished a state, that I arranged it in its present form with great difficulty."[15] Her wording tells the reader that the poem was left "unfinished" (a less scrupulous editor might well have glossed over this disclosure), that it required editorial intervention to be published in readable form, and that the production of a reading text was achieved "with great difficulty." Subsequent scholarship (notably that of Donald H. Reiman) has resulted in a more accurate text of the poem, but Mary Shelley does her best to describe facts pertinent to the poem's textual condition.

For another example of psychologizing, one might consider Susan Wolfson's interpretation of Mary Shelley's decision to close volume two of her edition of P. B. Shelley's prose with his final letter to her (signed "Ever, dearest Mary, Yours affectionately, S.").[16] Wolfson suggests that Mary Shelley's decision indicates her attempt "to define her status, for herself and for the world, as P. B. Shelley's enabling and loving reader—his best, and last, audience while he lived."[17] True, Mary Shelley could have concluded her second volume of *1840*, as Frederick L. Jones does his second volume of P. B. Shelley's letters, with the letter to Jane Williams, probably written the same day as the poet's last letter to his wife. In *1840*, the letter to Jane Williams precedes that to Mary Shelley. But Wolfson's surmise is no more than that: the last brick in an elegant edifice that is every bit as much a construction as the constructions of "Shelley" and "Mary Shelley" charted by Wolfson in the main body of her essay. The essay's idiom may be post-structuralist, but its cognitive mode at this point is sweepingly psycho-biographical. Wolfson posits an editor whose emotional investment in the activity of editing motivates the choices she makes about inclusion and ordering.

Yet if one is to talk about Mary Shelley's editing of the letters in *1840* in psychobiographical terms, the inclusion of the poet's final letter to Jane Williams merits favorable comment. It is safe to assert that Mary Shelley had complex feelings about Jane Williams, especially after her discovery in July 1827 that Williams had been making her "all falsely a fable to others" (*MWSJ* 506; see also 502–3), maligning her on grounds that included her supposed coldness to P. B. Shelley. Wolfson's Mary Shelley, an editor impelled by the wish to prove her special intimacy with P. B. Shelley, might have balked at publishing this letter; it is a letter whose lyrically cadenced final paragraph has much in common with the poet's late poems for Jane Williams: "How soon those hours passed, and how slowly they return, to pass so soon again, perhaps for ever, in which we have lived together so intimately, so happily! Adieu, my dearest friend! I only write these lines for the pleasure of tracing what will meet your eyes. Mary will tell you all the news. S" (*1840* 2:357).

Moreover, Wolfson overlooks the fact that the volume does not end with P. B. Shelley's signature (also vouchsafed to Jane Williams) but with his comment in a postscript, "I have found the translation of the Symposium" (*1840* 2:360). Mary Shelley's concluding with this postscript could be tortuously construed to support Wolfson's view that the editor was seeking to establish herself as P. B. Shelley's "enabling and loving reader." Yet, more centrally, the decision to close with this letter and this postscript serves a less oppressively egotistical motive; it reminds the reader that among the material made newly available by *1840* is *The Banquet — Translated from Plato* (*The Symposium*).

Mary Shelley's editing of this work brings out her strengths as an editor and reveals some of the problems with which she had to contend. One strength is her critical perceptiveness. In the preface to *1840*, she writes acutely about the virtues of P. B. Shelley's translation, arguing that, in contrast with the versions of Plato (by J. S. Mill) published in the *Monthly Repository* (1834–35), "Shelley commands language splendid and melodious as Plato, and renders faithfully the elegance and the gaiety which makes the Symposium as amusing as it is sublime" (ix). Her account of the "whole mechanism of the drama" (ix) brings out P. B. Shelley's ability to do justice to the different voices and attitudes of Plato's work. It is not Mary Shelley's fault that subsequent commentators have overemphasized P. B. Shelley's adoption of Platonic ideas and disregarded his significant debt to Plato's dialogic vitality.

A second strength revealed by her work on *The Symposium* is her sheer persistence. The production of a reading text of P. B. Shelley's translation of *The Symposium* cost Mary Shelley a great deal of effort, as her transcription of the work in Bodleian MS. Shelley adds. d. 8 reveals.[18] She transcribed this work during the years 1823–24 to serve as a press copy or backup copy of a press copy for the selection of prose that she originally intended to include in a volume of P. B. Shelley's unpublished poetry and prose.[19] The size of *Posthumous Poems,* however, ruled out the inclusion of prose. Sir Timothy Shelley's objections to the publication of his son's works foiled plans to bring out a separate edition of prose works, and Mary Shelley was required by William Whitton, Sir Timothy's solicitor, to give Thomas Love Peacock "the Manuscript of the prose writings," which included, Peacock told Whitton, "two *translations* from Plato."[20] It is likely that she gave Peacock either a manuscript of *The Symposium* that was in P. B. Shelley's hand or a transcription by her that was not the transcription in adds. d. 8.

From the outset, then, of Mary Shelley's plans to publish a work central to understanding P. B. Shelley's aesthetic, philosophical, erotic and ethical interests, she was in conflict with powerful forces. But her determination that the work should be published persisted, bearing fruit in *1840.* Press copy for this edition was supplied by her 1823–24 transcription in adds. d. 8. Marked by printers' fingerprints, the copy has signatures and the names of compositors written on it at intervals and must have been used in the printing house of Bradbury and Evans, the printers of *1840.* However, Mary Shelley did not feel able to publish the transcription as it stood, with its references to homosexuality in ancient Greece. In writing *A Discourse on the Manners of the Ancient Greeks Relative to the Subject of Love* to accompany his translation of *The Symposium,* P. B. Shelley himself was aware of the need to exercise "that delicate caution which either I cannot or I will not practise in other matters, but which here I acknowledge to be necessary." He goes on in the same letter to Peacock to say, "Not that I have any serious thought of publishing either this discourse or the *Symposium,* at least till I return to England, when we may discuss the propriety of it" (*PBSL* 2:29).

Twenty years on, Mary Shelley found herself preoccupied, as P. B. Shelley had been in 1818, by the "propriety" of publishing the translation and the essay. The result of her censoring both in *1840* was that for many years P. B. Shelley's readers encountered what James A. Notopoulos calls "the paradox of an essay which did not discuss what Shelley set out to do and a translation which omitted the very portions which the prefatory essay intended to discuss."[21] Yet we need not impute to Mary Shelley a foolish prudery, any more than we would think of ascribing to P. B. Shelley a dithering retreat from radical boldness in his preparedness to rework *Laon and Cythna* into *The Revolt of Islam.* That she accepted — at least in August 1818 — the force of P. B. Shelley's argument in *A Discourse* about the need to acknowledge cultural relativism is shown by her letter to Maria Gisborne: "Shelley translated the Symposium in ten days. . . . It is a most beautiful piece of writing, — I think you will be delighted with it — It is true that in many particulars it shocks our present manners, but no one can be a reader of the works of antiquity unless they can transport themselves from these to other times and judge not by our but by their morality" (*MWSL* 1:77).

The Reverend Dr. Folliott's two-edged remark in Peacock's *Crotchet Castle* (1831) illustrates and mocks the conventional response to Plato's *Symposium* in early nineteenth-century England: "I am aware, sir, that Plato, in his Symposium discourseth very eloquently touching the Uranian and Pandemian Venus: but you must remember that, in our Universities, Plato is held to be little better than a misleader of youth; and they have shown their contempt for him, not only by never reading him . . . but even by never printing a complete edition of him."[22] Hanging over Mary Shelley's head and that of *1840*'s publisher Edward Moxon was the threat of scandal and possible prosecution. In her editing of *1840* she was determined not to alienate P. B. Shelley from the readership which she had, at last, obtained for him by the publication of her editions of his poems. On October 8, 1839, she wrote to Moxon to withdraw P. B. Shelley's heterodox essay "on the Devil & Devils," which had been set up in proof, because she feared that "it would excite a violent party spirit against the volumes which otherwise I beleive [sic] will prove generally attractive" (*MWSL* 2:327).

With regard to *The Symposium* she consulted Leigh Hunt, who wrote penciled suggestions on the press copy (Bodleian MS. Shelley adds. d. 8).

Mary Shelley then made cuts and alterations in her 1839 hand, markedly different from her 1823–24 script. Collation with *1840* shows that she adopted many, though by no means all, of Hunt's proposed changes. But the fact that Mary Shelley kept the press copy shows the importance she attached to her original transcription. One of her copies of *1840,* which interleaves the text with blank pages, provides further evidence of her belief that her cut and altered text of *The Symposium* should and would one day be printed in its correct form. In this copy, now held in the Bodleian Library ([printed] Shelley adds. e. 19–20), Mary Shelley meticulously restores readings from her original 1823–24 transcription. It is noteworthy, too, that in the letter concerning the essay "On the Devil, and Devils" she writes: "When this Edition is sold I think of ⟨bringing⟩ printing all Shelley's prose, which I think will make two volumes similar to the poetical works—in that this Essay will of course appear" (*MWSL* 2:327). Quite possibly, had the opportunity presented itself, she would have published an unexpurgated text of *The Symposium* in an edition containing "all Shelley's prose."

An example where Mary Shelley did not act on Hunt's advice about the text of *The Symposium* occurs on page 66 of adds. d. 8. In Mary Shelley's transcription Phaedrus says "I cannot imagine a greater happiness and advantage to one who is in the flower of youth than an amiable lover, or to a lover than an amiable object of his love." With the addition of a comma after "a lover" this is the reading in *1840.* Hunt, however, had proposed "a loving friend" as an alternative to both "an amiable lover" and "a lover." A letter that Mary Shelley wrote to Hunt (October ?10, 1839) concerning his proposed changes casts light on her editorial vigilance:

> You have puzzled me much. What you said convinced me. You said: "Do as Mills, who has just phrased it so that the common reader will think common love is meant—the learned alone will know what is meant." Accordingly I read the Phaedrus & found less of a veil even than I expected—thus I was emboldened to leave it so that our sort of civilized love should be understood—Now you change all this back into friendship—which makes the difficulty as great as ever. I wished in every way ⟨to leave⟩ to preserve as many of Shelley's own words as possible—& I was glad to do so under the new idea which you imparted—but your alterations puzzle me mightily—I do not like not to abide by them—yet

they destroy your own argument that different sexes would be understood, & thus all is in confusion.

Accordingly I have left some & not others—where you seemed very
vehement—& your p. 192 I have altered & omitted as you mention—
but I could not bring myself to leave the word <u>love</u> out entirely from a
treatise on Love. (*MWSL* 2:327)

It is evident from this letter that Hunt had advised Mary Shelley in conversation to follow the example of J. S. Mill in his *Monthly Repository* translations, in which the word *love* was allowed to equivocate. However, Hunt's
changes to the press copy and the galley proofs (both, it seems, were sent
to him) struck Mary Shelley as being at odds with his advice, since they
frequently altered *love* and *lover* to *friendship* and *friend;* the result was to
highlight the homosexual implications of those passages where *love* and
lover were allowed to remain.

In the event, she made cuts, despite her dislike of "mutilations" (*MWSL*
2:301): omissions included the naming of Achilles and Patroclus as "lover"
and "beloved" (adds. d. 8, 69–70); a passage about the "affection and the
facility of lovers towards each other" (adds. d. 8, 76); large sections of
Aristophanes' explanation of sexual preference (adds. d. 8, 90–91); and
Alcibiades' account of his attempts to seduce Socrates (adds. d. 8, 138–43).
There are many changes made to mask homosexual implications: when
on page 72 Pausanias says (in the original transcription), "There ought to
be a law that none should love mere youths," Mary Shelley, responding
to a marginal pencil line made by Leigh Hunt, crosses out "mere youths"
and replaces it with "the very young," the reading in *1840*. Again, however,
the correct reading is restored by Mary Shelley in [printed] Shelley adds.
e. 19. Moreover, her editorial practice so far as *1840*'s version of *The Symposium* is concerned bears out her remark that she could not bring herself
"to leave the word <u>love</u> out entirely from a treatise on Love" as well as her
comment that she wished "in every way to preserve as many of Shelley's
<u>own</u> <u>words</u> as possible."

Often, as indicated, she resisted Hunt's suggested changes or, indeed,
her own alterations to the press copy. In addition to the example already
cited, one might take an example from adds. d. 8, 73: here the original
1823–24 transcription refers to those who "assert that it is dishonourable
to serve and gratify the objects of our love." With the insertion of a comma

after "assert," this is the version in *1840*. The press copy reveals, however, that Mary Shelley had thought of cutting the words after "dishonourable" and inserting "love is" in place of "it is."

Generally, Mary Shelley's decision to print a bowdlerized version of *The Symposium* in *1840* was tactical; the tactic, consciously and reluctantly deployed, served a long-term strategy of ensuring for P. B. Shelley the continuing admiration of the new readership that she had built up for him. But Mary Shelley was not so much falsifying P. B. Shelley (who is difficult, anyway, to see in unitive terms) as helping to foster the taste by which his work might be enjoyed. It is a tactic that receives support from P. B. Shelley's awareness of the need for "reformers" to "practise" "misrepresentation of their own true feelings and opinions." [23] Also to Mary Shelley's editorial credit is her attempt to consult the possibly more reliable version of *The Symposium* (not that in adds. d. 8), which she had been obliged to lodge with Peacock in 1824 or soon after (see *MWSL* 2:317 and 322, and *MWSL* 3:419). To sum up, Mary Shelley's editorial practice concerning *The Symposium* shows her making the best of a very tricky job: one notes that neither Hunt nor Moxon tried to talk her out of printing an expurgated version. In her preface to *1840* Mary Shelley remarks that in the work "we may suppose to have dignified the orgies of the last generation of free-spirited wits,—Burke, Fox, Sheridan, and Curran. It has something, too, of the license,—too much, indeed, and perforce omitted; but of coarseness, that worst sin against our nature, it has nothing" (x). The reference to "free-spirited wits" has an admiring tone that makes "perforce omitted" hint at criticism of early Victorian England.

Most damaging to Mary Shelley's reputation as an editor is the view that her editing was driven by the politically conservative wish to create P. B. Shelley as the "etherealized, disembodied, and virtually depoliticized poet" who, in Neil Fraistat's words, "emerged from her editions." Fraistat is less interested in singling Mary Shelley out for blame than in laying bare the workings of "an entire cultural apparatus." But he is committed to a view of Mary Shelley as "suppress[ing]" in her edition of P. B. Shelley's *Posthumous Poems* "Shelley's most ideologically controversial poems—for instance, 'The Mask of Anarchy' and the volume of 'popular songs' written for working-class reformers." [24] Though this is true (Mary Shelley appears to have decided to present the volume as "a specimen of how

[Shelley] could write without shocking any one" [*MWSL* 1:397]), it is not the whole truth.

Posthumous Poems was certainly a canny intervention in the literary marketplace, despite the fact that it ran into immediate trouble with the poet's father. Mary Shelley writes in a letter of June 20, 1824, that the poems [in *Posthumous Poems*] "are of more popular nature for the most part that [*than*] his former productions" (*MWSL* 1:430). This remark anticipates her later distinction, in the preface to the four-volume *Poetical Works* of 1839, between "two classes" of poems by P. B. Shelley, "the purely imaginative, and those which sprung from the emotions of his heart." [25] But, above all, the remark shows her wish to obtain a readership for P. B. Shelley's poetry. Mary Shelley's attempt in *Posthumous Poems* to shift the ground of the debate about P. B. Shelley's work is more justifiable than is sometimes allowed. By 1824, after years of polemical wrangling, the time was right for appreciation of the poetry's literary and aesthetic qualities.

Likewise, it is not clear that *Posthumous Poems* etherealizes, disembodies, and depoliticizes. It may have been "designed for consumption by the middle and upper classes," [26] but the fact that it was published by John and Henry L. Hunt would not have signaled appeasing quietism to a consumer. The publisher's views may well have influenced the decision to print unpublished pieces that, with luck, would not excite mere outrage. John Hunt had recently been successfully prosecuted for printing Byron's *The Vision of Judgment*, receiving a fine of £100 (shortly after *Posthumous Poems* was published). The seriousness with which Mary Shelley took the threat against John Hunt's liberty is evident in her expression of relief in a letter of June 20, 1824, that "this gentlem[an] has got off without imprisonment, and this long ⟨threat⟩ pending persecution is at last ended" (*MWSL* 1:430). *Posthumous Poems* does not so much depoliticize as keep its powder dry. After all, the volume's contents are far from apolitical: Julian and Maddalo debate the possibilities and limitations of the human condition; the Witch of Atlas engages in distinctly heterodox, if fantastical, activities; *The Triumph of Life* is saturated with contemporary political awareness; and the "Ode to Naples" celebrates in the author's Note (included by Mary Shelley) "the enthusiasm excited by the intelligence of the proclamation of a Constitutional Government at Naples." However idealizing her language, Mary Shelley does not shrink from referring, at the start of the second paragraph of her preface, to P. B. Shelley's "fearless enthusiasm in the cause, which he considered the most sacred upon earth, the improvement of the moral and physical state of mankind."[27] Fraistat's insistence on Mary Shelley's "class-coded language of sensibility"[28] ignores the degree to which that "code" admits of a libertarian reading.

At stake here are complex problems of reception: problems that include our own understanding of the ways in which P. B. Shelley's poetry is politically radical. Critics such as Fraistat and Wolfson can seem ill at ease with that side of P. B. Shelley which was happy to speak in elitist terms of an imagined audience. Because Mary Shelley follows P. B. Shelley's at times "elitist poetics of audience," it does not mean that she is unthinkingly expressing "ideological contradictions," or seeking, out of self-promotion or self-justification, to demonstrate "the editor's refined sympathy with her subject."[29] Wolfson, in fact, is attentive to the rhetoric of Mary Shelley's notes and prefaces; a long footnote (n. 34) offers a balanced account of the issues raised by Mary Shelley's editing practice. But on occasions Wolfson attributes to Mary Shelley the creation of myths about P. B. Shelley, where I see Mary Shelley as offering uncoercively a robustly evaluative insight. Of the popular songs of 1819, Mary Shelley writes justly that

> They are not among the best of his productions, a writer being always shackled when he endeavours to write down to the comprehension of those who could not understand or feel a highly imaginative style; but they show his earnestness, and with what heartfelt compassion he went home to the direct point of wrong—that oppression is detestable, as being the parent of starvation, nakedness and ignorance. Besides these outpourings of compassion and indignation, he had meant to adorn the cause he loved with loftier poetry of glory and triumph—such is the scope of the Ode to the Assertors of Liberty. (M 307)

Wolfson, who quotes this passage selectively, fails to point out that, despite Mary Shelley's reservations about the aesthetic quality of these poems, she does remark that they "show [Shelley's] earnestness, and with what heartfelt compassion he went home to the direct point of wrong—that oppression is detestable, as being the parent of starvation, nakedness and ignorance." For Wolfson, Mary Shelley merely "muddies" the "lines" of a "sentimental" picture of P. B. Shelley as "noble" altruist.[30] But what Mary Shelley's note offers is less elitist mythologizing than judicious critical appraisal; the editor brings out an unignorable issue of literary value.

It is the portrait of Mary Shelley as a sentimentalizing, depoliticizing editor whose lines need muddying. The grand narratives that materialist and feminist critiques of her editing are beginning to construct should be tested vigilantly. It is important, for example, to remember that during the period Mary Shelley assembled *Posthumous Poems* she was keeping alive the memory of P. B. Shelley's most "ideologically controversial" poems and prose. She did so in transcriptions made for safekeeping and possible future publication (in Bodleian MS. Shelley, adds. d. 6 and adds. d. 8 [prose] and adds. d. 7 and adds. d. 9 [poetry]) and for samizdat-like circulation among friends. For instance, she gave a fair copy of "To the Lord Chancellor" to Charles and Mary Cowden Clarke. This fair copy is bound with Cowden Clarke's copy of *Posthumous Poems* and the original, Pisan edition of *Adonais:* the volume is now in the Brotherton Collection, Leeds University Library (and is transcribed in *MYR: Shelley,* 8).

Again, Wolfson herself discusses Mary Shelley's dislike of "mutilations" in the case of the printing of *Queen Mab* in the first edition of the 1839 *Poetical Works* and her insistence on the complete restoration of omitted matter in the second edition of 1839.[31] Another area where Mary Shelley deserves praise is her treatment of P. B. Shelley's love poems to other women. Here she can be regarded as having "acted bravely."[32] More importantly, she also acted as a responsible editor seeking to publish the best text of a poem. When holograph manuscripts of poems to Jane Williams, such as "To Jane: The Invitation" and "To Jane: The Recollection," became available (see *M* 426), Mary Shelley included texts based on them in the second edition of the 1839 *Poetical Works.*

Mary Shelley did "construct" P. B. Shelley to the degree that she had considerable power over which of his works would be released and when, as well as over the critical terms in which those works might be discussed. Yet an understanding of her editing is best served not by a deconstruction of its motives and surmised effect but by a recognition that her practice shows that she was, indeed, "trying to make it as good" as she could.

14 : Mary Shelley's *Lives* and the Reengendering of History

GREG KUCICH

Amid the persisting solitude, painful memories, and "deep sorrows" of the 1830s, Mary Shelley found one refreshing literary "source" of what she called "interest & pleasure" (*MWSL* 2:257, 209) in her sustained work on a series of biographical lives for Dionysius Lardner's *Cabinet Cyclo-paedia*—a 133-volume popular encyclopedia published between 1829 and 1846, which featured contributions from some of the most distinguished writers of the early nineteenth century, including Walter Scott, Thomas Moore, Robert Southey, John Forster, James Mackintosh, J.C.L. de Sismondi, and John Herschel. Mary Shelley's biographical output for the *Cyclopaedia* was prodigious, amounting to the great majority of essays included in the three-volume *Lives of the Most Eminent Literary and Scientific Men of Italy, Spain and Portugal* (1835–37) and the two-volume *Lives of the Most Eminent Literary and Scientific Men of France* (1838–39), all energetically produced under the inspiration of what Mary Shelley describes as the special joy of "treading in unknown paths & dragging out unknown things. . . . There is no more delightful literary task" (*MWSL* 2:255; *LI* 1:256).[1] Her enthusiasm for that task surfaces in the crisp, intellectually spirited quality of her prose, which some of her more recent critics rank very highly amongst her overall writings. Paula Feldman commends her "considerable biographical ability." Johanna Smith emphasizes the aesthetic and political sophistication of her *Lives*. And William Walling finds them representing her "most solid and substantial" work "after *The Last Man*."[2] Despite these positive, though brief, notices and our increasing commitments to the work of "the Other Mary Shelley," such voluminous and significant writings as the *Lives* remain relatively unexamined in the history of Mary Shelley criticism.[3]

Several obvious factors have contributed to this neglect: Mary Shelley avowedly churned out her biographies to pay off mounting debts, which occasioned a traditional critical tendency to dismiss them as "hack" work;[4] until very recently, literature by women Romantic era writers outside of the major genres of fiction, poetry, drama, and literary criticism has not received substantial critical attention; moreover, attribution errors in W. H. Lyles's Mary Shelley bibliography have underrepresented the extensive volume of her biographical labor for the *Cabinet Cyclopaedia;*[5] and, perhaps most significant, ready access to this large body of work is severely restricted to modern readers because Mary Shelley's *Lives* have never been reproduced from the now obscure and hard-to-find *Cabinet Cyclopaedia.* That these conditions need to be rectified has already been implied by Anne Mellor's recent illustration of Mary Shelley's gendered critique of Romantic ideology in the *Lives,* particularly in her essay on Condorcet.[6]

Following that suggestion, I wish to argue for the significance of the *Lives* as a compelling type of historical revisionism, anticipatory of twentieth-century forms of feminist historiography and biography, that continues Mary Shelley's progressive gender politics throughout the 1830s. The revisionary history of the *Lives* manifests one of Mary Shelley's most substantial interventions in the gender ideologies of her time, even as it performs that critique in a somewhat muted and indirect manner. To recognize the historiographical functions and complexities of this intervention is to gain a more nuanced understanding of the mixture of reticence and critical politics that informs her later career, one of the most intensely debated issues in current Mary Shelley studies.[7]

Mary Shelley was always intrigued by the intersections of biography and history as interrelated modes of applying the life of the past to the politics of the present. The core narrative of *Frankenstein,* for instance, constitutes a form of biography—the Creature's narrative of Safie's life— that centers in a politicized reading by Safie and the Creature of Volney's history of oppressive government, *The Ruins of Empire.* Reflecting on the nature and function of her own biographical *Lives,* Mary Shelley claims that a successful sketch of a life entails not only "the biography of an individual" but also the political "history" of an era (*LF* 1:1). Biographical writing, she elaborates on another occasion, should form "a school . . . as it were . . . in which to study the philosophy of history" (*LI* 2:73). The search for "lessons," as she puts it (*LI* 1:293), from this school inspired an early fascination with biography and history that persisted throughout her life.

At seventeen, she commenced a life of Jean Baptise Louvet; she contributed biographical essays to the *Liberal* in the 1820s and proposed to John Murray a series of biographical projects, including lives of Madame de Staël, Empress Josephine, Columbus, Mahomet, the "English Philosophers," and "Celebrated women," as well as histories of chivalry, the conquests of Mexico and Peru, and the literature of England from Queen Anne to the French Revolution (*MWSL* 2:113–15). Much of her actual literary endeavors throughout the 1830s centered on biographical work for projects like the *Cabinet Cyclopaedia,* her edition of P. B. Shelley's writing, and her planned life of Godwin. Most of her overall fictional output assumed biographical and historical frameworks, and throughout this entire period of creative labor she consumed a prodigious amount of historical and biographical writing, including works by Alfieri, Barruel, Boswell, Gibbon, Godwin, Herodotus, Hume, Johnson, Catharine Macaulay, Plutarch, Robertson, Tacitus, Voltaire, Wollstonecraft . . . the list goes on. Some of these works she read with P. B. Shelley; many of them she studied independently.

The "lessons" they offered must have been profound to inspire and sustain such a massive, lifelong investment in historical reading and writing. By Mary Shelley's own account, the schooling was political in nature, and some of her recent critics have begun the important work of tracing the exact kind of political lessons she learned from the past and applied to the present in her own historiographical formats.[8] These findings indicate that a significant part of Mary Shelley's attraction to historical discourse stemmed from her recognition of its suitability for gender critique. That recognition was undoubtedly fostered by her particular schooling in a comprehensive effort by many of her female and some of her male contemporaries to rectify the gender inequalities of the present by reengendering, or feminizing, the history of the past. Mary Shelley's participation in this early form of feminist historiography culminated in her *Cyclopaedia* biographies, and the full extent of their gender revisionism can only be appreciated in relation to the broader patterns of her era's reengendering of history.

History became a foundational ground for all knowledge in the late eighteenth and early nineteenth centuries, and the "truth" it offered was, in Christina Crosby's recent phrase, "man's truth"—a gendered structure of understanding that excluded women and other marginalized groups from "historical and political life."[9] This structure's pivotal role in supporting systems of gender inequality helps explain what Stuart Curran characterizes as a "pervasive engagement with history" that runs throughout the period's writings by women, many of whom realized that their era's developing clash of gender ideologies would be fought out primarily on the grounds of history.[10] Individual examples of that struggle are beginning to figure prominently in new studies of women Romantic era writers;[11] but a comprehensive view of the patterns of historical revisionism practiced by many of the period's women writers has yet to be formulated. The elaborate detailing of such a project lies beyond the scope of this chapter, but I can begin to sketch here the general contours of the reengendering of history during the Romantic era by first drawing upon the recent theoretical work of feminist historiographers.

Rewriting the past in the service of present gender politics constitutes the driving force of current feminist historiography. However, as Joan Scott warns, that revisionary program does not simply entail recovering the stories of illustrious women.[12] Rather, a politically efficacious feminist historiography must alter the fundamental structures of historical representation in patriarchal versions of the past — challenging, as Elaine Showalter stresses, the "temporal categories" of "men's . . . history," which may "filter out women's experiences, values, and achievements," or, more radically, displacing the rhetorical and epistemological frames of understanding in traditional history with what Josephine Donovan calls a "women's way of seeing, a women's epistemology."[13]

Fostering such a new way of "seeing . . . women, and another way of seeing and understanding what counted as history," Scott contends, mobilizes one of the principal directives of feminist historiography: to interrogate the repressive dynamics of sex-gender systems in the past so as to dismantle their persisting formations in the present.[14] This way of reengendering the structures of knowledge and power in mainstream history comprises a unifying project for the group of feminist historians that Joan Scott and Ann-Louise Shapiro assemble in their new volumes, *Feminism and History* and *Feminists Revision History*.[15] Much as these contestatory practices are, indeed, newly revisioning the intersections of gender, history, and power, their strategies were anticipated by numbers of women Romantic era writers who, under different historical and political circumstances, also sought to feminize the structures of historical vision in order to correct the gender inequalities of their own time.

That many of the period's women writers were alert to and keenly critical of these masculine historical structures may be judged from Catherine Moreland's representative response to conventional historiography in Jane Austen's *Northanger Abbey*. "History, real solemn history," she declares, "tells me nothing that does not either vex or weary me. The quarrels of popes and kings, with wars or pestilences, in every page; the men all so good for nothing, and hardly any women at all—it is very tiresome."[16] The opposition of many women writers to this tiresome "solemn history" particularly centered on its totalizing inclination to delineate grand sweeps of historical process that subsume and efface individual subjects, particularly women, within universal paradigms of historical development.

For all of the rich variety of tropological, narrative, and political strategies that theorists like Walter Benjamin, Hayden White, and Benedict Anderson have uncovered in mainstream historical writing of the eighteenth and nineteenth centuries, many of these differing historical renderings share a common tendency to theorize their accounts of the past within abstract, totalizing frames of linear progress and decline.[17] The drama of this type of history subordinates human actors to such universal patterns of growth and degeneration, which may be construed variously as the liberal progressions of Whig history, the millennial advances of Priestly, Godwin, and the early advocates of the French Revolution, the cyclical patterns of destruction and renovation outlined by Volney, Condorcet, Cuvier, and Hegel, the brutal oscillations of supply and dearth in Malthus's population theory, or the degenerative motion of Gibbon's history of empire. Missing from all these highly theoretical accounts of history is the individualized story of the human subject, particularly the marginalized one.

Recent feminist critiques of Romantic ideology have demonstrated how totalizing, transhistorical systems of this sort remain deeply implicated in patriarchal codes of knowledge and law. The rights and privileges such histories support, however differently inflected in political terms, will always remain, in Tom Paine's famous and revealing title, "The Rights of Man." To contest such universalizing histories of "man's rights" is thus to challenge fundamentally the gender ideologies and subordinations that operate throughout much of Romanticism's dominant social and writing practices.

Such a challenge took the form of a more humanized historical epistemology, which replaces abstract patterns of historical development with localized evocations of the interior, often devastated lives of individual subjects within domestic communities that have been ravaged by social and political tyranny. These "histor[ies] of sorrowful interest," as Jane Austen phrases them in *Persuasion*,[18] were both produced and even theorized by many of the period's most prominent female writers—including Mary Wollstonecraft, who pauses significantly in her political history of the French Revolution to "weep" for the domestic sufferings of individual victims of revolutionary violence; Maria Edgeworth, who renounces in *Castle Rackrent* what she calls "heroic history" for "secret memoirs" and "private anecdotes" of loss and suffering; Mary Hays, whose *Female Biography* generally prioritizes the private "tears" and "sufferings" of historical figures like Joan of Arc over their public accomplishments; Joanna Baillie, whose "Introductory Discourse" subordinates the abstract military and political considerations of what she calls "real history" to the intricate griefs and passions of specific individuals grappling in sympathetic union with heavy burdens; Anna Jameson, who complains in her *Characteristics of Women* that "history . . . disdains to speak of [women]."[19]

Austen produced her own critique of such "real history" in her ebulliently parodic *History of England,* which dispenses with dates and political abstractions in favor of pitying the sorrows of victimized individuals, mostly women.[20] Catharine Macaulay presents the most complex and theoretically sophisticated form of this kind of personalized historicism in her widely read *History of England*—a work inspired, she announces in an explanatory preface, by "sympathising tenderness" for the "situation" of individuated "sufferers" whose broken ties of relation and affection cause her to "shed many tears."[21] The political significance of this revisionary historical attention to individual sufferings and sympathetic communities may be gauged by its recurrent promotion of something like the "ethic of care" that Anne K. Mellor, drawing on Carol Gilligan, finds so many women Romantic era writers using to oppose the abstract epistemologies and exclusionary gender politics of the period's masculine systems of writing and power.[22]

Now it would be reductive to claim that all women's historical writing of this era conformed to such a paradigm or that this paradigm exerted the only influence on Mary Shelley's historical consciousness. Nevertheless, she devoted considerable time throughout her life to the study of its various formulations in historiographical writings by Wollstonecraft, Edgeworth, Baillie, and Macaulay, among others. She adapted its general patterns for her own purposes as early as the Safie episode in *Frankenstein,* when she features Safie and the Creature weeping over the ruins of history.

In *The Last Man* and *Valperga* she formulates even more complex modes of personalized history, deploying the records of personal, domestic relations in order to condition the overall historical formats of her novels. One of Mary Shelley's most intriguing models for this ongoing effort to reengender the past emerges in the more specialized biographical form of revisionary history that female contemporaries like Mary Hays, Anna Jameson, Elizabeth Hamilton, Lucy Aikin, and Elizabeth Benger were actively developing in the early decades of the nineteenth century.

The general rise of biography as a major literary genre in the late eighteenth and early nineteenth centuries offered a unique set of problems and opportunities for women writers seeking to reformulate and personalize the structures of masculine history. Mainstream biography, as it developed through Johnson, Boswell, Southey, Scott, Hazlitt, and Lockhart, certainly grounds history in the lives of individuals, frequently recorded with extensive attention to character, psychic interior experience, and personal anecdotes. The trajectory of this interior focus, however, generally moves outward onto the larger stage of public events in an effort to demonstrate how personal character or choice both shapes and becomes conditioned by the grand flow of history, which is ultimately conceived and interpreted in terms of political, military, or cultural development. Locating the springs and turns, the shaping force of that sweep of public history, what Hazlitt, echoed by P. B. Shelley, famously called "The Spirit of the Age," remains one of the primary goals of delving into the personal lives of historical subjects.

It is precisely this outward, abstracting swing of mainstream biography that connects it with the period's historiography and simultaneously problematizes its adoption by those women writers striving to turn the flow of history back inward. For them to personalize history through the mediation of biography thus requires strategic revisioning of the genre similar to their interventions in mainstream historiography—writing "the history of the individual" in "domestic life," as Elizabeth Benger argues, instead of chronicling the public actions of "warriors and adventurers." [23] The standard "chart of [biographical] history," Benger complains, concentrates too frequently on "facts and dates, and . . . events," failing to engage what strikes her as the central stuff of history—the "secret chagrins and anxieties" of the individual historical subject, the "records of suffering and feeling" that speak most powerfully "to our sympathies" across the vast reaches of time.[24] In this provocation to revision the past through "domestic" histories of individual lives, female biographers like Benger found a number of inducements not available in the field of mainstream historiography.

Where the scientific aura of historiography resisted participation by all but the most aggressive women writers—Elizabeth Hamilton feared that historical writing "may be deemed too classical for a female pen"[25]—biography's more flexible generic amalgamation of memoirs, tributes, personal reminiscences, and narratives of friends and loved ones opened the field from early on to the kind of emotive discourse deemed appropriate for, and available to, women writers. That space for affect supplied an ideal basis for the kind of sympathetic engagement with an individuated past increasingly cultivated in the period's early forms of feminist historiography. Moreover, the prospect of selecting female biographical subjects or even groups of women made it possible to explore individual women's personal experience, domestic relations, and social achievements to a degree unheard of in standard historiographical inquiry.

Given these incentives, it is not surprising to find significant numbers of women writers attempting revisionary types of biography in prose and poetry: Lucy Aikin's *Epistles on Women* and her *Memoirs* of Queen Elizabeth, James I, and Charles I; Mary Hays's six-volume *Female Biography;* Anna Jameson's *Memoirs of Female Sovereigns;* Felicia Hemans's *Records of Woman;* Elizabeth Benger's *Memoirs* of Mary Queen of Scots, Anne Boleyn, and Elizabeth Hamilton; and Hamilton's own *Memoirs of the Life of Agrippina.* Much as these biographical works may differ in their structural formats and political priorities, many of them share a governing tendency to adapt the personalized dimensions of the genre into forms of feminist historiography that render the past, as Benger representatively puts it, as a sympathetic "school of suffering."[26] The model here for applying such reengendered modes of biography and history toward what Hays called "the advancement . . . of my sex . . . [in] the generous contention between the sexes for intellectual equality" anticipates current formulations of "feminist biography" as sympathetic modes of interiorized history that serve to critique sex-gender systems in the past and the present.[27]

These early and quickly developing experiments in "feminist biography" clearly intrigued Mary Shelley, who particularly admired the work of Hays and conceptualized biographical writing as a politically charged investment in "private history" capable of producing a new "philosophy of history" (*LI* 1:167; 2:73). Her interest in this specialized kind of new history quickened by her pragmatic recognition of a new income source, Mary Shelley fervently proposed that staggering range of biographical projects to John Murray in 1829–30. Her opportunity finally came with Lardner's invitation to produce the *Cyclopaedia* biographies, whose thematic, epistemological, and political structures all contribute to Mary Shelley's most comprehensive adaptation of the feminist historiographical procedures she had been cultivating throughout her writing career.

The controlling presence of that historiographical orientation in the *Lives* is traceable in Mary Shelley's recurrent characterization of her biographical essays as histories of the interior lives, or the *hearts,* of her subjects—she thinks of her Petrarch essay, for instance, as a "history of his heart" (*LI* 1:90); her Boccaccio sketch as a "history" of his emotional "attachment[s]" (*LI* 1:125); her life of Bernardo Pulci as a "private history"(*LI* 1:167). Although Mary Shelley acknowledges Samuel Johnson's biographical emphasis on "character" as a formative influence on this kind of interiorized history (*LI* 2:206), her own biographical method more specifically approximates her era's modes of feminist historiography in its sustained and fundamental attention to the life of the heart's social and domestic relations. The emotional ties of friendship, romantic love, and especially family connections make up the principal, though not exclusive, interest of most of her biographical essays. She devotes a considerable amount of space in her life of Petrarch, for instance, to the "family concord" that graced his upbringing, the generosity of his interactions "with many dear friends," and, of course, the "sympathy and esteem" that conditioned his lifelong adoration of Laura (*LI* 1:197). The life of Vittoria Colonna dwells extensively on the "utmost tenderness" exchanged between Vittoria and her spouse (*LI* 2:77). The life of Monti concentrates on the "warm heart" and "tenderness of feeling" he inherited from his parents, which "caused him to be idolized in his domestic circle" (*LI* 2:394). Such "ties of blood . . . [and] affection," as Macaulay puts it,[28] foregrounded within the broad field of public events and policy, constitute the essential record or "philosophy" of history worked out in Mary Shelley's *Lives.*

This continuous history of the heart's domestic affections gains a special resonance from Mary Shelley's uniquely personalized adaptation of the "sympathising tenderness" that Macaulay and other early practitioners of feminist historiography brought to their visions of the past. Mary Shelley's powerful form of this sympathy entailed her tendency to find recurrent versions of her own traumatic experience of shattering loss and broken affection in the domestic histories of her subjects.[29] Her *Lives* thus feature an array of grief-filled vignettes whose personal associations tantalizingly suggest the deepest forms of sympathetic identification: her special emphasis on mothers dying in childbirth in the lives of Rousseau and Lopé de Vega (*LF* 2:111; *LI* 3:24); her poignant treatment of the "distress" and "pain" brought to the "warm heart" of Cervantes by "the falling off of . . . [old] friends" (*LI* 3:160–61); her reflections on Petrarch's haunted memory of close friends who died young—"At this time Petrarch suffered the first of those losses which afterwards cast such gloomy shadows over his life" (*LI* 1:87); and, perhaps the most memorable of all these episodes, her account of Vittoria Colonna's mourning the early death of her husband for years afterward, "giving herself up entirely to sorrow . . . living in retirement . . . and dedicating herself wholly to memory" (*LI* 2:79).

This immersion in the personal calamities of others could give Mary Shelley a certain relief from her own harrowing memories, a Lethean solace she referred to as "the medicine of mind" issuing from the "quieter work" of biography (*MWSL* 3:92; *MWSJ* 532, 539). In some ways, then, biographical writing indulged her inclination to withdraw from public life and politics in her later years. But it also enabled her, through the mediation of biographical distance, to bring herself and her sorrows forward in ways she was otherwise reluctant to attempt, which is undoubtedly why she told Leigh Hunt that her life of Cervantes would "come home" (*MWSL* 2:293) and declared how much her readers would "sympathise in the intense and fond sorrow" of Vittoria Colonna (*LI* 2:79). If Macaulay frequently "shed many tears" over "the situation of [historical] sufferers," Mary Shelley fully *entered into* their situation, shed tears *with* them, and thereby produced one of her era's most emotionally charged forms of personalized history.

The public gender implications of that emphasis became acutely evident to Mary Shelley as soon as she joined the *Cyclopaedia* project in 1835, roughly halfway through its completion. She was the only female author in the series, a role prominently noted in advertised lists of the several dozen overall contributors and which constituted, in itself, something of a gendered intervention in masculine writing domains. Tensions accrued from that situation immediately, with Mary Shelley complaining that a gluttonous James Montgomery—the "Omnipresent Mr. Montgomery," she called him—swallowed up some of the best Italian lives (Dante and Ariosto) and botched the job by sexing it as the work of a man (*MWSL* 2:219, 222, 260).

Montgomery's life of Dante does betray a smirking tone of masculine con-descension—Beatrice is introduced as "the little lady" (*LI* 1:6)—and its general focus on Dante's public achievement and lack of interest in his personal or domestic situations implicate it even more significantly in the period's masculine historiography.

Many of the basic characteristics of that mode surface throughout the various historical and biographical contributions to the *Cyclopaedia* that preceded Mary Shelley's involvement. James Mackintosh characterizes his *History of England,* for instance, as a broad delineation of national mo-tions of progress (1:vi). E. E. Crowe adopts a lofty Hegelian philosophi-cal position for his *History of France,* claiming that the historian should "cast away . . . prejudices and passions" in the objective pursuit of fact and truth. Such an objectifying historical epistemology assumes literal em-bodiment in Harris Nicolas's *Chronology of History,* a one-volume compi-lation of "Tables, Calculations & Statements" on "the dates of Historical Events" that concisely represents the general historiographical spirit of the *Cyclopaedia's* earlier essays on the cultural past.[30] We know what a happily "prejudiced," date-free Jane Austen thought about such a historiographi-cal method. Mary Shelley's reaction may be judged from her final verdict on Montgomery's life of Dante: "I should have written it better" (*MWSL* 2:257). To produce "better" or, as I take her to imply, more personalized narratives within the impressive field of male historians assembled for the *Cyclopaedia* meant engaging in a particularly compelling form of histori-cal revisionism. Mary Shelley remained keenly attentive to the important gender politics of that challenge, refusing at one point to conduct research in the British Library because of its patriarchal atmosphere and working to include several women's biographies in the *Cyclopaedia Lives of Emi-nent . . . Men* (*MWSL* 2:260).

The stakes of these gender politics were raised dramatically by the cul-tural work that the *Cyclopaedia* was designed to perform. A product of the educational reform movements of the 1820s, the *Cyclopaedia* joined other diffusions of useful knowledge ventures in seeking to provide a rapidly expanding base of middle-class readers with cultural refinement and di-rection. Lardner and his publishers, Longman and the firm of John Taylor, specifically marketed their volumes to the "*general reader,*" to those non-specialists who, in the words of one of their advertisements, "seek that portion of information respecting [professional subjects] . . . which is generally expected from well-educated readers. . . . The present work will claim a place in the drawing-room and the boudoir."[31]

The type of upwardly mobile purchasers whom Lardner and his publishers expected to inhabit these book-filled drawing rooms and boudoirs may be recognized in the various product advertisements that pepper the *Cyclopaedia:* from table cutlery for "merchants, captains, families, [and] new-married couples" to treatises on female "accomplishments" for the "young lady" to medical pamphlets on tooth decay and the treatment of hernias — the hernia pamphlet available to be sent from a Charing Cross Road address to "any part of the world, *gratis.*"[32] In marketing cultural refinement, and sometimes medical relief, to this rising class of male and female consumers, the makers of the *Cyclopaedia* aimed, above all, to inculcate traditional British values and customs. Reviewers of the series, for example, found it teaching "gratitude" for the "blessings" of British government,[33] and the editors specifically directed such lessons at those new social groups and institutions acquiring prominence both at home and abroad: "Families resident in the Country . . . Emigrants . . . Libraries of Mechanics' Institutions, Literary and Philosophical Societies, The Army and the Navy, and of Colonial Institutions."[34]

Lardner's series became one of the most popular and successful purveyors of this conservative cultural conditioning, thanks to its distinguished cast of contributors, its innovative marketing strategy of offering "Cabinets," or subjects, for separate sale at only six shillings a volume, and its calculated pitches to the new purchasers of culture. Not even Lardner's eventual disgrace following his publicly scandalous liaison with the improbably named Mrs. Heaviside, wife of Captain Heaviside, seemed to dent the *Cyclopaedia*'s reputation as, in the words of a typical newspaper review, "one of the most valuable contributions that has ever been made to the cause of general knowledge and national education."[35] The national lessons it promoted were certainly conservative, but its mass educational appeal to a rising group of general readers, many of them clearly identified as female inhabitants of "the boudoir," also afforded special opportunities for a dissenting contributor like Mary Shelley to address, following Hays, a female readership's desire for "advancement" while participating more broadly in the shaping of social codes and practices for a newly ascendant class of readers.[36] For Mary Shelley, these circumstances made publishing her own form of feminist historiography in the *Cabinet Cyclopaedia* one of the most potentially influential contributions she could ever make to the gender reform movements of her time.[37]

Mary Shelley's alertness to this possibility of gender intervention registers in her habitual use of mediating biographical strategies to bring herself forward, both indirectly and more openly, on a variety of gender issues. Her views on patriarchal hierarchies and irresponsibility surface with trenchant irony, for instance, in her commentary on the actions of Goldoni's father when professional opportunities occasion his move to a new city. "Thus fortunately situated," Mary Shelley explains, "he resolved to have his son with him. He does not appear to have thought of inviting his wife also" (*LI* 2:215). The gender politics at work here become even more openly aggressive when Mary Shelley critiques unjust gender systems. In her life of Alfieri, for instance, she condemns the laws of primogeniture for "degrading" women and expresses "utmost abhorrence" at the moral degeneracy of the *cavalier servente* system (*LI* 2:248, 273). In contrast to her strictures against such historical examples of individual and institutional misogyny, Mary Shelley also celebrates societies noteworthy for their progressive gender relations. "No slur was cast by the [Renaissance era] Italians on feminine accomplishments," she contends. "Where abstruse learning was a fashion among men, they were glad to find in their friends of the other sex, minds educated to share their pursuits" (*LI* 2:75). Such analyses of the gender dynamics of the past certainly look to the present, sometimes obliquely yet often directly, giving Mary Shelley's *Lives* the overall shape of a sustained, if mediated, form of the gender critique she was loathe to conduct in a more openly polemical fashion.

Mary Shelley's most significant intervention in contemporary gender relations, however, entails a more specific application of her interiorized historiography to the clashing gender ideologies of her time. In tracing out the inner lives of her subjects, she consistently distinguishes between destructive types of egotism associated with masculine Romantic ideology and the kind of outward extension of emotional sympathies she had always promoted as the model of healthy personal and social relations. Examples of masculine egotism that injures women and children in particular recur throughout her *Lives* — such as Boccaccio's gratification of his own romantic passion for a married noblewoman, who is "humiliated" by their "secret intrigue"; or the selfish wrath of Marini's father, who expels his son from the family house for deviating from the professional career dictated by the father; or Ugo Foscolo's "worship of self," which leads to violent passions for women and makes "his own individuality the mirror in which the world was reflected" (*LI* 1:121; 2:174, 354).

Mary Shelley's most severe critique of such self-absorption centers on the individual she finds most responsible for contributing to its ideological elevation in her own time—who else but Rousseau. His selfish irresponsibility towards his lover and the five children he abandons to a Foundling Hospital appalls her: "he took her as a sort of convenience, and when inconveniences arose from the connection, he was disposed to get rid of them on the easiest possible terms" (*LF* 2:130–31). But Mary Shelley's ire burns hottest when she condemns Rousseau's insidious attempt to rationalize his behavior as part of a system of natural sublimity.

> In point of fact, nothing can be more unnatural than his natural man. The most characteristic part of man's nature is his affections. The protection he affords to woman—the cares required by his children; yet Rousseau describes his natural man as satisfying his desires by chance,— leaving the woman on the instant, while she, on her side, goes through child-bearing, child-birth, and child-nurture all alone. . . . He often dilates on simple pleasures—the charms of unsophisticated affections, and the ecstasy to be derived from virtuous sympathy—he, who never felt the noblest and most devoted passion of the human soul—the love of a parent for his child!" (*LF* 2:134–35, 130)

Mary Shelley rarely seethes like this in the *Lives,* and the extremity of her attack may very well derive from her awareness of how pervasively Rousseauist philosophies of egotism had infiltrated Romantic writing and social practices, sometimes in ways that struck very close to home. But her outrage also points to a corrective form of interior "affections," the outgoing "passion" or "sympathy" for others that cements domestic ties and forms the solid foundation for social and gender equality.

Various manifestations of this redemptive "sympathy," usually expressed within domestic communities, make up the core of Mary Shelley's revisionary historiography in the *Lives.* Numerous lives of poets, like the essay on Petrarch, attribute creative talent to the gentle nurturing of attentive parents who place the needs of their children before their own desires. Petrarch's father, for instance, initially resists his son's literary inclinations and tries to burn the youth's manuscripts of Roman authors; but the father relents upon hearing Petrarch's cries of anguish, "snatche[s] the remnants of Virgil and Cicero from the flames," and forever thereafter supports his son's literary ambitions (*LI* 1:64). Mary Shelley frequently presents related forms of domestic sympathy in siblings as well, perhaps most poignantly in her citation of Metastasio's letter to his brother on the death of their father: "I measure your sorrow by my own. . . . I thank you for your fraternal kindness in the midst of your affliction. Dear brother . . . if there is any thing that I can do to comfort you, demand it from me without reserve: your consolation will produce mine. My poor sisters!—how lost they will feel themselves! Take care of them, dear Leopold" (*LI* 2:207).

Mary Shelley's *Lives* also demonstrate how positive sympathy of this sort promotes harmonious gender relations based on mutual respect and consideration. Petrarch's outgoing concern for Laura's welfare, for example—just the opposite of Rousseau's inward love of self—enables him to control his destructive passion and avert disaster for them both. In the family politics of Mary Shelley's history, social and gender equality thus develop out of emotional sympathies nurtured within domestic circles. That chain of linked affections emerges most memorably in her portrait of Madame Roland, who learns from her mother's sheltering tutelage to "sympathise . . . with the emotions of others" and grows as an adult to extend that "tender sympathy" both to all of her loved ones and to the national causes of political justice and gender reform (*LF* 2:262, 271).

Reengendering history as the story of such sympathies, in a publishing format directly contesting more conventional historiography and marketed to a mass audience on the political rise, constituted one of Mary Shelley's strongest contributions to the persistence of those reform movements in her own time. Madame Roland's efforts, of course, had brought her to the scaffold, and Mary Shelley would always remain self-effacing and skeptical about her own endeavors to redeem the past and the present. But if she grew generally more publicly reticent as she aged, her comments on women's maturation in her final contribution to the *Cyclopaedia,* a life of Madame de Staël, suggest a certain kind of guarded confidence about her own sustained experiment with the politics of feminist historiography: "When young, they are open to such cruel attacks, every step they take in public may bring with it irreparable injury to their private affections, to their delicacy, to their dearest prospects. As years are added they gather courage; they feel the earth grow steadier under their steps; they depend less on others, and their moral worth increases" (*LF* 2:341). It would seem from the evidence of the *Cyclopaedia Lives* that the project of revisioning history helped give a maturing Mary Shelley the courage, steadiness, and self-worth to carry on her own political interventions, in however mediated a form, throughout even the darkest of times. That accomplishment gives her a special capacity among the female biographers and historians of her age to speak across the gap of time to feminist historiographers today, who continue, as Joan Scott puts it, to interrogate and change the ways in which "power is articulated," past and present, within the "primary field" of gender.[38]

15 : Blood Sisters

Mary Shelley, Liz Lochhead, and the Monster

E. DOUKA KABITOGLOU

The argument ad feminam, *all the old knives*
that have rusted in my back, I drive in yours,
ma semblable, ma soeur!

The cold felt cold until our blood
grew colder then the wind
died down and we slept

A woman in the shape of a monster
a monster in the shape of a woman
the skies are full of them

Adrienne Rich, "Snapshots of a Daughter-in-Law,"
"Phantasia for Elvira Shatayev," and "Planetarium"

Wanna know anything 'bout being a woman?
Well, better just ask us
I know her dramas, her traumas, and her fiascos
I know her sober
(but I know her better pissed)
I know her acid trips,
her abortions, and her analyst.
I know the Story of her Life —
each ironic twist.

She lent me her copy of Anais Nin
and we discovered we were Sisters Under the Skin.[1]

This is the way the Scottish poet Liz Lochhead, one of the most popular contemporary British women poets, begins her poem "True Confessions," which opens her collection *True Confessions and New Clichés*, 3, published in 1985, establishing a matrilineal model of textual relations (relations between texts authored by women)[2] depending on two assumptions—that texts are mothered[3] and that intertextuality is constitutive of meaning.[4] In her introduction to the volume, Lochhead confesses the following concerning the production of her performance poetry: "*True Confessions* in 1981 was an attempt at getting my stage nerve back after a disastrous premature version of *Blood and Ice*, my first try at a real play . . . ('I'd rather be at the dentist—Birmingham Evening News'). So would I, and the cast too" (*True Confessions and New Clichés*, 1).

The stage history of this "first try," demarcating her move from poetry to drama,[5] seems quite complicated, as we read in the revised edition of the play included in *Plays by Women*, 1988: "*Blood and Ice* was my first attempt at a stage play and my relationship with it has been as intense and almost as troubled as Mary Shelley's with her great novel—or the fictional Frankenstein's with his maimed and misunderstood creature. And as much of an ongoing passion too."[6] Lochhead continues her narrative of the play's vicissitudes, from its "first fumbling version—*Mary and the Monster*," to its disastrous production, which had provoked the sarcastic reviewer who'd said he would rather have been at the dentist. "And after reading the *Guardian* review I thought I'd rather be at the mortuary," she concedes. Tracing her engagement with the play "rewritten, totally, three times, living with and making for three years," her agonies and fights with directors, she concludes: "But despite the Bogey Men, I still love this play. More than anything else I have ever done. So I was glad to rewrite it substantially *again* for Winged Horse Touring Productions in Edinburgh in 1986. It'll never be perfect, or easy. But it's alive and kicking."[7]

Out of the four versions of the play, I will attempt an "intertextual" reading of the two published in *Plays by Women*, in 1985 and 1988. It surely makes for an interesting and complex relationship to Mary Shelley's two versions of *Frankenstein*, the 1818 and 1831 texts, calling for a comparative approach that examines Lochhead's dramatic biography of Mary Shelley as yet one more reader's response, attempting an exegesis of the nineteenth-century monstrous account of "the heart of darkness/darkness of the heart." But there is also Liz Lochhead's poetry.

In Lochhead's volume entitled *Dreaming Frankenstein and Collected Poems* (published in 1984),[8] the second poem is entitled "An Abortion" (significantly of an animal, not a human being), expounding a contemporary woman writer's version of the "myth of pregnancy" that was so powerfully explored by Mary Shelley, whose female anxieties of "birthing" were strategically displaced onto a male persona/mask.[9]

Spasms, strong, primeval
as the pulsing locomotion of some
terrible underwater creature
(*Dreaming Frankenstein*, 10)

In this poem and elsewhere, Lochhead emphasizes the grotesqueness of the female body, systematically avoiding and subverting what Teresa de Lauretis calls the cultural "representation of woman as image (spectacle, object to be looked at, vision of beauty—and the concurrent representation of the female body as the *locus* of sexuality, site of visual pleasure, or lure of the gaze)."[10] In a volume teeming with monsters, beasts, hags, furies, witches, (the) Grimm sisters, bulls, Caliban and the Minotaur, Bosch's and Brueghel's Hells—poetically representing what Jean Baudrillard calls "a culture of monstration, of demonstration, of productive monstrosity"[11]—Lochhead inserts three pieces drawing upon her obsession with the Mary Shelley myth: "Dreaming Frankenstein," "What the Creature Said," and "Smirnoff for Karloff," apparently inspired by the famous 1931 film version (with Boris Karloff acting the monster, fixing it into an authoritative cinematic representation).

I wish to quote the first one, "Dreaming Frankenstein,"[12] in full, not only because it constitutes an "abstract" of the play that I intend to discuss but also because it reveals both the "method" and the "truth" of literary production;[13] it yields answers to theoretical issues about the conditions of creativity, language, and writing, so rigorously formulated by Julia Kristeva, who asks: "In short, isn't art the fetish par excellence, one that badly camouflages its archaeology? At its base, isn't there a belief, ultimately maintained, that the mother is phallic, that the ego—never precisely identified—will never separate from her, and that no symbol is strong enough to sever this dependence?"; or, speaking of the mourning for the maternal object, she points to the loss of "the meaning—the value—of [the] mother tongue for want of losing the mother."[14]

She said she
woke up with him in
her head, in her bed.
Her mother-tongue clung to her mouth's roof
in terror, dumbing her and he came with a name
that was none of her making.

No maidservant ever
in her narrow attic combing
out her hair in the midnight mirror
on Hallowe'en (having eaten
that egg with its yolk hollowed out
then filled with salt)
— oh never one had such success as this
she had not courted.
The amazed flesh of her
neck and shoulders nettled
at this apparition.

Later, stark staring awake to everything
(the room, the dark parquet, the white high Alps beyond)
all normal in the moonlight
and him gone, save a ton-weight sensation,
the marks fading visibly where
his buttons had bit into her and
the rough serge of his suiting had chafed her sex,
she knew — oh that was not how —
but he'd entered her utterly.

This was the penetration
of seven swallowed apple pips.
Or else he'd slipped and healed her up secretly
again. Anyway
he was inside her
and getting him out again
would be agony fit to quarter her,
unstitching everything.

Eyes on those high peaks
in the reasonable sun of the morning,
she dressed in damped muslin
and sat down to quill and ink
and icy paper.
(*Dreaming Frankenstein,* 12)

The two texts of *Blood and Ice* I discuss (the 1985 and 1988 published versions) narrate the same events,[15] have the same dramatis personae (Mary Shelley and P. B. Shelley, Byron, Claire Clairmont, and the Swiss maid Elise), are phenomenological accounts of Mary Shelley's consciousness (as Lochhead emphatically informs us in her postscript to the play—"Mary Shelley, in whose consciousness my *entire play* takes place"), and use a similar structural technique—that of constant shifts in time between the play's "now" and the summer of 1816, when *Frankenstein* was conceived, as well as further back into Mary Shelley's childhood. In her dramatization, Lochhead attempts to duplicate the novel's structure of flashbacks instead of following a chronologically linear plot. Mary Shelley's all-enveloping consciousness, like a maternal womb or semiotic *chora,* acts as a frame narrative embedding the various incidents, making of the play an outgrowth of memory traces and retrospective reconstruction. "Literature, like hysteria," Kristeva remind us, is, after all, "a *staging* of affects both on the intersubjective level (characters) and on the intralinguistic level (style)."[16]

Yet the two plays differ crucially in two ways. The 1985 version is more of a representation of Mary Shelley's *reading,* rather than *writing,* of *Frankenstein,* and thus dramatizes the confrontation between Creator and Creature—and always under the sinister admonition of Byron, who seems fully aware of a text's potential for mischief:[17] "Have you read your book? Oh, I know you *wrote* it, have you read it though, recently? (*BI* 1985, 111). The 1988 text introduces a major innovation—it brings the Monster on stage as one of the main characters, who coauthors the book with Mary Shelley (addressed as "Frankenstein"). So we become witnesses to the writing process itself and Mary Shelley's psychological and textual engagement with her "creature." In the earlier version, the action's "now" is the year 1824 (spring)—the *terminus a quo* being the cue, "Lord Byron is dead. I wonder if Claire knows. . . . The news came yesterday" (*BI* 1985, 115); in the later version, Mary Shelley's stream of consciousness has as its point of departure (and return) a moment shortly after Percy's drowning in the summer of 1822. A radical digression can also be seen in the ending of the two plays, which I will discuss later.

The play fixates on "blood," — the sign of the whole cycle of woman's sexuality.[18] By employing and transforming the dominant imagery of the novel, the Promethean "fire and ice," the title suggests exactly Liz Lochhead's reading of her object of (textual) desire: *Frankenstein,* not as a "modern" but as a "female" Prometheus. The play consists of two acts. In the 1985 version, the stage directions set up the "mental" scene of a "ghostly nursery." The play opens with Mary Shelley alone, speaking to herself, in a sensation of "coldness," denoting a multiple cluster of ambivalent and contradictory significations that stitch together death, erotic frigidity, loneliness, dejection, sterility. The disembodied voices of P. B. Shelley, Byron, and Claire drag her into the past, as she re-members bits of lived experience that surface into consciousness: June 16th of 1816, Maison Chapuis, Montalègre, near Geneva — a period Mary Shelley later noted "was acting a novel, being an incarnate romance."[19] The scene fades into a tableau presenting Mary Shelley and Claire, in "filmy" clothes, standing on each side of stand with a double mirror,[20] and *"as if under a spell they begin to brush out their long hair slowly with silver hairbrushes, each other's image"* (*BI* 1985, 86).[21] Not only visually but also verbally, the scene highlights the "double" in both its uncanny and feminine, almost homoerotic, specificity:

> CLAIRE: Do you not think we are somewhat alike? *Oui?* Yes, Mary, we do resemble each other after all. Oh, not in colouring, no, but in bearing, in —
>
> MARY: How could we, we are not —
>
> CLAIRE: Not in blood, no. But we are closer perhaps than sisters, *oui?* Haven't we always shared everything? (*BI* 1985, 86)

The mirror scene, in which the two women form narcissistic reflections of each other, seamlessly unfolds into a discussion between Mary Shelley and Claire, bringing up reminiscences of Mary Godwin and P. B. Shelley courting "in the graveyard," the territory of the maternal.[22] The absent (dead) mother is the transcendental signified of the play.[23] She haunts (like in a gothic horror) not only Mary Shelley's memories and fantasies but everybody else's: from Claire's naive reminiscences — "That's Mary's famous mama!" (*BI* 1985, 89) — to Byron's sinister Coleridgean allusion to Mary Shelley's pendant[24] — "Oh yes, the lady she has hanging round her neck. The writer!" (91) — to Mary Shelley's awareness of her mother's monstrosity — "Yes, that 'Hyena in Petticoats' as all you male writers were pleased to call her" (91)[25] — to Elise's — "The marvellous Mary Wollstonecraft was very keen on freedom for Woman" (107) — to P. B. Shelley's — "Oh yes. She died. Yes, it *is* a terrible terrible thing that childbed was her deathbed" (113). The maternal grave is repeatedly posited as the primal scene for Mary Shelley — "CLAIRE: That was Mary's secret place. Her mother's grave. She would frighten me, tell me how her mother would come and haunt me" — whereas Mary Shelley's response establishes this horrific spot as the locus of autonomy and creativity: "There, I could be perfectly alone" (93).[26] To Mary Shelley's necrophiliac desire, her mother is literally a "text" that demands reinscription, resurrection,[27] but she is also the polymorphous site of prohibition, having set severe conditions for women's liberation in her *Vindication of the Rights of Woman:* the death of desire and female pleasure.[28] The basic polarity in this scene, as in the entire play, forms a relational structure that violates not only the traditional coupling of Mary Shelley–Percy and Byron-Claire, but also biographical information that presents Mary Shelley as a silent listener of — or, better, an eavesdropper upon — the philosophical exchanges conducted in her presence; "incapacity and timidity always prevented my mingling in the nightly conversations," she confesses.[29]

The roles of protagonist and antagonist in the play are held by Mary Shelley and Lord Byron. The subtext of an intense intellectual and sexual power game is established through minute details of speech and gesture. Byron, if anything, operates as a mirror, or double, to Mary Shelley, not of "sameness" (as in Claire's case) but of radical "otherness" — reflecting back to her what she chooses to forget or keep hidden. It is Byron, rather than P. B. Shelley, who persistently and almost ruthlessly enforces upon her her "unnameable" desire — to be a writer.

> BYRON: How about you, Mary? I'm sure you could astonish me. Aren't you a writer too? Mary Godwin?
> MARY: No, I don't want —
> SHELLEY: Mary writes very well. Oh, you do Mary. When you have a mind to. That novel you began, that promised —
> BYRON: Novel?

MARY: I did not complete it, it was worthless.

SHELLEY: Now, how could one with a parentage like yours write anything worthless?

MARY: I don't want to be a writer. (*BI* 1985, 91)

Her negation is more than a sign of modesty; it transpires the intense combination of pride and shame, anger and love that the act of writing, as the maternal topos, provokes in her — her ambivalence about female self-assertion and public performance. It is near this cue that Byron proclaims the celebrated literary competition that led to the birth of *Frankenstein:* "Listen, I'll set us a little contest. We shall all try our hand, shall we? . . . Who's going to write the most terrifying tale?" (*BI* 1985, 92). Wollstonecraft and Godwin, as members of Mary Shelley's personal "family romance," as historical figures, and as "texts" whose sociopolitical theories have significantly contributed to the cultural constructions of the time, constantly interface with the plot and rhetoric of *Blood and Ice.* Byron is the one to instigate Godwinian, and Shelleyan, idealistic notions of rationality and liberalism, the one who perceives not only Mary Shelley's Oedipal deadlock — "Poor Mary — Mary. Wearing her mother round her neck and her father on her sleeve" (94) — but also her ideological tensions, caught as she is between her mother's radicalism (the combination of equal rights and self-abnegating sexuality) and her father's utopianism. Parallel to his undermining of P. B. Shelley's idealism and liberalism, Byron systematically works on digging into Mary Shelley's "hiding places":

BYRON: Can you win the wager? I think perhaps you can. Who knows, you may find the damps and darks surprisingly agreeable. I sense you have a talent for it. Am I not right, Shelley, doesn't she? I sense it. I smell it. (*BI* 1985, 96)

In the Mary Shelley–Byron confrontation that follows, he ruthlessly "unclothes" her repressed anger at her husband's advanced sexual morals of "free love." Her demure justification of her own affair with P. B. Shelley's close friend, Thomas Jefferson Hogg,[30] as a "Noble Experiment" provokes an outburst from Byron that uniquely renders, I believe, the core of Lochhead's "reading" of Mary Shelley — and her novel — as a critique of the philosophizing away of sexual desire. With a masterful gesture of total rejection of P. B. Shelley (and his ideas) — "None of your cold-blooded laboratories of Sexual Relations" (100) — he winds up his rhetoric of seduction (simultaneously flicking her mother's pendant) closer and closer to Mary Shelley's nearly speechless (and willing) receptivity:[31]

> BYRON: Write that story! And, let me tell you it won't be made of nebulous ideas, pretty philosophies, or pointless, pointless politics! Everything I write is a creature who can only live by what he sees, hears, smells, tastes, touches and grabs, Mrs Shelley! (*BI* 1985, 101)

It is in the same night that Mary Shelley, sleeping next to P. B. Shelley, has the nightmare that gives birth to *Frankenstein* and articulates her ambivalence towards the creative act, her self-representation as a bearer of death, and her "creature" as the "sign" of the unrepresentable, a projection of indulged feminine desire in masculine form[32] — the subject of desire being, according to Freud, (always already) male.[33]

Act 2 opens with a scene and a setting that reestablish the mental frame of the "now" in 1824, from which the excursions into the past are undertaken. Mary Shelley is holding a copy of *Frankenstein* and a peculiar doll of her own resemblance, hiding under its skirt not the lower part of the body but another head in the resemblance of the maid, Elise. The doubleness of the enigmatic toy suggests the obscenity and horror of "something to see" — a head — in place of female genitals.[34] Byron is uppermost in Mary Shelley's mind — " 'Read your own story,' he said and now he is dead." As she begins reading her book, "and soon 'The Endeavour' was icebound" (*BI* 1985, 103), lights change and we are transferred to Bagni di Lucca in the summer of 1818. If in Act 1 Mary Shelley is cast in the problematic role of "daughter" to Mary Wollstonecraft's "mother,"[35] around the issue of incest, matricide,[36] guilt, and authorship, Act 2 focuses on the other "monstrosity" of Mary Shelley's life: infanticide or the undoing of children as obstacles to a woman's sexual and textual pleasure. Children killing mothers, mothers killing children — the imaginative stage is strewn with bodies.

Scene 7. Summer 1822 at Lerici. Mary Shelley reads her book or, rather, summarizes the part of Frankenstein's creation/destruction of the female monster. Upon the Creature's solemn pronouncement, "I shall be with you on your wedding night," P. B. Shelley enters. The total lack of communication between wife and husband is obvious as they speak at cross purposes — he of his new boat, she of his new mistress; he of the theory and practice of free love, she of the pain of abandonment and jealousy; he of the progress of medical science, she of childbeds that turn into death-beds;[37] he of his worship of female fecundity, she of women's suffering in the hands of men adoring Woman. Mary Shelley here "becomes" her natural and textual mother,[38] declaiming the fleshly desire that makes a woman hostage to the body—a body that in demanding physical satisfaction makes itself vulnerable to frustration and pain:

> MARY: When man and woman lie down together they are at once each other's strange wild savage beasts and each other's sacrificial victims. And Death sits at the bedhead. Oh, not the Little Death the poets talk of, the moment's love-swoon after which each animal feels a little sweetly sad. But the Death they talk about below stairs, down there, down among the women. (*BI* 1985, 114)[39]

As she tears at the last shreds of idealism,[40] the monstrous reality of death at childbirth (her mother's and woman's in general) arouses in her a feeling of sisterhood-in-blood to Elise and Claire and all women, a narcissistic, homosexual longing for the other-as-self. Double-doll in hand (which terrifies P. B. Shelley), she narrates yet another dream she had, of Elise stitching a Claire-doll, following instructions from "Mary Wollstonecraft's Pattern Book," and finishing with "a strong knot" at the joint "between the thighs." At this point P. B. Shelley enters her dream and begins to pull at the laces in sexual moves, lifting the dress that covers over the doll's head to reveal—"above the waist of your hellish creature . . . my belly, my loins, my thighs, my screaming vulva and my limbs tangled with your head and pulled you down, down, down" (*BI* 1985, 115). In an erotic delirium, Mary Shelley, lamenting the frustration of her emotional and sexual passion in a marriage that has deeply agonized her, reverses the orders of fiction and reality and projects the female monster's destruction onto her husband.[41] Seduced by erotic desire, she is yet "sewn up" according to her mother's "pattern" of the egalitarian family and denouncement of passion,[42] the prescriptive assault on female sexuality and pleasure that was posed as the grim condition for women's liberation.[43] The dream explodes Wollstonecraft's paradigm of women's psychic economy, which wants the sexual and the intellectual as mutually exclusive. The dream also signifies Mary Shelley's overwhelming surrender to uninhibited and all-consuming sexual experience.[44] The sublimated womb-turn-mind exacts its toll. Also, the image of a patchwork doll (like the patchwork monster) reflects a creativity conditioned by domesticity, mechanical rather than organic (in Romantic terms).

The play ends with Mary Shelley's monologue in Scene 8, which circles the narrative back into the frame of mind of the opening section. In a gesture of psychic dismemberment, she cathexes herself into all the characters of the drama:

> MARY: I thought: I am Frankenstein, the creator who loves creation and hates its results. Then I thought: no, I am the monster, poor misunderstood creature feared and hated by all mankind. And then I thought: it is worse, worse than that, I am the female monster, gross, gashed, ten times more hideous than any male counterpart, denied life, tied to the monster bed for ever. (*BI* 1985, 115)

Having identified with each and every one of her creatures, at last she recognizes the liberating power of the very act of writing: "But now I see who I am in my book. I am Captain Walton, explorer. Survivor" (115). Suspended between Walton's prudence and Frankenstein's adventurousness and also between a "blood bath" and a "bath of ice" — signifiers that constantly shift and slide in the drama as to offer no firm footing — she momentarily seems to achieve the (Romantic/Coleridgean) creative flight that reconciles oppositions and fuses the contraries of fire and ice: "The ice cannot stop you if your hot hearts say it shall not!" (116). It seems that the human mind can still impose meaning on the chaos of existence, categorizing and structuring, exercising linguistic control. The woman's fantasy of a possible return to a paradisal origin and maternal *jouissance* that can be imaginatively reached and verbally articulated apparently still holds. She "*sits down at her writing table*" (116).

In this version of the play, the monster, Frankenstein's creature, is only a verbal construct, an imaginative patchwork stitched out of numerous references to conditions of monstrosity and creaturehood made by the various characters, culminating in Mary Shelley's speaking of her miscarriage in the following figurative terms: "I wonder, was it a boy or a girl? Or a monster. What are little girls made of? Slime and snails and . . . What are monsters made of?" (*BI* 1985, 112). Here she very powerfully brings to the surface the literal monstrosity of female primary narcissism, the self-loathing of the body.

In the 1988 version of *Blood and Ice,* Lochhead brings the monster on stage, thus giving a local habitation and a name to imaginative grotesqueness, violence, and contamination, following the etymological imperatives of the word that signifies "saying" as "showing" (montrer, mostrare). What has probably intervened is Lochhead's attraction to the classical film version of the novel, James Whale's *Frankenstein* (1931), which allows for a transposition of cinematic semiology into her text.[45] I believe that the two editions of the play, like the two editions of *Frankenstein,* can provide a case study of the tensions and options that go into the formation of a text-in-process. Unlike Mary Shelley's 1831 revisions, which are in the direction of a criticism of imaginative indulgence, seeking a possible cohabitation of artistic needs and domestic obligations, Lochhead's rewriting severs all possibilities of a manageable reconciliation between the two, thereby enforcing the woman artist into a choice of either/or. Mary Shelley's revised version—shifting attention away from the monster's story—introduces a much stronger presence of the mysterious, of destiny, which turns humans into victims of forces they cannot control and presents the text as a cultural product of other people and external circumstances—an intertextual "patchwork."[46]

Mary Shelley, I think, conveniently resorts to the "death" of the author to get rid of the stain of creative boldness and egotistical imagination, for which she was censured. Lochhead's revised version, on the contrary, brings the Creature to the center of the drama, showing Mary Shelley, the (female) human, as victimizer and victim, collaborating with the forces of the semiotic that are now in full sway to overthrow (male) symbolic order in all its conventions and practices (mostly represented through her husband). If Mary Shelley's later text "defers" responsibility for the act of writing by claiming in the introduction that it was "only a transcript of the grim terrors of [her] waking dream," Lochhead's acknowledges full participation—and therefore guilty complicity—in a language that kills. A logocentrism that recognizes the "womb" as master signifier is in full sway here.

Lochhead's theatrical innovation not only sets the problem of visual representation of "monstrosity" as such,[47] but it also creates a new balance of powers and introduces a different narrative strategy. Without changing the plot substantially, Lochhead establishes a condensed mental time span that, while beginning with summer 1816, ends upon P. B. Shelley' s death— radically minimizing Byron's role. Byron's centrality is also undermined by the presence of the Creature, who now becomes Mary Shelley's "antagonist" and chief point of reference, if not interlocutor. With the marginalization of Byron and his heightened, heated speeches, the seductivenes of language gives its place to a silent seduction.[48] The play's emphasis has also shifted from the "scene of reading" to the "scene of writing," so we get a closer look at the psychic motions that accompany the production of the book rather than its reception or reader response on the part of Mary Shelley. In that sense, the play is theoretically closer to the Romantic aesthetics of creativity, although its ending is far less optimistic and positive. The play's rhythms, signifying the primal psychological impulses out of which the work grew, are also changed to incorporate the seesaw between semiotic and symbolic exchanges. Paradoxically, the Creature's mute or semiarticulate presence, acting as spectator and assessor of the action, usurps the category of the "real," giving a touch of unreality, a dreamlike sensation to the human interactions and transactions.

The ghostly nursery of the 1985 version is also gone. Scene 1 here highlights reflexivity through the presence of a "mirror," and we see Mary Shelley lying in a Fuselilike posture with her book on her chest in place of the original terrifying incubus,[49] duplicating Elizabeth Lavenza's pose after her murder by the monster and bringing into prominence the book's doubling of the daemonic unconscious. The Creature is the first to speak, unmistakably identifying the author with the protagonist of the story: "Why did you make me, Frankenstein?" (*BI* 1988, 83), thus exposing Mary Shelley's masculine persona as a cover strategy through which female desire can only be articulated. In my discussion of this version of the play, I intend to concentrate on the Creature's dramatic presence exclusively, which operates as a subtext (or choric commentary) to the dramatic action (or better conversation), and only refer to plot and the other characters where there is a significant divergence from the earlier work. The Creature's first description gives us "a glimpse of naked legs, and arm with a rag of seaweed like SHELLEY'S" (*BI* 1988, 85), alluding to P. B. Shelley's contribution to the repressed affects that torment Mary Shelley and also to the final "revenge" of the uncanny.

Lochhead's theatrical monster differs radically from its prototype in *Frankenstein;* in fact, it could be described as its "antitype" — as far as I can judge, of course, from the linguistic code of stage directions, the specular code as such being unavailable to me. Mary Shelley's fully articulate and verbally eloquent monstrosity, despite its social marginalization, betrays a complete integration into the symbolic order and Oedipal law of the father; the Shelleyan monster transgresses aesthetic and moral limits, but not linguistic ones. Lochhead counterposes what might be called a "semiotic" Creature that, despite its maleness, speaks a "m/other tongue"—it is the "sign" of the pre-Oedipal, the maternal body in a system of "generating substitutes for the forbidden mother."[50] Normally, as Julia Kristeva informs us, the "sign represses the *chora* and its eternal return," yet the monster, as an art object, marks "poetic animality," the "irruption of the motility threatening the unity of the social realm and the subject."[51]

In conceiving her Creature as inarticulate and linguistically childlike or animal-like—at the intersection of sign and rhythm, of the semiotic and the symbolic—Lochhead is probably following in the tradition of stage or film versions of the novel (more than a hundred film adaptations have been released), which, almost from the beginning (as early as 1823),[52] deprived the monster of its novelistic prerogative of high rhetoric.[53] The Creature in the play is extremely primitive, employing minimal, elliptical and paratactic language, with brief utterances, avoiding the first person pronoun identification and referring to himself with the deictic "This," evading a full disclosure of the subjectivity of monsterism. Furthermore, given that "deixis is the most significant linguistic feature—both statistically and functionally—in the drama" because it is "the primary means whereby language gears itself to the speaker and receiver," a way in which body language is "*inscribed* in the language itself," it definitely gestures towards origins.[54] The Creature speaks "poetry," the mother-tongue. It often takes its cues from the characters' conversation, as in, for instance, Claire's call—"Elise! Elise where are you, you tiresome creature! Come and help me make myself pretty"—to which it responds: "Frankenstein, why did you make This Not Beautiful?" (*BI* 1988, 86). Lochhead also emphasizes the semiotic nature of her Creature by allotting to it its own musical signature. The monster figures as a sign of the unsignifiable—the maternal *chora,* the maternal body.

The other innovation this version of the play introduces is a more clearcut visualization of Mary Shelley's inner split: her ego gradually becomes totally passive and receptive to the irruption of the semiotic forces from within:

CREATURE: Cry Hallelujah. . . . Frankenstein. For you have found
This. This has found you. What terrifies you will terrify

others. It is easy. Describe what haunts you. Frankenstein
you have thought of a story.

MARY *as in a dream, stands up,* CREATURE *leads her slowly to
her desk. She sits down, acceptance of her fate total, as if
hypnotised.*

CREATURE: Now write This.

She lifts pen, begins. Very slow fade as very slowly:

MARY/CREATURE (*in unison*):   It was on a dreary night in November
      . . . . (*BI* 1988, 99)

Act 2 presents more drastic changes from the earlier version of the
play than does Act 1, as it focuses on the actual writing of the book and
covers the period Mary Shelley was working on *Frankenstein* (June 1816–
May 1817), with the Creature permanently there, invisible to anyone but
her. As the stage directions suggest, the Creature is dressed "*in a strange
cloak. It is made of the same material as the backdrop so he can sometimes almost emerge out of it, or almost disappear, by merely turning*" (*BI*
1988, 100).[55] The Creature's presence radically alters the scopic economy
of the play, as human performance, particularly Mary Shelley's, is ob-
jectified under the monster's "spectatorship." Between them develops,
on both visual and verbal levels, what de Lauretis calls a "structure of
desire, of mutual seduction."[56]. Lochhead gives us an extended sample
of Creature-language, his subversive discourse, his "uncertain and inde-
terminate articulation": "Echolalic, vocalizing, lilting, gestural, muscular,
rhythmical."[57]

CREATURE: Cold. Cuckold. This is lonely. Men recoil from This, they
      are afraid. This is alive, they want to kill This. This will
      not die. This . . . woke up.
      Struggles with sound like babbling baby.
      Dark. This shivers. This is afraid. The light presses in on
      these eyes. The light hurts This. The light is worse than
      the dark. (*BI* 1988, 100)

The parallelism between the child's murder in the novel and the deaths
of Mary Shelley's own children comes out very strongly in the play,[58] but
so does her abortion, which is imaginatively associated with the ripping
apart of the female creature — an act denoting the primal drive pathway of
desire and its frustration, the undoing of female perverse sexuality con-

demned by Mary Wollstonecraft's notion of debased femininity — as well as the hideousness of birth as such:

> MARY   *like a zombie.* CREATURE *rocking*
> MARY   *as if in dream or hypnotised trance. Shaking her.*
> CREATURE: This hold. This love. Please . . .
> MARY: . . . I was now about to form another being . . .
> CREATURE: This saw you! She — This's She — She spread out. She not all come. Bits of She . . . One perfect eye. An eyelash. The curve of her cheek. Mess. Strings. Sinews. Bits with no skin. No skin to hold it in. Flesh. Bits where white bone show. Not built yet. Her heart not yet pumping. Her heart not yet in its cage. Not ready yet. Not time. Below the sheet a big mess of blood. You tore her to bits. You would not make her, you said —
> MARY: No. No. Foul abortion. I cannot cannot ever make another. (*BI* 1988, 110)

The scene indicates Mary Shelley's open revulsion against newborn life, the drama of guilt, dread, and flight from corrupt female flesh that murders, incarnating her mother's vindication of the rights of (rational) woman through the abortion of body.[59] But also, too perilously close to a narcissistic mirror image of herself, Mary Shelley/Frankenstein performs the ultimate act of triumphant castration on the desiring Creature[60] — matching horror for horror. "The body's inside," Kristeva argues, "shows up in order to compensate for the collapse of the border between inside and outside. It is as if the skin, a fragile container, no longer guaranteed the integrity of one's 'own and clean self.' "[61] After the final elimination of the dangerous sexual autonomy of the "bride," the roles are totally reversed; Mary Shelley seems to have turned into the disanimated automaton, passively surrendering to the Creature. In that, the creative process is reversed as she becomes the embodiment of the "uncanny," which, according to Freud's definition, marks the "uncertainty whether a particular figure . . . is a human being or an automaton."[62]

By now the Mary Shelley–Monster relationship has developed into a direct verbal exchange and a full communication that seems to render her unconscious wishes into "speech acts" — an "Adamic" language that ironically returns her to paradise lost in its destructive imaginative energy.[63] Mary Shelley surrenders to her terrified recognition that desire, once aroused, has its own impetus and logic, uncontrollably projecting itself into the natural and human world, becoming voracious, bleeding (and bleeding into) the object it invades. The Creature's performative utterance, "This kill!," is first translated into dream—P. B. Shelley's dream of strangling Mary Shelley—to which the Creature responds with the impatience of Mary Shelley's accomplice: "How long do you mean to be content?" (*BI* 1988, 113).

We know that by 1822 the Shelleys' marriage had broken down completely. Mary Shelley, devastated after her near-fatal miscarriage, wants to end the relationship. She cannot leave, so he must go. Like Lochhead's female in the poem "The Other Woman," her "right hand knows not what her left is doing."[64] The Creature undertakes to project those introjections, to enact the repressed murderous desires Mary Shelley's controlling ego cannot openly acknowledge—eliminate the bridegroom.[65] Mary Shelley seems to have relapsed into a childhood or primitive stage, where psychical and material reality are hardly distinguished, seduced into the (belief of) "omnipotence of thoughts" that gives birth to the uncanny, as Freud argues. In Kristeva's words, "the sign is not experienced as arbitrary but assumes a real importance."[66]

> MARY *very calmly begins to recount the final story, about* SHELLEY's *drowning as the creature picks up* SHELLEY's *now lifeless body and places it down on the chaise. Parody of the first time we saw him.* (*BI* 1988, 113)

As the human characters of the play—Byron, Claire, Elise—drift along with insubstantial declarations, wishes, or demands, to finally retreat as ghosts, the reality of Mary Shelley's homoerotic fixation and enforced companionship with her Creature is all that is left, lured as she is into "phantasmagoriana"—to use Polidori's term (*BI* 1985, 96)—the uncharted realms of female experience, of physicality and depression, the "dark region of the unnameable Thing" that promises no relief or rebirth:[67]

> CREATURE: Wrap yourself in furs, Frankenstein, for soon such ice
> and cold. No escape, except by the death of you, or This.
> *BI* 1988, 114)

Mary Shelley/Frankenstein admits to her incapacity to destroy her rival—son and lover—through fire or freezing. She is no longer the triumphant survivor of the 1985 version of the play, no longer granted a concluding monologue (by the elimination of Walton and its salutary frame). She is even deprived of language — the final word is now allocated to the presymbolic that threatens to engulf her:

CREATURE: Come, pursue This, chase This, till This shall catch you ...
Darkness and mist. (BI 1988, 114)

The game of erotic attraction and homicidal tactics continues, but its course seems already determined — quest and conquest becoming indeterminable, hunter and hunted blurring into one consciousness, a double syntax, a "death-bearing symbiosis."[68] Lochhead's 1988 Blood and Ice withdraws all desire of disentanglement from the embrace of monstrosity. In admitting her failure to eradicate her Creature, Mary Shelley seems to drift towards a negative (Kantian) sublime "of feminine disempowerment," nodding in the direction of "This thing of darkness I acknowledge mine."[69]

Like the poem "Smirnoff for Karloff," which takes its cue from the 1931 James Whale film version of the story, the poem "The Bride," in Lochhead's 1991 collection, Bagpipe Muzak,[70] de-monstrates "sisterhood":

I am the absolute spit of Elsa Lanchester.
A ringer for her, honestly,
down to the zigzag of lightning in my frightwig
and it's funny no one, me in-
cluded, ever noticed the resemblance before.
(Bagpipe Muzak 65)

The speaker, looking into the mirror on her wedding morning,[71] suddenly becomes aware that she looks like "Elsa Lanchester," the actress who played twin roles — the "monsteress" and Mary Shelley in the dramatized introduction, in James Whale's horror film The Bride of Frankenstein (1935).[72] In this version of the story, the female creature is not destroyed by its creator, so the Mary Shelley figure of the prologue is reincarnated as female monster, replete with frightening scars, frizzy hair, and a lightning bolt crossing through her.[73]

Lochhead, seeking identification with a figure that the "author" of Frankenstein had refused to create, having chosen instead to cross-dress in male garb the disruptive or disturbing forces — the monstrosity of female sexuality and creativity — reconfigures the cultural history of the myth, "birthing" that hideous progeny, female desire, whose symbolization had been problematic for Mary Shelley. Such doublings and triplings of (female) identity and its representation — Elsa Lanchester (actress) as Mary Shelley and as female monster, but also as Elizabeth Lavenza (Frankenstein's bride proper) — dissolving the boundaries between the novel, Mary Shelley's own life, and dramatic and cinematic readings of the original theme, suggest once more the instability of the book's "meanings," which allow it to become a modern "sign" for both the phenomenological and semiotic discourses: for the divided self as well as the floating signifier.[74] In our case, the return of the repressed referent, the female "teratogenesis" that shatters the culturally constructed feminine[75] — the "snow-white" mirror image of woman as "the beautiful object" — can come very appropriately from the concluding poem of *Dreaming Frankenstein*, called "Mirror's Song," which, through a savage castration,[76] bodies forth a triumphant surfacing of the female monster:

> Smash me looking-glass glass
> coffin, the one
> that keeps your best black self on ice.
> . . . .
> Smash me for your daughters and dead
> mothers, for the widowed
> spinsters of the first and every war
> let her
> rip up the appointment cards for the
> terrible clinics,
> the Greenham summonses, that date
> they've handed us. Let her rip.
> She'll crumple all the
> tracts and adverts, shred
> all the wedding dresses, snap
> all the spike-heel icicles
> in the cave she will claw out of —
> a woman giving birth to herself.
> (*Dreaming Frankenstein*, 68)

Notes

Chapter 1: "Not this time, Victor!"

1. For example, *Prometheus Bound, La Divina Comedia,* and *Paradise Lost.*

2. Mary Shelley referred to it as "a juvenile attempt of mine"(*MWSL* 1:71).

3. Mary Shelley commented at various times about how her works prognosticated the future. She perhaps would not have been surprised, then, when years later, Jane, Lady Shelley and Sir Percy Florence Shelley would adopt her neice, Bessie Florence Gibson, in somewhat similar circumstances.

4. Peter L. Thorslev Jr., "Incest as Romantic Symbol," *Comparative Literature Studies* 2 (1965): 56.

5. See, as examples, Margaret Homans, *Bearing the Word* (Chicago: Univ. of Chicago Press, 1986), 113-14, 302; Sandra M. Gilbert and Susan Gubar, *The Madwoman in the Attic* (New Haven: Yale Univ. Press, 1979), xi, xii, 6-17, 73; Mary Poovey, *The Proper Lady and the Woman Writer* (Chicago: Univ. of Chicago Press, 1984), x, xi, 138; Mary Jacobus, "Is There a Woman in This Text?" *New Literary History* 14 (1982): 117-41; Lee Sterrenberg, "Mary Shelley's Monster: Politics and Psyche in *Frankenstein,*" *The Endurance of Frankenstein,* ed. George Levine and U. C. Knoepflmacher (Berkeley: Univ. of California Press, 1979), 144; Patricia Meyer Spacks, *The Female Imagination* (New York: Avon Books, 1975), 2-6.

6. The condemnation of judicial systems in *Frankenstein* is internationalized by the story of the De Lacey family in France and Frankenstein's incarceration in Ireland.

7. A comparison of the 1818 and 1831 texts regarding the appearance of Lavenza can help clarify this important technique and its significance. In the *Frankenstein* of 1818, Lavenza has hazel eyes and an ample brow—the sign of intelligence—descriptive of the author herself; her dark auburn hair, however, is not a match. The 1831 Lavenza retains her ample brow, but her eyes are now blue—perhaps suggesting P. B. Shelley's family and her own children—but the "living gold hair" surely again reflects the author.

8. [Mary W. Shelley], Review of William Godwin's *Cloudesley, Blackwood's Edinburgh Magazine* 27 (May 1830): 712.

9. *MWSL* 2:260.

10. See *Mary Shelley,* ed. Betty T. Bennett, in *Lives of the Great Romantics III: Godwin, Wollstonecraft and Mary Shelley by Their Contemporaries* (London: Pickering and Chatto, 1999).

11. *Athenaeum* 484 (February 4, 1837): 74.

12. *The Iron Chest* was first performed in March 1796 at the Drury Lane Theatre.

13. *Spectator* 449 (February 4, 1837): 111, *Examiner* 1515 (February 4, 1837): 101, *Metropolitan* 18 (March 1837): 67, and *Monthly Review* 1 (March 1837): 376, in order.

14. *Literary Gazette, and Journal of the Belles Lettres,* 1046 (February 4, 1837): 66.

15. *MWSJ* 2:456.

Chapter 2: "To speak in Sanchean phrase"

1. Mary Shelley, "The English in Italy" (1826), in *The Mary Shelley Reader,* ed. Betty T. Bennett and Charles E. Robinson (New York: Oxford Univ. Press, 1990), 342.

2. On *History of a Six Weeks' Tour,* see: Betty T. Bennett, *Mary Wollstonecraft Shelley: An Introduction* (Baltimore: Johns Hopkins Univ. Press, 1998), 23–30; Angela D. Jones, "Lying Near the Truth: Mary Shelley Performs the Private," in *Iconoclastic Departures: Mary Shelley after* Frankenstein, ed. Syndy M. Conger, Frederick S. Frank, and Gregory O'Dea (Teaneck, N.J.: Fairleigh Dickinson Univ. Press, 1997), 19–34; Jeanne Moskal, Introductory Note to "History of a Six Weeks' Tour" and "Letters from Geneva I and II," in *The Novels and Selected Works of Mary Shelley,* gen. ed. Nora Crook with Pamela Clemit, 8 vols. (London: Pickering and Chatto, 1996), 8:1–8; Jacqueline M. Labbe, "A Family Romance: Mary Wollstonecraft, Mary Godwin, and Travel," *Genre* 25 (1992): 211–28; Robert Brinkley, "Documenting Revision: Shelley's Lake Geneva Diary and the Dialogue with Byron in *History of a Six Weeks' Tour,*" *Keats-Shelley Journal* 39 (1990): 66–82; E. B. Murray, "A Suspect Title-Page of Shelley's *History of a Six Weeks' Tour,*" *Papers of the Bibliographical Society of America* 88 (1989): 201–6; Elizabeth Nitchie, "Mary Shelley, Traveller," *Keats-Shelley Journal* 10 (1961): 29–42; and André Koszul, "Notes and Corrections to Shelley's 'History of a Six Weeks' Tour,'" *Modern Language Review* 2 (1906): 61–62.

3. Another script is provided by William Godwin's most recent novel, *Fleetwood* (1805).

4. Such political engagement has been one emphasis of the new edition of Mary Shelley's novels and selected works; see particularly the General Introduction by Betty T. Bennett (1:xlii–lxx; expanded into the *Introduction* cited above, n. 2) and the annotations to *Valperga* by Nora Crook (vol. 3) and to *Rambles in Germany and Italy* by Jeanne Moskal (in *Travel Writing,* vol. 8).

5. Parenthetical references cite Miguel de Cervantes Saavedra, *The Adventures*

of Don Quixote (1605, 1615); I have used the translation by J. M. Cohen (New York: Penguin, 1950).

6. Mary Shelley, "Life of Cervantes" in *Lives of the Most Eminent Literary and Scientific Men of Italy, Spain, and Portugal,* 3 vols. (London: Longman, Orme, Brown, Green and Longmans, 1837), 3:120–88; Godwin's assessment of *Don Quixote* appears at 3:182. This volume is also Vol. 88 of the *Cabinet of Biography,* conducted by the Rev. Dionysius Lardner (*Lardner's Cabinet Cyclopedia*).

7. William Godwin, *Lives of Edward and John Philips* (London: Longman, Hurst, Rees, Orme, and Brown, 1815), 255. Godwin's assessment of Philips's work as crude, in both language and sentiment (252–55), was shared by Peter Anthony Matteux, a later translator, who said that Philips "added a world of Obsenity and fribbling Conceits." Matteux is quoted in Edwin B. Knowles, "Cervantes and English Literature," in *Cervantes across the Centuries,* ed. Angel Flores and M. J. Bernardete (New York: Dryden Press, 1947), 285–86.

8. David Duff, *Romance and Revolution: Shelley and the Politics of a Genre* (Cambridge: Cambridge Univ. Press, 1994), 3.

9. Edmund Burke, *Reflections on the Revolution in France, and on the Proceedings in Certain Societies in London Relative to that Event,* ed. Conor Cruise O'Brien (Harmondsworth: Penguin, 1968); the entire passage occurs on 169–70.

10. Duff, *Romance and Revolution,* 3.

11. Helen Maria Williams, *Letters from France: containing many new anecdotes relative to the French Revolution,* 2d ed. (London, 1792), 4–5. For Williams's use of Burke, see Gary Kelly, *Women, Writing, and Revolution 1790–1827* (New York: Oxford Univ. Press, 1993), 44, 50.

12. Duff, *Romance and Revolution,* 3.

13. William Godwin, *Thoughts Occasioned by the Perusal of Dr. Parr's Spital Sermon, Preached at Christ Church, April 15, 1800: Being a Reply to the Attacks of Dr. Parr, Mr. Mackintosh, The Author of an Essay on Population, and Others* (1801; reprinted in Godwin, *Uncollected Writings [1785–1822]: Articles in Periodicals and Six Pamphlets,* facsimile reproductions, with an introduction by J. W. Maren and B. R. Pollin [Gainesville, Fla.: Scholars' Facsimiles and Reprints, 1968]), 351.

14. Peter H. Marshall, *William Godwin* (New Haven: Yale Univ. Press, 1984), 229.

15. Marshall, *Godwin,* 211–33. See Charles Lucas, *The Infernal Quixote. A Tale of the Day,* 4 vols. (London: W. Lane, 1801). On Lucas, see Nicola Trott, "Sexing the Critic: Mary Wollstonecraft at the Turn of the Century," in *1798: The Year of the Lyrical Ballads,* ed. Richard Cronin (New York: St. Martin's Press, 1998), 44–47.

16. Pamela Clemit, headnote to [Mary Wollstonecraft Shelley,] "Memoirs of William Godwin" and Mary Wollstonecraft Shelley, "Life of William Godwin" [1836–40], pp. ix–xxiv in *Lives of the Great Romantics III: Godwin, Wollstonecraft, and Mary Shelley by Their Contemporaries,* ed. Pamela Clemit, Harriet Devine

Jump, and Betty T. Bennett (London: Pickering and Chatto, 1999). More generally on this period, see Emily W. Sunstein, *Mary Shelley: Romance and Reality* (Baltimore: Johns Hopkins Univ. Press, 1991), 331–35.

17. Syndy McMillen Conger, "Multivocality in Mary Shelley's Unfinished Memoirs of Her Father," *European Romantic Review* 9 (1998): 303–22.

18. Throughout this section I rely on Rory Muir, *Britain and the Defeat of Napoleon, 1807–1815* (New Haven: Yale Univ. Press, 1996), esp. chap. 2; Simon Bainbridge, *Napoleon and English Romanticism* (Cambridge: Cambridge Univ. Press, 1995), chap. 3; Gabriel H. Lovett, *Napoleon and the Birth of Modern Spain,* 2 vols. (New York: New York Univ. Press, 1965), esp. chaps. 1, 3, 4, and 18; Charles E. Chapman, *A History of Spain* (New York: Macmillan, 1941), esp. 399–410 and 488–98; and F. J. MacCunn, *The Contemporary English View of Napoleon* (London: G. Bell and Sons, 1914), 107–16.

19. MacCunn, *Contemporary English View,* 108; Bainbridge, *Napoleon and English Romanticism,* 101.

20. Bainbridge, *Napoleon and English Romanticism,* 99. The quotation from Wordsworth is from the letter to R. E. Pasley, *Letters of William and Dorothy Wordsworth, The Middle Years, Part 1, 1806–1811,* ed. E. de Sélincourt, 2d ed., rev. Mary Moorman (Oxford: Clarendon Press, 1967), 1:480–81.

21. Muir, *Britain and the Defeat of Napoleon,* 37–38.

22. Quoted in Hedva Ben-Israel, *English Historians on the French Revolution* (Cambridge: Cambridge Univ. Press, 1968), 40.

23. William Wordsworth, *Concerning the Relations of Great Britain, Spain, and Portugal, to Each Other, and to the Common Enemy, at this Crisis; and Specifically as Affected by the Convention of Cintra* in *The Prose Works of William Wordsworth,* 3 vols., ed. W. J. Owen and Jane Worthington Smyser (Oxford: Clarendon Press, 1984), 1:227–28.

24. Samuel Taylor Coleridge, Letter to the Editor, *Courier,* December 7, 1809; reprinted as Letter 1 of "Letters on the Spaniards," in *The Collected Works of Samuel Taylor Coleridge,* 16 vols., gen. ed. Kathleen Coburn, Bollingen Series no. 75 (Princeton: Princeton Univ. Press, 1969–), 3.2:38.

25. Anne Plumptre, *A Narrative of a Three Years' Residence in France,* 3 vols. (London: J. Mawman, 1810), 3:847.

26. See William A. Borst, *Lord Byron's First Pilgrimage* (New Haven: Yale Univ. Press, 1948), 27.

27. [Sydney Owenson], Lady Morgan, *Florence Macarthy: An Irish Tale,* 4 vols. (1818; reprinted with an introduction by Robert Lee Wolff, no. 8 in series *Ireland: From the Act of Union 1800 to the Death of Parnell 1891* [New York: Garland, 1979]).

28. Ben-Israel, *English Historians,* 40–45.

29. Lovett, *Napoleon and the Birth of Modern Spain,* 2:833.

30. Linda Colley, *Britons: Forging the Nation 1701–1837* (New Haven: Yale Univ. Press, 1992), 258–59.

31. William Hazlitt, *The Complete Works of William Hazlitt*, 21 vols., ed. P. P. Howe (1930–34; New York: AMS Press, 1967), 19:164. On Hazlitt, see Bainbridge, *Napoleon and English Romanticism*, 183–207.

32. Byron, *Don Juan*, 13: st. 11. Byron dated Canto 13 February 12, 1823; it was published in a volume also containing Cantos 12 and 14 in December 1823. See *Byron's Don Juan: A Variorum Edition*, 4 vols., ed. Truman Guy Steffan and Willis W. Pratt (Austin: Univ. of Texas Press, 1971), 3:315, 358.

33. William Hazlitt, "Standard Novels and Romances," *Edinburgh Review* (March 1815), in Howe, ed., *Complete Works*, 16:8.

34. Marion Kingston Stocking, "Andrea Vaccà Berlinghieri," in Appendix C of *The Journals of Claire Clairmont*, ed. Marion Kingston Stocking, with the assistance of David Mackenzie Stocking (Cambridge: Harvard Univ. Press, 1968), 464–66; the quotation is from 464.

35. The characterization "fatal" was Henry Crabb Robinson's, quoted in *The Clairmont Correspondence: Letters of Claire Clairmont, Charles Clairmont, and Fanny Imlay Godwin, 1808–1879*, ed. Marion Kingston Stocking, 2 vols. (Baltimore: Johns Hopkins Univ. Press, 1995), 2:125. Charles Clairmont's letter appears on 119–24. I rely on Stocking's notes throughout this paragraph.

36. Indeed, her enthusiasm for Spanish culture endured. She devotedly read Spanish authors and sought recommendations and loans of books from John Bowring in 1826 and 1837 (*MWSL* 1:514, 2:288). The later request was connected with the Spanish biographies, which Mary Shelley enjoyed writing so much that she declared again, in 1835, "I wish I could go to Spain" (*MWSL* 2:255).

37. Catherine Belsey, "Constructing the Subject, Deconstructing the Text" (1985; reprinted in *Feminisms: An Anthology of Literary Theory and Criticism*, ed. Robyn R. Warhol and Diane Price Herndl [rev. ed; New Brunswick: Rutgers Univ. Press, 1997]), 657–73. See also Louis Althusser, *Lenin and Philosophy and Other Essays*, trans. Ben Brewster (London: New Left Books, 1971).

38. See Joan B. Landes, *Women and the Public Sphere in the Age of the French Revolution* (Ithaca: Cornell Univ. Press, 1988).

39. Mary Wollstonecraft, *Vindication of the Rights of Woman* (1792) in *The Works of Mary Wollstonecraft*, ed. Janet Todd and Marilyn Butler, 7 vols. (London: Pickering and Chatto, 1989), 5:255–56.

40. Belsey, "Constructing the Subject," 660–61.

41. Wollstonecraft, Preface to *Maria; or, the Wrongs of Woman*, in Todd and Butler, eds., *Works*, 1:83.

42. In a similar vein, Lucy Aikin, in *Epistles on Women* (1810), concluded her description of the idealized woman of chivalry with this complaint:

But say, this paragon, this matchless fair,
Trod she this care-crazed earth? No; . . . born of air,
A flitting dream, a rainbow of the mind,
The tempting glory leaves my grasp behind;
Formed for no rugged clime, no barbarous age,
She blooms in Fairyland the grace of Spenser's page. (emphasis added)

Lucy Aikin, *Epistles on Women, Exemplifying their Character and Condition in Various Ages and Nations* (1810), excerpted in *British Literature, 1780–1830,* ed. Anne K. Mellor and Richard E. Matlak (New York: Harcourt Brace, 1996), 831.

43. Mary Wollstonecraft, *Vindication of the Rights of Woman,* in Todd and Butler, *Works,* 5:96.

44. Judith Fetterley, Introduction to *The Resisting Reader* (1978); reprinted in Warhol and Herndl, eds., *Feminisms,* 569.

45. Charlotte Lennox, *The Female Quixote* (1752), ed. Margaret Dalziel (New York: Oxford Univ. Press, 1989), 381.

46. Mary Wollstonecraft, *Letters Written during a Short Residence,* in Todd and Butler, *Works,* 4:248. See Jeanne Moskal, "The Picturesque and the Affectionate in Mary Wollstonecraft's *Letters from Norway,*" *Modern Language Quarterly* 52 (1991): 263–94.

47. Rev. Richard Polwhele, *The Unsex'd Females: A Poem* (1798; reprinted in *The Unsex'd Females: A Poem by Richard Polwhele and The Female Advocate by Mary Ann Radcliffe,* ed. Gina Luria [New York: Garland, 1974]), 6 n.

48. Kelly, *Women, Writing, and Revolution,* 146.

49. Elizabeth Hamilton, *Memoirs of Modern Philosophers* (1800), 3 vols. (4th ed., Bath: R. Cruttwell, for G. C. and J. Robinson, 1804), 1:3; the phrase "female philosophers" occurs at 1:57.

50. Kelly, *Women, Writing, and Revolution,* 152, 149; the quotation is from 149.

51. I have consulted the second edition of Eaton Stannard Barrett's *The Heroine; or, the Adventures of Cherubina,* 3 vols. (London: Henry Colburn, 1814). See Gary Kelly, "Unbecoming a Heroine: Novel Reading, Romanticism, and Barrett's *The Heroine,*" *Nineteenth-Century Literature* 45 (1990), 220–41.

52. Mary Shelley's letter of August 15, 1832 suggests that the family also associated Sancho with a desire for solitude. Percy Florence, wanting to eat supper alone, obtains his mother's consent by saying he is imitating Sancho (*MWSL* 2:170).

53. In an earlier draft of *Frankenstein,* Mary Shelley wrote of Clerval, "Like Don Quixote his favourite study consisted in books of chivalry and romance, and when very young, I can remember that we used to act plays composed by him out of these books, the principal characters of which were Orlando, Robin Hood, Amadis and St. George." In the 1818 printing the phrase "like Don Quixote" was

omitted. See Charles E. Robinson, ed., *The Frankenstein Notebooks*, 2 vols. (New York: Garland, 1996), 1:11.

54. See Sunstein, *Mary Shelley*, 320; and Jean de Palacio, *Mary Shelley dans son oeuvre* (Paris: Klincksieck, 1969), 354. On *Lodore*, see Sharon L. Jowell, "Mary Shelley's Mothers: The Weak, the Absent, and the Silent in *Lodore* and *Falkner*," *European Romantic Review* 8 (1997): 298–322; and Lisa Vargo, "*Lodore* as an Imagined Conversation with Mary Wollstonecraft," a paper delivered at a conference devoted to Mary Shelley, University of Calgary, August 1997.

55. Charles E. Robinson, "Percy Bysshe Shelley, Charles Ollier, and William Blackwood: The Contexts of Early Nineteenth-Century Publishing," in *Shelley Revalued: Essays from the Gregynog Conference*, ed. Kelvin Everest (Leicester: Leicester Univ. Press, 1983), 184.

Chapter 3: The Impact of *Frankenstein*

1. For "horizons of expectations," see Wolfgang Iser, *Prospecting: From Reader Response to Literary Anthropology* (Baltimore: Johns Hopkins Univ. Press, 1989), and other works referred to in that book. The many biographical records of actual reviewing in the Romantic period show the extent to which reviewers were obliged and pressured to follow the general policy of the periodicals for which they wrote.

2. In William Hazlitt, *On Patronage and Puffing, Table Talk*, 2 (London: Colburn, 1824), 311.

3. Examples, notably one relating to Moore's *Lalla Rookh* (1817), for which a large sum was paid, can be found among the Longman Archives, Reading University Library.

4. E. B. Murray, ed., *The Prose Works of Percy Bysshe Shelley*, 1 (New York: Oxford Univ. Press, 1993). The piece was first published by T. Medwin in the *Athenaeum* (1832), and *The Shelley Papers* (1833). The three essays are written for an implied outside reader; they reveal no connection with the authors of the books and include some mild criticisms.

5. The specific phrase is "his labours." In the usage of the time, however, the phrase might also be read as gender neutral.

6. See Charles E. Robinson, "Percy Bysshe Shelley, Charles Ollier, and William Blackwood: The Contexts of Early Nineteenth Century Publishing," in *Shelley Revalued: Essays from the Gregynog Conference*, ed. Kelvin Everest (Leicester: Leicester Univ. Press, 1983) 183.

7. Frederick L. Jones ed., *The Letters of Percy Bysshe Shelley* (New York: Oxford Univ. Press, 1964) 1, 551. Another candidate for the third publisher known to have said no is Hookham, who published Peacock's novels.

8. The book is dated 1818 on the title page, but most copies appear to have been already sold to the distributors late in 1817. For the prices and print runs of the

various editions and the percentage changes in the fall in price in the nineteenth century, see the appendix.

9. The reviews, on which the following passage and the quotations are taken, are noted and summarized in W. H. Lyles, *Mary Shelley: An Annotated Bibliography* (New York: Garland, 1975), 168.

10. The copy in the Codrington Library, All Souls College Library, Oxford, carries a long advertisement describing Lackington's other publications in the associated genres, including *The Magus or Celestial Intelligencer, Lives of the Alchemystical Philosophers, Apparitions, or The Mysteries of Ghosts, Hobgoblins, and Haunted Houses, The Life, Prophecies and Predictions of Merlin Interpreted,* and Toland's *Critical History of the Celtic Religion, Tales of the Dead.*

11. *The Collected Letters of Thomas and Jane Welsh Carlyle* (Durham, N.C.: Duke Univ. Press, 1970), 1:124.

12. Quoted in Steven Earl Forry, *Hideous Progenies, Dramatizations of Frankenstein from the Nineteenth Century to the Present* (Philadelphia: Univ. of Pennsylvania Press, 1990), ix.

13. Account transcribed in *Shelley and His Circle* (Cambridge: Harvard Univ. Press, 1961-), 5:397, from the manuscript in the Bodleian.

14. Godwin to Mary Shelley, July 22, 1823. Quoted in Forry, *Hideous Progenies,* 3, from an unpublished letter in the Huntington Library, California.

15. *Morning Post,* August 23, 1823, quoted in Forry, *Hideous Progenies,* 37.

16. *Frankenstein* was still advertised in the *London Catalogue of Books,* 1835.

17. Bentley Archives, British Library. See also Royal A. Gettman, *A Victorian Publisher: A Study of the Bentley Papers* (London: Cambridge Univ. Press, 1960).

18. From 1800 to 1810, the average price of three-volume novels (three deckers) was about 12 shillings, in the following decade about 25 shillings. After Scott's *Ivanhoe* (1820), at 30 shillings, Hope's *Anastasius* set a new high of 31.5 shillings, a level at which the price of most new novels was maintained, despite the continuing fall in the costs of manufacturing, until the end of the century.

19. The Waverley novels, sold to the trade at 3.8 shillings for retail at 5 shillings were often "undersold" at 4 shillings. See John J. Barnes, *Free Trade in Books* (Oxford: Oxford Univ. Press, 1964), 6. Reprints of The English Classics produced by Dove, Scott, and Webster and other publishers at this time were cheaper than Bentley's, for example.

20. Bentley Archives. Figures confirmed by printing records in the Strahan/ Spottiswoode Archives, British Library. An account page reproduced in Gettman, *A Victorian Publisher,* 52, treats the first two impressions as one.

21. As I calculate, this represents twenty-eight years from 1818 or twenty-eight years from 1831.

22. A repair, effected by soldering in a plug that stands out as not quite aligned, can be seen on page 35, where, in the 1849 impression, the word *modern* in the

running title has been replaced. This appears to have been an error on the part of the repairer, for it is the word *Prometheus* that had become worn. The engraved title page was also dropped in the later impressions, perhaps because that plate had become too worn.

23. *The Letters of Mary Wollstonecraft Shelley,* ed. Betty T. Bennett (Baltimore: Johns Hopkins Univ. Press, 1980–88), 2:299.

24. *The Hodgson Parlour Library* edition (see appendix) is a possible exception. I have found no record among the Bentley archives either of permission having been given or of a complaint of piracy. Since Hodgson's edition is taken from the 1831 version, it would have been hard for the publisher to claim that this edition was not infringing upon copyright.

25. Sir Herbert Maxwell, *Life and Times of . . . William Henry Smith* (1893), vol. 1, especially 49–58. This was noted, for example, by Charles Knight in *Passages of a Working Life,* 3 vols. (1865), 3, 17, referring to an observation made in 1851. *The Parlour Library* and *The Novelist, A Collection of Standard Novels,* like *The Romancist and Novelist's Library,* also contained many foreign titles.

26. For prices see Gettman, *A Victorian Publisher,* 51, and Michael Sadleir, *XIX Century Fiction: A Bibliographical Record* (London: Constable, 1951), 2:97. The prices noted in these books are, however, mainly for new volumes appearing in the series for the first time. The dates when the prices of existing titles like *Frankenstein* were reduced are not all known. Impressions for all the *Bentley's Standard Novels* were in general for shorter runs than the 1,000 suggested as normal in the mid-thirties in a letter noted by Gettman, *A Victorian Publisher,* 51.

27. "Inventory of Stereotypes," 1861, Bentley Archives.

28. It does not appear, for example, in the *Catalogue of W. H. Smith's Subscription Library* (1872), John Johnson Collection, Bodleian Library.

29. Mary Wollstonecraft Shelley, *Frankenstein: The Original 1818 Text,* ed. James Rieger (New York: Pocket Books, 1974), xx; Mary Shelley, *Frankenstein,* ed. with an introduction by Maurice Hindle (London: Penguin, 1985), 8; Mary Shelley, *Frankenstein, Or, The Modern Prometheus* (New York: Modern Library, 1993), ix; Mary Wollstonecraft Shelley, *Frankenstein: The Original 1818 Text,* ed. D. L. Macdonald and Kathleen Scherf (Peterborough, Ontario: Broadview Press, 1994), 35.

30. From a sample of circulating library catalogs in the Bodleian Library.

31. Advertisement for the Series in copies of books published in Routledge's *World Library.*

32. Mrs. Julian Marshall, *The Life and Letters of Mary Wollstonecraft Shelley* (London: Bentley, 1889), 1:139, 143.

33. Lucy Maddox Rossetti, *Mary Shelley* (London: W. H. Allen, 1890), 109.

34. Richard Church, *Mary Shelley* (London: Gerald Howe, 1895), 52.

35. In vol. 2, chap. 5 of the 1818 version.

36. Quoted in Forry, *Hideous Progenies*, 5.

37. For the mass reading of *Don Juan* see William St Clair, "The Impact of Byron's Writings," Andrew Rutherford, ed., *Byron, Augustan, and Romantic* (London: Macmillan, 1990).

38. *John Bull*, July 29, 1823, quoted in Forry, *Hideous Progenies*, 5.

39. *Theatrical Observer*, August 9, 1823.

40. *Court Circular and Royal Gazette of Fashion, Literature, The Fine Arts, Music, and the Drama* 1, no. 7 (August 16, 1823), not known to Forry. Quoted from a copy in the author's collection. Unfortunately I have been unable to find a copy of the earlier issue, which is said to have contained a fuller review.

41. I have been unable to find a more exact figure. Capacity at the time was normally measured in terms of money, that is, gross nightly takings. It is clear from figures given by witnesses to the House of Commons Select Committee on Dramatic Literature, 1832, that the English Opera House was comparable in size to the Haymarket, which held between 1,600 and 1,700.

42. The boxes held 1,230 persons, the pit 1,090, and the galleries 1,512. "Second prices" offered boxes for 3 shillings, pit for 1.5, and lower gallery for 1, based on information from a playbill for a performance on August 27, 1828.

43. Evidence by the theater managers to the Select Committee on Dramatic Literature, *Parliamentary Papers*, 1832.

44. In several movies he was renamed Egor and made famous by Marty Feldman.

45. *The Vampyre* was written by Byron's doctor, John William Polidori, one of the party at Diodati in 1816. *The Vampyre* achieved some fame, partly because it was falsely attributed to Byron. For its original publication, see *Shelley and His Circle*, 6:777–81. Despite public denials by Byron, Galignani of Paris, whose editions were widely read in Britain during the first half of the century, continued to include the piece among Byron's works, although with a disclaimer. In the 1880s and 90s, when *Frankenstein* first reached its mass popular readership, *The Vampyre* was also on sale in a cheap edition, still falsely attributed to Byron.

46. E.g., in *Theatrical Observer* for August 2, 1823.

47. The print runs of the Everyman edition, for example, appear to have been modest. See the appendix.

48. Notably Chris Baldick, *In Frankenstein's Shadow* (New York: Oxford Univ. Press, 1987).

Chapter 4: From *The Fields of Fancy* to *Matilda*

1. *Mathilda*, in *The Mary Shelley Reader*, ed. Betty T. Bennett and Charles E. Robinson (New York: Oxford Univ. Press, 1990), 173–246; *Matilda* [retitled from

Mathilda], ed. Janet Todd, in one vol. with Mary Wollstonecraft, *Mary* and *Maria* (London: Pickering and Chatto, 1991; Harmondsworth: Penguin Books, 1992); *Mathilda*, ed. Elizabeth Nitchie, Extra Series 3 of *Studies in Philology* (Chapel Hill: Univ. of North Carolina Press, 1959).

2. Nitchie, introduction to *Mathilda,* vii–xv; U. C. Knoepflmacher, "Thoughts on the Aggression of Daughters," in *The Endurance of Frankenstein: Essays on Mary Shelley's Novel,* ed. George Levine and U. C. Knoepflmacher (Berkeley: Univ. of California Press, 1979), 113–15; Peter Dale Scott, "Vital Artifice: Mary, Percy, and the Psychopolitical Integrity of *Frankenstein,*" ibid., 183–85; William Veeder, *Mary Shelley and Frankenstein: The Fate of Androgyny* (Chicago: Univ. of Chicago Press, 1986), 217–18; Terence Harpold, " 'Did you get Mathilda from Papa?': Seduction Fantasy and the Circulation of Mary Shelley's *Mathilda,*" *Studies in Romanticism* 28 (1989): 49–67.

3. Anne K. Mellor, *Mary Shelley: Her Life, Her Fiction, Her Monsters* (London: Routledge, 1988), 191–200; Kate Ferguson Ellis, "Subversive Surfaces: The Limits of Domestic Affection in Mary Shelley's Later Fiction," in *The Other Mary Shelley: Beyond* Frankenstein, ed. Audrey A. Fisch, Anne K. Mellor, and Esther H. Schor (New York: Oxford Univ. Press, 1993), 227–29. For a broader view, see Katherine C. Hill-Miller, *"My Hideous Progeny": Mary Shelley, William Godwin, and the Father-Daughter Relationship* (Newark: Associated Univ. Presses, 1995), 101–27, and Margaret Davenport Garrett, "Writing and Re-writing Incest in Mary Shelley's *Mathilda,*" *Keats-Shelley Journal* 45 (1996): 44–60.

4. *Matilda* [retitled from *Mathilda*] and *The Fields of Fancy,* in M 5–67, 351–405 (the spelling of all quotations follows the idiosyncrasies of the original); Nitchie includes only chapter one of *The Fields of Fancy* (90–101).

5. Knoepflmacher, "Thoughts on the Aggression of Daughters," 113; Jane Blumberg, *Mary Shelley's Early Novels* (London: Macmillan, 1993), 225, n. 20; see Pamela Clemit, *The Godwinian Novel: The Rational Fictions of Godwin, Brockden Brown, Mary Shelley* (Oxford: Clarendon Press, 1993), 35–69, 139–74. For a discussion of *Matilda* in relation to a different configuration of novels, see Tilottama Rajan, "Mary Shelley's *Mathilda:* Melancholy and the Political Economy of Romanticism," *Studies in the Novel* 26, no. 2 (summer 1994): 43–68.

6. M 350, 388, 410.

7. See Emily W. Sunstein, *Mary Shelley: Romance and Reality,* 2d ed. (Baltimore: Johns Hopkins Univ. Press, 1991), 168–79.

8. *MWSJ* 294, 296; Betty T. Bennett, introduction to "Relation of the Death of the Family of the Cenci, Bodleian MS. Shelley adds. e. 13," trans. Mary Shelley, ed. Betty T. Bennett, in vol. 10 of *The Bodleian Shelley Manuscripts* (New York: Garland, 1992), 163.

9. E.g. Knoepflmacher, "Thoughts on the Aggression of Daughters," 115; Veeder, *Mary Shelley and Frankenstein,* 217–18. For a discussion that does recog-

nize the novella's artistry, published after this essay was completed, see Charlene E. Bunnell, "*Mathilda*: Mary Shelley's Romantic Tragedy," *Keats-Shelley Journal* 46 (1997): 75–96.

10. P. B. Shelley translated the *Symposium* from July 7 to 20, 1818, and Mary Shelley transcribed his translation from July 20 to August 6, 1818 (*MWSJ* 217–20, 220–22).

11. Mary Shelley read Dante's *Purgatorio* with P. B. Shelley in February and August 1819 (*MWSJ* 248, 294–95).

12. Nitchie, introduction to *Mathilda*, ix; exceptions are Harpold, "'Did you get Mathilda from Papa?'" 51; Rajan, "Mary Shelley's *Mathilda*," 46; and Garrett, "Writing and Re-writing Incest," 48–50.

13. According to Mary Shelley's preface to P. B. Shelley's *Essays, Letters from Abroad, Translations and Fragments* (1840), he also planned to use the figure of Diotima as the instructress of the Greek stranger in his unfinished tale, "The Coliseum," begun in late 1818 (*M* 335).

14. E.g. Nitchie, "Introduction," ix; Todd, "Introduction," xviii.

15. Mary Wollstonecraft, "Extract of The Cave of Fancy. A Tale" (written 1787, published 1798), ed. Marilyn Butler and Janet Todd, in vol. 1 of *The Works of Mary Wollstonecraft* (London: Pickering and Chatto, 1989), 199, 206.

16. E.g. *PJ* 115–16, 125, 470; cf. *PBSL* 1:81, 162, 201.

17. Blumberg, *Mary Shelley's Early Novels*, 225, n. 20; cf. Muriel Spark, *Mary Shelley: A Biography* (Harmondsworth: Sphere Books, 1988), 150, and Rajan, "Mary Shelley's *Mathilda*," 49.

18. Mary Shelley to Maria Gisborne (November 9, 1819), *MWSL* 1:112.

19. *MWSJ* 308 and n.; Sunstein, *Mary Shelley*, 179.

20. For Mary Shelley's unsuccessful attempts to retrieve *Matilda* between January and June 1822, see *MWSL* 1:215, 218, 224, 229, 237, and *Maria Gisborne and Edward E. Williams, Shelley's Friends: Their Letters and Journals,* ed. Frederick L. Jones (Norman: Univ. of Oklahoma Press, 1951), 76, 82 (hereafter *MGJL*). That she retained a copy is clear from the fact that she read it aloud to Edward and Jane Williams in August and September 1821 (*MWSJ* 377, 379).

21. Blumberg, *Mary Shelley's Early Novels*, 225, n. 20.

22. Harpold, "'Did you get Mathilda from Papa?'" 63.

23. Mary Shelley began a translation of Alfieri's *Myrrha* in September 1818 (*MWSJ* 226); for a fuller discussion of her use of this play, and of its Ovidian source, see Garrett, "Writing and Re-writing Incest," 51–56.

24. Thomas Medwin, *The Life of Percy Bysshe Shelley: A New Edition,* ed. H. Buxton Forman (New York: Oxford Univ. Press, 1913), 252; Medwin went so far as to suggest that *Matilda* was a fictional rewriting of *Myrrha*.

25. E.g. Harpold, "'Did you get Mathilda from Papa?'" 59; William Godwin, *Things as They Are; or The Adventures of Caleb Williams,* ed. Pamela Clemit,

vol. 3 of *Collected Novels and Memoirs of William Godwin* (London: Pickering and Chatto, 1992), 110, 118, 124 (hereafter *CW*).

26. See *M* 404–5.

27. See *PJ* 10–13.

28. For a fuller discussion of the material summarized in the next two paragraphs, see a longer version of this essay in *Romanticism* 3 (1997): 152–69.

29. Shelley read *Oedipus Tyrannus* to Mary Shelley from September 19 to 24, 1818 (*MWSJ* 226–27).

30. *Purgatorio*, 28–29. (References are to *The Vision; or Hell, Purgatory, and Paradise, of Dante Alighieri*, translated by the Rev. H. F. Cary [London, 1814].) For P. B. Shelley's admiration of the episode of "Matilda gathering flowers" in Canto 28, of which he translated lines 1–51 at around this time, see *PBSL* 2:112.

31. *M* 19–20; *Purgatorio*, 28.50–53; for Mary Shelley's dramatic treatment of the myth of Proserpine, see *M* 72–91; *M* 34.

32. See Clemit, *The Godwinian Novel*, 115–58, 198–99.

33. Cf. *M* 363–64.

34. Milton, *Comus*, lines 672–13; *Paradise Lost*, 9.710–14. (References are to *John Milton*, ed. Stephen Orgel and Jonathan Goldberg [New York: Oxford Univ. Press, 1991].)

35. Mark Philp, *Godwin's Political Justice* (London: Duckworth, 1986), 16–23; on P. B. Shelley and Godwin, see P. M. S. Dawson, *The Unacknowledged Legislator: Shelley and Politics* (Oxford: Clarendon Press, 1980), 33–176; M. H. Scrivener, *Radical Shelley: The Philosophical Anarchism and Utopian Thought of Percy Bysshe Shelley* (Princeton: Princeton Univ. Press, 1982), 35–76; Pamela Clemit, "Shelley's Godwin, 1812–1817," *Durham University Journal* 85 (1993): 189–201.

36. See Hill-Miller, *"My Hideous Progeny,"* 46–50.

37. *CW* 273, 275; see also Philp, *Godwin's Political Justice*, 113–17.

38. See *PJ* 18.

39. *CW* 273.

40. See Philp, *Godwin's Political Justice*, 24, 95.

41. Cf. Sunstein, *Mary Shelley*, 172–73. For Mary Shelley's active involvement in the writing of *The Cenci*, see Bennett's introduction to "Relation of the Death of the Family of the Cenci," 161–70, and *M* 283 and n.

42. See *M* 358–59.

43. See *PJ* 53.

44. Cf. *E* 222.

45. E.g. *M* 32.

46. For a discussion of *Matilda* in relation to the feelings of the actual victims of father-daughter incest, see Hill-Miller, *"My Hideous Progeny,"* 102–5.

47. Mary Shelley reread *Mandeville* from April 21 to 23, 1818 and (volume one only) on March 6, 1819 (*MWSJ* 206, 251).

48. Godwin praised *The Cenci* in a letter to Mary Shelley of March 30, 1820 (C. Kegan Paul, *William Godwin: His Friends and Contemporaries,* 2 vols. [London: Henry S. King, 1876], 2:272); his dismissal of *Prometheus Unbound* is noted by Maria Gisborne in her journal entry for August 22, 1820 (*MGJL* 45); Godwin to Mary Shelley, February 14–18, 1823 (*MWSL* 1:323 n.).

Chapter 5: Mathilda as Dramatic Actress

1. Although Betty Bennett and I in *The Mary Shelley Reader* (New York: Oxford Univ. Press, 1990) (hereafter *MSR*) used the standard spelling of "Mathilda" for both the heroine and the title of this novella, I here adopt the convention of the new Pickering and Chatto edition and denominate the novella *Matilda* and the heroine "Mathilda."

2. *Mathilda,* ed. Elizabeth Nitchie, Extra Series 3 of *Studies in Philology* (Chapel Hill: Univ. of North Carolina Press, 1959).

3. Mary Shelley's relationship with her mother, Mary Wollstonecraft, is suggested by Safie's relationship with her mother, who "instructed her daughter . . . and taught her to aspire to higher powers of intellect" (*F* 92).

4. Charlene E. Bunnell, "*Mathilda*: Mary Shelley's Romantic Tragedy," *Keats-Shelley Journal* 46 (1997): 75–96.

5. Audra Dibert Himes, "'Knew shame, and knew desire': Ambivalence as Structure in Mary Shelley's *Mathilda,*" in *Iconoclastic Departures: Mary Shelley after* Frankenstein, ed. Syndy M. Conger, Frederick S. Frank, and Gregory O'Dea (Madison: Fairleigh Dickinson Univ. Press, 1997), 115–29, quotation from 121. See also in the same volume: Judith Barbour, "'The meaning of the tree': The Tale of Mirra in Mary Shelley's *Mathilda*" (98–114); and Ranita Chatterjee, "*Mathilda*: Mary Shelley, William Godwin, and the Ideologies of Incest" (130–49). For a convenient and full listing of the earlier, mainly biographical readings of *Matilda,* see Himes, "'Knew shame and knew desire,'" 127, n. 3. For another worthwhile essay that suggests "a measure of ambiguity about Mathilda's guilt" but does not sufficiently pursue that point, see Margaret Davenport Garrett, "Writing and Rewriting Incest in Mary Shelley's *Mathilda,*" *Keats-Shelley Journal* 45 (1996): 44–60.

6. The sexual overtones of the "extactic moments" (*M* 14) in Mathilda's dreams of meeting her father are repeated by other phrases in her narrative: e.g., she was "attracted and enchanted" (*M* 16) by her father, whose return brings her "hours of intense delight" (*M* 18) as well as "the ravishing delight of beholding his smile" (*M* 25); she "leant against a tree" at the moment of confrontation, when her father confesses his passion for her, after which she feels "as if stung by a serpent" (*M* 28); thereafter she confesses to herself that she considers her father "a lover, there was madness in the thought, yet he was my lover" (*M* 37). This confession precedes the scene in which Mathilda discovers her dead father: "the bed within

instantly caught my eye; something stiff and straight lay on it, covered by a sheet; the cottagers looked aghast"; and, again, "never more hear his voice; no caress, no look? All cold, and stiff, and dead!" (*M* 39, 40). These lines repeat her father's own words about "the hell of passion which has been implanted in [him] to burn untill all be cold, and stiff, and dead" (*M* 35).

One of the most suggestive passages recounts part of Mathilda's dream of her pursuing her father: "he held his course right on towards the brink and I became breathless with fear lest he should plunge down the dreadful precipice; I tried to augment my speed, but my knees failed beneath me, yet I had just reached him; just caught a part of his flowing robe, when he leapt down and I awoke with a violent scream. I was trembling and my pillow was wet with tears; for a few moments my heart beat hard" (*M* 31–32).

7. *The Poems of John Dryden,* ed. James Kinsley, 4 vols. (Oxford: Clarendon Press, 1958), 4:1545–64.

8. See the story of Feliciana of the Voice, in Miguel de Cervantes, *The Trials of Persiles and Sigismunda, a Northern Story,* trans. Celia Richmond Weller and Clark A. Colahan (Berkeley: Univ. of California Press, 1989), esp. 193–222. For a fascinating exploration of this episode in Cervantes' novel, see Diana de Armas Wilson, *Allegories of Love: Cervantes's Persiles and Sigismunda* (Princeton: Princeton Univ. Press, 1991), esp. chap. 9 ("Some Perversions of Pastoral: Feliciana de la Voz" 200–222). Wilson's remarks on this Cervantes story — and her reading of it against two other incest-charged tales, Myrrha and her son Adonis as well as Mary and her son Christ, suggest ways that Mary Shelley might have read the narrative in May 1819 just before she began *Matilda.* Wilson's analysis has a haunting kind of application to Mary Shelley's novella — e.g., Wilson writes that Cervantes in this tale "is preoccupied with three questions: female desire, its interdiction by patriarchal law, and its flight into elemental nature as a place for coming into voice" (200).

9. *The Captain* (4.4) in *The Works of Francis Beaumont and John Fletcher,* 10 vols., ed. A. R. Waller (Cambridge: Cambridge Univ. Press, 1907), 5:298–99.

Chapter 6: Between Romance and History

The last eight paragraphs of this essay also appear in the Introduction to my edition of *Valperga* (Peterborough: Broadview Press, 1998).

1. Mary Favret, "Mary Shelley's Sympathy and Irony: The Editor and Her Corpus," in *The Other Mary Shelley: Beyond* Frankenstein, ed. Audrey A. Fisch, Anne K. Mellor, and Esther H. Schor (New York: Oxford Univ. Press, 1993), 19.

2. Tilottama Rajan, "Autonarration and Genotext in Mary Hays' *Memoirs of Emma Courtney*" *Studies in Romanticism,* 32 (1993): 149–76. See also Rajan,

"Mary Shelley's *Mathilda:* Melancholy and the Political Economy of Romanticism," *Studies in the Novel* 26, no. 2 (1994): 60–61.

3. William Godwin, *Enquiry Concerning Political Justice and Its Influence on Morals and Happiness*, ed. F. E. L. Priestley, 3 vols. (Toronto: Univ. of Toronto Press, 1946), 1:238 (hereafter *PJ*).

4. Hans Kellner, *Language and Historical Representation: Getting the Story Crooked* (Madison: Univ. of Wisconsin Press, 1989), 41–43.

5. Henry Hallam, *History of Europe During the Middle Ages*, 3 vols. (1818; rpt., New York: Colonial Press, 1900), 1:328.

6. See Ian Duncan, *Modern Romance and Tranformations of the Novel: The Gothic, Scott, Dickens* (Cambridge: Cambridge Univ. Press, 1992), 1–19. William Godwin, "Of History and Romance," (hereafter *HR*) in *Things as They Are; or, The Adventures of Caleb Williams*, ed. Maurice Hindle (London: Penguin, 1988), 372.

7. Jon Klancher, "Godwin and the Genre Reformers: On Necessity and Contingency in Romantic Narrative Theory," *Romanticism, History, and the Possibilities of Genre*, ed. Tilottama Rajan and Julia Wright (Cambridge: Cambridge Univ. Press, 1997), 27–35. Klancher's article is seminal in foregrounding a turn in Godwin's thinking between *Political Justice* and *The Enquirer,* which he sees as explicable in terms of the qualification of "necessity" by "contingency."

8. Ibid., 28. Joseph Priestley, *The Doctrine of Philosophical Necessity Illustrated* (London: J. Johnson, 1777), 15, 20. Priestley defines a "contingent event" as one "that does not depend upon any previous known circumstances" and does not conform to existing laws of cause and effect. However, he is more of a necessitarian than Leibniz or Godwin, insisting that "nothing can be known *to exist* but what does exist."

9. On the Romantic reception of Leibniz see Catherine Wilson, "The Reception of Leibniz in the Eighteenth Century," in *The Cambridge Companion to Leibniz,* ed. Nicholas Jolley (Cambridge: Cambridge Univ. Press, 1995), 467–70. By Godwin's time Leibniz was a canonical figure: Sir William Drummond includes a chapter on him in his *Academical Questions* (London: Cadell and Davies, 1805).

10. All parenthetical references to Leibniz are to *Basic Writings,* trans. George R. Montgomery (La Salle: Open Court, 1902). I refer to the *Discourse on Metaphysics* as *D,* to the "Correspondence with Arnauld" as *C,* and to *The Monadology* (cited by section number) as *M.*

11. Godwin uses the term *contingency* in *PJ* 1:384, as well as in *Thoughts on Man: His Nature, Productions and Discoveries* (1831; rpt., New York: Augustus M. Kelley, 1969), 230. In the latter, Godwin, like Leibniz, associates contingency (and also possibility) with man, and the predictable operation of laws of cause and effect with nature: "Hence arises the idea of contingency . . . and the opinion that, while, in the universe of matter, every thing proceeds in regular course, and nothing has happened or can happen, otherwise than as it actually has been or will

be, in the determinations and acts of living beings each occurrence may be or not be . . . both issues being equally possible till that decision has been made."

12. Gilles Deleuze, *The Fold: Leibniz and the Baroque,* trans. Tom Conley (Minneapolis: Univ. of Minnesota Press, 1993), 59.

13. Margaret D. Wilson, "Leibniz's Dynamics and Contingency in Nature," in *Motion and Time, Space and Matter,*m ed. Peter K. Machamer and Robert G. Turnbull (Columbus: Ohio State Univ. Press, 1976), 371.

14. The fragment form constitutes a further connection between Leibniz and Romanticism, as evidenced particularly in the work of Johann Gottfried Herder and Friedrich Schlegel.

15. Martin Heidegger, *Schelling's Treatise on the Essence of Human Freedom,* trans. Joan Stambaugh (Athens, Ohio: Ohio Univ. Press, 1985), 9.

16. Leibniz concedes that this is a "contingent" truth: "it cannot be demonstrated that God makes that which is most perfect, since the contrary does not imply a contradiction" ("On Freedom and Possibility," in *Philosophical Essays,* ed. and trans. Roger Ariew and Daniel Garber [Indianapolis: Hackett, 1989], 20).

17. The occurrence of the term *substance* as well as *aggregation* seems to echo Leibniz or at least suggests a way of thinking between materialism and idealism that is congenial to Leibniz's thought.

18. I refer to Godwin's account of the composition of *Caleb Williams* in his preface to the 1832 edition of *Fleetwood* (in Hindle, ed., *Things as They Are; or The Adventures of Caleb Williams*), 351. See also Wilson, who sees Herder as having been mainly interested by Leibniz's theory of *"petites perceptions"* ("Leibniz's Dynamics," 467).

19. William Godwin, *St. Leon, a Tale of the Sixteenth Century,* ed. Pamela Clemit (New York: Oxford Univ. Press, 1994), 435.

20. William Godwin, *History of the Commonwealth from Its Commencement to the Restoration of Charles the Second,* 4 vols. (London: Henry Colburn, 1824), 4:vi (hereafter *HC*). One can contrast Godwin's emphasis on general history in this book for adults with the greater emphasis on romance and individual history in his books for children, for instance his *History of Rome: From the Building of the City to the Ruin of the Republic* (6th ed., London: Baldwin and Cradock, 1835).

21. The passage referred to is in 3.8. However, similar turning points occur in 1.5 (43), 1.8 (68), 2.7 (173), and 2.9 (192). The first of these points occurs when Castruccio meets Scoto, *after* he has already killed a man; yet we are told, "Hitherto his mind had been innocence . . . and the tenderness of his nature seemed to render it impossible for him to perpetrate a deed of harshness or inhumanity" (43). Despite Scoto and Galeazzo, as late as 2.4 the narrator can still say, "though there lurked in his heart the germ of an evil-bearing tree, it was as yet undeveloped and inanimated" (151).

22. Georges Bataille, "The Psychological Structure of Fascism," in *Visions of*

Excess: Selected Writings: 1927–1939, ed. and trans. Allan Stoekl (Minneapolis: Univ. of Minnesota Press, 1985), 148–49, 158, 154.

23. Ibid., 141.

24. J. C. L. Simonde de Sismondi, *Histoire des Républiques Italiennes du Moyen Âge,* 3d ed., 12 vols. (Paris: Furne et Cie, 1840), 3:395.

25. Hallam, *History,* 1:303; Sismondi, *Histoire,* 1.5:292.

26. Hallam, *History,* 1:328.

27. Louis Green, *Castruccio Castracani: A Study on the Origins and Character of a Fourteenth-Century Italian Despotism* (Oxford: Clarendon Press, 1986), 4–5.

28. Godwin writes: "I am not contented to observe such a man upon the public stage, I would follow him into his closet. I would see the friend and the father of the family" (*HR* 364).

29. Gilles Deleuze, *Bergsonism,* trans. Hugh Tomlinson and Barbara Habberjam (New York: Zone Books, 1991), 97.

Chapter 7: Future Uncertain

I have benefitted greatly from having access to Kelvin Everest's edition of "Mazenghi," published in *The Poems of Shelley,* vol. 2, ed. Kelvin Everest and Geoffrey Matthews (New York: Longman, 2000). I would also like to thank Mrs. Maryse L'Hoste-Morton for reviewing my translation of Sismondi. I acknowledge with gratitude the financial support of the Department of English Literary and Linguistic Studies and the Staff Travel Fund of the University of Newcastle upon Tyne and the assistance of the staff of the Bodleian Library, the British Library, Cambridge University Library, the Literary and Philosophical Society of Newcastle upon Tyne, the National Library of Scotland, and the Robinson Library of the University of Newcastle upon Tyne.

1. For English interest in Italian history in the Romantic period, see C. P. Brand, *Italy and the English Romantics: The Italianate Fashion in Early Nineteenth-Century England* (Cambridge: Cambridge Univ. Press, 1957), 187–95.

2. I am indebted here to the analyses of the aesthetics of Burckhardt's *Civilization of the Renaissance in Italy,* in David Norbrook, "Life and Death of Renaissance Man," *Raritan* 8 (1989): 89–110, and in Paul Hamilton, *Historicism* (New York: Routledge, 1996), 23–26.

3. See Betty T. Bennett, "The Political Philosophy of Mary Shelley's Historical Novels: *Valperga* and *Perkin Warbeck,*" in *The Evidence of Imagination: Studies of Interactions between Life and Art in English Romantic Literature,* ed. Donald H. Reiman, Michael C. Jaye, and Betty T. Bennett (New York: New York Univ. Press, 1978), 358: "*Valperga; or the Life and Adventures of Castruccio, Prince of Lucca* suggests that the story is about one or the other. The two cannot coexist; confrontation must erupt."

4. *V*'s misprint of "every" for "ever" in this passage has been corrected.

5. P. B. Shelley's use of the word *fiction* suggests his awareness that many of Machiavelli's anecdotes about Castruccio (which Lockhart quotes extensively and with relish in his review) were lifted from Diogenes Laertius's *Lives of the Philosophers* (see Niccolò Machiavelli, "The Life of Castruccio Castracani," in *Machiavelli: The Chief Works and Others,* 3 vols., ed. and trans. Allan Gilbert (Durham, N.C.: Duke Univ. Press, 1965), 2:559 n. 4).

6. *Blackwood's Edinburgh Magazine* 13 (1823): 283.

7. Ibid., 284.

8. Machiavelli, "The Life of Castruccio Castracani," 555.

9. William Hazlitt, "Coriolanus," *The Complete Works of William Hazlitt,* 21 vols., ed. P. P. Howe (London: Dent, 1930–34), 4:214.

10. Niccolò Machiavelli, *The Prince,* ed. Peter Bondanella, trans. Peter Bondanella and Mark Musa (New York: Oxford Univ. Press, 1984), 52.

11. I quote from Peter Bondanella's introduction, ibid., xv.

12. *Posthumous Poems of Percy Bysshe Shelley* (London: John and Henry L. Hunt, 1824), 257.

13. J. C. L. Simonde de Sismondi, *Histoire des Républiques Italiennes du Moyen Âge,* 2d ed., 16 vols. (Paris: Treuttel et Würtz, 1818), 8:142–43:

Les Florentins ne croyoient guère possible d'ouvrir une brêche aux murs de Pise, en sorte qu'ils se proposoient de réduire la ville par la famine, tandis que leur armée attaquoit successivement les divers châteaux du territoire. Les Pisans, de leur côté, s'efforçoient de se pourvoir de vivres; ils envoyèrent quelques galères chercher des blés en Sicile: l'une d'elles, surprise à son retour par des vaisseaux que les Florentins avoient fait armer à Gênes, se réfugia sous la tour de Vado. Un Florentin, nommé Pierre Marenghi, qui erroit loin de sa patrie, frappé d'une sentence capitale, saisit cette circonstance pour rendre à ses concitoyens un service signalé. Il s'élança du rivage, un flambeau à la main, et s'approcha de la galère à la nage, malgré les traits qu'on lançoit contre lui. Percé de trois blessures, il continua longtemps à se soutenir sous la proue, en soulevant son flambeau, jusqu'à ce que le feu se fût communiqué à la galère ennemie de manière à ne plus s'éteindre. Elle brûla en face de la tour de Vado, tandis que Pierre Marenghi regagna le rivage. Il fut rappelé ensuite dans sa patrie avec honneur.

Sismondi's source for the story of Marenghi, referred to in *Histoire* 8:143 n, is Matteo Palmieri's *De Captivitate Pisarum liber* in Lodovico Muratori, *Rerum Italicarum Scriptores,* 25 vols. (Mediolani, 1723–51) 19 [1731]: 165–94 (176), a work to which the Shelleys appeared to have access.

14. For a brief examination of "Mazenghi," see Alan M. Weinberg, *Shelley's Italian Experience* (Basingstoke: Macmillan, 1991), 98–100.

15. The quotation is from the fourth line of a stanza in Bodleian MS. Shelley e.4, fol. 49ʳ. See P. M. S. Dawson, ed., *Bodleian MS. Shelley e.4: A Facsimile Edition with Full Transcription and Textual Notes* (New York: Garland, 1987), 196–97. I am indebted to Kelvin Everest for allowing me access to his convincing argument that this stanza is associated with "Mazenghi."

16. *Valperga* and Sismondi's *Histoire* refer to *Vado;* in the ms. of "Mazenghi" P. B. Shelley writes both *Vada* and *Vado;* a map in *Hand-Book for Travellers in Northern Italy* (London: John Murray, 1843) refers to *Vado;* the modern name is *Vada.*

17. The *OSA* text of "Mazenghi" (which is misleadingly entitled "Marenghi") is unsatisfactory but is referred to here as currently the most widely available version of the poem. To absorb the poem's full significance, it is worth consulting Dawson's edition referred to above, 168–97.

18. "Now again she paused, and thought that all the shows this world presents were dearly bought at the price of one drop of human blood. She doubted the purity of her own motives; she doubted the justification which even now she was called upon to make at the tribunal of her conscience, and hereafter before that of her God" (*V* 212).

19. For Sismondi's engagement with Enlightenment historiography, see H. O. Pappé, "Sismondi's System of Liberty," *Journal of the History of Ideas* 40 (1979): 251–66.

20. *Blackwood's Edinburgh Magazine* 13 (March 1823): 284.

21. For a useful contextualizations of Sismondi's *Histoire,* see Norbrook, "Life and Death," 94–95.

22. For a brief summary of its publication history, see Sismondi, *Histoire* (1818) 1:xvi n: "Les deux premiers volumes parurent à Zurich en 1807; les tomes 3 et 4, aussi à Zurich en 1808; les tomes 5 à 8, à Paris, en 1809, avec une seconde édition des quatre premiers; les tomes 9 à 11, en juin 1815; les tomes 12 à 16, en janvier 1818."

23. *Quarterly Review* 7 (1812): 357–74. The quotations are from 363 and 362. The essay is attributed to John Herman Merivale in H. Shine and H. C. Shine, *The Quarterly Review under Gifford. Identification of Contributors, 1809–1824* (Chapel Hill: Univ. of North Carolina Press, 1949), 31.

24. William Hazlitt, review of Sismondi, *De La Littérature du Midi de l'Europe,* 4 vols. (Paris, 1813), *Edinburgh Review* 25 (1815) 31; reprinted in *Complete Works* 16:24.

25. *MWSL* 1:137: "I am too much depressed by its [i.e., England's] enslaved state, my inutility; the little chance there is for freedom; & the great chance there is for tyranny to wish to be witness of its degradation step by step." For an engaging account of the complexities of nationalist politics in Italy during the Romantic period, see Adrian Lyttelton, "The National Question in Italy," in *The National*

Question in Europe in Historical Context, ed. Mikuláš Teich and Roy Porter (Cambridge: Cambridge Univ. Press, 1993), 63–105.

26. On English reaction to political events in Italy during the Romantic period, see Brand, *Italy and the English Romantics*, 196–214.

27. For my gloss on the history of Geneva in this period I am indebted to the annotation supplied by the Pickering and Chatto editors in volumes 1 and 8 of their edition. For a detailed, critical examination of Geneva's aristocratic republicanism and an account of its turbulent history, including the revolution of 1782 and the Napoleonic period, see L. Simond, *Switzerland; Or, A Journal of a Tour and Residence in that Country, in the Years 1817, 1818, and 1819*, 2 vols. (London: John Murray, 1822), esp. 1:508–46 and 2: chaps. 32–38.

28. *The Diary of Dr. John William Polidori 1816*, ed. W. M. Rossetti (London: Elkin Mathews, 1911), 106.

29. See, for example, Lee Sterrenburg, "Mary Shelley's Monster: Politics and Psyche in *Frankenstein*," in *The Endurance of Frankenstein: Essays on Mary Shelley's Novel*, ed. George Levine and U. C. Knoepflmacher (Berkeley: Univ. of California Press), 143–71; Franco Moretti, "Dialectic of Fear," in *Signs Taken for Wonders: Essays in the Sociology of Literary Forms*, trans. Susan Fischer, David Forgacs, and David Miller (New York: Verso, 1983; rev. ed. 1988), 83–108; Chris Baldick, *In Frankenstein's Shadow: Myth, Monstrosity, and Nineteenth-century Writing* (New York: Oxford Univ. Press, 1987), chaps. 2 and 3.

30. Jean de Palacio, *Mary Shelley dans son oeuvre: Contribution aux études shelleyennes* (Paris: Éditions Klincksieck, 1969), 48. On Dantean elements in *Valperga*, see esp. 47–61.

31. See Hunt's preface to *The Liberal. Verse and Prose from the South* (London: John Hunt, 1822–23), 1:xii. On *The Liberal*, see William H. Marshall, *Byron, Shelley, Hunt, and* The Liberal (Philadelphia: Univ. of Pennsylvania Press, 1960). The quote is from Lyttelton, "The National Question in Italy," 72.

32. *The Liberal* 2:281–97.

33. Of the treatment of Manfred in *Purgatorio* 3: 103 ff, Mary Shelley comments, "Dante sweetly and pathetically dwells on the wrongs and virtues of Manfred, and places him on the high road to heaven" (*GV* 138 n). She wrote a short story about his son, "A Tale of the Passions," *The Liberal* 1:289–325 (reprinted in *CT* 1–23), and planned a tragedy about him, referred to in *MWSJ* 442 n. 2 and possibly alluded to in *MWSL* 1:412, 413 n. 5.

34. Karl Marx, *The Eighteenth Brumaire of Louis Bonaparte* (1852), in *Surveys from Exile: Political Writings*, vol. 2, ed. David Fernbach (Harmondsworth: Penguin, 1973), 146.

35. In the context of Euthanasia's parallel function in *Valperga* to that of the poet in *A Defence*, it is worth noting that Claire Clairmont in a letter to Mary refers

to Euthanasia as "Shelley in female attire," *The Clairmont Correspondence: Letters of Claire Clairmont, Charles Clairmont, and Fanny Imlay Godwin,* 2 vols., ed. Marion Kingston Stocking (Baltimore: Johns Hopkins Univ. Press, 1995), 2:341.

36. "Be mindful that in a short time you will die." (My translation differs slightly from that given in *V* 326 n. a).

37. Her name is surely a subtle and ironic reworking of David Hume's patently ironic sentence, "Absolute monarchy, therefore, is the easiest death, the true *Euthanasia* of the BRITISH constitution": Essay 7, "Whether the British Government Inclines More to Absolute Monarchy, or to a Republic," in *Essays Moral, Political, and Literary,* ed. Eugene F. Miller (Indianapolis: Liberty *Classics*, 1985; rev. ed. 1987), 53. Joseph Lew's discussion of the significance of her name in the context of Mary Shelley's reading of Hume's essay seems inattentive to the argument of Hume's essay and to Mary Shelley's politics; see Joseph Lew, "God's Sister: History and Ideology in *Valperga,*" in *The Other Mary Shelley: Beyond* Frankenstein, ed. Audrey A. Fisch, Anne K. Mellor, and Esther H. Schor (New York: Oxford Univ. Press, 1993), 162.

Chapter 8: Reading the End of the World

1. The journal entry reads: "The last man! Yes I may well describe that solitary being's feelings, feeling myself as the last relic of a beloved race, my companions extinct before me" (*MWSJ* 476–77).

2. For readings of this kind, see especially: Jane Blumberg, *Mary Shelley's Early Novels* (Iowa City: Univ. of Iowa Press, 1993); Anne K. Mellor, *Mary Shelley: Her Life, Her Fiction, Her Monsters* (New York: Routledge, 1985); Victoria Middleton, *Elektra in Exile: Women's Political Fiction* (New York: Garland, 1988). These critics offer rich, nuanced readings of *The Last Man* in the context of Mary Shelley's life. My purpose here is not to disagree with those readings but to expand that view to take into account currents in the larger literary culture.

3. I use *she* to refer to the editor, chiefly to avoid the cumbersome *he/she* construction. However, the editor is a fictional personae and should neither be conflated with Mary Shelley herself nor necessarily be gendered as female. It is significant that neither the editor nor the editor's companion are gendered in the text.

4. In these examples of Scott and Macpherson, of course, it was the question of authenticity that got these authors into trouble; however, it is the formal and rhetorical implications of the editor that interest me.

5. Jon Klancher, *The Making of English Reading Audiences, 1790–1832* (Madison: Univ. of Wisconsin Press, 1987), 3.

6. For excellent discussions of Scott's uses of the narrative frame, see especially: Patricia S. Gaston, *Prefacing the Waverley Prefaces: A Reading of Sir Walter*

Scott's Prefaces to the Waverley Novels (New York: Peter Lang, 1991); James Kerr, *Fiction against History: Scott as Storyteller* (Cambridge: Cambridge Univ. Press, 1989); Jane Millgate, *Walter Scott: The Making of the Novelist* (Toronto: Univ. of Toronto Press, 1984); Fiona Robertson, *Legitimate Histories: Scott, Gothic and the Authorities of Fiction* (New York: Oxford Univ. Press, 1991).

7. Walter Scott, *Old Mortality,* ed. Angus Calder (London: Penguin Classics, 1985), 65.

8. Ross Chambers, *Story and Situation: Narrative Seduction and the Power of Fiction* (Minneapolis: Univ. of Minnesota Press, 1984), 8. A number of other critics have also explored the role of the reader in generating meaning, as well as the etymological links between the words *author* and *authority,* most notably Edward Said in *Beginnings: Intention and Method* (New York: Columbia Univ. Press, 1985); and Jonathan Culler, *On Deconstruction: Theory and Criticism after Structuralism* (Ithaca: Cornell Univ. Press, 1989).

9. A number of critics have examined the connection between Adrian and P. B. Shelley. For example, Terence Dawson claims that Mary Shelley's sympathies do not lie entirely with the freedom-loving republican but more with the ambitious Lord Raymond; See Dawson, "Re-Collecting Shelley: A Reading of Mary Shelley's *The Last Man,*" *Shelley: 1792–1992,* ed. James Hogg (Lewiston: Edwin Mellen Press, 1993), 246–60. Steven Goldsmith argues that the relationship between Lionel and Adrian parallels that of Mary Shelley and P.B. Shelley; see Goldsmith, "Of Gender, Plague, and Apocalypse: Mary's *The Last Man,*" *Yale Journal of Criticism* 4 (1990): 129–73. Jane Blumberg distinguishes Mary Shelley's admiration and love for P. B. Shelley the man and her critique of his ideas; see Blumberg, *Mary Shelley's Early Novels,* 139–40.

10. Morton D. Paley sees the plague as an image of the French Revolution or, more precisely, as another of the apocalyptic figurations of that event that were current in the cultural discourse; See Paley "*Le Dernier Homme:* The French Revolution as the Failure of Typology," *Mosaic* 24 (1991): 67–76. Lee Sterrenburg also views it as a revolutionary image in "*The Last Man:* Anatomy of Failed Revolutions," *Nineteenth-Century Fiction* 33 (1978): 324–47.

11. Jane Aaron traces the gendering of the plague throughout the novel, arguing that it becomes a "covert and subversive" revenge on "a patriarchal system dependent upon the repression of female lives and female self-expression"; see Aaron, "The Return of the Repressed: Reading Mary Shelley's *The Last Man*" *Feminist Criticism: Theory and Practice,* ed. Susan Sellers (Toronto: Univ. of Toronto Press, 1991), 9–21.

12. William Walling, *Mary Shelley* (New York: Twayne, 1972). Anne K. Mellor also makes this identification in *Mary Shelley.*

13. Mellor, *Mary Shelley,* 164; Blumberg, *Mary Shelley's Early Novels,* 153.

14. In her edition of *The Last Man* (Toronto: Broadview Literary Texts, 1997),

Anne McWhir includes an excerpt from Godwin's proposal. According to William St. Clair, this was one of Mary Shelley's favorite works by her father, and she would sometimes take a copy to her mother's grave in St. Pancras Churchyard to read. *The Godwins and the Shelleys: The Biography of a Family* (London: Faber and Faber, 1989), 367. William Godwin, "Essay on Sepulchres," vol. 6 of *Political and Philosophical Writings of William Godwin,* ser. ed. Mark Philp (London: Pickering and Chatto, 1993), 6. Further references cited parenthetically.

15. Jane Blumberg reads Mary Shelley's early novels through the lens of an un-published essay, probably written between 1814 and 1815, entitled "The History of the Jews." There, Blumberg argues, Mary Shelley began her exploration of the theme of revolution and the process of distinguishing her political vision from her husband's; Mary Shelley completes this process in *The Last Man.*

16. For references and allusions to Cassandra throughout Mary Shelley's work, see Barbara Jane O'Sullivan, "Beatrice in *Valperga:* A New Cassandra," in *The Other Mary Shelley: Beyond* Frankenstein, ed. Audrey A. Fisch, Anne K. Mellor, Esther H. Schor (New York: Oxford Univ. Press, 1993), 140–58.

17. *Dictionary of Mythology, Folklore and Symbols,* s.v. "Sibyl"; Audrey A. Fisch also discusses the public function of Sibylline books in "Plaguing Politics: AIDS, Deconstruction, and *The Last Man*" in Fisch, Mellor, and Schor, eds., *The Other Mary Shelley,* 270.

Chapter 9: *Kindertotenlieder*

1. Leigh Hunt, "Deaths of Little Children," originally published in the *Indicator,* April 5, 1820, reprinted in *Essays and Sketches,* ed. R. Brimley Johnson (London: Oxford Univ. Press, 1906), 10.

2. In "*Frankenstein* and the Uses of Biography," *Approaches to Teaching Shelley's* Frankenstein, ed. Stephen C. Behrendt (New York: Modern Language Association of America, 1990), Betty T. Bennett argues for the likelihood that Mary Shelley gives William Frankenstein the name of her own son because "William's death was for her the worst thing she could imagine. The idea is consistent in terms of *Frankenstein* because this worst death is in fact the climax of the book" (91). I similarly argue that Evelyn's death, which so closely mirrors William Shelley's death from malaria, in 1819, is the worst death in *The Last Man.*

3. Mary Poovey notes that "disappointment and grief" characterize *The Last Man:* "In the empty world the plague leaves behind, Shelley's nightmare of her own maturity is fully dramatized; its defining characteristics . . . are pain, loss, and grief." She further argues that Mary Shelley "in treating her own suffering, rejects psychological complexity for a simplified indulgence of self-pity"; Mary Poovey, *The Proper Lady and the Woman Writer: Ideology and Style in the Work of Mary Wollstonecraft, Mary Shelley, and Jane Austen* (Chicago: Univ. of Chicago Press,

1984), 153, 155. Anne Mellor, on the other hand, argues that "writing *The Last Man* enabled Mary Shelley to distance herself from her emotional response to the loss of both P. B. Shelley and Byron," and further notes that "in Idris Mary Shelley projects both her own obsessive grief for her dead Clara Everina and William (the death of Verney's last son, Evelyn, is a detailed description of William Shelley's death from malaria)"; Anne Mellor, *Mary Shelley: Her Life, Her Fiction, Her Monsters* (New York: Methuen/Routledge, 1988), 152, 154. In *The Last of the Race*, Fiona Stafford locates the origin of the novel in bereavement: "Mary Shelley's decision to embark on a novel describing the decimation of the entire human race (bar the narrator) was directly related to the traumas of losing her husband and children. . . . Mary Shelley is interesting, too, in that she suffered the loss of her mother in infancy—a condition that frequently renders the losses of adult life more difficult to overcome." She sees *The Last Man* as "an expression and study of grief," and argues that the writing of the novel was therapeutic: "The projection of feelings into an imaginary world, where a personal situation could be given separate life, seems to have had the cathartic effect of purifying, reducing, and eventually ending previously uncontrollable emotions"; Fiona Stafford, *The Last of the Race: The Growth of a Myth from Milton to Darwin* (Oxford: Clarendon Press, 1994), 7–8, 124, 221.

4. Mary Jacobus, *First Things: The Maternal Imaginary in Literature, Art, and Psychoanalysis* (New York: Routledge), 107. For Jacobus, "*The Last Man* prompts one to ask . . . in what ways the writing of melancholia might affect the consolidation of authorial identity, making it possible to mourn, and hence, memorialize the dead" (107). Drawing upon Kristeva's notion of writing, "(writing springing out of that very melancholia) [as] the only counter depressant," a "cure" of writing that "demands the elimination of the mother," Jacobus argues that "because literary creation (in Kristeva's words) 'bears witness to the affect' and at the same time to the 'imprint of separation and beginning of the symbol's sway,' Verney's identification with maternal sadness—his ventriloquization of Melancholy—provides an organizing identity for the bereaved author-daughter" (112–13). Melanie Klein, on the other hand, regards the revivification of the internal parents as crucial in the resolution of mourning: "If greater security in the inner world is gradually regained, and feelings and inner objects are therefore allowed to come more to life again, re-creative processes can set in, and hope return" (Melanie Klein, "Mourning and Its Relation to Manic-Depressive States," in *Contributions to Psychoanalysis, 1921–45* [London: Hogarth Press, 1948], 327).

5. Quoted in Emily Sunstein, *Mary Shelley: Romance and Reality* (Boston: Little, Brown, 1989), 174.

6. Clare Gittings, *Death, Burial, and the Individual in Early Modern England* (London: Croom Helm, 1984), 58.

7. Colin Murray Parkes, *Bereavement: Studies of Grief in Adult Life* (London:

Tavistock, 1972), 140; Parkes quotes G. Gorer's *Death, Grief, and Mourning in Contemporary Britain* (London: Crescent, 1965).

8. Irving G. Leon, *When a Baby Dies: Psychotherapy for Pregnancy and Newborn Loss* (New Haven: Yale Univ. Press, 1990), 71, 27. Here Leon is referring specifically to perinatal loss, yet in comparing such loss to that of an older child, he later notes, "Usually the magnitude of grief in perinatal bereavement is not as severe as that of mourning the older child. . . . Death of the older child involves a greater degree of object loss than that of perinatal bereavement" (72).

9. See, for instance, Jane Littlewood's synopsis in *Aspects of Grief: Bereavement in Adult Life* (London: Tavistock, 1992), 144, of research studies comparing mothers' and fathers' reactions to the death of their child.

10. Jeremy Holmes cites several studies confirming Freud's linking of depression with childhood loss in *John Bowlby and Attachment Theory* (London: Routledge, 1993), 185.

11. Littlewood, *Aspects,* 58.

12. Paula Feldman, "Mary Shelley and the Literary Annuals" and Judith Pascoe, "Poetry as Souvenir: Mary Shelley in the Annuals," papers presented at "Mary Wollstonecraft Shelley in Her Times," New York, May 1997, both attest to the regular presence in the popular nineteenth-century literary annuals of women's poems mourning the deaths of infants and children.

13. M. H. Abrams, *A Glossary of Literary Terms* (New York: Harcourt Brace Jovanovich, 1985), 51. In *The English Elegy: Studies in the Genre from Spenser to Yeats* (Baltimore: Johns Hopkins Univ. Press, 1985), Peter Sacks notes that "the difficulty in identifying with predominantly male symbols of consolation greatly complicates the woman's work of mourning" (13). And Celeste M. Schenck argues that women poets significantly revised the elegiac tradition: whereas "the masculine elegy marks a rite of separation that culminates in ascension to stature . . . the female elegy is a poem of connectedness" (Schenck, "Feminism and Deconstruction: Re-Constructing the Elegy," *Tulsa Studies in Women's Literature* [April 1986]: 15). Schenck notes that women elegists "deploy writing as a strategy for prolonging attachment, a means of deferring resolution or radical separation" (22–23), an observation that holds true for the *Kindertotenlieder* discussed here.

14. In Charlotte Elliott, *Hours of Sorrow Cheered and Comforted* (London: J. Booth, 1869), 112. See also in the same volume "On the Anniversary of a Child's Death," "On an Infant Who Lived Only a Few Months," and "Epitaph."

15. *The Poetical Works of Caroline Bowles Southey: Collected Edition* (Edinburgh: William Blackwood, 1867), 128.

16. "Graves of Infants," in *The Poems of John Clare,* ed J. W. Tibble (London: J. M. Dent, 1935), 466; "Dirge of a Child," in *The Poetical Works of Mrs. Felicia Hemans* (New York: Thomas Y. Crowell, n.d.), 331.

17. Mary Masters, *Familiar Letters and Poems on Several Occasions* (London: D Henry and R. Cave, 1755), 137.

18. Tibble, ed., *The Poems of John Clare*, 2:92.

19. Amelia Opie, *Lays for the Dead* (London: Longman, Rees, Orme, Brown, Green, and Longman, 1840), 81.

20. Sigmund Freud, *The Future of an Illusion,* reprinted in *The Freud Reader,* ed Peter Gay (New York: W. W. Norton, 1989), 734.

21. Anne McWhir has traced patterns of imagery associated with pestilence throughout the novel in "Mary Shelley, Disease, and the Infected Text," paper presented at "Mary Wollstonecraft Shelley in Her Times," New York, May 1997.

22. Klein, "Mourning," 337–38.

23. Hanna Segal describes the normal resolution of the infantile depressive position in *Introduction to the Work of Melanie Klein* (London: Hogarth Press and the Institute of Psychoanalysis, 1973), 92. Emily Sunstein's account of Mary Shelley's infancy and early childhood in *Mary Shelley,* however, attests to major and minor disruptions in her care that may have complicated the normal process. Because of Mary Wollstonecraft's puerperal fever, her newborn daughter was given to a wet nurse on her third day and brought to Wollstonecraft's sickbed from time to time. She was then taken to Maria Reveley's house on the day of Wollstonecraft's death, where she became "frighteningly ill" (19). Brought back to Godwin's house on her eighteenth day, Mary Shelley was cared for by Louisa Jones, who left the household when Mary Shelley was fifteen months old, "an age when fears of abandonment are said to be particularly strong" (26). Jones later returned, looking after the two-year-old Mary Shelley when Godwin took a long vacation, during which Mary Shelley "worried that he had given her to her sitters" (26). As noted above, Holmes suggests that "early loss of the mother, especially if accompanied by disruption and lack of care, makes a person more vulnerable to depression when faced with adversity in adult life" (*John Bowlby and Attachment Theory,* 185); it seems clear that Mary Shelley experienced both significant early disruptions and later adversity.

24. Jean-Michel Petot makes this observation in *Melanie Klein,* trans. Christine Trollope (Madison, Conn.: International Univ. Press, 1991), 2:52.

25. Hanna Segal, "A Psycho-Analytical Approach to Aesthetics." In *New Directions in Psycho-Analysis,* ed. M. Klein, P. Heinmenn, and R. Money-Kyrle (London: Tavistock, 1955), 390.

26. Klein, "Mourning," 321. Marc A. Rubenstein relates "the great movement of yearning and searching with respect to lost motherhood which pervades [*Frankenstein*]" to Mary Shelley's losses of both her mother and her daughter: "To know that Mary Shelley's mother died giving birth to her, and that she herself lost her first child two weeks after it was born, is to know much about the origins of

Frankenstein" (Rubenstein, " 'My Accursed Origin': The Search for the Mother in *Frankenstein,*" *Studies in Romanticism* 15 [spring 1976]: 174). Betty T. Bennett, in the general introduction to *Novels and Selected Works of Mary Shelley,* ed. Nora Crook et al. (London: W. Pickering, 1996), xxxiii–xxxiv, argues that the deaths of Mary Shelley's next two children were similarly entwined for her with the death of Mary Wollstonecraft:

> The two children for her represented more than her union with P. B. Shelley, and more than renewal after her first lost child. One may speculate that a primary motivation, conscious or not, in Mary Shelley's interest in having children related to her own mother's life and death. Rather than an unwilling sexual and maternal partner, as Mary Shelley has been sometimes characterized, through the deliberate act of child-bearing and child-rearing she celebrated and forgave both her mother and herself for her own birth. At the same time, she forgave Wollstonecraft's death, that left her mother-less. With her own children, she could secure the mother-child affection that she imagined would have been hers had Mary Wollstonecraft lived.

Bennett's speculation is consistent with Klein's notion of maternal regression: "A mother identifies with her own mother (or with the mother she wishes she had) and tries to provide nurturant care for the child. At the same time, she reexperiences herself as a cared-for child, thus sharing with her child the possession of a good mother" (Chodorow, *The Reproduction of Mothering: Psychoanalysis and the Sociology of Gender* [Berkeley: Univ. of California Press, 1978], 90). The loss of the child therefore would therefore necessarily involve reexperiencing the loss of the mother.

27. Segal, "A Psycho-Analytical Approach," 390.

28. Sigmund Freud, "The Case of Schreber," in *The Complete Psychological Works of Sigmund Freud,* trans. and ed. James Strachey (London: Hogarth Press and the Institute of Psycho-analysis, 1958), 7:68.

29. Judith Hughes notes this agreement in *Reshaping the Psychoanalytic Domain: The Work of Melanie Klein, W. R. D. Fairbairn, and D. W. Winnicott* (Berkeley: Univ. of California Press, 1989), 85. Freud postulates that Schreber viewed the people he saw as "cursorily improvised" because he had "withdrawn from the people in his environment and from the external world generally the libidinal cathexis which he has hitherto directed on to them. Thus everything has become indifferent and irrelevant to him . . . The end of the world is the projection of this internal catastrophe; his subjective world has come to an end since his withdrawal of his love from it" (70). Such decathexis from permanently lost libidinal objects, however, constitutes the work of mourning, as described by Freud in "Mourning and Melancholia," *Complete Psychological Works,* vol. 14: while decathexis prompts the catastrophe for the paranoiac, it is only accomplished painfully and gradu-

ally by the mourner in response to loss. Both the mourner and the paranoiac seek to rebuild the world, the paranoiac by the work of his delusions, according to Freud: "the delusional formation which we take to be the pathological product, is in reality an attempt at recovery, a process of reconstruction" ("Schreber," 71). Mary Shelley's projection of catastrophe may ultimately have served to promote decathexis, but, unlike Schreber's, hers did not stem from it.

30. C. Fred Alford makes this point in *Melanie Klein and Critical Social Theory: An Account of Politics, Art, and Reason Based on Her Psychoanalytic Theory* (New Haven: Yale Univ. Press, 1989), 111–12.

31. Segal, "A Psycho-Analytical Approach," 399. Joan Riviere has explored other literary representations of such fantasies, stating that "the projection of persecutory phantasies concerning the inner world has manifestly found its most widespread expression in the myths of frightful and horrible forces of existence, e.g. as in nether worlds, notably in the Hell of medieval times. . . . Hell is a mythological projection of a personal region within the individual in which all one's own 'bad,' cruel, torturing and destructive impulses are raging against the 'badness' of others and vice versa." "The Unconscious Phantasy of an Inner World Reflected in Examples from Literature," in *New Directions in Psycho-Analysis,* ed. M. Klein, P. Heinmenn, and R. Money-Kyrle (London: Tavistock, 1955), 365.

32. See, for example, Mary Shelley's journal entries of October 7 and 10, 1822, and May 31, 1823; her letters of February 19 and May 31, 1823, to Jane Williams, of November 27, 1823 to Marianne Hunt, and of March 4, 1836, to Maria Gisborne, remarking at the birth of Jane Williams's daughter, "I envy her even to bitterness in the possession of a little girl" (*MWSL* 2:266). I argue that Mary Shelley's maternal bereavement also shaped the unlikely reunions and obsessive and idealized relations between mothers and children in *Lodore* and *Falkner.* In a poignant passage from *Rambles in Germany and Italy,* she speaks directly of the anguish of traveling to Venice along the same road she took with the dying Clara: "this road was as distinct in my mind as if traversed yesterday. . . . I saw those before me long departed; and I was agitated again by emotions—by passions—and those the deepest a woman's heart can harbour—a dread to see her child even at that instant expire—which then occupied me," *TW* 269). According to Sunstein, "She spoke of William, whose portrait hung on her bedroom wall, on her deathbed" (*Mary Shelley,* 383).

Chapter 10: Politicizing the Personal

1. Anne Kostelanetz Mellor, *Mary Shelley: Her Life, Her Fiction, Her Monsters* (New York: Routledge, 1988).

2. Mary Jacobus, *Reading Woman: Essays in Feminist Criticism* (New York: Columbia Univ. Press, 1986), 278–82, and Jacobus, *First Things: The Maternal*

Imaginary in Literature, Art, and Psychoanalysis (New York: Routledge, 1995), 63–82.

3. Eileen Janes Yeo, ed., *Mary Wollstonecraft and 200 Years of Feminisms* (London: Rivers Oram Press, 1997); Jane Blumberg, *Mary Shelley's Early Novels: "This Child of Imagination and Misery,"* (Iowa City: Univ. of Iowa Press, 1993); Audrey A. Fisch, Anne K. Mellor, and Esther H. Schor, eds., *The Other Mary Shelley: Beyond Frankenstein* (New York: Oxford Univ. Press, 1993); and Syndy M. Conger, Frederick S. Frank, and Gregory O'Dea, eds., *Iconoclastic Departures: Mary Shelley after* Frankenstein (Madison: Fairleigh Dickinson Univ. Press, 1997).

4. Gary Kelly, *The English Jacobin Novel 1780–1805* (Oxford: Clarendon Press, 1976); Pamela Clemit, *The Godwinian Novel: The Rational Fictions of Godwin, Brockden Brown, Mary Shelley* (Oxford: Clarendon Press, 1993).

5. Gary Kelly, *English Fiction of the Romantic Period 1789–1830* (London: Longman, 1989).

6. Gita May, *Madame Roland and the Age of Revolution* (New York: Columbia Univ. Press, 1970).

7. Claire Tomalin, *The Life and Death of Mary Wollstonecraft* (London: Weidenfeld and Nicolson, 1974).

8. Pierre Bourdieu, *The Rules of Art: Genesis and Structure of the Literary Field*, trans. Susan Emanuel (Stanford: Stanford Univ. Press, 1996), 120, 121, 163, 220.

Chapter 11: Mary Wollstonecraft Godwin Shelley

1. Mary Douglas, "Judgements on James Frazier," *Daedalus* 107, no. 4 (fall 1978): 161.

2. Take for example Harriet Devine Jump's Introduction to *Women's Writing of the Romantic Period 1789–1836: An Anthology* (Edinburgh: Edinburgh Univ. Press, 1997). Anthologies are important because they may represent all that students know of "lesser" women writers, and this one is especially worrying because it reprints the briefest of snippets, provides no individualized contexts, and frames female cultural and literary contribution as decline. "Revolutionary feminism effectively ceased to exist" after the 1790s, and "acceptably 'feminine' discourses such as educational writing showed a new caution," favoring "a safer construction of woman associated with the domestic and familial sphere" (xiv). To assume that educational and travel writing are necessarily conservative and to read spherist metaphors as historic facts perpetuates clichés that demand reconsideration.

3. Because my take on this explanatory paradigm (together with comprehensive documentation) is detailed elsewhere, the full argument and references are not repeated here: see my " 'Completing the Union': Critical *Ennui*, the Politics of Narrative, and the Reformation of Irish Cultural Identity," *The Intersections of the*

Public and Private Spheres, ed. Paula R. Backscheider and Timothy Dykstal, *Prose Studies: History, Theory, Criticism* 18, no. 3 (December 1995): 41–77; and " 'Like the Pictures in a Magic Lantern': Gender, History, and Edgeworth's Rebellion Narratives," *Special Issue: Writing Women/Writing Power, Nineteenth-Century Contexts: An Interdisciplinary Journal* 19, no. 4 (1996): 373–412. Recent overviews warning against narrow readings of "public" and "private" spheres also support the cultural importance this essay assigns to women's literary production: especially important are John Brewer, "This, That, and the Other: Public, Social, and Private in the Seventeenth and Eighteenth Centuries," *Shifting the Boundaries: Transformation of the Languages of Public and Private in the Eighteenth Century,* ed. Dario Castiglione and Lesley Sharpe (Exeter: Univ. of Exeter Press, 1995), 1–21; Lawrence E. Klein, "Gender and the Public/Private Distinction in the Eighteenth Century: Some Questions about Evidence and Analytic Procedure," *The Public and the Nation, Eighteenth-Century Studies* 29, no. 1 (fall 1995): 97–109; Anthony J. La Volpa, "Conceiving A Public: Ideas and Society in Eighteenth-Century Europe," *Journal of Modern History* 64, no. 1 (March 1992): 79–116; Bruce Robbins, "Introduction: The Public as Phantom," *The Phantom Public Sphere,* ed. Bruce Robbins (Minneapolis: Univ. of Minnesota Press, 1993), vii–xxvi; and, most thoroughly, Jeff Weintraub, "The Theory and Politics of the Public/Private Distinction," *Public and Private: Perspectives on a Grand Dichotomy,* ed. Jeff Weintraub and Krishan Kumar, *Morality and Society* (Chicago: Univ. of Chicago Press, 1997), 1–42. Scholars in American studies, the field in which "domestic ideology" began its modern career two decades ago, are now embracing more inclusive views of women's roles in social life than are most students of French and British history: see, for example, Karen V. Hansen, "Making the Social Central: An Introduction," *A Very Social Time: Crafting Community in Antebellum New England* (Berkeley: Univ. of California Press, 1994), 1–28; and her "Rediscovering the Social: Visiting Practices in Antebellum New England and the Limits of the Public/Private Dichotomy," *Public and Private,* ed. Weintraub and Kumar, 268–302; and Sandra F. VanBurkleo, "Little Monarchies," review of *Founding Mothers and Fathers: Gendered Power and the Forming of American Society,* by Mary Beth Norton, *Women's Review of Books* 13, no. 12 (September 1996): 23–24. Essential studies include Craig Calhoun, ed., *Habermas and the Public Sphere* (Cambridge: MIT Press, 1992); Oskar Negt and Alexander Kluge, *Public Sphere and Experience: Toward an Analysis of the Bourgeois and Proletarian Public Sphere,* trans. Peter Labanyi, et al. (Minneapolis: Univ. of Minnesota Press, 1993); and Johanna Meehan, ed., *Feminists Read Habermas: Gendering the Subject of Discourse* (New York: Routledge, 1995). For Habermas's initial formulation, see Jürgen Habermas, *The Structural Transformation of the Public Sphere: An Inquiry Into a Category of Bourgeois Society,* trans. Thomas Burger and Frederick Lawrence, 1962 (Cambridge: MIT Press, 1992), esp. 14–26. Donald H. Reiman's valuable analysis of editorial and interpretive practices, *The*

Study of Modern Manuscripts: Public, Confidential, and Private (Baltimore: Johns Hopkins Univ. Press, 1993), uses these terms in related but more specialized ways. Like Betty T. Bennett, to whose enormous labors in authoritatively editing the letters all Mary Shelley scholars are indebted, Reiman appreciates the author as editor and notes the constraints that public gossip imposes on literary practices.

4. So pervasive is this recent cult of confessional autobiography veiled as criticism that it has inspired its own anthology, H. Aram Veeser, ed., *Confessions of the Critics* (New York: Routledge, 1996). Curiously, even when a critic seeks to situate *Frankenstein* within an explicitly Habermasian (and potentially more valuable) schema of public and private spheres instead of the more familiar pairing of conduct-book private woman and political-public man, the author's confessional secrets are still further foregrounded and Mary Shelley the Enlightened public author obliterated: Patricia McKee states that "Shelley cuts off psychological depths from social production and insists on the need to hide them." Again considered a one-book writer, the creator of Frankenstein and his creature is blamed for contributing "much to the identification of secrecy with private life" in the nineteenth century. If the tale's "double meanings . . . are in absolute and irresolvable conflict" so that the "ostensible or surface meaning" has "no meaning except the obfuscation of the hidden meaning," then "knowledge is not productive of discriminations but can only reproduce irresolvable antagonisms, both within the self and between self and others." Patricia McKee, *Public and Private: Gender, Class, and the British Novel (1764–1878)* (Minneapolis: Univ. of Minnesota Press, 1997), 67–70.

5. The letter to Frances Wright of September 12, 1827, richly conveys Mary Shelley's complex attitude toward her heritage:

> The memory of my Mother has been always the pride & delight of my life; & the admiration of others for her, has been the cause of most of the happiness . . . I have enjoyed. Her greatness of soul & my father [*sic*] high talents have perpetually reminded me that I ought to degenerate as little as I could from those from whom I derived my being. . . . you must not fancy that I am what I wish I were, and my chief merit must always be derived, first from the glory these wonderful beings have shed [? *around*] me, & then for the enthusiasm I have for excellence & the ardent admiration I feel for those who sacrifice themselves for the public good. (*MWSL* 2:3–4)

Until Bennett's own biography appears to supplement the letters and journals now available, her overviews remain foundational: see her "Feminism and Editing Mary Wollstonecraft Shelley: The Editor And?/Or? the Text," in *Palimpsest: Editorial Theory in the Humanities*, ed. George Bornstein and Ralph G. Williams (Ann Arbor: Univ. of Michigan Press, 1993), 67–96; "Finding Mary Shelley in Her Letters," in *Romantic Revisions*, ed. Robert Brinkley and Keith Hanley (Cambridge:

Cambridge Univ. Press, 1992), 291–306; "General Introduction," in *The Novels and Selected Works of Mary Shelley,* vol. 1, *Frankenstein or The Modern Prometheus,* ed. Nora Crook (London: William Pickering, 1996), 1:xiii–lxx; and "Editing Mary Wollstonecraft Shelley: A Bicentary Review," *Keats-Shelley Journal* 47 (1997): 23–28.

6. Recent work gendering "Romanticism" (still a markedly masculinist terrain) raises issues central to analysis of this period's literature. As both noted Romanticists and feminist literary critics observe, the female presence unsettles, perhaps undoes, what twentieth-century criticism has conventionally understood as "Romanticism." Susan J. Wolfson suggests that "insofar as the set of epistemic, discursive, and political concerns most aptly described as 'Romanticism' are still sufficiently and significantly different from what characterizes the wider contemporaneous literary culture, the 'Romantic' canon must remain select and exclusive of other discourses, whether those of women's writing or . . . genres beyond the ones that have defined this canon and its place in subsequent literary history and culture." If revisionary work succeeds in expanding the canon, "what will the field of Romanticism . . . look like? . . . Will Romanticism itself be consumed, or demoted to a relative phenomenon within this enlargement? Will we continue to value the descriptive usefulness and analytic power of the very name 'Romanticism'?" Susan J. Wolfson, review of *The Romantics and Us,* ed. Gene W. Ruoff, and *Romantic Revolutions,* ed. Kenneth R. Johnston et al., *Studies in Romanticism* 32, no. 1 (spring 1993): 130. Because she speaks as a feminist critic instead of a Romantic specialist, Susan K. Lanser's taxonomy of six possible relationships between "Romanticism" and "women writers" is especially valuable. She notices, for example, how "Romantic" functions as an honorific at the same time that much women's writing of this period is not conventionally "Romantic," a problem not satisfactorily resolved by binarizing Romanticism into masculine and feminine forms, "Review Essay: Writing Women into Romanticism," *Feminist Studies* 23, no. 1 (spring 1997): 167–90. In practice, counting women in mostly privileges poetry, the quintessentially "Romantic" genre: see Harriet Kramer Linkin, "Taking Stock of the British Romantics Marketplace: Teaching New Canons through New Editions?" *Special Issue: Gendering Romanticisms, Nineteenth-Century Contexts: An Interdisciplinary Journal* 19, no. 2 (1995): 111–23.

7. Lady Louisa Stuart, for one, thought not; she considered Mary Shelley not as the harbinger of a new Romantic novel but as a stylistic throwback to outmoded sentimental fiction. Writing to Sir Walter Scott (April 24, 1826), she complains of her

long bad cold, such as reduces one to trash and slops, novels and barley-water, and amongst the books my friends kindly sent me to while away time was the first volume of one puffed in the newspaper, *The Last Man,* by the authoress of *Frankenstein.* I would not trouble them for any more of it, but really there were sentences in it so far exceeding those Don Quixote ran mad in trying to comprehend, that I could not help copying out a few of them; they would have turned Feliciano de Silva's own brains. For example: — "Her eyes were impenetrably deep; you seemed to discover space after space in their intellectual glance, and to feel that the soul which was their soul comprehended an universe of thought in its ken." And this: "The overflowing warmth of her heart, by making love a plant of deep root and stately growth, had attuned her whole soul to the reception of happiness."

I amused myself with turning the metaphor to matter of fact. The overflowing warmth of the stove, by making the geranium strike root and grow vigorous, tuned the pianoforte to the reception of God save the King. Since the wonderful improvement that somebody who shall be nameless, together with Miss Edgeworth and one or two more, have made in novels, I imagined such stuff as this had not ventured to show its head, though I remember plenty of it in the days of my youth. So for old acquaintance-sake I give it welcome. But if the boys and girls begin afresh to take it for sublime and beautiful, it ought to get a rap and be put down. (*The Letters of Lady Louisa Stuart,* intro. R. Brimley Johnson [New York: Dial Press, 1926], 209–10)

8. For a classic exposition of the dangers in conflating advice on female behavior and women's actions, see Jay Mechling, "Advice to Historians on Advice to Mothers," *Journal of Social History* 9, no. 1 (fall 1975): 44–63. As he points out, not only do official pronouncements often contradict what readers do, but their actual behavior and their own perceptions of what they do are also frequently at odds. Although he is speaking about maternal care in particular, his caveats on "fatal circularity" equally apply to more general conduct-book advice on gender, the staple source for spherist readings of women's culture: "the exact relationship between the real and the ideal in any system of cultural behavior is something to be tested, not posited" (47). For the latest version of conduct books as key to female fiction, see Penelope Joan Fritzer, *Jane Austen and Eighteenth-Century Conduct Books* (Westport, Conn: Greenwood Press, 1997).

9. William Hazlitt, *Conversations of James Northcote,* in *The Complete Works of William Hazlitt,* ed. P. P. Howe (London: J. M. Dent, 1932), *Conversation* 17, 11:287.

10. Mechling, "Advice to Historians," 56.

11. Johanna M. Smith, "'Cooped Up': Feminine Domesticity in *Frankenstein,*" in *Mary Shelley: Frankenstein,* ed. Johanna M. Smith, Case Studies in Contemporary Criticism (Boston: St. Martin's Press, 1992), 270–85, quoted at 274–76. Anne K. Mellor's feminist analysis of P. B. Shelley's collaborative activities in *Mary*

Shelley: Her Life, Her Fictions, Her Monsters (London: Methuen, 1988) similarly reads them as impositions that weakened the original text. Smith does concede that working with another might be empowering, although she opts for a different interpretation. The private collaboration as public authorial empowerment view has recently been elaborated persuasively by Zachary Leader, "Parenting *Frankenstein*," in *Revision and Romantic Authorship* (Oxford: Clarendon Press, 1996), 167–205. What is at issue is not only the often discussed differences between the 1818 and 1831 texts but also those interventions and revisions prior to the original publication.

12. See, for example, the sample syllabi for adolescents and young adults in Anne H. Lundin and Carol W. Cubberley's 1995 overview, *Teaching Children's Literature: A Resource Guide with Directory of Courses* (Jefferson, N.C.: Mcfarland, 1995); and the innovative bracketing of Mary Shelley's tale with thematically related young adult novels in a recent series on curricular reform for today's more reluctant high school readers in Teri S. Lesesne, "Exploring the Horror Within: Themes of the Duality of Humanity in Mary Shelley's *Frankenstein* and Ten Related Young Adult Novels," in *Adolescent Literature as a Complement to the Classics,* vol. 2, ed. Joan F. Kaywell (Norwood, Mass.: Christopher-Gordon, 1995), 187–97. *Frankenstein* is regularly marketed and shelved as a thriller for young adults in mass-market bookstores, and elite antiquarian book dealers often follow suit (see, for example, the 1998 Catalogue 44 of *Children's Books* from Oxford-based M. and D. Reeve, entry 486). Unsurprisingly, recent teen narrators carry on in *The Last Man* (1826) tradition as well; twenty-first-century Los Angeles on the verge of apocalypse is the setting for Cynthia Kadahota's futurism of physical, spiritual, and cultural displacement, *In the Heart of the Valley of Love,* 1992 (Berkeley: Univ. of California Press, 1997). For an excellent overview of the tradition of cultural critique and revision in literature about and for the young, see Millicent Lenz, *Nuclear Age Literature for Youth: The Quest for a Life-Affirming Ethic* (Chicago: American Library Association, 1990).

13. The plasticity of Mary Shelley's progeny adapts itself equally to Orientalism, British racial discourse and xenophobia, aesthetics, and the scientific knowledge industry; see, for example, Joseph W. Lew, "The Deceptive Other: Mary Shelley's Critique of Orientalism in *Frankenstein*," *Studies in Romanticism* 30, no. 2 (summer 1991): 255–83; H. L. Malchow, "Frankenstein's Monster and Images of Race in Nineteenth-Century Britain," *Past and Present* 139 (May 1993): 91–130; Elizabeth A. Bohls, "Standards of Taste, Discourses of 'Race,' and the Aesthetic Education of a Monster: Critique of Empire in *Frankenstein*," *Eighteenth-Century Life* 18, new ser. 3 (November 1994): 23–36; and Alan Rauch, "The Monstrous Body of Knowledge in Mary Shelley's *Frankenstein*," *Studies in Romanticism* 34, no. 2 (summer 1995): 227–54. Gendered readings are, of course, too numerous to cite, but notably, recent discussion attends to a battle of the sexes within such read-

ings over time: see especially Ellen Cronan Rose, "Custody Battles: Reproducing Knowledge about *Frankenstein*," *New Literary History: Philosophical Resonances* 26, no. 4 (autumn 1995): 809–32. For still another take on a text whose "performance of gender can solicit readers differently," see Bette London, "Mary Shelley, *Frankenstein*, and the Spectacle of Masculinity," *PMLA* 108, no. 2 (March 1993): 253–67, quoted at 264. The latest spin on the story as family tragedy shifts the argument from parents and offspring to siblings: see William Crisman, " 'Now Misery Has Come Home': Sibling Rivalry in Mary Shelley's *Frankenstein*," *Studies in Romanticism* 36, no. 1 (spring 1997): 27–41.

Simultaneously, however, interpretation of *Frankenstein* as religious and/or scientific allegory revives, with the 1818 and 1831 versions likened to a "paradigm shift" in the author's attitudes toward science, as in Naomi Heatherington, "Creator and Created in Mary Shelley's *Frankenstein*," *Keats-Shelley Review* 11 (1997): 1–39, quoted at 29; as she acknowledges, Heatherington is developing Marilyn Butler's reading in her introduction to *Frankenstein or The Modern Prometheus: The 1818 Text* in the World's Classics series (New York: Oxford Univ. Press, 1994), ix–liii. Likewise, the tale's relation to previous and subsequent Gothic traditions can be endlessly recycled, as in Jerrold E. Hogle's Kristeva-influenced " 'Frankenstein' as Neo-Gothic: From the Ghost of the Counterfeit to the Monster of Abjection," in *Romanticism, History, and the Possibilities of Genre*, ed. Tilottama Rajan and Julia M. Wright (Cambridge: Cambridge Univ. Press, 1998), 176–210. The extensive bibliographies appended to these recent studies (and they are far from complete) underscore what Butler calls the tale's "reputation as the most protean and disputable of even Romantic texts" (vi).

14. Long after Hinton's meteoric rise, Jay Daly, the author of the *Presenting S. E. Hinton* volume in the Twayne Young Adult Authors series (New York: Twayne, 1989), entitled his opening chapter, "Who Is This S. E. Hinton and Where Did He Come From?" and still startles some readers by revealing that "Susie" is a woman, one who uses her initials because girls in her youth were passive mirrors of men who "never got to *do* anything," 1. Unless the book has been assigned in a class, most teenagers seem unaware of the author's gender.

15. Probably like most people working in this period, I collect mass-market *Frankenstein* spinoffs, which proliferate even faster than academic analyses of Mary Shelley's first novel. The latest—found in a drugstore discount bin—is entitled *The Mammoth Book of Frankenstein*, ed. Stephen Jones (New York: Carroll and Graf, 1994), and features the originary "classic of science fiction and horror" plus a host of more recent "electrifying tales of cursed creation," complete with an appalling cover: a snarling, scarred old monster with seven bleeding silver plates in his head, a far cry from the educable creature of Mary Shelley's tale (xiv, 2).

16. How and why Trelawny's misrepresentations were institutionalized is wor-

thy of critical study; even in his editor's introduction, he comes across as exemplary of masculinist Romanticism at its worst, mouthing libertarian sentiments and behaving like a beast, especially toward native women and bluestockings, "the barren sect of mouldy, virgin blues": Edward John Trelawny, *Adventures of a Younger Son,* ed. William St Clair (London: Oxford Univ. Press, 1974), 87.

17. Mary Poovey, *The Proper Lady and the Woman Writer: Ideology as Style in the Works of Mary Wollstonecraft, Mary Shelley, and Jane Austen* (Chicago: Univ. of Chicago Press, 1984), 143; she is quoting from Elizabeth Nitchie, *Mary Shelley: Author of "Frankenstein,"* 1953 (rpt., Westport, Conn.: Greenwood Press, 1970), xii. Trelawny emphasizes Mary Shelley's jealousy and loneliness as much as her supposed conventionality, accusing her of "even affect[ing] the pious dodge, such was her yearning for society," *Letters of Edward John Trelawny,* ed. H. Buxton Forman (London: Oxford Univ. Press, 1910), 229. Had Poovey gone to the primary source, she would have found much more evidence for her interpretation of Shelley as "proper lady"; see, for example, Trelawny's further epistolary slanders, 209, 225, 232, 234, 239–40, and 259–60; and his public dismissal of Mary Shelley as her husband's "exact opposite," whose limited capacity can be judged by her novels written after his death, which were "more than ordinarily commonplace and conventional," Trelawny, *Records of Shelley, Byron, and the Author,* 2 vols. (London: Basil Montagu Pickering, 1878), Appendix 1, 2:229. Trelawny's hurtful impact on Mary Shelley and her subsequent reputation is outlined in *MWSJ* 558 n, Nitchie, *Mary Shelley,* 11.

This equation of *Matilda* with Mary informs not only Nitchie's discussion in the 1953 biographical study but also the first publication of the novelette and her 1943 overview. In her introduction to the work's initial printing, Nitchie states that "it would be hard to find a more self-revealing work" as a "document" in the understanding of the daughter, husband, and father: "The three main characters are clearly Mary herself, Godwin, and Shelley, and their relations can easily be reassorted to correspond with actuality," *Mathilda* [and *The Fields of Fancy*], ed. Elizabeth Nitchie, extra ser. 3 *Studies in Philology* (Chapel Hill: Univ. of North Carolina Press, 1959), vii. Even before seeing all three of the notebooks containing the *Mathilda-Matilda* versions, Nitchie, like most subsequent critics, takes for granted that "certainly Mary is Mathilda," torturing the tale's Shelley figure "and herself with her grief," "Mary Shelley's *Mathilda*: An Unpublished Story and Its Biographical Significance," *Studies in Philology* 40, no. 3 (July 1943): 454.

18. Victorian scholarship is increasingly concerned not with the stereotypical "angel in the house" but with the permeability and instability of "masculine" and "feminine" domains and with women's exploitation of boundaries and borderlands. See, for instance, Elizabeth Langland, *Nobody's Angels: Middle-Class Women and Domestic Ideology in Victorian Culture* (Ithaca: Cornell Univ. Press, 1995); and

Anne Digby, "Victorian Values and Women in Public and Private," in *Victorian Values*, ed. T. C. Smout, *Proceedings of the British Academy* 78 (New York: Oxford Univ. Press, 1992), 195–215.

19. Chapter 1, 175–76, of *Mathilda* as reprinted from Elizabeth Nitchie's 1959 first public presentation of the 1819 tale in Betty T. Bennett and Charles E. Robinson, ed., *The Mary Shelley Reader* (New York: Oxford Univ. Press, 1990). Subsequent page references in the text refer to the *Reader*. Now that multiple versions and variants, including spellings of the heroine's name, are available for detailed comparison in vol. 2 of *The Novels and Selected Works of Mary Shelley*, ed. Pamela Clemit (London: William Pickering, 1996), the scholar interested in authorial writing processes faces a daunting task that could, but probably will not, transform thinking about easy identification of author and narrator. This text, however, does not completely supersede Nitchie's original two versions and notes or her 1943 commentary on the fragmented originals, and some notes are factually inaccurate.

20. Although Janet Todd neatly aligns *Matilda* with the Romantic incest theme in Byron and P. B. Shelley and argues that "it is probable that Shelley's own interest helped inspire his wife," one wonders, given the daughter's own confessions of father worship, whether the husband's influence was necessary; there was, of course, a collaborative (or incestuous) writing project between the two young authors, introduction, *Mary Maria Matilda,* by Mary Wollstonecraft and Mary Shelley (Harmondsworth: Penguin, 1992), xxii. The novella has only recently become available in paperback for classroom use, and Todd usefully outlines (and simplifies) the relations between the mother's and daughter's tales.

21. Rev. Richard Polwhele, *The Unsex'd Females: A Poem, Addressed to the Author of "The Pursuits of Literature"* (London: Cadell and Davies, 1798), 8–9. We do not always remember that Polwhele's famous title comes from the voluminous versifier T. J. Mathias, to whom he dedicates his poem, nor does our indignation at Polwhele's gross retelling of Mary Wollstonecraft's tragic history let us register the recognition and sometimes generous praise Polwhele accords women writers. Were they not influential and dangerous, he would not be writing the poem, which, in the *Anti-Jacobin Review and Magazine*'s understatement, is "of a political cast," a vindication of Anglican Christian Britain "at this awful crisis of church and state": review of *The Unsex'd Females, Anti-Jacobin Review and Magazine* 3 (May 1799): 27, 33.

22. Myrrha's father is horrified when he finally calls for lights to see his eager bedmate; the outcast girl's bole splits to give birth not to a monster but to a gorgeous babe, washed by the mother tree's sweet tears: see "The Story of Cinyras and Myrrha" in Ovid's *Metamorphoses,* trans. Rolfe Humphries (Bloomington: Indiana Univ. Press, 1961), Book 10: 243–51. In contrast, as several critics argue, Shelley's tale of incest (mediated through Alfieri's *Myrrha* and P. B. Shelley's

Cenci), is linked with the writer's child loss and mourning, the private experience of dead children punitively projected onto the public, guilty protagonist of the rewritten version of *Matilda,* usually taken as the "final" version of "The Fields of Fancy," although neither was published in the author's lifetime. The existence or erasure of the original "Oriental" vision frame, derived in part from Wollstonecraft's *The Cave of Fancy,* controls how the daughter's protagonist must be read, as noted below. First published by Godwin in the fourth volume of the *Posthumous Works,* where it is labeled "Extract of the Cave of Fancy. A Tale, [Begun to be written in the year 1787, but never completed]," it is reprinted in *The Works of Mary Wollstonecraft,* ed. Janet Todd and Marilyn Butler (New York: New York Univ. Press, 1989), 1:185–206.

23. Godwin's comments on *Matilda* are not wholly hostile or imperceptive; he admired "very highly" some parts, notably the pursuit and "the catastrofe [*sic*] which closes it." His chief objection remains a problem in recent studies: "Mathildas [*sic*] protestation at the beginning . . . that she has not to reproach herself with any guilt; but, yet, in proceeding one is apt to lose sight of that protestation," so wretched is the heroine-narrator: quoted in *Maria Gisborne and Edward E. Williams, Shelley's Friends: Their Journals and Letters,* ed. Frederick L. Jones (Norman: Univ. of Oklahoma Press, 1951), 44. For Gisborne's own high valuation and Mary Shelley's attempts to get the manuscript back, see 27, 76, and 82; and also *MWSL* 1:225, 229, 237. To his credit, Godwin had taken responsibility for Wollstonecraft's daughter by Gilbert Imlay; Janet Todd's "Thoughts on the Death of Fanny Wollstonecraft," *Gender, Art, and Death* (New York: Continuum, 1993), 120–35, helps contextualize the family's fear of scandal and what she calls "the contagion of suicide," quoted at 131. Like Godwin, Thomas Medwin considered Mary Shelley's subject "disgusting," however "delicately treated": he thought the tale the product of youthful taste "not so refined as at present" and was "not surprised that it should never have made its appearance," *The Life of Percy Bysshe Shelley: A New Edition,* ed. H. Buxton Forman (New York: Oxford Univ. Press, 1913), 252.

24. The 1823 piece is partially reprinted in Bennett and Robinson's *Mary Shelley Reader* (329–33), quoted at 331. A central document in rethinking public and private in the author's work, the essay celebrates the *I* in Burton, Montaigne, Rousseau, Boswell's Johnson, Lady Mary Montagu's letters, and above all her own mother's Scandinavian travels: "this sensitive, imaginative, native, suffering, enthusiastic pronoun, spreads an inexpressible charm over Mary Wollstonecraft's Letters from Norway," 332. In her review of Godwin's *Cloudesley* (1830), she quotes evocatively from her mother's travel book; her review is reprinted in vol. 2 of the Pickering and Chatto edition of *The Novels and Selected Works of Mary Shelley,* ed. Pamela Clemit, as are the full text of "Giovanni Villani" and the two versions of *Matilda.* Because we now know that the author of the review is the daughter of the

novelist and the travel writer to whom she alludes, we necessarily read the public endorsement of the mother's autobiographical narrative mode in a different way from that of the original audience.

25. Two recent misidentifications of key allusions in the mother's and daughter's works illustrate these points, for both displace Enlightenment legacies for personalist poetics. Critiquing my early reading of Wollstonecraft's late travels as deftly balancing rational argument and Romantic sensibility, thus managing an "organic integrity" that eludes "the public/private dichotomy," Esther H. Schor argues instead that Wollstonecraft represents her reasoned observations as "the effusions of sensibility," adopting "a diminutive ('little hero'), feminine persona derived from sentimental fiction." But the source for the "I" in the Advertisement to Wollstonecraft's travel book ("I could not avoid being continually the first person—'the little hero of each tale'"), which goes unidentified in all previous editions (from Joseph Johnson to Sylva Norman, Richard Holmes, and the 1989 *Works,* ed. Todd and Butler), is an ambitious man, not a weepy woman. Wollstonecraft appropriates Edward Young's first satire to the Duke of Dorset on the marvelous effect of fame from his well-known *Love of Fame, the Universal Passion: In Seven Characteristical Satires,* 2d rev. ed. (London: J. Tonson, 1728), Satire 1:10, "It makes *dear self* on well-bred tongues prevail,/And *I* the *little hero* of each Tale." See Mitzi Myers, "Wollstonecraft's *Letters Written . . . in Sweden: Toward Romantic Autobiography,*" *Studies in Eighteenth-Century Culture,* ed. Roseann Runte (Madison: Univ. of Wisconsin Press, 1979), 8:165–85, quoted at 166; and Schor, "Mary Shelley in Transit," in *The Other Mary Shelley: Beyond* Frankenstein, ed. Audrey A. Fisch, Anne K. Mellor, and Esther H. Schor (New York: Oxford Univ. Press, 1993), 235–57, quoted at 254, n. 9, and 238.

Similarly, when the Pickering and Chatto editors (2:17) unaccountably describe the hero of Frances Sheridan's *Nourjahad* (a Shelley allusion in *Matilda* and elsewhere) as "pass[ing] vast periods of time in a state of sleep or suspended animation" when he merely *thinks* he does, they erase the Enlightenment trickery Nourjahad's friend employs to cure his solipsism. Nourjahad is a deluded narcissist, not a Romantic visionary; the slip here epitomizes alternative readings of the framed and frameless *Matilda* versions. I discuss the relationship between the *I* in Wollstonecraft's Scandinavian travel letters and her daughter's work, including *Matilda* and its intertextualities, in other work in progress.

26. From the huge literature on the daddy's girl–family romance explanatory model for the writers cited (and more), Cora Kaplan, "Wicked Fathers: A Family Romance" (on Browning), in *Sea Changes: Culture and Feminism* (London: Verso, 1990), 191–211, exemplifies a nuanced approach. What is striking, however, is that (just as with incest), the father-daughter dyad is as welcome on the bestseller charts as in academic journals: a recent instance is Carmen Renee Berry and Lynn Barrington, *Daddies and Daughters* (New York: Simon and Schuster, 1998).

27. Reviews of Fisch, Mellor, and Schor, eds., *The Other Mary Shelley,* typically laud the collection's collaborative editorship as reminiscent of Shelley's own authorial practices, yet they also fault the subject matter for insufficiently "othering" the author and her work: which "Mary Shelley" is "the other" and why do many of the contributors traverse the same ground? Above all, suggests Elizabeth A. Fay, how come the volume cannot answer the canonical conundrum of why this writer's publications — and, one might add, those of her cohort — "should have been so easy to forget" by the twentieth-century literary establishment, "Review. The Othering of Romantic Studies: Prisms and Art," *College English* 57, no. 3 (March 1995): 346–47; see also Gary Kelly's review in *Keats-Shelley Journal* 43 (1994): 202–4.

28. Robert Southey quoted in Ford K. Brown, *The Life of William Godwin* (London: J. M. Dent; New York: E. P. Dutton, 1926), 134; for Godwin's aim and the book's reception, see my "Godwin's *Memoirs* of Wollstonecraft: The Shaping of Self and Subject," *Studies in Romanticism* 20, no. 3 (fall 1981): 299–316, and its references. Godwin's literary caution was hard won; as Southey notices in praising a later work, "His folly in thus eternally making himself a mark for abuse is inconceivable. Come kick me — is his eternal language. Yet is the man a good creature — brimfull of benevolence — as kind hearted as a child would wish. It should be known to his credit that he is a father to Imlays child [Wollstonecraft's daughter Fanny]," *New Letters of Robert Southey,* ed. Kenneth Curry, 2 vols. (New York: Columbia Univ. Press, 1965), 1:246 (August 17, 1801).

29. For thoughtful critiques of cropping Mary Shelley to fit preconceived critical paradigms, see Bennett's overviews, cited in note 6 above; and Rose, "Custody Battles." Bennett makes a strong case for Mary Shelley's private letters as illuminating guides to her public authorship not only in her introductions to the letter volumes and the reader but also in "Finding Mary Shelley in Her Letters." For another shrewd assessment of Mary Shelley's adroit use of "feminine" rhetoric as mask for a "belief in her own authorial talents that is not wholly consistent with her fear of appearing before the public in writing," see James P. Carson, "Bringing the Author Forward: *Frankenstein* through Mary Shelley's Letters," *Criticism* 30, no. 4 (fall 1988): 431–53, quoted at 431. If critics can abate their familial fixation, Shelley's later literary career may well yield the hard data about women writers' professional exploitation of "minor" genres that Paula R. Feldman is uncovering in Felicia Hemans's contributions to annuals. I am grateful to Professor Feldman for sharing her findings before their appearance as "The Poet and the Profits: Felicia Hemans and the Literary Marketplace," *Keats-Shelley Journal* 46 (1997): 148–76.

30. Two decades after publication, *The Endurance of* Frankenstein: *Essays on Mary Shelley's Novel,* ed. George Levine and U. C. Knoepflmacher (Berkeley: Univ. of California Press, 1979), remains invaluable. As those familiar with the

nineteenth-century reviews of what was regularly termed the "Godwin school of novels" will notice, Pamela Clemit's subtitle to *The Godwinian Novel: The Rational Fictions of Godwin, Brockden Brown, Mary Shelley* (Oxford: Clarendon Press, 1993), recapitulates, yet narrows the initial way this fictional subset was framed (works by Thomas Jefferson Hogg and John Gibson Lockhart were also considered gloomily "Godwinian"); Maggie Kilgour, *The Rise of the Gothic Novel* (London: Routledge, 1995). Instead of attributing distinctive generic attributes to the author's disordered psyche, scholars interested in marketplace dynamics might make more use of archival research. Reading the reviews in Burton R. Pollin's neglected *Godwin Criticism: A Synoptic Bibliography* (Toronto: Univ. of Toronto Press, 1967) in their original locales chastens twentieth-century assumptions about which authors and what genres count.

31. Diane F. Sadoff's review, however, finds Hill-Miller's punishing father-authorizing daughter model a problem in relation to the critic's own positioning of her book. That is, in omitting Harold Bloom and Freud, "the biggest daddy of all," Hill-Miller replicates in her own analysis the strategies her subject is said to deploy, eliding her own theoretical incest just as *Matilda*'s author erases the physical from her problematics of desire and power. Diane F. Sadoff, review of Hill-Miller, *Keats-Shelley Journal* 95 (1996), 211.

32. Hill-Miller's " 'The Skies and Trees of the Past': Anne Thackeray Ritchie and William Makepeace Thackeray" in *Daughters and Fathers,* ed. Lynda E. Boose and Betty S. Flowers (Baltimore: Johns Hopkins Univ. Press, 1989), 361–83, precedes *"My Hideous Progeny": Mary Shelley, William Godwin, and the Father-Daughter Relationship* (Newark: Univ. of Delaware Press; London: Associated Univ. Presses, 1995).

33. "Until I knew Shelley I may justly say that [Godwin] was my God — & I remember many childish instances of the excess of attachment I bore for him," *MWSL* 1:296 (December 5, 1822). Movingly expressing her loneliness at Harrow, Mary Shelley again recalls the covert sensibility of her early years, "except that Mrs Godwin had discovered long before my excessive & romantic attachment to my father," *MWSL* 2:215 (October 30–November 17 1834). Mary Shelley's judicious assessment of her son's less than transcendent capacities in this letter might be usefully compared with Godwin's reading of her character when she was in her early teens: "she is singularly bold, somewhat imperious, and active of mind. Her desire of knowledge is great, and her perseverance in everything she undertakes almost invincible," C. Kegan Paul, *William Godwin: His Friends and Contemporaries,* 2 vols. (London: Henry S. King, 1876), 2:214.

34. Betty T. Bennett's witty dismantling of Kenneth Branagh's visual misreading of Shelley's first novel simultaneously demonstrates the tale's versatility and makes a case for its continuing public relevance: "Hate at First Sight: How Kenneth

Branagh Misunderstood Mary Shelley's *Frankenstein*," *TLS* 4778 (November 18, 1994): 16–17.

35. Most recent analysis, like that of Judith Lewis Herman, with Lisa Hirschman, *Father-Daughter Incest* (Cambridge: Harvard Univ. Press, 1981), positions violation of the incest taboo as "a paradigm of female sexual victimization," 4; indicatively, Hope Edelman's chap. 5, "Daddy's Little Girl," in *Motherless Daughters: The Legacy of Loss* (New York: Bantam Doubleday Dell, 1994), pays special attention to incest. For a Jungian (and more literarily amenable) interpretation of the "father-daughter wound," see Linda Schierse Leonard, *The Wounded Woman: Healing the Father-Daughter Relationship* (Boston: Shambhala, 1985). Elizabeth Wilson, "Not in This House: Incest, Denial, and Doubt in the White Middle-Class Family," *Yale Journal of Criticism* 8, no. 1 (spring 1995): 35–58, typifies the ever-expanding critical literature on incest, just as recent celebrity revelations demonstrate the public appetite for the prurient that is the popular analogue to contemporary academia's sexualized critical theory. In critiquing "incest's sudden commonplaceness" as plot device in late twentieth-century female fiction, Anne Roiphe explores its recent "cultural reasons for coming to prominence" as indicative of changing notions of men and the family, *Fruitful. Living the Contradictions: A Memoir of Modern Motherhood*, 1996 (New York: Penguin, 1997), 57. Historically contextualizing "Incest as the Meaning of the Gothic Novel," Ruth Perry similarly links the incestuous contrivances of eighteenth-century Gothic fiction to "a real change in family relations"; I am grateful to Professor Perry for prepublication access to her contribution for a special issue of *The Eighteenth Century: Theory and Interpretation, Constructions of Incest in Restoration and Eighteenth-century England*, ed. Ellen Pollak, 39, no. 3 (1998): 261–78.

36. For an alternative, politicized reading of *Lodore* (1835) based on Bennett's scholarship, see the introduction to Lisa Vargo's recent edition in the Broadview Literary Texts series (Peterborough, Canada: Broadview Press, 1997). Indicatively, Vargo takes as her epigraph Fanny Derham's faith in the reformist force of woman's words: "Words have more power than any one can guess; it is by words that the world's great fight, now in these civilized times, is carried on; I never hesitated to use them, when I fought any battle for the miserable and oppressed. People are so afraid to speak, it would seem as if half our fellow-creatures were born with deficient organs; like parrots they can repeat a lesson, but their voice fails them, when that alone is wanting to make the tyrant quail": vol. 3, chap. 1, 316 in this edition. Outlining why the Pickering and Chatto edition is "clearly a milestone," a welcome corrective to the "politically conservative" characterization of the later work he links with Anne Mellor, Michael Baron especially dwells on *Falkner*, hitherto unread and now found "thrilling": "Romantic Riches," *Women: A Cultural Review* 8, no. 2 (autumn 1997): 244–46.

37. For a striking example of the sophisticated voyeur who simultaneously critiques and revels, see Marilyn May, "Publish and Perish: William Godwin, Mary Shelley, and the Public Appetite for Scandal," *Papers on Language and Literature* 26, no. 4 (fall 1990): 489–512. Richly insightful as they are, the studies cited above stress (albeit in different ways) familial dynamics and autobiographical revelation: see Gonda's chap. 4, "Schedoniac Contours: The Sins of the Fathers in Gothic Fiction," linking Mary Shelley's story with her husband's drama; Terence Harpold, "'Did you get Mathilda from Papa?': Seduction Fantasy and the Circulation of Mary Shelley's *Mathilda*," *Studies in Romanticism* 28, no. 1 (spring 1989): 49–67; Tilottama Rajan, "Mary Shelley's *Mathilda*: Melancholy and the Political Economy of Romanticism," *Studies in the Novel: The Romantic Novel*, ed. Scott Simpkins, 26 no. 2 (summer 1994): 43–68; Margaret Davenport Garrett, "Writing and Re-writing Incest in Mary Shelley's *Mathilda*," *Keats-Shelley Journal* 45 (1996): 44–60, quoted at 59. As Gonda, Todd, and others note, Mathilda's name not only echoes Dante, as Romanticists often assume, but is also favored for heroines in Gothic fiction, especially the incest prone.

38. Shelley, "Valerius: The Reanimated Roman," in *Mary Shelley: Collected Tales and Stories*, ed. Charles E. Robinson (Baltimore: Johns Hopkins Univ. Press, 1976), 333. In a fragmentary version of this same story, however, the point of view shifts from the Roman's to that of his daughterly guide, Isabell Harley, whose closing commentary can be read as ambiguously incestuous, 343–44; and there are still other tales, like "The Elder Son," 244–65, whose widowed father and loving daughter have been taken as covertly self-referential by Emily Sunstein and others. The parricidal stigma attached to the innocent daughter in "The Mourner," 81–99, as well as *Matilda*, is read as critique of the bourgeois family by Kate Ferguson Ellis, "Subversive Surfaces: The Limits of Domestic Affection in Mary Shelley's Later Fiction," in Fisch, Mellor, and Schor, eds., *The Other Mary Shelley*, 220–34.

39. Charleen E. Bunnell, "*Mathilda*: Mary Shelley's Romantic Tragedy," *Keats-Shelley Journal* 46 (1997): 75–96, quoted at 80. Similarly indicating a more generically adroit and less self-absorbed novelist is A. A. Markley, "'Laughing That I May Not Weep': Mary Shelley's Short Fiction and Her Novels," *Keats-Shelley Journal* 46 (1997): 97–124.

40. Bunnell makes the tale's exorbitant affect and hyperbolic style Mathilda's rather than Mary Shelley's ("*Mathilda*," 92), so that the narrative excesses figure as thematic, but the stylized language and affective indulgence of a tragic heroine can be found in some of Mary Shelley's journal entries as well, especially in those immediately after her husband's drowning. Mary Shelley herself thinks of *Matilda* as prophetic of that tragedy in her letters: see *MWSL*, 1:247 (August 15, 1822), 336 (May 3, 1823). For devirilized heroes, see Claudia L. Johnson, *Equivocal Beings: Politics, Gender, and Sentimentality in the 1790s: Wollstonecraft, Radcliffe, Burney, Austen* (Chicago: Univ. of Chicago Press, 1995); and Margaret Waller, *The*

Male Malady: Fictions of Impotence in the French Romantic Novel (New Brunswick: Rutgers Univ. Press, 1993). Situating the father's multiple failings within these literary traditions obviously ironizes Garrett's interpretation of *Matilda* as "a metaphorical narrative" of "any woman's excessive dependence upon a male protector" (Garrett, "Writing and Re-writing Incest," 45).

41. What Godwin refused to give back and what Mary Shelley possessed, like much else about this tale, remains murky: the journals record a September 4, 1821, reading of "Matilda to Jane": *MWSJ* 1:379. Had the Wollstonecraft-derived Oriental frame survived to suggest the heroine's growth toward a more rational self-knowledge, Mathilda's tale might be construed as part of an Enlightenment narrative, as in William D. Brewer, "Mary Shelley's *Valperga:* The Triumph of Euthanasia's Mind," *European Romantic Review* 5, no. 2 (winter 1995): 133–48.

42. Peter Thorslev, Jr., "Incest as Romantic Symbol," *Comparative Literature Studies* 2, no. 1 (1965): 41–58; Eugene Stelzig, " 'Though It Were the Deadliest Sin to Love as We Have Loved': The Romantic Idealization of Incest," *European Romantic Review* 5, no. 2 (winter 1992): 230–51; and *The Letters of Percy Bysshe Shelley,* ed. Frederick L. Jones (Oxford: Clarendon Press, 1964), 2:154 (November 16, 1819). The complementary studies of James B. Twitchell illustrate the gamut from trash to high art with particular reference to incest and *Frankenstein:* see Twitchell, *Forbidden Partners: The Incest Taboo in Modern Culture* (New York: Columbia Univ. Press, 1987), *Preposterous Violence: Fables of Aggression in Modern Culture* (New York: Oxford Univ. Press, 1989), and *Carnival Culture: The Trashing of Taste in America* (New York: Columbia Univ. Press, 1992).

43. Poovey, *The Proper Lady and the Woman Writer,* 114.

Chapter 12: Poetry as Souvenir

1. Southey to Allan Cunningham, Esq., February 24, 1828, *The Life and Correspondence of Robert Southey,* vol. 5, ed. Charles Cuthbert Southey (1849–50; rpt., St. Clair Shores, Mich.: Scholarly Press, [1969]), 322.

2. S. M. Ellis, *William Harrison Ainsworth and His Friends* (London: John Lane, 1911), 160.

3. Peter Manning's essay on Wordsworth in the *Keepsake* directed my attention to many of the sources I drew on in what follows; it also articulates an important association between the annuals' promise of refinement and the productions of Romantic poets. Manning, "Wordsworth in the *Keepsake,* 1829," in *Literature in the Marketplace,* ed. John O. Jordan and Robert I. Patten (Cambridge: Cambridge Univ. Press, 1995), 44–72.

4. In an effort to garner enough information to be able to make generalizations about these anthologies, I examined approximately fifty volumes kept by British men and women during the period from 1790 to the middle of the

nineteenth century. Any sampling of these private albums is an idiosyncratic survey, hostage to the vagaries of collecting habits through the years. Commonplace books either kept by someone with a claim to fame or an association with another famous person (witness the preservation of Dorothy Wordsworth's commonplace book) or with an inscription by a celebrity (for example, a poem in Byron's hand) are much more likely to have been preserved than books with no such claim on the collector's interest. Commonplace books are frequently sliced up by booksellers, who are more interested in the drawings and engravings often pasted on their pages than in the written matter which is the focus of my interest. Scholars of Romantic era literature and culture owe a debt of gratitude to William St Clair, who has amassed a fascinating collection of these ephemeral volumes from London bookstalls. St Clair's collection provided by far the largest single source for my study.

5. Although commonplace books were kept by both men and women, the fact that, of those extant, a much greater number were in the possession of women than men points to the gendered aspect of this kind of collecting activity. Also, the existence of commonplace books compiled by fathers and brothers for daughters and sisters suggests that the perusal of a commonplace book—particularly one given the imprimatur of masculine literary authority—was a fully sanctioned female pastime. The commonplace book compiled by Thomasine Leigh early in the second decade of the nineteenth century by "a friend and brother" and the one presented to Emma Garland by her father in 1825 provide good examples of books compiled by men for women. On the gendering of collecting practices, see Ellen Gruber Garvey's discussion of trade card scrapbooks in *The Adman in the Parlor: Magazines and the Gendering of Consumer Culture, 1800s to 1910s* (New York: Oxford Univ. Press, 1996). See also Naomi Schor's treatment of postcard collecting in "*Cartes Postales:* Representing Paris, 1900," *Critical Inquiry* 18, no. 2 (1992): 188–244.

6. Susan Stewart, *On Longing: Narratives of the Miniature, the Gigantic, the Souvenir, the Collection* (1984; Durham, NC: Duke Univ. Press, 1993), 136.

7. Bradford Allen Booth, *A Cabinet of Gems* (Berkeley: Univ. of California Press, 1938), 6.

8. Preface to the *Keepsake,* ed. William Ainsworth Harrison (London: Thomas Davison, 1828), 14.

9. Ibid.

10. Arjun Appadurai, "Introduction: Commodities and the Politics of Value," in *The Social Life of Things: Commodities in Cultural Perspective,* ed. Arjun Appadurai (Cambridge: Cambridge Univ. Press, 1986), 11.

11. *Juvenile Forget Me Not,* ed. Mrs. S. C. Hall (London: N. Hailes, 1829), 230.

12. Frederick Winthrop Faxon, *Literary Annuals and Gift-Books* (Boston: Boston Book Co., 1912), xxvii.

13. Igor Kopytoff, "The Cultural Biography of Things: Commoditization as Process," in *The Social Life of Things: Commodities in Cultural Perspective,* ed. Arjun Appadurai (Cambridge: Cambridge Univ. Press, 1986), 82.

14. Southey to Allan Cunningham, in *Life and Correspondence,* ed. Charles Cuthbert Southey, 339.

15. Judith Pascoe, *Romantic Theatricality: Gender, Poetry, and Spectatorship* (Ithaca: Cornell Univ. Press, 1997), 130–62.

16. Richard Holmes, "The Romantic Circle," *New York Review of Books,* April 10, 1997, 34.

17. Sonia Hofkosh, "Disfiguring Economies: Mary Shelley's Short Stories," in *The Other Mary Shelley: Beyond "Frankenstein",* ed. Audrey A. Fisch, Anne K. Mellor, and Esther H. Schor (New York: Oxford Univ. Press, 1993), 205.

18. Judith Pike, "Resurrection of the Fetish in *Gradiva, Frankenstein,* and *Wuthering Heights,*" in *Romantic Women Writers: Voices and Countervoices,* ed. Paula R. Feldman and Theresa M. Kelley (Hanover, N.H.: Univ. Press of New England, 1995), 157.

19. *Keepsake,* ed. William Ainsworth Harrison (London: Hurst, Chance, and Co., 1831), 84.

20. Mary Shelley, "On Reading Wordsworth's Lines on Peele Castle," in *Romanticism: An Anthology,* ed. Duncan Wu (Cambridge: Blackwell Publishers, 1994), 1083.

21. Bette London, "Mary Shelley, *Frankenstein,* and the Spectacle of Masculinity," *Publications of the Modern Language Association of America* 108 (1993): 253.

22. Ibid., 255.

23. Shelley, "On Reading Wordsworth's Lines," 1083.

Chapter 13: "Trying to make it as good as I can"

A slightly different version of this essay has appeared in *Romanticism* 3, no. 2 (1998).

1. Neil Fraistat, "Illegitimate Shelley: Radical Piracy and the Textual Edition as Cultural Performance," *Publications of the Modern Language Association of America* 109 (1994), 409–23; see also what Fraistat describes as "an earlier version" of this essay in *Shelley: Poet and Legislator of the World,* ed. Betty T. Bennett and Stuart Curran (Baltimore: Johns Hopkins Univ. Press, 1996), 105–13 (the quoted phrase is on 105); Mary Favret, "Mary Shelley's Sympathy and Irony: The Editor and Her Corpus," in *The Other Mary Shelley: Beyond "Frankenstein,"* ed. Audrey A. Fisch, Anne K. Mellor, and Esther H. Schor (New York: Oxford Univ. Press, 1993), 17–38; Susan J. Wolfson, "Editorial Privilege: Mary Shelley and Percy Shelley's Audiences," in ibid., 39–72; Lisa Vargo, "Close Your Eyes and Think of Shelley: Versioning Mary Shelley's *The Triumph of Life,*" in *Evaluating Shelley,* ed.

Timothy Clark and Jerrold E. Hogle (Edinburgh: Edinburgh Univ. Press for Univ. of Durham, 1996), 215–24.

2. *Constructing* and *reconstructing* are central terms in Wolfson, "Editorial Privilege," esp. 45, 51 and 56; see also Fraistat, "Illegitimate Shelley," 419, n. 5.

3. Favret, "Mary Shelley's Sympathy and Irony," 27.

4. Emily W. Sunstein, *Mary Shelley: Romance and Reality* (Baltimore: Johns Hopkins Univ. Press, 1991), 393.

5. Fisch, Mellor, and Schor, eds., *The Other Mary Shelley*, 9.

6. Favret, "Mary Shelley's Sympathy and Irony," 27, 26.

7. See *The "Defence of Poetry" Fair Copies* (New York: Garland, 1994), ed. Michael O'Neill, vol. 20 of the *Bodleian Shelley Manuscripts* (hereafter *BSM* 20), and *Fair-Copy Manuscripts of Shelley's Poems in European and American Libraries*, ed. Donald H. Reiman and Michael O'Neill (New York: Garland, 1997), vol. 8 of the *Shelley* volumes in the series *The Manuscripts of the Younger Romantics* (hereafter *MYR: Shelley* 8). Quotations from my transcriptions of Bodleian MS. Shelley adds. d. 8 (in *BSM* 20) appear by kind permission of the Bodleian Library, Oxford.

8. Wolfson, "Editorial Privilege," 59.

9. Murray dedicates the volume "To the memory of Mary Wollstonecraft Shelley who gathered together and preserved the manuscripts which made possible this edition of her husband's prose," *The Prose Works of Percy Bysshe Shelley, Volume 1*, ed. E. B. Murray (Oxford: Clarendon Press, 1993), [v].

10. Betty T. Bennett, "Finding Mary Shelley in Her Letters," in *Romantic Revisions*, ed. Robert Brinkley and Keith Hanley (Cambridge: Cambridge Univ. Press, 1992), 303. See also the same critic's "Feminism and Editing Mary Wollstonecraft Shelley: The Editor and?/or? the Text," in *Palimpsest: Editorial Theory in the Humanities*, ed. George Bornstein and Ralph G. Williams (Ann Arbor: Michigan Univ. Press, 1993), 67–96. Bennett's caution in the latter essay against "viewing Mary Shelley's works though a single prism and without reliance on a factually evidenced context of her own works and era" (67) is one with which my essay is in sympathy.

11. Vargo, "Close Your Eyes and Think of Shelley," 216, 221.

12. Mary Shelley is quoted from P. B. Shelley, *Posthumous Poems* (London: John and Henry L. Hunt, 1824), 85.

13. Vargo, "Close Your Eyes and Think of Shelley," 222.

14. Quoted from Jerome J. McGann, *The Textual Condition* (Princeton: Princeton Univ. Press, 1991) in Vargo, 215.

15. Shelley, *Posthumous Poems*, vii.

16. *Essays, Letters from Abroad, Translations and Fragments, by Percy Bysshe Shelley*, ed. Mrs. Shelley, 2 vols. (London: Moxon, 1840 [1839]), 2:360 (hereafter *1840*).

17. Wolfson, "Editorial Privilege," 62.

18. Transcribed in *BSM* 20, 260–451.

19. See *BSM* 20, 122 for fuller details.

20. Roger Ingpen, *Shelley in England: New Facts and Letters from the Shelley-Whitton Papers* (London: Kegan Paul, Trench, Trubner, and Co., 1917), 582, 583.

21. James A. Notopoulos, *The Platonism of Shelley: A Study of Platonism and the Poetic Mind* (Durham, N.C.: Duke Univ. Press, 1949), 390.

22. *The Works of Thomas Love Peacock,* ed. H. F. B. Brett-Smith and C. E. Jones, 10 vols. (London: Constable, 1924–34), 4:95.

23. "On Christianity," in Murray, ed., *Prose Works,* 262.

24. Fraistat, "Illegitimate Shelley," 410, 411.

25. *Matilda, Dramas, Reviews and Essays, Prefaces and Notes,* ed. Pamela Clemit, vol. 2 of *The Novels and Selected Works of Mary Shelley,* gen. ed. Nora Crook with Pamela Clemit, 8 vols. (London: Pickering and Chatto, 1996), 256 (hereafter *M*). This edition is used for Mary Shelley's Notes to P. B. Shelley's 1839 *Poetical Works* (first in four volumes, then in one volume) because it is now the standard modern scholarly text and is more widely available than the first editions. The preface to *1840,* though available in *M,* is quoted from the first edition because the main body of the text of *1840* is not included in *M.*

26. Fraistat, "Illegitimate Shelley," 412. Fraistat acknowledges, but rather brushes aside, the fact that "John Hunt . . . was widely identified with radical publications," 420, n. 11.

27. P. B. Shelley, *Posthumous Poems,* 113, iii–iv.

28. Fraistat, "Illegitimate Shelley," 411. Fraistat argues interestingly in a footnote that "Shelley produced a body of self-conflicted poetry" that opened his work "to several sorts of appropriation," 419, n. 7.

29. Wolfson, "Editorial Privilege," 42, 44.

30. Ibid., 42.

31. Ibid., 49–50.

32. Jane Blumberg, *Mary Shelley's Early Novels* (Basingstoke: Macmillan, 1993), 169.

Chapter 14: Mary Shelley's *Lives* and the Reengendering of History

I wish to thank Jeanne Moskal, Lisa Vargo, and William St Clair for their stimulating conversation and the many helpful suggestions they offered at the Mary Shelley Bicentennial Conference in New York, "Mary Wollstonecraft Shelley in Her Times" (May 22–24, 1997).

1. The following abbreviations are used parenthetically throughout this ar-

ticle: *LI* for *Lives of the Most Eminent Literary and Scientific Men of Italy, Spain, and Portugal*, 3 vols. (London: Longman, 1835–37); *LF* for *Lives of the Most Eminent Literary and Scientific Men of France*, 2 vols. (London: Longman, 1838–39).

2. Paula R. Feldman, "Biography and the Literary Executor: The Case of Mary Shelley," *The Papers of the Bibliographical Society of America* 72 (1978): 287; Johanna M. Smith, *Mary Shelley* (New York: Twayne, 1996), 128–44; William Walling, *Mary Shelley* (New York: Twayne, 1972), 132.

3. There has been no sustained critical study of the *Lives* since the earliest periodical reviews appeared. The major scholarly books on Mary Shelley only give them passing reference, and they receive little mention in important recent collections of essays on Mary Shelley's lesser-known works: *The Other Mary Shelley: Beyond* Frankenstein, ed. Audrey A. Fisch. Anne K. Mellor, and Esther H. Schor (New York: Oxford Univ. Press, 1993); *Iconoclastic Departures: Mary Shelley after* Frankenstein, ed. Syndy M. Conger, Frederick S. Frank, and Gregory O'Dea (Madison, N.J.: Farleigh Dickinson Univ. Press, 1997).

4. Morse Peckham, "Dr. Lardner's *Cabinet Cyclopaedia*," *The Papers of the Bibliographical Society of America* 45 (1951): 46.

5. W. H. Lyles, *Mary Shelley: An Annotated Bibliography* (New York: Garland, 1975). Precise attribution of all the biographical essays in *LI* and *LF* is notoriously problematic, and the exact number of essays Mary Shelley contributed to these volumes remains contested. Lardner employed multiple authors for both sets of biographies and left specific attributions indefinite in his contents pages and advertisements. The "Analytical Catalogue of Lardner's Cabinet Cyclopaedia," describing the entire 133-volume series and inserted in many of the individual volumes, lists the contributors to *LI* as "Mrs. Shelley, Sir. D. Brewster, J. Montgomery, &c."; it presents *LF* under the title of "Shelley's Lives of Authors of France" but designates authorship of these lives as "Mrs. Shelley, and others" ("Analytical Catalogue," in *LF*, 1:7). Nevertheless, it is possible to verify multiple Mary Shelley contributions to *LI* and *LF*, many of which go unnoticed by Lyles. He only cites her composition of the lives of Petrarch, Boccaccio, and Machiavelli in volume one of *LI*, for instance (37), but Mary Shelley affirmed on different occasions that she also contributed the lives of d'Medici, Ficino, Mirandola, Poliziano, Bernardo, and Luigi Pulci, Ferrara, Burchiello, Bojardo, and Berni (*MWSL* 2:219, 222). Lyles acknowledges that Mary Shelley wrote the lives of Metastasio, Goldoni, Alfieri, Monti, and Foscolo in volume two of *LI* (37), but Mary Shelley told Maria Gisborne that most of the additional lives in that volume — including those of Guicciardini, Vittoria Colonna, Guarini, Chiabrera, Tassoni, Marini, and Filicaja — "are mine" (*MWSL* 2:257).

For the first two volumes of *LI*, then, Mary Shelley produced all but the lives of Dante, Ariosto, Tasso, and Galileo. Lyles suggests that she "possibly" contributed all of the essays to volume three of *LI*, with the exception of the life of Ercilla

(38). William Walling is more conclusive, affirming that Mary Shelley definitely wrote all of the lives in volume three except for the Ercilla essay (*Mary Shelley*, 128). Smith argues on the basis of internal evidence that Mary Shelley also composed the life of Ercilla (*Mary Shelley*, 131). Where Lyles is silent on the number of Mary Shelley essays in *LF*, Walling traces her presence everywhere in both volumes (*Mary Shelley*, 128–32). Smith makes a more discriminating and convincing argument that she contributed little to volume one but wrote all of the essays in volume two of *LF* (*Mary Shelley*, 131). Although some of these overall attributions remain speculative, the record of solid evidence confirms that Mary Shelley produced nearly three quarters of the 1,756 printed pages that comprise *LI* and *LF*, possibly even more but conclusively much more than Lyles's bibliography indicates. To avoid any questionable citation in this article, I will confine my discussion of Mary Shelley's *Cyclopaedia Lives* to those definitively verifiable essays she contributed to the three volumes of *LI* and volume two of *LF*.

6. Anne K. Mellor, *Mary Shelley: Her Life, Her Fictions, Her Monsters* (London: Methuen, 1988), 84, 86.

7. The editors of the most recent collection of essays on Mary Shelley, *Iconoclastic Departures*, ed. Conger, Frank, and O'Dea, foreground this question in their introduction and present the entire volume as a sustained, if somewhat uncomplicated, argument for a persistently radical Mary Shelley: "[Our] contributors also share the conviction that, even if Mary Shelley, after P. B. Shelley's death, gradually retired from public life according to the wishes of his relatives, she retained a resistant, resiliently radical attitude toward many of the established orders of her day that is easily recovered by a careful look beyond her 'feelings' to the productions of her literary 'imagination'" (10).

8. Gregory O'Dea, drawing on Hayden White's theories of "metahistory," argues that Mary Shelley interrogates the socially constructed nature of historical fact in *The Last Man* and critiques the false epistemologies and values such conventional forms of historicism support; O'Dea, "Prophetic History and Textuality in Mary Shelley's *The Last Man*," *Papers on Language and Literature* 28 (1992): 283–304. Joseph Lew focuses more specifically on the gender politics of Mary Shelley's historiography in *Valperga*, showing how she deploys historical frameworks to contest the masculinist politics of Romantic ideology; Lew, "God's Sister: History and Ideology in *Valperga*," in Fisch, Mellor, and Schor, eds., *The Other Mary Shelley*, 159–81. Ann M. Frank Wake finds Mary Shelley constructing a more specific kind of history of women in the historical formats of *Valperga* and *Perkin Warbeck*, which critiques the gender politics of the past and the present; "Women in the Active Voice: Recovering Female History in Mary Shelley's *Valperga* and *Perkin Warbeck*," in Conger, Frank, and O'Dea, eds., *Iconoclastic Departures*, 235–59. James P. Carson shows how Mary Shelley grounds the narrative of *Valperga* in a historical vision prioritizing affect over public events; Carson, "'A Sigh of

Many Hearts': History, Humanity, and Popular Culture in *Valperga*," in Conger, Frank, and O'Dea, eds., *Iconoclastic Departures,* 167–92. Johanna Smith suggests that Mary Shelley consistently utilizes biographical narrative in the *Cyclopaedia Lives* to expose the social injustice of sex-gender systems in the past as well as the present; Smith, *Mary Shelley,* 128–44.

9. Christina Crosby, *The Ends of History: Victorians and "the Woman Question"* (New York: Routledge, 1991), 1.

10. Stuart Curran, "Women Readers, Women Writers," in *The Cambridge Companion to British Romanticism,* ed. Stuart Curran (Cambridge: Cambridge Univ. Press, 1993), 191.

11. Jane Rendall, "Writing History for British Women: Elizabeth Hamilton and the *Memoirs of Agrippina*," in *Wollstonecraft's Daughters: Womanhood in England and France 1780–1920,* ed. Clarissa Campbell Orr (Manchester: Manchester Univ. Press, 1996), 79–93; Antoinette Burton, " 'Invention Is What Delights Me': Jane Austen's Remaking of English History," in *Jane Austen and Discourses of Feminism,* ed. Devoney Looser (New York: St. Martin's Press, 1995), 35–50; Nanora Sweet, "History, Imperialism, and the Aesthetics of the Beautiful: Hemans and the Post-Napoleonic Moment," in *At the Limits of Romanticism: Essays in Cultural, Feminist, and Materialist Criticism,* ed. Mary A. Favret and Nicola J. Watson (Bloomington: Indiana Univ. Press, 1994), 170–84; Gary Kelly, *Women, Writing, and Revolution 1790–1827* (Oxford: Clarendon Press, 1993), 236–46, 269–74; Greg Kucich, "Romanticism and Feminist Historiography," *Wordsworth Circle* 24 (1993): 133–40.

12. Joan Wallach Scott, "Introduction," in *Feminism and History,* ed. Joan Wallach Scott (New York: Oxford Univ. Press, 1996), 1–13.

13. Elaine Showalter, "Women's Time, Women's Space: Writing the History of Feminist Criticism," in *Feminist Issues in Literary Scholarship,* ed. Shari Benstock (Bloomington: Indiana Univ. Press, 1987), 31; Josephine Donovan, "Toward a Women's Poetics," ibid., 98.

14. Scott, "Introduction," *Feminism and History,* 3.

15. *Feminists Revision History,* ed. Ann-Louise Shapiro (New Brunswick, N.J.: Rutgers Univ. Press, 1994); Scott, ed., *Feminism and History.*

16. Jane Austen, *Northanger Abbey,* ed, Anne Henry Ehrenpreis (London: Penguin, 1985), 123.

17. Walter Benjamin, "Theses on the Philosophy of History," in *Illuminations,* ed. Hannah Arendt (New York: Schoken Books, 1968), 253–64; Hayden White, *Metahistory: The Historical Imagination in Nineteenth-Century Europe* (Baltimore: Johns Hopkins Univ. Press, 1974); Benedict Anderson, *Imagined Communities: Reflections on the Origin and Spread of Nationalism,* 2d. ed. (London: Verso, 1991).

18. Jane Austen, *Persuasion,* ed. D.W. Harding (London: Penguin, 1985), 57.

19. Mary Wollstonecraft, *An Historical and Moral View of the Origin and Progress of the French Revolution and the Effect It Has Produced in Europe,* ed. Janet M.

Todd (Delmar, New York: Scholars' Facsimiles and Reprints, 1975), 163; Maria Edgeworth, *Castle Rackrent,* ed. George Watson (New York: Oxford Univ. Press, 1980), 2; Mary Hays, *Female Biography; or Memoirs of Illustrious and Celebrated Women, of All Ages and Centuries,* 6 vols. (London: Richard Phillips, 1803), 1:167, 169; Joanna Baillie, "Introductory Discourse," in *British Literature 1780–1830,* ed. Anne K. Mellor and Richard E. Matlak (New York: Harcourt Brace College Publishers, 1996), 443; Anna Jameson, *Characteristics of Women: Moral, Political, and Historical,* 2 vols. (London: Saunders and Otley, 1832), 1:xvii.

20. Austen describes herself on the title page as "a partial, prejudiced, & ignorant Historian," and announces that "There will be very few Dates in this History"; Austen, *The History of England from the Reign of Henry the 4th to the Death of Charles the 1st,* ed. Deirdre Le Faye (London: British Library, 1993), xv.

21. Catharine Macaulay, *The History of England,* 8 vols. (London: Nourse, 1764–83), 8: 59, 6: xii; Macaulay, *Letters on Education: With Observations on Religion and Metaphysical Subjects* (London: Dilly, 1790), 177.

22. Anne K. Mellor, *Romanticism and Gender* (New York: Routledge, 1993), 3.

23. Elizabeth Benger, *Memoirs of the Life of Mary Queen of Scots,* 2d. ed., 2 vols. (London: Longman, 1823), 2:52, and *Memoirs of the Late Elizabeth Hamilton,* 2 vols. (London: Longman, 1818), 1:1.

24. Benger, *Memoirs of the Life of Mary Queen of Scots,* 2:52, and *Memoirs of the Late Elizabeth Hamilton,* 1:1; Elizabeth Benger, *Memoirs of the Life of Anne Boleyn, Queen of Henry VIII,* 3d. ed. (Philadelphia: John E. Potter, n.d.), 150.

25. Quoted by Benger, *Memoirs of the Late Elizabeth Hamilton,* 2:41.

26. Benger, *Memoirs of the Life of Anne Boleyn,* 1:34.

27. Hays, *Female Biography,* 1:iv. For recent theorizations of "feminist biography," see Bell Gale Chevigny, "Daughters Writing: Toward a Theory of Women's Biography," in *Between Women: Biographers, Novelists, Critics, Teachers and Artists Write about Their Work on Women,* ed. Carol Ascher, Louise DeSalvo, Sara Ruddick (Boston: Beacon, 1994), 357–79; Elizabeth Kamarck Minnich, "Friendship between Women: The Art of Feminist Biography," *Feminist Studies* 11, no. 2 (1985): 287–305; and Peggy Rosenthal, "Feminism and Life in Feminist Biography," *College English* 36 (1974): 180–88.

28. Macaulay, *The History of England,* 6:xiii.

29. Emily W. Sunstein comments on this form of identification in *Mary Shelley: Romance and Reality* (Baltimore: Johns Hopkins Univ. Press, 1991), 224. Such intense identifications with biographical subjects, according to Minnich, can be traced in the "conversational" format of much recent "feminist biography" ("Friendship between Women," 292).

30. James Mackintosh, *History of England,* 10 vols. (London: Longman, 1830), 1:v; E. E. Crowe, *The History of France,* 3 vols. (London: Longman, 1830), 1:330; "Analytical Catalogue," in *LF* 1:5.

31. "Analytical Catalogue," in *LF* 1:1; Quoted by Peckham, "Dr. Lardner's *Cabinet Cyclopaedia*," 41.

32. "Analytical Catalogue," in *LF* 1:1; "Advertisement," in *The History of Poland* (London: Longman, 1831), 3.

33. Quoted by Smith, *Mary Shelley,* 131.

34. "Analytical Catalogue," in *LF* 1:1.

35. Ibid.

36. Although Lardner's *Cyclopaedia* generally projected a conservative social agenda, the diversity of its contributors allowed for a range of political positions, some of which — like Mary Shelley's and Sismondi's — differed considerably from the ideological mainstream of the overall venture.

37. William St Clair has determined, from his research at the Spottiswoode Archive in the British Library, that the print run of Mary Shelley's *Lives* ran to several thousand copies for each volume from the *Cabinet Cyclopaedia,* a number considerably higher than the average for her novels.

38. Joan Scott, "Gender: A Useful Category of Historical Analysis," *Feminism and History,* 169.

Chapter 15: Blood Sisters

1. Liz Lochhead, *True Confessions and New Clichés* (Edinburgh: Polygon, 1985), 3. "Would ye, o my sisters, really possess modesty, ye must remember that the possession of virtue, of any denomination, is incompatible with ignorance and vanity! ye must acquire that soberness of mind, which the exercise of duties, and the pursuit of knowledge, alone inspire, or ye will remain in a doubtful dependent situation, and only be loved whilst ye are fair!" Mary Wollstonecraft, *Vindication of the Rights of Woman* (Harmondsworth: Penguin, 1972, 1985), 239.

2. Liz Lochhead (interviewed by Colin Nicholson): "I'm very ambivalent about women: they're people with problems too. I get at them because I am one. I'm allowed to. Although I am a feminist, I don't want to give my writing back only to women, I don't want to be a feminist separatist, nor do I want to 'solve the world' solely for woman because I find that position too bleak," Colin Nicholson, *Poem, Purpose, and Place: Shaping Identity in Contemporary Scottish Poetry* (Edinburgh: Polygon, 1992), 204.

3. "Each woman participates in the symbolic 'conception' of the other: they are 'mothers' *birthing* each other into language *through trust,*" Liz Yorke, *Impertinent Voices: Subversive Strategies in Contemporary Women's Poetry* (London: Routledge, 1991), 128.

4. Liz Lochhead (inteviewed by Rebecca E. Wilson): "I wouldn't mind being called a female poet, because I think my poetry is a pursuit of the feminine. Robert Graves says all poetry is anyway, but mine is a female pursuit of the feminine,

whereas his is about a male pursuit of the feminine," *Sleeping with Monsters: Conversations with Scottish and Irish Women Poets,* ed. Gillean Somerville-Arjat and Rebecca E. Wilson (Edinburgh: Polygon, 1990), 11.

5. "Lochhead's plays resist and challenge traditional representations of femininity by re-configuring cultural stories and myths with women characters, problematising traditional feminine signifiers, and foregrounding the material conditions which may affect women's cultural construction," Jan McDonald and Jennifer Harvie, "Putting New Twists to Old Stories: Feminism and Lochhead's Drama," in *Liz Lochhead's Voices,* ed. Robert Crawford and Anne Varty (Edinburgh: Edinburgh Univ. Press, 1993), 135.

6. Liz Lochhead, *Blood and Ice,* in *Plays by Women,* vol. 4, ed. Michelene Wandor (London: Methuen, 1985; rev. ed. 1988), 115.

7. Ibid., 115, 116. Liz Lochhead (inteviewed by Rebecca E. Wilson):

> Why would Mary Shelley write about monsters? I was haunted by that phrase from Goya: "The sleep of reason produces monsters." If you try to force things to be too rational the dark and untidy bits will well up and manifest themselves in quite concrete ways. So I stopped reading about Mary Wollstonecraft and began to read about Mary Shelley and became more and more interested in the companions she had who were pulling her in two different ways and what they meant to her, and the whole thing began to be written, a bit like a great big fat poem. All the different things it threw up were different aspects of self. When you read the book you're both creator and monster and a lot of the other characters as well. (Somerville-Arjat and Wilson, *Sleeping with Monsters,* 13)

8. Liz Lochhead (interviewed by Colin Nicholson): "I found myself taking on these myths, and some of the poems are jokes in a vein of feminist reductionism, But the book as a whole was an attempt to find the muse. If you are a female looking for the white goddess, where can you find it but within yourself? The search was for an internal, as opposed to an external or male muse," Nicholson, *Poem, Purpose, and Place,* 212.

9. "Just as Wollstonecraft's invocation of reason is really a transvaluation of feeling, so her masculine persona [in *Vindication of the Rights of Men*] is really a cover for the feminine position she has all along retained," Mary Poovey, *The Proper Lady and the Woman Writer: Ideology as Style in the Works of Mary Wollstonecraft, Mary Shelley, and Jane Austen* (Chicago: Univ. of Chicago Press, 1984), 68.

10. Teresa de Lauretis, *Alice Doesn't: Feminism, Semiotics, Cinema* (Bloomington: Indiana Univ. Press, 1994), 37.

11. Jean Baudrillard, *Seduction,* trans. Brian Singer (New York: St. Martin's Press, 1990), 35.

12. Liz Lochhead, *Dreaming Frankenstein and Collected Poems* (Edinburgh: Polygon, 1984). Dorothy McMillan points out the elements of "magical penetration and birth structure" and the conjunction of "language, the female and creativity," with the monster as "both self created and a created self," a "demon lover" and "a monstrous child," Dorothy Porter McMillan, "Liz Lochhead and the Ungentle Art of Clyping," in Crawford and Varty, eds., *Liz Lochhead's Voices*, 29.

13. Liz Lochhead (interviewed by Colin Nicholson):

Mary Shelley was herself uncertain, When she wrote about the competition which was organised to get her to write the story she says — "I did not sleep, nor could I be said to dream, just by my side stood that pale student of unhallowed arts, looking down at me with yellow, pale and watery eyes." And in that sentence she has already become the monster.

In some way it is to do with her own creativity being monstrous to her. Maybe the confusion which so many people still share, about who is Frankenstein and who the monster, is a sharing of that reality because it concerns a split psyche. And what books of this kind have in common is that sense of not sleeping or dreaming but being compelled to write. So "Dreaming Frankenstein" concerns having a male muse, which is a part of yourself. This aspect became more interesting to me, and Mary Shelley's disgust at her own creativity, her self-disgust, comes out very strongly in the way that Frankenstein is the villain of the book, and the monster very quickly becomes the hero. (Nicholson, *Poem, Purpose, and Place*, 218–19)

14. Julia Kristeva, *Revolution in Poetic Language*, trans. Margaret Waller (New York: Columbia Univ. Press, 1980), 65, and *Black Sun: Depression and Melancholia*, trans. Leon S. Roudiez (New York: Columbia Univ. Press, 1987), 53.

15. Liz Lochhead, *Blood and Ice*, Hereafter *BI* 1985 and *BI* 1988.

16. Kristeva, *Black Sun*, 179.

17. For an interesting discussion on "the book as monster," beginning with the statement that books can "behave monstrously towards their creators, running loose from authorial intention and turning to mock their begetters by displaying a vitality of their own," see chap. 3, "The Monster Speaks," in Chris Baldick's critical work, *In Frankenstein's Shadow: Myth, Monstrosity, and Nineteenth-century Writing* (Oxford: Clarendon Press, 1987), 30–62.

18. Luce Irigaray: "Woman is the guardian of the blood. But as both she and it have had to use their substance to nourish the universal consciousness of self, it is in the form of *bloodless shadows* — of unconscious fantasies — that they maintain an underground subsistence"; it is "blood that still recalls a very ancient relationship with the mother," Luce Irigaray, *Speculum of the Other Woman*, trans. Gillian C. Gill (Ithaca: Cornell Univ. Press, 1993), 225, 364. For a discussion on menstrual

blood as one of the strongest primitive taboos, see René Girard, *Violence and the Sacred* (Baltimore: Johns Hopkins Univ. Press), 33–36.

19. Peter Dale Scott, "Vital Artifice: Mary, Percy and the Psychopolitical Integrity of *Frankenstein*," in *The Endurance of* Frankenstein: *Essays on Mary Shelley's Novel*, ed. George Levine and U. C. Knoepflmacher (Berkeley: Univ. of California Press, 1979), 173.

20. "Psychoanalytically speaking, the precursor of the mirror is the mother's face, in which the child first sees itself reflected," Claire Kahane, "The Gothic Mirror," in *The M/Other Tongue: Essays in Feminist Psychoanalytic Interpretation,* ed. Shirley Nelson Garner et al. (Ithaca: Cornell Univ. Press, 1985), 344.

21. Baudrillard speaks of "*the incestuous relation we maintain with our own image*"; he asserts that the "double is an imaginary figure that, like the soul or one's shadow, or one's image in a mirror, haunts the subject with a faint death that has to be constantly warded off," *Seduction*, 69, 168.

22. "Her brief, secret courtship with Percy Shelley was largely conducted in St. Pancras' Churchyard, where Mary took her books to read beside her mother's grave; she read and reread the works of both her father and her mother while she was growing up" (Poovey, *The Proper Lady and the Woman Writer*, 120).

23. Luce Irigaray asserts that culture has "forced us to repress the female genealogies" and to enter into "relations that bear no relation to blood, which is love-hated" and "repressed because it is associated with female-maternal genealogies," Irigaray, *Sexes and Genealogies,* trans. Gillian G. Gill (New York: Columbia Univ. Press, 1993), 160; it has also been argued that in the work of contemporary women writers "the image of the mother emerges as both a sublime metaphor *and* as partaking of the real, the concrete, the material, the physical *bloody* milky rawness of the body" (Yorke, *Impertinent Voices,* 116).

24. Muriel Spark reminds us of the importance of Coleridge for Mary, noting that "it had not gone for nothing that she had heard, while still a child, a rendering of the *Ancient Mariner* from the poet's own lips; and she was never released from the enthralment of the poem," Muriel Spark, *Mary Shelley* (London: Cardinal, 1988), 158.

25. Mary "undoubtedly read most of the reviews of her mother's *Posthumous Works,* reviews in which Mary Wollstonecraft was attacked as a 'philosophical wanton' and a monster," Sandra M. Gilbert and Susan Gubar, *The Madwoman in the Attic: The Woman Writer and the Nineteenth-century Literary Imagination* (New Haven: Yale Univ. Press), 222.

26. Jessica Benjamin uses the term *intersubjectivity* to define the experience of "inner space" associated with the "space between self and other — the paradox that we need to experience being alone in the presence of the other," Jessica Benjamin, "A Desire of One's Own: Psychoanalytic Feminism and Intersubjective Space," in

Feminist Studies/Critical Studies, ed. Teresa de Lauretis (Bloomington: Indiana Univ. Press, 1986), 96.

27. Anne Mellor argues that Mary Shelley's novels systematically point towards the notion of a "social construction of mothering as a learned rather than instinctual practice," Anne K. Mellor, *Romanticism and Gender* (New York: Routledge, 1993), 83. Given the peculiar conditions of Mary's relation to her mother, it would be interesting to further probe into what Margaret Homans calls the "literal language shared between mother and daughter: a language of presence, in which the presence or absence of referents in the ordinary sense is quite unimportant," Margaret Homans, *Bearing the Word: Language and Female Experience in Nineteenth-century Women's Writing* (Chicago: Univ. of Chicago Press, 1986), 18.

28. "Is it possible that a human creature could have become such a weak and depraved being . . . dissolved in luxury? . . . Such a woman is not a more irrational monster than some of the Roman emperors. . . . Women are everywhere in this deplorable state." Mary Wollstonecraft, *Vindication of the Rights of Woman* (Harmondsworth: Penguin, 1972, 1985), 131. Cora Caplan draws our attention to the fact that "only by understanding why Wollstonecraft wanted women to become full members of the middle-class, can we make sense of the negative and prescriptive assault on female sexuality that is the *leitmotif* of *A Vindication,*" Cora Kaplan, *Sea Changes: Essays on Culture and Feminism* (London: Verso, 1986), 35.

29. Poovey, *The Proper Lady and the Woman Writer,* 121.

30. "Percy's urgent desire to link Mary and Hogg, despite Mary's initial feeling that she was quite satisfied with Percy alone, lends further support to the suggestion that Percy was here trying to negotiate a sexual *quid pro quo* with Mary, her affair with Hogg for his affair with Claire," Mellor, *Mary Shelley,* 30.

31. It has been argued that "Mary Shelley and Byron developed their own narratives of the divided self needing or seeking completion in *Frankenstein* and in *Manfred,*" Charles E. Robinson, *Shelley and Byron: The Snake and the Eagle Wreathed in Fight* (Baltimore: Johns Hopkins Univ. Press, 1976), 45.

32. For a reading of *Frankenstein* as a representation of masculine desire, as "the monstrosity of masculine desire itself, the tendency of males (such as Percy) to disrupt the potential harmony of feminine space ideologized for Shelley as the domestic arrangements of nineteenth-century society," see Marlon B. Ross, *The Contours of Masculine Desire: Romanticism and the Rise of Women's Poetry* (New York: Oxford Univ. Press, 1989), 113–14; for the tensions arising between Mary Shelley and P. B. Shelley on matters of gender and authorship, see the chapter entitled, "The Limits of Rivalry: Revisioning the Feminine in a Community of Shared Desire" (ibid., 112–54).

33. Furthermore, "given the restrictions on the expression of female sexuality in eighteenth-century society, women were encouraged to view their sexuality as

a function of *male* initiative, a response to present and future relationships, not a self-expression at all" (Poovey, *The Proper Lady and the Woman Writer*, 110).

34. René Girard reminds us that "the double and the monster are one and the same thing. . . . There is no monster who does not tend to duplicate himself or to 'marry' another monster, no double who does not yield a monstrous aspect upon close scrutiny" Girard, *Violence and the Sacred*, 160.

In a paper "entitled 'Medusa's Head,' Freud reiterated his theory that 'the terror of castration . . . is linked to the sight of something,' the female genitals; and similarly 'the sight of Medusa's head makes the spectator stiff with terror, turns him to stone,' " de Lauretis, *Alice Doesn't*, 135.

35. It is also noted by Laurie Langbauer that in "Wollstonecraft's fiction, mothers and daughters supplant fathers and sons," enjoying "a union and happiness denied to men," Laurie Langbauer, "Motherhood and Women's Writing in Mary Wollstonecraft's Novels," in *Romanticism and Feminism*, ed. Anne K. Miller (Bloomington: Indiana Univ. Press, 1988), 209.

36. On "the streak of incest that darkens *Frankenstein*" and on the possible contribution to this incest-obsession of Mary Shelley's by the "famously incestuous author of Manfred," see Gilbert and Gubar, *The Madwoman in the Attic*, 229. In her discussion of Kristeva's notion of matricide, Elisabeth Bronfen maintains that "by turning the mother into an image of death the necessary aggression can be preserved while the culpability of matricide is effaced. However, if an autonomy from the maternal is not achieved, if the maternal is not renounced, madness ensues," Elisabeth Bronfen, *Over her Dead Body: Death, Femininity, and the Aesthetic* (Manchester: Manchester Univ. Press, 1992), 135.

37. "Death and birth were thus as hideously intermixed in the life of Mary Shelley as in Frankenstein's 'workshop of filthy creation,' " Ellen Moers, *Literary Women: The Great Writers* (Garden City, N.Y.: Doubleday, 1977), 142.

38. "Endlessly studying her mother's works and her father's, Mary Shelley may be said to have 'read' her family and to have been related to her reading, for books appear to have functioned as her surrogate parents, pages and words standing for flesh and blood," Gilbert and Gubar, *The Madwoman in the Attic*, 223.

39. Girard emphasizes the two functions of blood: as contaminating and purifying—the second guaranteed as a cleansing of violence through the ritual of sacrifice (*Violence and the Sacred*, 36); Bataille also groups it together with incest as taboos that "spring from the general horror of violence," "the taboos associated with menstruation and the loss of blood at childbirth. These discharges are thought of as manifestations of internal violence; blood in itself is a symbol of violence." Georges Bataille, *Erotism: Death and Sensuality*, trans. Mary Dalwood (San Francisco: City Lights Books, 1986), 54.

40. In the chapter devoted to Mary Shelley, "Bearing Demons: Frankenstein's

Circumvention of the Maternal," Homans focuses on the marital problems arising out of Percy's disappointment with Mary Shelley's "substantiality, and therefore her inadequacy for fulfilling his visionary requirements. *Frankenstein* is the story of what it feels like to be the undesired embodiment of romantic imaginative desire" (Homans, *Bearing the Word*, 108).

41. It has been noted that various remarks by Percy Shelley "show that the Erotic dichotomy between spirit and flesh makes woman herself seem like a horridly sensual idea. Shelley applies to her his general Erotic view of humans as mere beasts ('apes asses geese') and, forgoing the 'antique courtesy' of courtly love, let alone the feminist recognition of integral otherness, he reduces to animal physicality the women whom he finds inadequate spiritually," William Veeder, *Mary Shelley and Frankenstein: The Fate of Androgyny* (Chicago: Univ. of Chicago Press, 1986), 107–8.

42. It has been argued that for Wollstonecraft "marriage should be based on friendship between equals," and that "the distrust of sexuality which [she] displays is evidence that she has taken over a masculine conception of the rational individual and an opposition between mind and body, reason and passion that is central to the male point of view." Karen Green, *The Woman of Reason: Feminism, Humanism and Political Thought* (Cambridge: Polity Press, 1995), 96–99.

43. "For it is the right use of reason alone which make us independent of everything—excepting the unclouded reason—'Whose service is perfect freedom'" (Wollstonecraft, *Vindication*, 226).

44. "For Wollstonecraft, female desire was a contagion caught from the projection of male lust, an ensnaring and enslaving infection that made women into dependent and degenerate creatures, who nevertheless had the illusion that they acted independently" (Kaplan, *Sea Changes*, 158). Kaplan also notes that "reason may be the psychic heroine of *A Vindication*, but its gothic villain, a polymorphous perverse sexuality, creeping out of every paragraph and worming its way into every warm corner of the text, seems in the end to win out" (ibid., 45–46).

45. For a detailed account of the transposition of Mary Shelley's novel into the visual arts, see Albert J. Lavalley, "The Stage and Film Children of *Frankenstein*: A Survey," in Levine and Knoepflmacher, eds., *The Endurance of* Frankenstein, 243–89.

46. Keir Elam reminds us of "the *intertextual* basis of the theatrical frame" in the sense that a play relates not only to other texts and performances but also to "extra-theatrical and non-dramatic intertextual influences." Keir Elam, *The Semiotics of Theatre and Drama* (London: Methuen, 1980), 93–94.

47. "The body here becomes monstrously *visible*, it becomes the sign of a monster called desire" (Baudrillard, *Seduction*, 33).

48. "Seduction, as an original form, is considered related to the state of the 'primal phantasy' and thus treated, according to a logic that is not longer its own,

as a residue, a vestige, or screen/formation in the henceforth triumphant logic and structure of psychic and sexual reality" (ibid., 56).

49. On Mary Wollstonecraft's strong emotional attachment to the Swiss painter Henry Fuseli and its consequences, see Moira Ferguson and Janet Todd, *Mary Wollstonecraft* (Boston: Twayne Publishers, 1984), 11–12, 71–72.

50. Homans, *Bearing the Word, 7.*

51. Julia Kristeva, *Powers of Horror: An Essay on Abjection,* trans. Leon S. Roudiez (New York: Columbia Univ. Press, 1984), 14, and *Revolution in Poetic Language, 79–80.*

52. "The first dramatic adaptation of her novel was already playing at the English Opera House, Richard Brinsley Peake's significantly named *Presumption: or the Fate of Frankenstein.* Three changes from the novel are particularly significant. The stage Monster does not speak, and has the mind of an infant," Marilyn Butler, "Introduction," in Mary Wollstonecraft Shelley, *Frankenstein or the Modern Prometheus: The 1818 Text,* ed. Marilyn Butler (Oxford: Oxford Univ. Press, 1994), xlvii.

53. William Nestrick notes that "several stage versions introduced speechlessness but kept the rapidity of movement attributed to him in the novel. Enacting the novel on stage or screen makes the audience face his physical aspect, a reversal of the way the reading audience enters into the creature's highly articulate monologue," William Nestrick, "Coming to Life: *Frankenstein* and the Nature of Film Narrative," in Levine and Knoepflmacher, eds., *The Endurance of* Frankenstein, 295.

54. Elam, *The Semiotics of Theatre and Drama,* 26, 27, 142.

55. The Creature "might have died of hunger and exposure had he not found berries he instinctively ate, water to drink, and a cloak in which to wrap himself." Butler, "Introduction," xxxiv.

56. Teresa de Lauretis, *Practice of Love: Lesbian Sexuality and Perverse Desire* (Bloomington: Indiana Univ. Press, 1984), 152.

57. Julia Kristeva, *Desire in Language: A Semiotic Approach to Literature and Art,* trans. Leon S. Roudiez (New York: Columbia Univ. Press, 1980), 133, and *Tales of Love,* trans. Leon S. Roudiez (New York: Columbia Univ. Press, 1987), 126.

58. Ellen Moers supports the view that "*Frankenstein* is a birth myth, and one that was lodged in the novelist's imagination" because of her own experience of maternity; she further argues that it was Mary Shelley's "chaotic experience" with motherhood and pregnancy—its persistence, its insecurity, its unlawfulness—that found an imaginative outlet in writing: "So are monsters born" (*Literary Women,* 140).

59. In *Vindication,* "Wollstonecraft implies that female sexuality might be more voracious—and hence more blameworthy—than male desire. . . . The suspicion Wollstonecraft reveals here that female appetite might be the precipitating

cause of women's cultural objectification also helps account for her vehement disgust with female physicality" (Poovey, *The Proper Lady and the Woman Writer*, 75–76).

60. De Lauretis argues that the object of desire for a woman is not the mother but "the subject's own body-image, the denied and wished for female body which castration threatens with non-existence, and disavowal makes attainable by a compromise fantasy," producing "the ambivalent or contradictory perception of having and not having a body: having a body designated as female, and yet not having a female body that can be narcissistically and libidinally invested" (*Practice of Love*, 288).

61. Kristeva, *Powers of Horror*, 53.

62. Sigmund Freud, "The 'Uncanny,'" in *Art and Literature*, the Pelican Freud Library, vol. 4 (Harmondsworth: Penguin, 1985), 347. Judith Pike, in her discussion of *Frankenstein*, introduces the notion of the automaton as developed by Lacan, for whom "the return of the repressed figures as the automaton," that is as "the insistence of the sign"; and beyond the automaton there is a more terrifying encounter, "the encounter with the real of the maternal body," experienced by Frankenstein in his dream "as a traumatic vision of incest and necrophilia." Judith Pike, "Resurrection of the Fetish in *Gradiva, Frankenstein*, and *Wuthering Heights*," in *Romantic Women Writers: Voices and Countervoices*, ed. Paula R. Feldman and Theresa M. Kelley (Hanover: Univ. Press of New England, 1995), 156–57.

63. "Many critics have noticed that *Frankenstein* (1818) is one of the key Romantic 'readings' of *Paradise Lost*" (Gilbert and Gubar, *The Madwoman in the Attic*, 221).

64. Lochhead, *Dreaming Frankenstein*, 93. Liz Lochhead (interviewed by Colin Nicholson): "If an actress performs a poem like 'The Other Woman,' . . . she has to decide which of what might be equal ambiguities to emphasise. The other will then become a sub-text," Nicholson, *Poem, Purpose, and Place*, 221.

65. According to Benjamin, a subject of desire is "an agent who can will things and make them happen" ("A Desire of One's Own," 87).

66. Freud, "The 'Uncanny,'" 367; Julia Kristeva, *Strangers to Ourselves*, trans. Leon S. Roudiez (New York: Columbia Univ. Press, 1991), 186.

67. Kristeva, *Black Sun*, 164.

68. Ibid., 250. Girard uses the term *monstrous double* to refer to "unrecognized reciprocity. The monstrous double is also to be found wherever we encounter an 'I' and an 'Other' caught up in a constant interchange of differences" (Girard, *Violence and the Sacred*, 164).

69. Barbara Claire Freeman, *The Feminine Sublime: Gender and Excess in Women's Fiction* (Berkeley: Univ. of California Press, 1995), 77. Liz Lochhead (interviewed by Colin Nicholson) refers to the material of her recent work, "the Draculas and the Frankensteins. That work was very much concerned with a part

of the monster we carry inside us, though I'm not really in the business of reducing them. I'm trying to explain them, to make people take responsibility for them, as Prospero does when he says of Caliban 'This thing of darknes I acknowledge mine'" (Nicholson, *Poem, Purpose, and Place*, 209).

70. Liz Lochhead, *Bagpipe Muzak* (Harmondsworth: Penguin, 1991). For a prose version of the poem, see Somerville-Arjat and Wilson, *Sleeping with Monsters*, 14–16.

71. Liz Lochhead (like Mary Shelley) seems to fulfill what Barbara Johnson sees as "recent trends in scholarly as well as popular literature," that is, she covers the three crucial questions that "can be seen to stand at the forefront of today's preoccupations: the question of mothering, the question of the woman writer, and the question of autobiography." Barbara Johnson, "My Monster/My Self," in *Mary Shelley's Frankenstein*, ed. Harold Bloom (New York: Chelsea House, 1987), 55.

72. "In *The Bride of Frankenstein*, Frankenstein and his crazed collaborator Dr. Praetorius undertake what neither Mary Shelley nor her hero could quite bring themselves to do—embody woman as fully monstrous," Mary Jacobus, *Reading Woman: Essays in Feminist Criticism* (New York: Columbia Univ. Press, 1986), 103.

73. Kristeva reminds us that "Freud noted that the archaic, narcissistic self, not yet demarcated by the outside world, projects out of itself what it experiences as dangerous or unpleasant in itself, making of it a *double*, uncanny and demoniacal" (*Strangers to Ourselves*, 185).

74. And, of course, literature "has undergone a major process of revision in the last quarter of a century, having reached the point where it no longer signifies objects meriting sacred devotion but 'a particular manner of reading and deciphering signs.'" Fred Botting, "Introduction," in *Mary Shelley: Frankenstein*, ed. Fred Botting (London: Macmillan, 1995), 1.
Mellor informs us that the

> semiotic significance of *Frankenstein* was recognized in the first dramatic production of the novel. H. M. Milner's play bill for *Frankenstein: or, The Man and the Monster. A Romantic Melodrama, in Two Acts*, first performed at the Royal Cobourg Theatre in London on July 3, 1826, listed the monster in the dramatis personae thus: "********** [played by] Mr. O. Smith." Milner thus drew attention to the unknowability, the purely fictive semantic significance, of the creature. Mary Shelley commented approvingly when she saw Thomas Cooke in the role on August 29, saying that "this nameless mode of naming the unnameable is rather good." (Mellor, *Mary Shelley*, 133–34)

Kristeva traces the origin of the unrepresentable to the "affect confined within an unnameable mother" (Kristeva, *Tales of Love*, 311); and Baudrillard explains the attraction of nonrepresentability in his assertion that only "signs without referents, empty, senseless, absurd and elliptical signs, absorb us" (Baudrillard, *Seduction*, 74).

75. Mary Russo gives an interesting presentation of "taboos around the female body as grotesque (the pregnant body, the aging body, the irregular body)" in her discussion of the presence of the female body in carnival situations. Mary Russo, "Female Grotesques: Carnival and Theory," in *Feminist Studies/Critical Studies*, ed. de Lauretis, 214.

76. McMillan argues that the poem "continues the figure of painful and destructive birth. The 'best black self' which lies coffined in ice behind the surface of the mirror is to be released by the gazing subject who is self-commanded to smash 'the looking-glass glass/coffin' to release a Kali-like self whose whirling arms trash the offensive accoutrements of constructed femininity" (McMillan, "Liz Lochhead and the Ungentle Art of Clyping," 29).

Kaja Silverman reminds us of Freud's correlation between castration, forbidden activity, and the female genitals, in the little boy's violent emotions when looking at a girl, "through 'horror of the mutilated creature or triumphant contempt for her.'" Kaja Silverman, *The Acoustic Mirror: The Female Voice in Psychoanalysis and Cinema* (Bloomington: Indiana Univ. Press, 1988), 13.

Contributors

𝐵ETTY 𝒯. 𝐵ENNETT is Distinguished Professor of Literature at the American University. Editor of the letters of Mary Shelley and consulting editor of the Pickering and Chatto edition of Mary Shelley's works, she has also most recently been responsible for presenting the early biographical accounts of Mary Shelley and has written *Mary Wollstonecraft Shelley: An Introduction,* published by the Johns Hopkins University Press (1998). She is currently working on a biography of Mary Shelley.

𝒫AMELA 𝐶LEMIT is Reader in English Studies at the University of Durham and author of *The Godwinian Novel* (1993). Editor of several volumes in the Pickering and Chatto editions of the works of William Godwin and Mary Shelley, she is currently writing a biography of Godwin.

𝒮TUART 𝐶URRAN is Vartan Gregorian Professor of English at the University of Pennsylvania. His edition of Mary Shelley's *Valperga* appeared in 1998.

ℰ. 𝒟OUKA 𝒦ABITOGLOU is professor of English and chair of the School of English at the Aristotle University of Thessaloniki. She has recently edited *Logomachia: Forms of Opposition in English Language/Literature* (1994) and the symposium *Women/Poetry in Britain and Greece* (1998).

𝒢ARY 𝒦ELLY is professor of English at the University of Alberta and a Fellow of the Royal Society of Canada. His most recent publication is an edition of *Bluestocking Feminism* for Pickering and Chatto.

𝒢REG 𝒦UCICH is associate professor of English at the University of Notre Dame. He is author of *Keats, Shelley, and Romantic Spenserianism* and coeditor of *Nineteenth-Century Contexts: An Interdisciplinary Journal.*

He is completing a book on women writers of the Romantic era and historiography.

JEANNE MOSKAL is professor of English at the University of North Carolina at Chapel Hill and the author of *Blake, Ethics, and Forgiveness* (1994). Editor of Mary Shelley's travel writings in the Pickering and Chatto edition, she is writing a book on British women travel writers and the politics of the 1790s.

MITZI MYERS teaches at the University of Los Angeles. She is coeditor of the forthcoming Pickering and Chatto edition of the works of Maria Edgeworth as well as editor of several volumes in that series. She has two studies of Edgeworth in progress, including a literary life.

MICHAEL O'NEILL is professor of English at the University of Durham. His publications include *The Human Mind's Imaginings: Conflict and Achievement in Shelley's Poetry* (1989) and *Romanticism and the Self-Conscious Poem* (1997).

JUDITH PASCOE is associate professor of English at the University of Iowa. She is the author of *Romantic Theatricality: Gender, Poetry, and Spectatorship* (1997) and editor of *Mary Robinson: Selected Poems* (1999).

TILOTTAMA RAJAN is professor of English and director of the Centre for the Study of Theory and Criticism at the University of Western Ontario. She has written widely on fiction by women of the Romantic era and is editor of Mary Shelley's *Valperga* (1998).

CHARLES E. ROBINSON is professor of English at the University of Delaware and the Executive Director of the Byron Society of America. He has published a number of books and articles on the English Romantics, including four editions of Mary Shelley's works, the latest of these being *The Frankenstein Notebooks* (1996), a diplomatic edition of the manuscripts of Mary Shelley's novel.

MICHAEL ROSSINGTON is Lecturer in English Literature at the University of Newcastle upon Tyne. He has recently completed editions of P. B.

Shelley's *The Cenci* (2000) and Mary Shelley's *Valperga* (2000) and is writing a study of P. B. Shelley and history.

WILLIAM ST CLAIR, FBA, FRSL, is a Fellow of Trinity College, Cambridge. Among his publications is *The Godwins and the Shelleys, the Biography of a Family* (1989).

CONSTANCE WALKER is professor of English at Carleton College, where she is chair of the English Department. She has previously published essays on P. B. Shelley and on representations of the passions in eighteenth- and nineteenth-century literature.

SAMANTHA WEBB is assistant professor of English at the University of Montevallo. She is currently working on a book of images of authorship in English Romantic prose.

Index

adultery, 66, 156
Agrippa, Cornelius, 4
Aikin, Lucy, 204; *Epistles on Woman*, 205, 237–38 n. 42
Ainsworth, William Harrison, 173, 176
Alfieri, Vittorio, 210; *Myrrha*, 68, 78, 79, 84, 85, 200, 244 nn. 23, 24
Althusser, Louis, 28
Amulet, 176
Anderson, Benedict, 202
Anniversary, 175
annuals, 173–84
Anti-Jacobin Review, 270 n. 21
Appadurai, Arjun, 176
Ariosto, 207
Aristotle, 105
Atlantic Monthly, 177
Austen, Jane, 44, 47, 155; *History of England*, 203; *Northanger Abbey*, 202; *Persuasion*, 203
Austria, 111

Bage, Robert, 150
Bagni di Lucca (Italy), 222
Baillie, Joanna, "Introductory Discourse," 203
Baldick, Chris, 288 n. 17
Barbauld, Anna Laetitia, 150
Baron, Michael, 275 n. 36
Barruel, l'Abbé Augustin, 200
Barrett, Eaton Stannard, *The Heroine*, 32–33
Bataille, Georges, 97, 291 n. 39
Baudrillard, Jean, 216, 289 n. 21, 292 n. 47, 292–93 n. 48, 295–96 n. 74

Beaumont, Sir George, 181
Beckford, William, 43, 45
Belsey, Catherine, 28–29
Benger, Elizabeth, 204–5, *Memoirs*, 205
Benjamin, Jessica, 289–90 n. 26, 294 n. 65
Benjamin, Walter, 202
Bennett, Betty T., 65, 187, 250 n. 3, 256 n. 2, 260 n. 26, 274–75 n. 34, 280 n. 10
Bentley, Richard, 21, 35, 44–47, 241 n. 26
biography, 199, 204–5
Birmingham *Evening News*, 215
Blackwood's Edinburgh Magazine, 176
Bloom, Harold, 274 n. 31
Blumberg, Jane, 67, 128, 130
Boccaccio, 206, 210; *The Decameron*, 83–84, 87
Bonaparte, Joseph, 23
Bonaparte, Napoleon, 18, 23–24, 25, 97, 111, 112
Booth, Bradford Allen, 175
Bosch, Hieronymus, 216
Boswell, James, 200, 204, 271 n. 24
Botting, Fred, 295 n. 74
Bourdieu, Pierre, 159
Branagh, Kenneth, 274–75 n. 34
British Critic, 42
British Library, 208
Bronfen, Elizabeth, 291 n. 36
Brontë family, 153
Browning, Elizabeth Barrett, 166
Browning, Robert, 78
Brueghel, Pieter, 216
Bulwer, Edward (later, Bulwer Lytton), 45, 153

Duff, David, 20
Duvillard, Louise ("Elise"), 218, 220, 222, 223, 227, 230

Edgeworth, Maria, 45, 166, 174, 265–66 n. 7; *Castle Rackrent,* 203
Edinburgh, 215
Edinburgh Review, 24, 25
education, 4–5, 6, 7, 9, 11, 14, 15, 66–67, 124–27, 150, 170, 210, 211, 244 n. 13
Elam, Keir, 292 n. 46
Elío, Francisco, 27
Eliot, George, 153
Elliott, Charlotte, 137
Ellis, Kate Ferguson, 276 n. 38
England: and imperialism, 12; and the Napoleonic Wars, 23–28, 159; and politics, 23–25, 111, 147, 149, 156, 157, 158, 159, 202, 252 n. 25, 254 n. 37; Victorian society in, 1, 8, 17, 48, 54–55, 120, 142, 153, 194
equality, 7, 73; of sexes, 14

family romance, 164–68, 272 n. 26
fantasies, persecutory, 261 n. 31
Favret, Mary, 88, 185, 186
Faxon, Frederick Winthrop, 177
Fay, Elizabeth, 273 n. 27
Feldman, Paula, 198
females: body of, 216, 223, 224, 229, 288–89 n. 18, 296 n. 75; in novels, 15; and politics, 15–17, 29, 32–33; position in society of, 3, 4–5, 6, 11, 28–29, 89; as writers, 147–59, 160–61, 164, 220–21
Fenwick, Eliza, 152
Ferdinand "the Beloved," Prince (Spain), 23, 25–27
Ferrier, Susan, 45, 47
Fetterley, Judith, 29–30, 35
Fisch, Audrey A., 186, 283 n. 8
Fletcher, John: *The Captain,* 68, 84; *Cupid's Revenge,* 83, 87
Florence (Italy), 98, 108, 115
Forget-me-not, 175

Forster, John, 198
Foscolo, Ugo, 210
Fournier, Louis-Edouard, *Funeral of Shelley,* 182–83
Fox, Charles James, 194
fragment, as literary form, 249 n. 14
Fraistat, Neil, 185, 194, 196, 281 nn. 26, 28
France, 89
Frank, Frederick S., 283 n. 7, 283–84 n. 8
Frankenstein, or the Demon of Switzerland, 52
French Constitution (1791), 23
French Revolution, 20, 24, 25, 26, 112, 147, 148–49, 150, 202, 203
Freud, Sigmund, 144, 145, 260–61 n. 29, 274 n. 31, 291 n. 34, 294 n. 62, 295 n. 73, 296 n. 76; *The Future of an Illusion,* 138
Friendship's Offering, 175
Fuseli, Henry, 226, 293 n. 49

Galt, John, 45
Garrett, Margaret Davenport, 170, 276–77 n. 40
gender: and history, 198–213, 258 n. 13; roles, 3, 5–6, 7, 14, 18, 28, 29–33, 89, 160
Geneva (Switzerland), 112–13, 219, 253 n. 27
Germany, 89, 99
Gettmann, Royal A., 241 n. 26
Gibbon, Edward, 200, 202
Gilbert, Sandra, 166, 289 n. 25, 291 nn. 36, 38
Gilbert and Sullivan, *Patience,* 53
Gilligan, Carol, 203
Girard, René, 288–89 n. 18, 291 nn. 34, 39, 294 n. 68
Gisborne, John, 179
Gisborne, Maria (Reveley), 33–34, 65, 67, 179, 180, 186, 191, 259 n. 23, 271 n. 23
Gittings, Clare, 136, 138, 141
God, 93, 95
Godoy, Manuel, 23
Godwin, Mary Jane, 2, 21, 274 n. 33

Robertson, William, 200
Roiphe, Anne, 275 n. 35
Roland, Jean-Marie, 148, 153
Roland, Marie, 148–49, 153, 212
romance, 19–21, 29–31, 33, 35, 89, 90–91, 95, 96–98, 101–2, 104, 219
romantic reviews, 39, 239 n. 1
Romanticism, 1, 3, 17, 88, 89, 119–33, 147–59, 265 n. 6; and medievalism, 103–4
Ross, Marlon B., 290 n. 32
Rossetti, Lucy Maddox, 50
Rothwell, Richard, 169
Rousseau, Jean-Jacques, 50, 112–13, 118, 207, 211, 212; *La Nouvelle Hélöse*, 158
Routledge, 49
Rubenstein, Marc A., 259–60 n. 26
Russo, Mary, 296 n. 75

Sadleir, Michael, 241 n. 26
Sadoff, Diane F., 274 n. 31
St. Pancras, 289 n. 22
Schelling, Friedrich, 94, 95
Schlegel, Friedrich, 249 n. 14
Schor, Esther H., 186, 283 n. 8
Schreber, Dr. Daniel, 144
Scott, Joan, 213; *Feminism and History*, 201
Scott, Walter, 20, 48, 54, 90, 122, 155, 173, 198, 204, 265 n. 7; *Old Mortality* in *Tales of My Landlord*, 122, 123–24, 129, 131, 132; *Waverly* novels, 44
Segal, Hanna, 143
sexual desire, 190–94, 221–22, 223–24, 229–30, 231–32, 290 n. 32, 293–94 n. 5, 294 nn. 60, 65
Shakespeare, William, 14, 17; *As You Like It*, 78; *Hamlet*, 118; *King John*, 80; *Macbeth*, 140; *The Tempest*, 78
Shapiro, Ann-Louise, *Feminists Revision History*, 201
Shelley, Clara, 65, 82, 134–35, 139–40, 141, 144, 145, 146, 261 n. 32
Shelley, Jane, Lady, 233 n. 3

Shelley, Mary Wollstonecraft Godwin: artistry of, 64, 67–70, 75, 88, 106, 119–33, 134–46, 147–59, 178, 179, 180, 243–44 n. 9, 257 n. 3, 276 n. 39, 276 n. 40; and autonarration, 88; biographical elements in writings of, 9, 147, 199, 206–7, 261 n. 32; biographical imposition on writings of, 76–77, 120, 127, 160, 164, 167, 189, 269 n. 17; and biography, 198–213; and *Don Quixote*, 18–25, 28–37, 238–39 n. 53; and editing, 131–32, 185–97, 200, 280 n. 10, 281 nn. 26, 28; elopement of, 18, 19, 21, 33, 162, 289 n. 22; and Godwin, 19, 21–22, 64, 120, 135–36, 169, 221, 289 n. 22, 291 n. 38; Godwinian influence on works of, 67, 72–75, 88, 95, 167–68, 200; health of, 21; and history, 89, 90, 96–97, 101, 106, 198–213, 283–84 n. 8; and Jacobinism, 20–21, 112–13, 147–48; journal entries of, 19, 166, 186, 277 n. 41; letters of, 119, 166, 171–72; and maternity, 134–46, 169, 211, 216, 257 n. 4, 258 n. 8, 259–60 nn. 23, 26, 290 n. 27, 291 n. 37, 293 n. 58; and mourning, 134–46; mourning of, for P. B. Shelley, 119–20, 139, 143, 180, 182, 276 n. 40; and necessity, 96–97; and P. B. Shelley, 160, 166, 174, 290 nn. 30, 32, 291–92 n. 40; and P. B. Shelley's themes / techniques, 64, 73–75, 88, 101, 127; and politics, 118, 120–21, 125, 150–51, 152, 153, 254 n. 37, 283 n. 7, 286 n. 36; and politics of gender, 18, 100–101, 107; politics of, in *Frankenstein* and *Faulkner*, 4, 6, 8, 11–13, 15–17; reformist politics of, 1, 27–28, 37, 168, 252 n. 25; and Spain, 237 n. 36; and travel writing, 18, 19, 37–38; and Wollstonecraft, 30, 147, 165–66, 167, 169, 221–23, 264 n. 5, 271 n. 24, 272 n. 25, 290 n. 27, 291 n. 38; and Wollstonecraft's death, 5, 143, 145; and Wollstonecraft's feminism, 33, 89,

163, 220; at Wollstonecraft's grave, 9, 219, 289 n. 22; and writing about P. B. Shelley, 171–72. Works: "The Choice," 139, 143; "The Dirge," 180, 181, 182, 183; "The Elder Son," 276 n. 38; "The English in Italy," 18; *Essays, Letters from Abroad, Translations and Fragments by Percy Bysshe Shelley*, 188–89, 191, 192; *Falkner*, 1, 8–17, 146, 168–69, 261 n. 32, 275 n. 36; *The Fields of Fancy*, 64–70, 76–78; *Frankenstein*, 64, 112–13, 120, 126, 135, 155, 156, 158, 168–69, 171, 203, 215, 290 n. 31; adaptations of—, 43, 51–54, 60–61, 62, 227, 268 n. 15, 274–75 n. 34, 288 n. 13, 292 n. 45, 293 nn. 52, 53, 295 nn. 72, 74; —, compared with *Faulkner*, 1–16; critical readings of, 264 n. 4, 267–68 n. 13, 294 n. 63; —, and death, 145, 178, 180, 291 n. 37; —, as frame tale, 76–77, 199; influence of—, 38–63, 162, 218–32; introduction to—, 33; publishing history of—, 41–50, 57–60; reputation of—, 42–43, 48, 50, 162–63; *The Fields of Fancy*, 76–78, 81–82, 83; "Giovanni Villani," 114–15, 165, 273 n. 24; *History of a Six Weeks' Tour*, 18–21, 27, 32, 34, 35, 37, 112, 118; *The Last Man*, 8, 17, 77, 89, 98, 119–33, 135, 139, 140, 142, 143, 144, 145, 155, 156, 166, 198, 204, 256–57 n. 3, 265–66 n. 7, 283 n. 8; biographical elements in—, 119–20, 131–32, 135, 138–46, 256–57 n. 3; *Lives of the Most Eminent . . . Men of France (Cabinet Cyclopaedia)*, 198, 199, 207, 211, 212, 282–83 n. 5, 284 n. 8, 286 nn. 36, 37; *Lives of the Most Eminent . . . Men of Italy, Spain, and Portugal (Cabinet Cyclopaedia)*, 22, 35, 198, 199, 206, 207–8, 210, 211–12, 282–83 n. 5, 284 n. 8, 286 nn. 36, 37; *Lodore*, 30, 33–35, 166, 168–69, 261 n. 32, 275 n. 36; *Matilda*, 64–75, 76–87, 119, 166, 168–69, 170, 244 n. 20,

247 n. 8, 272 n. 25, 274 n. 31, 276 nn. 37, 38, 40; biographical elements in—, 64–65, 69, 82–83, 87, 88, 90, 135, 164–65, 269 n. 17, 270–71 n. 22; "Memoirs of Godwin," 21–22, 75; "The Mourner," 276 n. 38; "On Reading Wordsworth's Lines on Peele Castle," 181–82, 183; *The Poetical Works of Percy Bysshe Shelley* (4 vols.), 186, 195; *Posthumous Poems of Percy Bysshe Shelley*, 108, 187, 188, 194, 196; *Rambles in Germany and Italy*, 36–37, 261 n. 32; "Recollections of Italy," 77; review of Godwin's *Cloudesley*, 271 n. 24; "A Tale of the Passions," 253 n. 33; "Valerius: The Reanimated Roman," 170, 276 n. 38; *Valperga*, 8, 37, 75, 88–102, 103–18, 119, 155, 158, 166, 204, 249 n. 21, 283–84 n. 8

Shelley, Percy Bysshe, 16, 51, 52, 111, 153, 156, 158, 251 n. 5, 269 n. 17, 274 n. 33, 290 n. 30; and Dante, 245 n. 30; death of, 119–20; and *Frankenstein*, 40, 41–42, 43, 256 n. 2; and Godwin, 5 21, 72, 145; and history, 103, 107, 109–10, 118; and Lochhead's *Blood and Ice*, 218–23, 226, 230; and *Matilda*, 65, 76, 119, 270 n. 20; and poetry, 104, 110; and politics, 20, 26, 27, 107, 118, 150–51, 152, 153; as Quixote, 21, 27, 29; travels of, 19; and women, 291–91 n. 40, 291 n. 41; work of, 1, 64, 178. Works: *Adonais*, 197; *Alastor*, 41; *The Cenci*, 73–75, 81, 245 n. 41, 270–71 n. 22; "The Coliseum," 244 n. 13; *Defence of Poetry*, 115, 116, 125; *A Discourse on the Manners of the Ancient Greeks Relative to the Subject of Love*, 190–91; "England in 1819," 110, 188; *Essays, Letters from Abroad, Translations and Fragments by Percy Bysshe Shelley*, 188–90, 191, 192; "To Jane" ("The Keen Stars Were Twinkling"), 187; "To Jane: The Invitation," 197; "To Jane: The Recollection," 197; "Julian and Maddalo," 195; *Laon and*

Library of Congress Cataloging-in-Publication Data

Mary Shelley in her times / edited by Betty T. Bennett
and Stuart Curran.
    p.   cm.
Includes bibliographical references and index.
ISBN 0-8018-6334-1 (alk. paper)
1. Shelley, Mary Wollstonecraft, 1797–1851 — Criticism and
interpretation. 2. Literature and history — England — History —
19th century. 3. Women and literature — England — History — 19th
century. I. Bennett, Betty T. II. Curran, Stuart.
PR5398 .M27   2000
823'.7 — dc21

                                        99-057227